THE CAMBRIDGE COMPANION TO
THE CISTERCIAN ORDER

This volume presents the composite character of the Cistercian Order in its unity and diversity, detailing the White Monks' history from the Middle Ages to the present day. It charts the geographical spread of the Order from Burgundy to the peripheries of medieval Europe, examining key topics such as convents, liturgy, art, agriculture, spiritual life and education, providing an insight into Bernard of Clairvaux's life, work and sense of self, as well as the lives of other key Cistercian figures. This *Companion* offers an accessible synthesis of contemporary scholarship on the Order's interaction with the extramural world and its participation in, and contribution to, the cultural, economic and political climate of medieval Europe and beyond. The discussion contributes to the history of religious orders, and will be useful to those studying the twelfth-century renaissance, the apostolic movement and the role of religious life in medieval society.

Mette Birkedal Bruun is Professor of Church History at the University of Copenhagen. She is the author of *Parables: Bernard of Clairvaux's Mapping of Spiritual Topography* (2007), and the co-editor of *Negotiating Heritage: Memories of the Middle Ages* (with Stephanie Glaser, 2008) and *Commonplace Culture in Western Europe in the Early Modern Period I* (with David Cowling, 2011).

T0384766

CAMBRIDGE COMPANIONS TO RELIGION
A series of companions to major topics and key figures in theology and religious studies. Each volume contains specially commissioned chapters by international scholars which provide an accessible and stimulating introduction to the subject for new readers and non-specialists.

Other titles in the series

THE CAMBRIDGE COMPANION TO CHRISTIAN DOCTRINE
edited by Colin Gunton (1997)
9780521471183 hardback   9780521476959 paperback

THE CAMBRIDGE COMPANION TO BIBLICAL INTERPRETATION
edited by John Barton (1998)
9780521481441 hardback   9780521485937 paperback

THE CAMBRIDGE COMPANION TO DIETRICH BONHOEFFER
edited by John de Gruchy (1999)
9780521582582 hardback   9780521587815 paperback

THE CAMBRIDGE COMPANION TO KARL BARTH
edited by John Webster (2000)
9780521584760 hardback   9780521585606 paperback

THE CAMBRIDGE COMPANION TO JESUS
edited by Markus Bockmuehl (2001)
9780521792615 hardback   9780521796781 paperback

THE CAMBRIDGE COMPANION TO FEMINIST THEOLOGY
edited by Susan Frank Parsons (2002)
9780521663274 hardback   9780521663809 paperback

THE CAMBRIDGE COMPANION TO MARTIN LUTHER
edited by Donald K. McKim (2003)
9780521816489 hardback   9780521016735 paperback

THE CAMBRIDGE COMPANION TO ST PAUL
edited by James D. G. Dunn (2003)
9780521781558 hardback   9780521786942 paperback

THE CAMBRIDGE COMPANION TO POSTMODERN THEOLOGY
edited by Kevin J. Vanhoozer (2003)
9780521790628 hardback   9780521793957 paperback

THE CAMBRIDGE COMPANION TO JOHN CALVIN
edited by Donald K. McKim (2004)
9780521816472 hardback   9780521016728 paperback

THE CAMBRIDGE COMPANION TO HANS URS VON BALTHASAR
edited by Edward T. Oakes, SJ and David Moss (2004)
9780521814676 hardback   9780521891479 paperback

THE CAMBRIDGE COMPANION TO REFORMATION THEOLOGY
edited by David Bagchi and David Steinmetz (2004)
9780521772242 hardback   9780521776622 paperback

Continued at the back of the book

Frontispiece Fountains (England), chapter house and southern transept of the church, © THOC.

THE CAMBRIDGE COMPANION TO

THE CISTERCIAN ORDER

Edited by Mette Birkedal Bruun

 CAMBRIDGE
UNIVERSITY PRESS

CAMBRIDGE UNIVERSITY PRESS
Cambridge, New York, Melbourne, Madrid, Cape Town,
Singapore, São Paulo, Delhi, Mexico City

Cambridge University Press
The Edinburgh Building, Cambridge CB2 8RU, UK

Published in the United States of America by Cambridge University Press, New York

www.cambridge.org
Information on this title: www.cambridge.org/9781107001312

First published 2013

Printed and bound in the United Kingdom by the MPG Books Group

A catalogue record for this publication is available from the British Library

Library of Congress Cataloguing in Publication data
The Cambridge companion to the Cistercian order / edited by Mette Birkedal Bruun.
    pages   cm. – (Cambridge companions to religion)
Includes bibliographical references and index.
ISBN 978-1-107-00131-2 (hardback) – ISBN 978-0-521-17184-7 (paperback)
1. Cistercians. I. Bruun, Mette Birkedal.
BX3402.3.C36 2012
271'.12–dc23
2012018815

ISBN 978-1-107-00131-2 Hardback
ISBN 978-0-521-17184-7 Paperback

Contents

List of figures   *page* ix

Notes on contributors   xi

Preface   xv
METTE BIRKEDAL BRUUN

List of abbreviations   xvii

Introduction: withdrawal and engagement   1
METTE BIRKEDAL BRUUN AND EMILIA
JAMROZIAK

Part I *History*

1   Foundation and twelfth century   25
    MARTHA G. NEWMAN

2   The Cistercian Order 1200–1600   38
    PETER KING

3   The Cistercian Order since 1600   50
    MICHAEL CASEY OCSO

Part II *Structure and materiality*

4   Centres and peripheries   65
    EMILIA JAMROZIAK

5   The Cistercian community   80
    JAMES FRANCE

6   Constitutions and the General Chapter   87
    BRIAN PATRICK MCGUIRE

7   Nuns   100
    ELIZABETH FREEMAN

8   Agriculture and economies   112
    CONSTANCE HOFFMAN BERMAN

9   Art   125
    DIANE J. REILLY

10   Libraries and scriptoria   140
DAVID N. BELL

11   Cistercian architecture or architecture of
the Cistercians?   151
THOMAS COOMANS

Part III   *Religious mentality*

12   Bernard of Clairvaux: his first and greatest
miracle was himself   173
CHRISTOPHER HOLDSWORTH

13   Bernard of Clairvaux: work and self   186
M.B. PRANGER

14   Early Cistercian writers   199
E. ROZANNE ELDER

15   The spiritual teaching of the early
Cistercians   218
BERNARD MCGINN

16   Cistercians in dialogue: bringing the world
into the monastery   233
WIM VERBAAL

17   Preaching   245
BEVERLY MAYNE KIENZLE

18   Liturgy   258
NICOLAS BELL

Map of Cistercian monasteries   268

Primary sources   269

Further reading   283

Index   301

Figures

Frontispiece Fountains (England), chapter
   house and southern transept of the church,
   © THOC.

9.1   Gregory the Great, Moralia in Job (Dijon,
      BM MS 173, fol. 29), © Dijon, Bibliothèque
      municipale.   *page* 127

9.2   Clairvaux Bible (Troyes, BM MS 27, fol. 104v),
      © Troyes, Bibliothèque municipale.   131

9.3   Tile floor from Byland Abbey, © Emma
      Johnson.   132

9.4   Knotwork window from Obazine Abbey,
      © MOSSOT.   134

9.5   Seal of St Bernard, © Can Stock Photo Inc./
      Morphart   137

11.1 Eberbach (Germany), interior of the abbey
      church to the choir, © THOC-SOFAM.   154

11.2 Pontigny (France), abbey church seen from the
      south, © THOC-SOFAM.   155

11.3 Fontenay (France), façade of the church from the
      west, © THOC-SOFAM.   155

11.4 Villers (Belgium), northern transept of the
      church, © THOC-SOFAM.   156

11.5 Rievaulx (England), choir and transept of the
      abbey church, © THOC-SOFAM.   158

11.6 Sénanque (France), cloister and church,
      © THOC-SOFAM.   162

11.7 Fountains (England), chapter house and southern
      transept of the church, © THOC-SOFAM.   162

11.8 Le Thoronet (France), eastern gallery of the
      cloister, © THOC-SOFAM.   163

11.9   Caduin (France), late medieval cloister gallery,
© THOC-SOFAM.   166

11.10   Herkenrode (Belgium), gate house of the
nunnery, © THOC-SOFAM.   167

Map 1   Cistercian monasteries, 1098–1675. Based
on a map from R.A. Donkin, *The Cistercians:
Studies in the Geography of Medieval England
and Wales* (Toronto, 1978). Reproduced with
the permission of the Pontifical Institute of
Medieval Studies.   268

Contributors

David N. Bell is Professor Emeritus of Religious Studies, Memorial University of Newfoundland. Among his publications are *Understanding Rancé: The _irituality of the Abbot of La Trappe in Context* (2005); *What Nuns Read: Books and Libraries in Medieval English Nunneries* (1995); *An Index of Authors and Works in Cistercian Libraries in Great Britain* (1992); and *The Image and Likeness: The Augustinian Spirituality of William of Saint Thierry* (1984).

Nicolas Bell is Curator of Music Manuscripts, British Library, London. He is the author of *The Las Huelgas Music Codex: A Companion Study to the Facsimile* (2003) and several articles on medieval music. He is General Secretary of the Henry Bradshaw Society, founded in 1890 for the editing of rare liturgical texts.

Constance Hoffman Berman is Professor of History, University of Iowa. She is the author of *The Cistercian Evolution: The Invention of a Religious Order in Twelfth-Century Europe* (2000/2010) and *Medieval Agriculture, the Southern French Countryside, and the Early Cistercians* (1986), and the editor of *Medieval Religion: New Approaches* (2005) and *Women and Monasticism in Medieval Europe: Sisters and Patrons of the Cistercian Order* (2002).

Mette Birkedal Bruun is Professor of Church History, University of Copenhagen. She is the author of *Parables: Bernard of Clairvaux's Mapping of Spiritual Topography* (2007), and co-editor, with David Cowling, of *Commonplace Culture in Western Europe in the Early Modern Period I: Reformation, Counter Reformation and Revolt* (2011) and, with Stephanie Glaser, of *Negotiating Heritage: Memories of the Middle Ages* (2008).

Michael Casey OCSO is a monk of Tarrawarra Abbey, Australia. He is the author of *Athirst for God: Spiritual Desire in Bernard of Clairvaux's Sermons on the Song of Songs* (1987). Casey is editor of *Tjurunga: An Australasian Benedictine Review* and is on the Advisory Board of *Cistercian Studies Quarterly*, *Cistercian Publications*, the *Monastic Wisdom* series and *Thomas Merton Annual*.

Thomas Coomans is Professor of Architectural History and Conservation, University of Leuven. He is the author of *L'abbaye de Villers-en-Brabant: construction, configuration et signification d'une abbaye cistercienne gothique*, Cîteaux: Studia et documenta 11 (2000) and is a member of the editorial boards of *Cîteaux: Commentarii cistercienses* and *Bulletin monumental*.

E. Rozanne Elder is Director of the Centre for Cistercian and Monastic Studies and Professor of History, Western Michigan University. She is the editor of, amongst other publications, *Praise No Less Than Charity: Studies in Honor of M. Chrysogonus Waddell* (2002); *The New Monastery: Texts and Studies on the Early Cistercians* (1998); *The Contemplative Path: Reflections on Recovering a Lost Tradition* (1996); and *The Joy of Learning and the Love of God: Essays in Honor of Jean Leclercq* (1995).

James France is the author of *Separate but Equal: Cistercian Lay Brothers 1120–1350* (2012); *Medieval Images of Saint Bernard of Clairvaux* (2007); *The Cistercians in Medieval Art* (1998); and *The Cistercians in Scandinavia* (1992).

Elizabeth Freeman is Senior Lecturer in Medieval European History, University of Tasmania. She is the author of *Narratives of a New Order: Cistercian Historical Writing in England, 1150–1220* (2002) and has written numerous articles on Cistercian topics.

Christopher Holdsworth is Professor Emeritus of Medieval History, University of Exeter. He is the author of *Rufford Charters*, 4 vols. (1972–81) and co-editor, with Diana Greenaway and Jane Sayers, of *Tradition and Change: Essays in Honour of Marjorie Chibnall* (Cambridge, 1985/2002) and, with Hilary Costello, *A Gathering of Friends: The Learning and Spirituality of John of Forde* (1996).

Emilia Jamroziak is Senior Lecturer in Medieval History, University of Leeds. She is the author of *The Cistercian Order in Medieval Europe: 1090–1500* (in press); *Survival and Success on Medieval Borders: Cistercian Houses in Medieval Scotland and Pomerania from the Twelfth to the Late Fourteenth Century* (2011); and *Rievaulx Abbey and Its Social Context 1132–1300: Memory, Locality and Networks* (2005), and co-editor, with Janet Burton, of *Religious and Laity in Western Europe 1000–1400: Interaction, Negotiation, and Power* (2006).

Beverly Mayne Kienzle is John H. Morison Professor of the Practice in Latin and Romance Languages, and Lecturer on Medieval Christianity and Director of Language Studies, Divinity School of Harvard University. She is the author of *Hildegard of Bingen's Gospel Homilies: Speaking New Mysteries* (2009) and *Cistercians, Heresy and Crusade (1145–1229): Preaching in the Lord's Vineyard* (2001), and editor of *The Sermon*, Typologie des sources du moyen âge occidental 81–3 (2000). Kienzle is co-editor, with Pamela J. Walker, of *Women Preachers and Prophets through Two Millennia of Christianity* (1998) and, with Jacqueline Hamesse, Debra Stoudt and Anne Thayer, of *Medieval Sermons and Society: Cloister, City, University* (1998).

Peter King is Lecturer Emeritus in Medieval History, St Andrews University. He is the author of *Western Monasticism* (1999) and *The Finances of the Cistercian Order in the Fourteenth Century* (1985) and co-editor, with A.O. Johnsen, of *The Tax Book of the Cistercian Order* (1979).

Bernard McGinn is Naomi Shenstone Donnelley Professor Emeritus, Divinity School of the University of Chicago. He has written extensively on medieval apocalyptic traditions and on the history of mysticism and spirituality and is currently engaged upon a seven-volume history of Western Christian mysticism under the general title, *The Presence of God* (four volumes have appeared to date).

Brian Patrick McGuire is Professor Emeritus of Medieval History, Roskilde University. He is the author of *Brother and Lover: Aelred of Rievaulx* (1994); *The Difficult Saint: Bernard of Clairvaux and His Tradition* (1991); *Friendship and Community: The Monastic Experience 350–1250* (1988/2010); and *The Cistercians in Denmark, Their Attitudes, Roles, and Functions in Medieval Society* (1982), and editor of *A Companion to Bernard of Clairvaux* (2011).

Martha G. Newman is Chair for the Department of Religious Studies and Associate Professor of History and Religious Studies, University of Texas at Austin. She is the author of *The Boundaries of Charity: Cistercian Culture and Ecclesiastical Reform, 1098–1180* (1996) and has written numerous articles on Cistercian life.

M.B. Pranger is Professor Emeritus at the Department of Religion, University of Amsterdam. He is the author of *Eternity's Ennui: Perseverance and Temporality in Augustine and Western Literature* (2010); *The Artificiality of Christianity: The Poetics of Monasticism* (2003); and *Bernard of Clairvaux and the Shape of Monastic Thought: Broken Dreams* (1994).

Diane J. Reilly is Associate Professor of Art History, Indiana University, Bloomington. She is the author of *The Art of Reform in Eleventh-Century Flanders: Gerard of Cambrai, Richard of Saint-Vanne and the Saint-Vaast Bible* (2006), and co-editor, with Susan Boynton, of *The Practice of the Bible in the Middle Ages: Production, Reception and Performance in Western Christianity* (2011).

Wim Verbaal is Professor of Latin Language and Literature, Ghent University. He is the author of *Een middeleeuws drama* (2004) on Bernard of Clairvaux and Peter Abelard. He is the co-editor, with Yanick Maes and Jan Papy, of *Latinitas perennis*, vol. I, *The Continuity of Latin Literature* (2007), and vol. II, *Appropriation and Latin Literature* (2009).

Preface

The ambition behind this volume is double. It is to offer an up-to-date cross-disciplinary introduction to the Cistercian Order and to reflect the character and interests of current scholarship. The content is structured in three sections. The first treats, in three chapters, the history of the Order from its foundation until today. Then follow two thematic sections, the main focus of which is the medieval period. The first, 'Structure and materiality', deals with the Order's organisation, its material culture and agricultural production, and with the ever-present dynamic between unity and diversity. The second, 'Religious mentality', centres on authors and educators and on the ideas, texts, preaching and music which emerged from Cistercian monasteries. The chapters stand as individual essays on different aspects of the Order – and not necessarily in unison. In this sense this volume mirrors the composite nature of the Order, and of the research into it.

Sincere thanks are due to all of the authors for their brave and spirited response to the academic challenge, not to mention the severe word limit, and to Terryl N. Kinder and I. Gorevich as well as Laura Morris and Anna Lowe of Cambridge University Press.

Mette Birkedal Bruun

Abbreviations

AASS	Acta Sanctorum, ed. Société des Bollandistes (Antwerp, Paris, Brussels, 1643–1940)
ASOC	*Analecta Sacri Ordinis Cisterciensis*
BHL	Bibliotheca hagiographica latina antiquae et mediae aetatis, ed. Société des Bollandistes *et al.* (Brussels, 1898–1901 and later)
Canivez, *Statuta*	J.-M. Canivez (ed.), *Statuta capitulorum generalium ordinis cisterciensis*, 8 vols. (Louvain, 1933–41)
CCCM	Corpus Christianorum Continuatio Medievalis
CF	Cistercian Fathers Series
Choisselet/ Vernet	D. Choisselet and P. Vernet (eds.), *Les 'Ecclesiastica officia' cisterciens du XIIème siècle. Texte latin selon les manuscrits étudiés de Trente 1711, Ljubljana 31 et Dijon 114*, La documentation cistercienne 22 (Reiningue, 1989)
COCR	*Collectanea ordinis cistercensium reformatorum*
CS	Cistercian Studies Series
CSQ	*Cistercian Studies Quarterly*
Ep	*Epistola*
McGinn, *Growth*	B. McGinn, *The Presence of God*, vol. ii, *The Growth of Mysticism: Gregory the Great through the Twelfth Century* (New York, 1994)
MGH	Monumenta Germaniae historica
PL	*Patrologia Latina*, ed. J.P. Migne, 221 vols. (Paris, 1846–95)
RB	*Regula Benedicti* / Rule of Benedict
RTAM	*Recherches de théologie ancienne et médiévale*
S	Sermon
SBOp	*Sancti Bernardi opera*, ed. J. Leclercq, H.M. Rochais and C.H. Talbot, 8 vols. (Rome, 1957–77)
SCh	Sources chrétiennes
VP	*Vita Prima*
Waddell, *Lay*	C. Waddell (ed.), *Cistercian Lay Brothers: Twelfth-Century Usages with Related Texts*, Cîteaux: Studia et Documenta 10 (Brecht, 2000)

Waddell,
Narrative   C. Waddell (ed.), *Narrative and Legislative Texts from Early Cîteaux*, Cîteaux: Studia et Documenta 9 (Brecht, 1999)
Waddell,
Statutes   C. Waddell (ed.), *Twelfth-Century Statutes from the Cistercian General Chapter*, Cîteaux: Studia et Documenta 12 (Brecht, 2002)

Works by Aelred of Rievaulx
Spec   *Speculum caritatis*

Works by Bernard of Clairvaux
Ann   *Sermo in annuntiatione domini*
Apo   *Apologia ad Guillelmum abbatem*
Asspt   *Sermo in assumptione Beatae Mariae Virginis*
Csi   *De consideratione*
Ded   *Sermo in dedicatione ecclesiae*
Dil   *De diligendo Deo*
Div   *Sermo de diversis*
Gra   *De gratia et libero arbitrio*
Humb   *Sermo in obitu domni Humberti*
Miss   *Homilia super 'Missus est' in laudibus virginis matris*
Nat   *Sermo in nativitate domini*
Pre   *De praecepto et dispensatione*
QH   *Sermo super psalmum 'Qui habitat'*
SC   *Sermo super Cantica canticorum*
Sent   *Sententiae*
V Mal   *Vita sancti Malachiae*
V Nat   *Sermo in vigilia nativitatis domini*

Works by William of Saint Thierry
Aenig   *Aenigma fidei*
Cant   *Expositio super Cantica canticorum*
Contemp   *De contemplando Deo*
Ep frat   *Epistula ad fratres de Monte Dei*
Med   *Meditativae orationes*
Nat am   *De natura et dignitate amoris*
Nat corp   *De natura corporis et animae*
Spec   *Speculum fidei*

Introduction: withdrawal and engagement

METTE BIRKEDAL BRUUN AND
EMILIA JAMROZIAK

How are we to comprehend the Cistercian Order? How do we examine
and represent a phenomenon which has existed for over 900 years and
spread across the world, which has built monumental architecture and
produced a wide array of texts, tilled land and cultivated minds, seen
schisms and sought concord? How do we grasp the basic tenor, the fluc-
tuations, the varied responses to widely different conditions within one
overall scholarly framework?

An influential trend in Cistercian scholarship has viewed the history of the White Monks as a tug-of-war between 'ideals' and 'reality'.
The assumption is that the Order was founded on a set of ideals, crys-
tallised in twelfth-century legislation and foundation narratives: lofty
aspirations – whether for isolation from the world and its ways, for
repudiation of tithes, ownership of serfs and other allegedly corrupting
practices or for harmony and uniformity within the Order and its communities. The reality is, then, all those factors which cause appropriation, modulation and abolition of these ideals, synchronically as well
as diachronically: local conditions, extramural powers, pragmatism or
the impact of individual figures. Louis Lekai, seminally, set the dichotomy as a motto for his momentous *The Cistercians: Ideals and Reality*
(1977) and, in a definitive article, employed the collision between ideals
and reality as a key to the dating of the Cistercian decline: the Order's
fourteenth-century fall from its initial ideals, pushed by the overpow-
ering force of reality.[1] Seen in this light, ideals become synonymous
with 'true Cistercianness' in the shape of unanimity, strictness and
absence of ambiguity, whereas reality stands for distortion, deviation
and equivocation.

Recent scholarship has challenged Lekai's dichotomy. There is a
growing sense that its robust segregation produces a fragmented understanding of the Cistercian history and culture.[2] But much remains to be
done if we want to understand the complexity of the Order, its history
and its relation to society without losing sight of its fundamental ideas:

if we want to examine, in an integrated way, its matter without neglecting its spirit – and vice versa.

The Cistercian Order is multifaceted, and the field of Cistercian studies is broad and complex. One of the roads to an integrated approach to the White Monks goes by way of consciousness of the different disciplinary approaches, their interrogatory horizons and scholarly aims. Riding roughshod over nuances and specialisations, we may divide Cistercian studies into two overall approaches: two groups of scholars with different objectives, methodologies and questions for the material. Each of the groups is too heterogeneous to be seen as a single scholarly unit, school or tradition, but let us, briefly and for the sake of overview, consider the composite corpus of Cistercian scholarship as two distinct approaches.

One approach, involving historians, archaeologists and historians of architecture and art, focuses on organisation and materiality, on Cistercian life as it was lived at a particular time and place. These scholars study their material in its historical and physical context as shaped by contemporary conditions. They search for the political, economic, social and spiritual *Sitz-im-Leben* of the Cistercians' texts, buildings and artefacts, and their search may be informed by theories formulated within, for example, sociology, anthropology and cultural studies. This approach has brought forth studies of watermills and granges, of individual houses and their edifices, and it has fostered monastic archaeology as a specific discipline.[3] Twentieth-century pioneers are scholars such as the British historian David Knowles (1896–1974) and the American historian Bennett D. Hill (1934–2005), whose specialised research focused on particular national or regional aspects.

Earlier generations of scholarship took their cue directly from the Cistercian legislation and material remains, but since the 1970s a broader variety of sources have been employed to throw light on the Order and its handling of land, buildings, production and societal relations. This change of focus has come with a shift from an interest in unity to an interest in diversity – and with an ambition to comprehend the medieval idea of unity in diversity.

The other approach, represented by historians, theologians, philologists and literary scholars, centres on the spiritual world and religious mentality of the White Monks. These scholars study the handling of the biblical and patristic legacy and examine the Cistercians as students and teachers of doctrinal issues such as the image of God in man or the relationship between Fall, restoration and beatitude, and they examine differences in the teaching of, for example, Bernard of Clairvaux,

William of Saint Thierry and Aelred of Rievaulx. Their methodological tools come from philology, rhetoric, literary studies, philosophy and theology, and a considerable portion of their work has been carried out in connection with editions and translations.

Some of these scholars are concerned with the systematisation of spiritual categories such as the Bernardine degrees of love, and they seek more or less coherent representations of the spiritual worldview that underpins Cistercian life. The French historian of philosophy Étienne Gilson (1884–1978) may be considered a founding figure for such a systematising approach.[4] Others are interested in the Cistercian texts as palimpsests of biblical, liturgical and patristic utterances, rhetorically complex and carefully edited. Scholarly foundations for this approach have been laid by, for example, the Dutch philologist Christine Mohrmann (1903–88) and the Benedictine scholar Jean Leclercq (1911–93).[5] The issues studied in this scholarly area are examined as themes which have been conceptualised and formulated in a specific intellectual and religious climate, but connections can also be traced across centuries in, for example, a search for Augustinian influences, ruptures and continuities in anthropology and ecclesiology across the Christian tradition, or the reception of biblical phrases through liturgical texts. Focus is directed to systems of belief as well as to linguistic, rhetorical and literary structures.

Evidently interests overlap: scholars concerned with legislation look at religious motivation and rhetorical strategies; scholars orientated towards spirituality may take manuscript traditions and the material embeddedness of spiritual principles into consideration. The idea is not to make strict divisions but to sketch various perspectives within Cistercian studies.

A central motif in Cistercian scholarship is the tension between withdrawal and engagement, between the wilderness and the world. On the one hand, foundation narratives and legislation state repeatedly that the White Monks must found, and do found, their houses in inhospitable areas far from human habitation. On the other hand, historical and archaeological evidence attests to an abundance of cases where Cistercians appropriated land which was already cultivated, or took over existing monastic houses; and charters, wills and letters point to a wide range of interactions between abbeys and the surrounding society.

At a first glance, the tension between wilderness and engagement may seem like a case of 'ideals' versus 'reality': as if the Cistercians aspired to withdrawal from society but in reality succumbed to engagement with it. In fact, withdrawal and engagement are two sides of one and the same thing: the Cistercian ethos in its field of tension between earthly life and heavenly beatitude, between the monastic tradition and the conditions of a specific time and place and between the individual houses and the Cistercian Order at large – at a given moment and across the ages.

It takes both approaches to understand this ethos. The idea of the wilderness is soon dissolved if examined from the point of view of physical and material conditions. But if considered as a 'written world', the trope of the wilderness abounds in information about the Cistercians – and information about their societal relations too. Engagement is best approached from a perspective attuned to social exchange, authority and power. When examined from this angle, it does in fact turn out that the Cistercian engagement with the world hinges on both significant spiritual factors and elements central to the monastic tradition.

MBB/EJ

WITHDRAWAL

Older historical scholarship took the Cistercian wilderness mythology at face value. But in the 1980s the narrative of the Cistercian settlement in the desert was increasingly contested and it has now been abandoned, owing to archaeological evidence, the redating of key documents and a less literal reading of the narrative sources.[6] After this turn, the Cistercian claim that the Order settles in the wilderness has appeared somewhat dubious. The suspicion of hypocrisy is not new. It was voiced already by Walter Map, ever critical of the Order:

> So they choose a proper place to abide in, a place not uninhabitable but inhabited, clean, fertile, responsive to tillage, receptive of crops … a place outside the world in the heart of the world, remote from men in the midst of men, as wishing not to know the world yet to be known of it.[7]

But how are the references to Cistercian solitude to be understood if we want to move beyond scepticism? Ernst Robert Curtius has already warned us that medieval descriptions of landscapes are permeated by rhetorical principles and elements inherited from Antiquity.[8] Seen in this light, it is unsurprising that the representations of Cistercian sites are shaped less by topographical than by rhetorical factors. When dealing with Cistercian descriptions of wildernesses, we are not looking at physical circumstances or literal meaning, but at the spiritual and rhetorical mentality of the Order – in Waddell's words: a spiritual climate, in Newman's: a metaphorical condition[9] This is a condition imbued with the language of the Bible and the early Christian Fathers.

In *Exordium Cistercii* from the mid or late 1130s (that is, the second generation of the Order),[10] Robert of Molesme and his monks are described as purposeful *milites Christi* (soldiers of Christ):

> After many labors, therefore, and exceedingly great difficulties … they at length attained their desire and arrived at Cîteaux – at that time a place of horror and of vast solitude. But judging that the harshness of the place was not at variance with the strict purpose they had already conceived in mind, the soldiers of Christ held the place as truly prepared for them by God: a place as agreeable as their purpose was dear.[11]

The place is in concordance with their aim. The passage hinges on the phrase *locum tunc scilicet horroris et vastæ solitudinis* ('at that time a place of horror and of vast solitude') from Deuteronomy 32.10, which was to become a key reference in Cistercian foundation narratives.[12] In its biblical context the phrase alludes to the desert where God sustained his people during their forty years of wandering. In *Exordium Cistercii* it conveys the hostility of the terrain (which did in fact accommodate a chapel, a cabin for three serfs and a main road),[13] but in a way which lifts the site into a typologically tinged sphere.

The conglomeration of desert asceticism and *militia Christi* harks back to the Egyptian Desert Fathers, and the text makes the Cistercian founders heirs to both Moses, the desert-wanderer, and Anthony, the paradigmatic fourth-century hermit. Such aspirations belong to the second generation of Cistercians rather than the first,[14] but when ascribing them to the first generation, the authors secure a connection between themselves, the founders, the early Christian Fathers and the biblical text. Their portrait of the wilderness of Cîteaux and its cultivation posits a past for the Order, which is in keeping with its mid-twelfth-century present and constructs a topographical antecedent in harmony with the Order's ethos at this point. Later foundation narratives took the cue and thus stressed the association of new houses with the primordial foundation at Cîteaux.

The wilderness hovers between the literal and the metaphorical. It represents the site and may take its bearings from a physical topography, but its key function is to point out spiritual and ascetic co-ordinates. The wilderness is a pliant narrative topos. On the one hand, it brings with it a cluster of basic implications: withdrawal from society and exposure to harsh climates and hostile forces. On the other hand, it is easily modulated and transferred: the sylvan thickets or soggy marsh-lands of Western Europe can readily be seen as analogous to the stony desert of Thebes, the habitat of the Desert Fathers, or to the unspecified desert of Exodus. The wilderness may even be invested with different qualitative nuances: it can be hostile and diabolic, but it can also be contemplatively flavoured and indicate proximity to God.

In short, the wilderness is a topos, which connotes the weight of legitimacy and the power of uniformity; it is stamped with the mark of constancy that comes with prescriptive and normative genres. The idea of the wilderness links Cistercians everywhere and at all times to a legacy and a 'foundation mythology'. But at the same time it func-tions as a repository of various characteristics and implications, and it may easily be adapted to different circumstances and rhetorical needs.

Already the two foundation narratives *Exordium Cistercii* and *Exordium Parvum* represent two different shades of wilderness repre-sentations. They agree that the nature of Cîteaux was hostile and unin-habitable and thus in concord with the ascetic aim of Robert and his companions. They also agree that no sooner had the monks reached the wild than they began to cut it down and create a monastic civilisa-tion. But whereas *Exordium Cistercii* stresses the *militia Christi* motif, *Exordium Parvum*, which dates from before 1147, directs its focus to the life of the men of God (*viri Dei*) in its contrast to secular life:

> Understanding upon arrival that the more despicable and
> unapproachable the place was to seculars, the more suited it was
> for the monastic observance they had already conceived in mind,
> and for which sake they had come there, the men of God, after
> cutting down and removing the dense grove and thornbushes,
> began to construct a monastery there.[15]

The place is fitting because it is the exact opposite of the world, just as Cistercian life in its orientation towards God – as envisaged by the founders, according to the second-generation authors – is the exact opposite of secular life.

Surprisingly, perhaps, Bernard of Clairvaux is no great champion of the wilderness. He associates the desert with the life of the hermit as opposed to the cenobitic (communal) life in the monastery, and he warns against it. To a nun in Troyes, who was tempted by the hermit-age, he writes, for example: 'For anyone wishing to lead a bad life the desert supplies ample opportunity. The woods afford cover, and solitude assures silence.'[16] But it is telling of the flexibility of the topos that when he does describe the Cistercian monastery as a desert, it is a desert which is almost unrecognisable as such:

> The southern region is the cloister or the desert ... and the 'southern plain' [Gen. 13.1] represents the communal life, a spiritual mode of living among good people. The paradise of the cloister, facing the sweet mildness of the favourable south wind, flourishes, as it were, with as many flowers as it abounds in virtues.[17]

Bernard turns the desert into a blossoming paradise; nonetheless, it retains an associative connection to the basic idea of the Cistercians as desert-dwellers.

Whenever there is a need to assert monastic legitimacy, the foundation is called upon. It is typical that Armand-Jean de Rancé's (1626–1700) reform at La Trappe engendered not only a renewed interest in the Rule of Benedict and its proper meaning, but also an evocation of the wilderness topos and its inherent link to the origin of the Order. Two examples will suffice. La Trappe was founded in the 1140s, and Rancé was not a cultivator in the same way as the first founders. Nonetheless, the official visitor Dominique Georges, abbot of Val-Richer, comes close to making such a claim in the report he presented to the General Chapter in 1686. In the section dedicated to the material state of the monastery, Georges describes La Trappe before and after Rancé's reform. The 'before' conjures up a wilderness, which is the consequence of material and spiritual decay: nature is creeping in and has overtaken monastic civilisation – a well-known topos of deterioration.[18] The passage is so vivid that we almost forget that Georges's visitation took place in November 1685, more than twenty years after the situation he describes:

> When entering the cloister you saw a completely ruined roof, which, at the slightest rainfall, would cause flooding of the cloister ... parlours served as stables for the horses. The refectory was a refectory in name only. Monks and seculars gathered there to play *boules* when heat or bad weather prevented them from playing outside. The dormitory was abandoned and uninhabited; it served as a retreat only for night birds ... The monastery had no garden; it was surrounded by poor soil, in which grew thorns, bushes and trees. But the worst thing was that, owing to the highway built around a hundred years earlier close to the monastic walls, you saw nothing there but vagabonds, criminals and assassins. Men and women gathered in the woods nearby and there, as in a safe haven, hid to commit every sort of crime.[19]

Rancé had the highway relocated and thus reinforced the withdrawal by, so to speak, moving the world further away. The passage describes the wild muddle of animals, climatic elements, plants and vices allegedly disciplined by the reformer. In his portrait of the transformation of this Babylonian anarchy into an orderly and well-structured civilisation, Georges brings Rancé's reform close to the foundation at Cîteaux despite widely different circumstances. The visitor was countering the internal scepticism as to the reform voiced at the General Chapter of 1684 and elsewhere; the wilderness topos corroborates his comprehensive vindication of its genuine Cistercian character.[20]

In 1670, sixteen years before Georges's report, Louis XIV's historiographer André Félibien des Avaux visited La Trappe.[21] He penned his impressions in a *carte de visite*, the *Description de l'abbaye de la Trappe*, which was printed in several editions and translated into English. Félibien recounts his first impression of the scenery with verve:

> This monastery is situated in a wide valley, and the forest and the hills that surround it are so positioned that they seem to want to hide it from the rest of the world. They ... make access so difficult that it is hard to get there without the directions of a guide. There once was a road from Mortagne to Paris that ran behind the garden walls ... the Abbot had it redirected so that the surroundings of their monastery were less frequented. Thus there is nothing more desolate than this desert. And even though there are several towns and villages around it at a distance of three leagues, it seems that one is in an unknown region in another country.[22]

La Trappe remains a wilderness, but the tenor of Félibien's wilderness differs significantly from Georges's. It is represented as so far removed from the world that it almost seems to hover in a tension between absence and presence.

In fact, hundreds of visitors travelled to La Trappe each year,[23] and it is difficult not to agree with the nineteenth-century theologian and abolitionist Mary Schimmelpenninck's dry remark:

> It is repeatedly said that, on an average, this seclusion is visited by six thousand strangers every year; and that from 12 to 15 hundred poor are fed there ... twice every week. It seems difficult to conceive how a road can be untracked, which is passed a hundred and sixty thousand times every year.[24]

But, again, the description is about spiritual temper rather than topographical layout. Rancé's reform revolved around withdrawal from the world through penitence, silence and fasting; the *carte de visite* is permeated by this drift which, in Félibien's version, makes for joyful tranquility. The description of the wilderness which accommodates the monastery chimes in with the visitor's overall description of the ascetic regime at La Trappe as a serene haven: it is a place in harmony with the spirit of the reform.

Félibien's text was sometimes paired with an apocryphal volume of regulations and thus made to serve an internal purpose for the monks of La Trappe.[25] But it was written for an external addressee, Jeanne de Schomberg, duchesse de Liancourt (1600–1674), who belonged to the lay entourage of Port-Royal. The historiographer begins his description with a concession: 'Madame, it is not without reason that I fear not to be able to satisfy entirely your pious curiosity, for I have difficulties making you a description of La Trappe which corresponds to the elevated idea one must have of it.'[26] Félibien portrays both La Trappe and his own awe of its life while feeding the duchess's vision of austere penance. His aesthetically flavoured representation of the severe isolation of La Trappe caters to a taste for penitential piousness and solitude which was in fashion among the duchess and her peers.[27] People talked about Rancé and La Trappe, and the monastery and its reformer seem to have qualified as interesting news; for example, Marie Dupré attached a *carte de visite* from La Trappe to a letter to the comte de Bussy-Rabutin alongside gossip about deaths, love affairs and new admissions to the Academy.[28]

Rancé maintained a comprehensive correspondence and offered moral instruction to men and women, lay as well as religious.[29] Many aristocrats came to the monastery for retreats, partaking for a while in its withdrawal from society. The guests were met with signboards instructing them not to address the monks and later had their own refectory so as not to disturb the community. They were lodged immediately outside the walls in the former abbatial lodge with its own garden (a favourite retreat for Louis XIV's cousin, Mme de Guise), in an apartment which traversed the wall or more centrally next to the lay brothers' quarters.[30] Together with Rancé's extensive correspondence and reputed charisma, representations such as Félibien's extended the penitential spirit of La Trappe beyond the monastic walls, thus, as it were, inverting the withdrawal it celebrated. For the king it even became possible to pay a virtual visit to La Trappe by way of a model (fourteen by sixteen feet), complete with needy people at the gate made of enamel, with fruit trees and flowers made of silk. It was offered to the monarch in 1708 with the words: 'Now your Majesty can visit this famous monastery in one glance.'[31]

There are five centuries between the uninhabitable thickets of the foundation narratives and Bernard's allegorical desert-paradise on the one hand and Georges's Babylonian chaos and Félibien's peaceful solitude on the other. There are differences of genre between the foundation texts, the draft sermon, the visitation report and the description intended for an aristocratic laywoman. There are differences of historical context between the twelfth-century textual consolidation of a successful Order, or the rhetorical mastery of its primary figure, and the texts written in the seventeenth-century cultural and religious climate with its particular aesthetic and penitential preferences and the specific textual needs provoked by Rancé's reform. Finally, there are significant differences between the wildernesses represented; from the impenetrable vegetation of Cîteaux to the flowery fertility in Bernard's text, from the degeneracy and villainy of La Trappe before Rancé to the placid isolation that, according to Félibien, came after. Nonetheless, they all qualify as wildernesses. Each of these representations of a monastic site makes a claim to an overall desert mythology that connotes ascetic estrangement from the world and spiritual aspiration for the love of God. They all play a part in the construction of uniformity, coherence and legitimacy, but they also represent widely different individual emphases and adaptations.

As Félibien's *carte de visite* shows, the written wildernesses are not only employed to reinforce the internal coherence of the Order. Paradoxically, the solitude, this icon of isolation, may also play a role in the engagement of the monastery with the surrounding society – and in the engagement of this society with the monastery.

MBB

ENGAGEMENT

The withdrawal from the world is only half of the Cistercian story. Engagement and service to the world was just as important as being 'in the desert'. The nature of the Cistercian obligations to the wider society and the connections resulting from them was a subject carefully rethought and reshaped by the Cistercian leaders. The precise form of the monastic engagement in the individual abbeys was linked to the character of different regions and localities and strongly rooted in the pre-existing monastic traditions and expectations of the lay world.

The central role of the monks has always been to intercede on behalf of the world, a tradition of which Cistercian were a part. At the core of the monastic–lay relationships was the reciprocity in the form of material support given to the monasteries in return for the prayers. By giving donations to the monasteries lay people acknowledge the ideals and vocations, which they themselves could not attain, but through their material gifts they could directly benefit from monks' prayers and good works.[32] Sometimes the grant from a lay person was accompanied by counter-gift from the monks for the donor, which marked the formation of the reciprocity obligation. It was usually a small amount of money, an object, a pair of gloves or cloak, or more valuable items such as a horse or cow, which not only represented the good will of the monks, but were also a symbolic representation of the transfer of property and promise of prayers. The counter-gift emphasised the lasting nature of the relationship resulting from the donation. When given to the close relatives of the donors, especially children or spouses, they were meant to prevent their objections to the alienation of the family inheritance.[33] We can find examples of substantial counter-gifts for the relatives of the donors in many parts of Europe. In Burgundy a late twelfth-century grant of pasture to Reigny Abbey was accompanied by a series of counter-gifts to the relatives of the donor. His wife received a cow, his oldest son a brooch, his second son a cape and each of his daughters two solidi.[34] In the charters of grants to Yorkshire Cistercian houses in the twelfth and thirteenth century we find relatively frequent references to the circumstances of the counter gift – the donors received them because of 'necessity' or even 'pressing necessity', so a fairly substantial counter-gift allowed them to become benefactors of a Cistercian monastery even if their resources were very limited.[35] Donations accompanied by counter-gifts were not 'secret sales', but even outright sales to a monastery were believed to provide spiritual benefits. In the eyes of the monks and the laity alike, material and spiritual gains were not mutually exclusive.

The donation ceremony, a solemn ritual, was a method of strengthening the security and permanency of the grant. It was a common practice across Europe that the donor, his family, kin group, witnesses, local people, the abbot and representatives of the monastic community took a walk along the boundaries of the donated land (known as the perambulation), often marking it in some way, for example by crosses cut on the trees, later replaced by permanent stone markers. In this way the line was entrusted to the memory of the locality as the agreed boundary in order to prevent future conflicts. At the time of the emergence of the Cistercian Order the use of charters was already fairly widespread in Western Europe, whilst in Central-Eastern Europe in the twelfth century charters became increasingly important and valued as legal proof of rights to a property. The charters were sealed by both the recipient and the donors, if he, or she, had their own seal. A further solemn act of the donation ceremony required donors to place the charter of grant on the high altar of the abbey as a promise that its terms would not be broken. It was one of the very few situations when a lay person was allowed into the most sacred space of the Cistercian church, which was normally out of bounds to outsiders. The act, on one hand, gave a sense of prestige and privilege, and on the other, evoked the fear of ecclesiastical punishment if the grant was revoked.

The circle of benefactors and neighbours who formed a sphere of the abbey's friends and supporters was very important in the life of any Cistercian community. The bond was particularly valued if there was continuity over several generations. Neighbours and friends frequently witnessed charters issued by and for the abbey. Even when such individuals ceased to be active benefactors themselves, their presence as witnesses was a manifestation of their continuing support. As in any human relationship, the links between Cistercian houses and lay people were subject to change. There never was a perfect uniformity in the attitudes of particular families or kin groups within the same generation and across time. As Constance Bouchard describes it, 'the laymen, especially with the change in the generations, had a continually shifting view of what their relationship could or should be'.[36] With the decrease in land donations in the thirteenth century in most of Western Europe, the support for Cistercian houses was manifested by the witnessing already mentioned, smaller piecemeal donations, exchanges of property, grants of objects, especially church furnishings, windows, liturgical vessels, vestments or books.

Within the monastic tradition there were a number of established forms of liturgical commemoration, which the Cistercians continued. One of the oldest practices was writing down the names of individuals in special books. Such volumes (or sometimes rolls) are named differently by the historians – *libri vitae, libri mortuorum*, obituary or mortuary rolls or necrologies – but the function was the same: commemorating friends and supporters of an abbey. Prayers for the dead were not only an obligation on the living, but also helped to create ties between monasteries and subsequent generations of benefactors' families and were the key element of the reciprocity circle. The Cistercian Order inherited a long and established Benedictine tradition of commemoration, which Cluniac houses had developed further – not only performing daily liturgy for the benefit of an ever-growing number of individuals, but also distributing charity to the poor in the name of their dead benefactors and friends.[37]

The Cistercians introduced radical changes to this burdensome custom. They abolished the principle of individual commemoration, replacing it with annual cumulative prayers for different groups of people. On 11 January the White Monks prayed for all the benefactors of the Order and on 20 November for the members of other Orders, which were in prayer confraternity with the Cistercians – Cluny, Carthusians, Augustinian Canons and Premonstratensians, the Benedictine abbey of Monte Cassino and several houses in Burgundy.[38] The individual *familiares* of the Order were prayed for on 17 September (from 1187 on 15 September). Each day the Cistercians celebrated a special mass, except on certain holy days (Good Friday, Holy Saturday, Christmas, Easter and Pentecost), for all the dead members and *familiares* of the Order. Later, an additional mass was added, in honour of the Virgin Mary, for all the benefactors of the Order. Despite these provisions, there was a strong demand for individual commemoration, and the General Chapter had granted such a privilege by 1200 to some fifty individuals – royalty and high nobility – including King Louis of France, King Richard I of England and Matthew, chancellor of the king of Sicily. Individual houses also compiled their own list of benefactors, but excluded individual commemoration of the monks' relatives, causing protestations and discussions at the General Chapter in 1180.[39] The belief in the great intercessory power of Cistercian prayers is also exemplified by a flurry of requests in the thirteenth century for prayers directed to the General Chapter from various European monarchs for their own and their families' salvation – Philip III of France (1270–1285), Charles I of Sicily (1266–1282), Alfonso X of Castile (1252–1284), James I of Aragon (1213–1276) and Edward I (1272–1307).[40]

This particular exclusivity of entry into the Cistercian prayer community made it very desirable and gave the abbeys a useful tool for 'rewarding' individuals, who were, for a variety of reasons, particularly significant.[41] From the thirteenth century noting down names of departed friends and supporters and their commemoration became an established element of the Cistercian role. In the early fifteenth-century copy of the necrology from Pelplin Abbey in Pomeralia, the scribe added an explanation of the privileges which the lay people who were members of the fraternity would receive. By the agreement of the Chapter and according to the regulations of the Order, the confraters were granted the spiritual benefits derived from of all the masses, vigils, alms, prayers and charitable works performed by the monks in Pelplin Abbey 'until the end of the world'.[42] The entry into individual lists kept at particular abbeys was so advantageous for the salvation of the soul of those people listed because they automatically partook in the benefits of all activities of the Cistercian abbeys.[43] In the late Middle Ages many houses entered into 'individual agreements' with lay people to set up permanent liturgical commemorations. King Valdemar IV Atterdag of Denmark (d. 1375) bequeathed 50 silver marks for daily masses for his soul and a yearly pittance for all the monks in his remembrance consisting of a three-course meal and a barrel of German beer at Esrum Abbey.[44]

Burials were one of the principal manifestations of the intercessory function of the monastic houses. In principle, Cistercian monasteries were very restrictive in allowing access for lay people; in practice, we can observe a great variety of attitudes towards lay burials in the abbeys. As in many other aspects of the relationship with the wider world, the Cistercians inherited an established tradition. Burials in close proximity to the relics of the saints 'benefited' from closeness to regularly performed masses and other liturgical activities. As such, they were much desired by lay people for their intercessory power and social prestige. The Benedictine and Cluniac houses were real 'magnets' for lay burials, and commemoration was central to their monastic role. When the Cistercian movement emerged, there was clearly an idea that patrons are entitled to be buried in 'their' monasteries. The General Chapter was well aware of these expectations, but for the donors burial in a Cistercian monastery was not an automatic privilege. In 1180 a Cistercian statute forbade secular burials in the monastic churches except for kings, queens, bishops and archbishops; this prescription was frequently repeated until 1316.[45]

Early on, there was a clear understanding of the importance of such burials as a tool for creating and sustaining key relationships with the outside world, as clarified by several statutes. By *c.* 1147 an abbey's servants who died within the precincts were allowed to be buried in the monastic cemetery alongside a limited number of 'friends' and *familiares* and their wives. As a response to growing pressure the General Chapter allowed burials of founders and anybody else who could not be refused without 'causing a scandal' in 1179. The codification of 1202 listed types of people who could be buried in Cistercian houses – founders, their descendants (patrons) and guests, two familiars with their wives, servants and travellers. Further clarification issued in 1217 by the General Chapter indicated that, by the early thirteenth century, lay burials were a widespread phenomenon. The statute stated that lay people in Cistercian cemeteries were subject to a licence from the parish priest of the 'applicant' in question.[46] Many of the early regulations appear not to have been implemented with great vigour, and in fact there was a widespread acceptance of lay burials. For example Melrose Abbey in Scotland accepted a significant number of male and female interments in the 1180s, several of them in the chapter house.

The position of the General Chapter appears to have changed in the course of the thirteenth century. The explicit prohibitions ceased; instead, the specific locations of the burials came under sustained scrutiny. The statutes focused on the ban on interments in chapter houses and churches. We have a number of General Chapter rulings to punish abbots who allowed lay burials in chapter houses or monastic churches in the late twelfth and first half of the thirteenth century, but there was clearly no consistency. The cases involved only houses in France and Germany, not elsewhere, where burials of laity were rife. It was a process that could not have been stopped, and by 1300 Cistercian churches were open to a much wider spectrum of lay people. This created a further need for more burial spaces, which led to the creation of special chapels located on the parameter of the east end and the nave.[47]

The influence of older traditions also led to foundations of Cistercian houses specifically as family necropoleis just as had been the case amongst Benedictine houses. Sorø Abbey, founded by the Hvide family in the early 1160s, was described in the Sorø Donation Book (created c. 1210) as founded 'in honour of God and as a family sepulchre', whilst Bishop Peder of Roskilde described the monastery in his charter thus: 'as is well known, [it] was founded by our ancestors as a burial for our family'.[48] Sometimes this role was remarkably long-lasting. Doberan Abbey was continuously used by the patrons, the dukes of Mecklenburg, as their necropolis until the Reformation. Not only male houses functioned as multi-generational mausolea. It was even more common for nunneries to have such a role. The Cistercian nunnery in Trzebnica was founded by Duke Henry the Bearded of Silesia and his wife Hedwig in 1202 as their burial place. The founders were particularly generous in the endowment and the subsequent grants, whilst the monastic church provided an impressive setting for the ducal mausoleum and the liturgical commemorations. The first abbess was Gertrud, the daughter of the founders. She succeeded in securing the canonisation of her mother in 1268, thus making Trzebnica Abbey a thriving pilgrimage destination.[49]

By the late thirteenth century Cistercian houses were not only accessible for burial to those at the very top of society. Many abbeys across Europe attracted lay burials of lesser nobility or even wealthy peasants. Such burials were frequently a type of 'counter-gift'. References to lay burials appeared in the charters of grants with the phrase 'with the body', which means that the donor expected burials as a counter-gift.[50] Such individuals were usually buried in the monastic cemetery outside the walls of the church. The thirteenth-century requests for burials in Fountains Abbey show a cross-section of Yorkshire society, including a substantial number of peasants and several cases of burials from the same family over three generations.[51]

Unsurprisingly, monastic chronicles, such as the *Chronicle of Melrose Abbey*, noted who was buried and where as a reminder of the commemorative obligations. The *Liber ordinarius* of Bebenhausen from the fifteenth century reminded the community about its obligation to perform masses for the dead for those 'who are lying with us in the chapter house'.[52] Whilst the eternal presence of patrons and benefactors through burials left many physical remains and written references, the presence of living lay persons within the Cistercian precincts was also very important yet left far less evidence in the sources.

Among many of the 'founding myths' of the Cistercians in the *Exordium Parvum* is a story that until the abbacy of Harding the dukes of Burgundy held court in Cîteaux, but then the practice was abolished, which symbolised the end of lay interference.[53] It is true that the Cistercians were protective of their own spaces and select-ive in the admission of outsiders, but they were also guided by the Rule of Benedict and their own regulations – especially *Ecclesiastica Officia* – which put hospitality among the chief monastic obligations. The prescription to show kindness to guests was frequently repeated by the General Chapter.[54] The number of guests at Cistercian houses was probably lower than in the Benedictine houses, but they remained an important part of the White Monks' ethos. In their hospitality rit-uals Cistercians tried to follow precisely the prescriptions of the Rule of Benedict, for example the custom of prostration before guests and washing of hands and feet as symbols of humility. These were practised by the Benedictines and Cluniacs in an abbreviated form, for which Cistercians criticised them harshly.[55]

The guests were accommodated in the guest houses, which were located in such a way, usually west of the lay brothers' range, as to minimise contact with the monastic community. Food played a major role in the hosting of guests and a separate kitchen catered for the abbot and his guests. They were offered much richer food than the community, but had to fast on the prescribed days. One of the reasons for the development of impressive abbatial residences was precisely the need for providing high-status space for entertaining important guests. It is clear that the practice of eating with lay guests was common in Cistercian monasteries but it continued to be a 'grey area' for the Order's authorities. During the visitation of Hailes Abbey conducted by Abbot Herman of Stratford in 1394, he reminded the community that secular persons must not eat regularly in the monastery, which was qualified by the statement that this can be done if 'very great advantage to the community would come from this'.[56] Not all guests were equal, and the type and quality of the accommodation and food made a clear differentiation. By the end of the twelfth century Cistercian and Benedictine abbots operated 'a two-tier system of hospitality': selected guest dined with them, whilst the common guests ate in the guest hall.[57]

Engagement in the world, bonds with patrons and benefactors and the intercessory obligations of the White Monks were not a contradiction of the ideal of withdrawal, but a central element of being a Cistercian community. Prayers for lay people, burials and hospitality were all key elements of an ancient monastic tradition which the White Monks inherited in the same way as the desert imagery. At the same time it was also a pragmatic tool for creating and sustaining relationships with the outside world without which no religious institution could survive. Across Europe, in different regions and localities, Cistercian abbeys encountered well-established ideas of their potential benefactors about their function as monastic houses. The idea of desert and withdrawal, engagement with and connection to the world were equally important aspects of 'Cistercianness' and we must not try to separate them, even if this is so alien to our modern sensibilities.

EJ

Notes

1   The work was a revision of *The White Monks: A History of the Cistercian Order* (Okauchee, WI, 1953), elaborated and translated into French (1957) and German (1958). See also L.J. Lekai, 'Ideals and Reality in Early Cistercian Life and Legislation', in *Cistercian Ideals and Reality*, ed. J.R. Sommerfeldt, CS 60 (Kalamazoo, MI, 1978), pp. 4–29; K. Elm *et al.* (eds.), *Die Zisterzienser: Ordensleben zwischen Ideal und Wirklichkeit* (Cologne, 1981); and F.J. Felten and W. Rösener (eds.), *Norm und Realität: Kontinuität und Wandel der Zisterzienser im Mittelalter* (Berlin, 2009).

2   For instance C. Bouchard, 'Cistercian Ideals versus Reality: 1134 Reconsidered', *Cîteaux*, 39 (1988), 217–31; C. Bouchard, *Holy Entrepreneurs: Cistercians, Knights, and Economic Exchange in*

Twelfth-Century Burgundy (London and Ithaca, NY, 1991), pp. 185–7; M.G. Newman, *The Boundaries of Charity: Cistercian Culture and Ecclesiastical Reform 1098–1180* (Stanford, CA, 1996); J. Burton and J. Kerr, *The Cistercians in the Middle Ages* (Woodbridge, 2011); E. Jamroziak, *Survival and Success on Medieval Borders: Cistercian Houses in Medieval Scotland and Pomerania from the Twelfth to the Late Fourteenth Century* (Turnhout, 2011).

3   See Thomas Coomans's chapter in this volume.

4   É. Gilson, *La théologie mystique de Saint Bernard* (Paris, 1934), trans. *The Mystical Theology of Saint Bernard* (London, 1940; repr. Kalamazoo, MI, 1990).

5   C. Mohrmann, 'Observations sur la langue et le style de St Bernard'; SBOp 2, pp. ix–xxxiii; J. Leclercq, *Recueil d'études sur Saint Bernard et ses écrits*, vol. III (Rome, 1969).

6   See, for example, for Great Britain, R.A. Donkin, *The Cistercians: Studies in the Geography of Medieval England and Wales* (Toronto, 1978), pp. 31–51 and 179–80; for Scandinavia, J. France, *Cistercians in Scandinavia*, CS 131 (Kalamazoo, MI, 1992), pp. 10–11; for eastern central Europe, W. Schich, 'Zum Wirken der Zisterzienser im östlichen Mitteleuropa im 12. und 13. Jahrhundert', in *Zisterziensische Spiritualität: Theologische Grundlagen, funktionale Voraussetzungen und bildhafte Ausprägungen im Mittelalter*, ed. C. Kasper and K. Schreiner (St Ottilien, 1994), pp. 269–94 (pp. 279–81); and for Germany, W. Ribbe, 'Die Wirtschaftstätigkeit der Zisterzienser im Mittelalter: Agrarwirtschaft', in *Die Zisterzienser: Ordensleben zwischen Ideal und Wirklichkeit*, ed. K. Elm *et al.* (Cologne, 1981), pp. 203–36 (pp. 203–4). See further C.H. Berman, *Medieval Agriculture, the Southern French Countryside, and the Early Cistercians* (Philadelphia, PA, 1986), pp. 7–10, and the chapters by Constance H. Berman and Emilia Jamroziak in this volume.

7   'Locum igitur ad habitaculum habilem eligunt; eligunt non inhabitabilem sed inhabitatum, mundum, fecundum, responsalem frugibus, non ineptum seminibus … locum extra mundum in corde mundi, semotum ab hominibus hominum in medio, seculum scire nolentes, a seculo sciri uolentes.' Walter Map, *De nugis curialium* 1.24, ed. and trans. M.R. James *et al.* (Oxford, 1983), pp. 74–5.

8   E.R. Curtius, *European Literature and the Latin Middle Ages* (Princeton, NJ, 1973; first pub. in English 1953; first pub. in German 1948), pp. 183–202.

9   Waddell, *Narrative*, p. 401, n.8; Newman, *The Boundaries of Charity*, pp. 69, 94–6.

10   Waddell, *Narrative*, p. 161.

11   *Exordium Cistercii* 1: 'Igitur post multos labores … tandem desiderio potiti Cistercium devenerunt, locum tunc scilicet horroris et vastæ solitudinis. Sed milites Christi loci asperitatem ab arcto proposito quod iam animo conceperant non dissidere iudicantes, ut vere sibi divinitus præparatum tam gratum habuere locum quam carum propositum.' Trans. Waddell, *Narrative*, p. 400.

12 See J.-B. Auberger, *L'unanimité cistercienne primitive: mythe ou réalité?* Cîteaux: Studia et Documenta 3 (Achel, 1986), pp. 121–4, and E. Freeman, *Narratives of a New Order: Cistercian Historical Writing in England, 1150–1220* (Turnhout, 2002), pp. 158–9.

13 Waddell, *Narrative*, p. 401, n.8.

14 B. Ward, 'The Desert Myth', in *One Yet Two: Monastic Tradition East and West*, ed. B.M. Pennington, CS 29 (Kalamazoo, MI, 1976), pp. 183–99 (pp. 183–6); H.E.J. Cowdrey, 'The English Background of Stephen Harding', in *The New Monastery*, ed. E.R. Elder, CF 60 (Kalamazoo, MI, 1998), pp. 57–77 (p. 68); Auberger, *L'unanimité*, for instance, pp. 173–4; M.B. Bruun, 'The Wilderness as *lieu de mémoire*: Literary Deserts of Cîteaux and La Trappe', in *Negotiating Heritage: Memories of the Middle Ages*, ed. M.B. Bruun and S. Glaser (Turnhout, 2008), pp. 21–42.

15 *Exordium Parvum* 3: 'Ad quem viri Dei venientes, locumque illum tanto religioni quam animo iamiamque conceperant, et propter quam illuc advenerant, habiliorem quanto sæcularibus despicabiliorem et inaccessibilem intelligentes, nemoris et spinarum densitate præcisa ac remota, monasterium ibidem … construere cœperunt.' Trans. Waddell, *Narrative*, p. 421; for the dating see p. 230.

16 'Nam volenti perperam agere, et desertum abundantiam habet, et nemus umbram, et silentium solitudo.' *Ep* 115.1; SBOp 7, p. 294; B. Scott James (trans.), *The Letters of St Bernard of Clairvaux*, intro. B.M. Kienzle (Stroud and Kalamazoo, MI, 1998; first pub. 1953), p. 180.

17 'Regio australis est claustrum, vel eremus … et per australem plagam socialis vita et spiritualis bonorum conversatio designatur. Claustralis vero paradisus ad suavem spirantis austri clementiam, quasi tot floribus vernat, quot virtutibus abundat.' *Sent* III.91; SBOp 6.2, p. 140, trans. F. Swietek, *The Parables and the Sentences*, CF 55 (Kalamazoo, MI, 2000), p. 290; see also *Div* 42.2; SBOp 6.1, p. 258.

18 See Peter King's chapter in this volume.

19 'En entrant dans le Cloître on voyoit un toit ruiné, qui à la moindre pluye le remplissoit d'eau … les Parloirs servoient d'écuries. Le Refectoire n'en avoit plus que le nom. Les Moines & les Seculiers s'y assembloient pour joüer à la boule, lorsque la chaleur ou le mauvais temps ne leur permettoit pas de joüer dehors. Le Dortoir estoit abandonné & inhabité; il ne servoit de retraite qu'aux oiseaux de nuit … Le Monastere estoit sans jardin, & il estoit environné d'une terre ingrate, plantée d'épines, de buissons & d'arbres. Mais le comble des maux estoit, que par le moyen du grand chemin qu'on avoit fait depuis environ cent ans auprés des murailles du Monastere, on ne voyoit que vagabonds, que scelerats, qu'assassins. Les hommes & les femmes s'assembloient dans le bois qui est tout proche, & là comme dans un azile assuré ils se cachoient pour commettre toute sorte de crimes.' Dominique Georges, 'Proces Verbal de l'ètat spirituel & temporel de l'Abbaïe de la Trappe', in Pierre Maupeou, *La vie du très-reverend père dom Armand Jean Le Bouthillier de Rancé* (Paris, 1709), Book 4, pp. 251–71 (pp. 265–6).

20 J.D. Leloczky (ed.), *Constitutiones et Acta Capitulorum Strictioris Observantiae Ordinis Cisterciensis (1624–1687)* (Rome, 1967), pp. 223–4.

21 C. Waddell, 'The Cistercian Dimension of the Reform of La Trappe', in *Cistercians in the Late Middle Ages*, ed. E.R. Elder, CS 64 (Kalamazoo, MI, 1981), pp. 102–61 (p. 129); D.N. Bell, *Understanding Rancé: The Spirituality of the Abbot of La Trappe in Context*, CS 205 (Kalamazoo, MI, 2005), pp. 312–13. 'Avaux' is sometimes written 'Abaux'.

22 'Cette Abbaye est située dans un grand valon; & la forest, & les colines qui l'environnent, sont disposées de telle sorte, quelles semblent la vouloir cacher au reste de la terre. Elles … rendent les aproches si difficiles, qu'il est même mal-aisé d'y arriver sans le secours d'un guide. Il y avoit autrefois un chemin pour aller de Mortagne à Paris … Monsieur l'Abbé neantmoins l'a fait changer, afin que les environs de leur Monastere soient moins frequentez. Aussi n'y a t'il rien de plus solitaire que ce desert; car encore qu'il y ait plusieurs Villes & Bourgades à trois lieuës à l'entour, il sembles pourtant qu'on soit dans une terre étrangere, & dans un autre pays.' Félibien des Avaux, 'Description de l'abbaye de la Trappe a Madame la Duchesse de Liancour', in *Reglemens de l'Abbaye de Nôtre-Dame de la Trappe* (Paris, 1718), pp. 3–4.

23 A.J. Krailsheimer, *Armand-Jean de Rancé, Abbot of la Trappe: His Influence in the Cloister and the World* (Oxford, 1974), p. 84.

24 M.A. Galton Schimmelpenninck (trans. and commentary), *Narrative of a tour taken in the year 1667, to La Grande Chartreuse and Alet by Dom Claude Lancelot* (London, 1813), p. 254.

25 Krailsheimer, *Armand-Jean de Rancé*, pp. 85–7.

26 'Madame, ce n'est pas sans raison que je crains de ne pas contenter entierement vôtre pieuse curiosité, parce qu'il est bien difficile que je vous fasse une description de l'Abbaye de la Trappe, qui puisse répondre à la haute idée qu'on en doit avoir.' Félibien, 'Description', p. 1.

27 B. Beugnot, *Le discours de la retraite au XVIIe siècle: loin du monde et du bruit* (Paris, 1996), esp. pp. 235–56; D. Stanton, 'The Ideal of of "repos" in Seventeenth-Century French Literature', *L'Esprit Créateur*, 15 (1975), 79–104.

28 Letter of 22 June 1672; *Lettres de Mademoiselle de Montpensier … Marquise de Lambert* (Paris, 1806), p. 180.

29 A.J. Krailsheimer (ed.), *Armand-Jean de Rancé: Correspondance*, 4 vols. (Paris and Cîteaux, 1993); trans. (partial) A.J. Krailsheimer, *The Letters of Armand-Jean de Rancé, Abbot and Reformer of La Trappe*, 2 vols., CS 80 and 81 (Kalamazoo, MI, 1984).

30 Plan in *Description du plan en relief de l'Abbaye de la Trappe presenté au Roy par le Frere Pacôme* (Paris, 1708); Bell, *Understanding Rancé*, pp. 327–8.

31 *Description du plan en relief*, pp. 19–20.

32 I.F. Silber, *Virtuosity, Charisma, and Social Order: A Comparative Sociological Study of Monasticism in Theravada Buddhism and Medieval Catholicism* (Cambridge, 1995), pp. 37–172.

33 Bouchard, *Holy Entrepreneurs*, pp. 87–94.

34 *Ibid.*, p. 89.

35 E. Jamroziak, 'Making and Breaking the Bonds: Yorkshire Cistercians and Their Neighbours', in *Perspectives for an Architecture of Solitude: Essays on Cistercians, Art and Architecture in Honour of Peter Fergusson*, ed. T. N. Kinder (Turnhout, 2004), pp. 64–5.

36 Bouchard, *Holy Entrepreneurs*, p. 175.

37 J. Wollasch, 'Gemeinschaftsbewusstsein und soziale Leistung im Mittelalter', *Frühmittelalterliche Studien*, 9 (1975), 268–86.

38 Waddell, *Statutes*, 1192:12, 1193:5, 1194:9, 1196:61, 1198:14, 1200:1, 1201:4, 1201:50.

39 *Ibid.*, 1180: 8.

40 *Ibid.*, 1273: 68, 69, 70, 71, 72, 73.

41 J. Wollasch, 'Neue Quellen zur Geschichte der Cistercienser', *Zeitschrift für Kirchengeschichte*, 84 (1973), 188, 227, 230–1; Canivez, *Statuta*, 1187: 9, 1180: 8; B. Lackner, 'The Liturgy of Early Citeaux', in *Studies in Medieval Cistercian History Presented to Jeremiah F. O'Sullivan*, ed. M.B. Pennington (Shannon, 1971), p. 29; P. Orliński, *Cysterskie nekrologi na Pomorzu Gdańskim od XIII do XVII wieku* (Toruń, 1997), pp. 32–3.

42 'Liber mortuorum Pelplinensis', in *Monumenta Poloniae Historica*, vol. IV, p. 124: 'de communi consensus nostri capituli omnium missarum, psalmorum, vigillarum, disciplinarum id est castigacionum corporum, elemosinarum, oracionum, laborum et omnium spiritualium beneficiorum ac omnium bonorum, que fiunt in ecclesia nostra et que nunc procurata sunt et usque in finem mundi procurari poterunt, participles facimus fraternitatem in predictis omnibus secundum Cisterciensis ordinis consuetudinem largientes.'

43 Orliński, *Cysterskie nekrologi*, p. 43.

44 K. Erslev (ed.), *Repertorium Diplomaticum Regni Danici Mediaevalis* (Copenhagen, 1896–8), vol. II, no. 3210; B. P. McGuire, *The Cistercians in Denmark: Their Attitudes, Roles, and Functions in Medieval Society*, CS 35 (Kalamazoo, MI, 1982), p. 223.

45 Waddell, *Statutes*, 1180:5; codifications in 1202, 1220, 1237, 1257, 1289 and 1316.

46 J. Hall, 'The Legislative Background to the Burial of Laity and Other Patrons in Cistercian Abbeys', *Cîteaux*, 56 (2005), 364–9; J. Hall *et al.*, 'Table of Legislation Concerning the Burial of Laity and other Patrons in Cistercian Abbeys', *Cîteaux*, 56 (2005), 373–418.

47 M. Untermann, *Forma Ordinis: Die mittelalterliche Baukunst der Zisterzienser* (Munich and Berlin, 2001), pp. 89–90.

48 K. Esmark, 'Religious Patronage and Family Consciousness: Sorø Abbey and the "Hvide Family", c. 1150–1250', in *Religious and Laity in Western Europe 1000–1400: Interaction, Negotiation, and Power*, ed. E. Jamroziak and J. Burton (Turnhout, 2006), p. 101; *Scriptores rerum Danicarum*, vol. IV, p. 476; *Diplomatarium Danicarum*, first series, vol. IV, no. 41.

49 M. Kutzner, *Cysterska architektura na śląsku w latach 1200–1330* (Toruń, 1969), p. 22; P. Wiszewski, 'Cysterki trzebnickie w społeczeństwie

śląskim (czwarta ćwierć XIII wieku – pierwsza połowa XIV wieku)', in *Cystersi w Społeczeństwie Europy Środkowej*, ed. A.M. Wyrwa and J. Dobosz (Poznań, 2000), pp. 705–6.
50 J. Wardrop, *Fountains Abbey and Its Benefactors*, CS 91 (Kalamazoo, MI, 1987), pp. 260–75.
51 *Ibid.*, pp. 263–75.
52 'apud nos in capitulo legitur', J. Sydow, *Die Zisterzienserabtei Bebenhausen*, Germania Sacra NF 16: Bistum Konstanz (Berlin, 1984), p. 118.
53 *Exordium Parvum* 17.4; C. Rudolph, 'The Principal Founders and the Early Artistic Legislation of Cîteaux', in *Studies in Cistercian Art and Architecture*, 3, ed. M.P. Lillich (Kalamazoo, MI, 1982), pp. 16–17.
54 *RB*, chapter 53; 'Instituta Generalis Capituli apud Cistercium', in Waddell, *Narrative*, clause 1, p. 454; Choisselet/Vernet, chapters 87, 120.
55 J. Sonntag, *Klosterleben im Spiegel des Zeichenhaften. Symbolisches Denken und Handeln hochmittelalterlicher Mönche zwischen Dauer und Wandel, Regel und Gewohnheit* (Münster, 2008), pp. 582–96.
56 C. Harper-Bill, 'Cistercian Visitation in the Late Middle Ages: The Case of Hailes Abbey', *Historical Research*, 53 (1980), 103–14 (p. 110).
57 J. Kerr, 'The Symbolic Significance of Hospitality', in *Self-Representation of Medieval Religious Communities*, ed. A. Müller and K. Stöber (Berlin, 2009), pp. 125–41 (p. 130).

Primary sources

Félibien des Avaux, A., 'Description de l'abbaye de la Trappe a Madame la Duchesse de Liancour', in *Reglemens de l'Abbaye de Nôtre-Dame de la Trappe* (Paris, 1718)
Georges, D., 'Proces Verbal de l'ètat spirituel & temporel de l'Abbaïe de la Trappe', in Pierre Maupeou, *La vie du très-reverend père dom Armand Jean Le Bouthillier de Rancé* (Paris, 1709), Book 4, pp. 251–71
Krailsheimer, A.J. (ed.), *Armand-Jean de Rancé: Correspondance*, 4 vols. (Paris and Cîteaux, 1993); trans. (partial) A.J. Krailsheimer, *The Letters of Armand-Jean de Rancé, Abbot and Reformer of La Trappe*, 2 vols., CS 80 and 81 (Kalamazoo, MI, 1984)
Leloczky, J.D. (ed.), *Constitutiones et Acta Capitulorum Strictioris Observantiae Ordinis Cisterciensis (1624–1687)* (Rome, 1967)
Waddell, C. (ed.), *Narrative and Legislative Texts from Early Cîteaux*, Cîteaux: Studia et Documenta 9 (Brecht, 1999)
  Twelfth-Century Statutes from the Cistercian General Chapter, Cîteaux: Studia et Documenta 12 (Brecht, 2002)

Part I

History

1 Foundation and twelfth century

MARTHA G. NEWMAN

In 1098 a small group of monks left the Burgundian monastery of Molesme to establish a new monastery in the forest of Cîteaux, about 25 km south of the town of Dijon. By the end of the twelfth century this one community had spawned an international monastic Order with over 500 abbeys of men and an indeterminate number of women, spread from Spain to the Baltic, from Scotland to Sicily. Over the course of the century Cistercian monks became powerful figures in the ecclesiastical hierarchy, Cistercian writings and spiritual ideas influenced the prevailing religious culture and many Cistercian monasteries became centres for economic and technological change.

Scholars have long debated the character of the new community at Cîteaux and the process by which the Cistercian Order formed. They have argued about Cîteaux's relationship to older forms of monasticism and to movements of monastic and ecclesiastic reform, about the nature of the documents that claim to describe the foundation of this new Order and about the Order's ideals and organisational structure. They have questioned the influence of its spiritual leaders, and the extent to which they articulated a unified Cistercian culture. They have asked whether this Order included women's houses as well as those of men. And they have debated whether the monks' political activities, economic success and growing status distinctions within their communities illustrate their early ideals or instead demonstrate a quick decline from their initial reform.

Many of these debates stem from efforts to place the Cistercians into the paradigms used to describe eleventh- and twelfth-century monasticism. Over the last fifty years the study of monastic reform has been shaped by two converging developments. Catholic theologians and confessional historians, interested in returning to the sources of their Christian faith (*ressourcement*), sought to find in the early texts of religious Orders their guiding spirit and ideals. At the same time secular

scholars incorporated into their work ideas from Max Weber's sociological analysis of charisma and bureaucracy, and they employed Victor
Turner's concepts of 'communitas' and 'liminality' to describe the
intense relationships of those living outside normal social structures.
Medieval monasteries appeared examples of liminal and charismatic
communities. The two groups of scholars have influenced one another
and together have made the contrast between 'ideal' and 'reality' and
the cycle of charismatic reform, institutionalisation and decline central
themes of medieval religious history.

Yet early Cistercian history fits uneasily into these paradigms, for
a number of reasons. First, it is hard to contrast a 'reformed' Cîteaux
with a 'traditional' Molesme. The abbey of Molesme was established
in 1075 as a community of hermits, and the men who founded the new
monastery at Cîteaux – the abbot Robert, his prior Alberic and his secretary Stephen Harding – had held positions of leadership at Molesme.
Initially, Cîteaux followed similar customs, adopting Molesme's liturgical books and allowing the Duke of Burgundy to hold court in its
enclosure. Only some decades later, once they had composed their
Exordium Cistercii, did Cistercian monks articulate language contrasting their life to that at Molesme. Second, there is scant evidence for the
charismatic character of Cîteaux's founders; we have remarkably little
material about these men at all. Robert of Molesme quickly disappeared
from the Cistercians' twelfth-century lists of abbots, and there are neither contemporary *vitae* of Alberic and Stephen Harding nor evidence
for their cults. And third, the Cistercians' earliest texts express their
organisational concerns more than abstract spiritual ideals.

Many of the new religious movements of the eleventh and early
twelfth centuries were indeed inspired by a charismatic leader who
sought to live a life in imitation of Christ and the apostles, and they
only gradually adopted a rule and customary. But the first Cistercians
did not innovate in this way nor seek to enact an apostolic poverty,
an evangelism or an extreme asceticism. Rather, like the monks of
Vallombrosa (who may well have influenced them), they sought to
follow the Benedictine Rule and to create an organisation that would
maintain their understanding of these observances. This nascent institution unified and regulated Cistercian communities, but it also provided an environment that could incorporate and refine prevailing
spiritual ideals and expressions. The Cistercians' ideals developed and
changed over time, and this flexibility within an administrative structure helped make them the most popular and influential of the new
monastic groups of the twelfth century.

FOUNDATION AND DOCUMENTS

Early Cistercian history once seemed straightforward. Robert, the abbot of Molesme, along with Alberic and the Englishman Stephen Harding, became dissatisfied with the wealth and political status of Molesme and, with permission of Hugh of Die, papal legate and arch-bishop of Lyons, established a new community in the forest of Cîteaux. An assembly of ecclesiastics soon ordered Robert to return to Molesme, but Alberic and Stephen Harding remained at the new monastery and became its first abbots. Under Stephen Harding the monastery began to grow, admitting a large group of young aristocrats, including Bernard of Fontaines-lès-Dijon and his companions and relatives, and founding its first affiliated abbey, La Ferté, in 1113. By 1115 the new monastery at Cîteaux had created five affiliates; by 1118 the affiliates began to found their own offspring. During these years Stephen Harding wrote the Charter of Charity that bound the communities together, instituted uniform monastic customs, created a process of visitation between the founding abbey and its affiliates and established a yearly General Chapter of abbots. In 1119 Pope Calixtus II approved this charter.

Since the 1940s the documents that provided this clear and straightforward history have been the subject of much disagreement. Scholars of the early Cistercians are blessed, or cursed, with two twelfth-century foundation narratives: the *Exordium Parvum* and the *Exordium Cistercii*. There are also multiple versions of the *Carta Caritatis*, and various collections of statutes from the General Chapter. Scholars have long disagreed about the dating of these texts and their possible authors. They divide into two camps. On one side are those who see in the documents' inconsistencies an effort by the Cistercians to hide irregularities and rewrite their history. In the 1940s and 1950s Jean Lefèvre suggested that Cîteaux's foundation was unauthorised and that the narrative documents were composed later to disguise this fact. More recently Constance Berman has argued that the Charter of Charity dates from 1165, and that the monks subsequently wrote the narrative documents to backdate the formation of the Order. Her hypothesis suggests that the Cistercian Order was initially a loose affiliation of both male and female communities; only after an institutional structure developed in the 1160s did women's houses begin to be excluded. Opposed to Lefèvre and Berman are scholars who assume the early Cistercian documents are essentially what they claim to be and were written in the first decades of the twelfth century. While the details of their arguments vary, these scholars have generally assumed that the Calixtus II approved a version of the Charter of Charity in 1119, that the *Exordium Parvum* was composed in the early 1120s at Cîteaux and that the *Exordium Cistercii* came from Clairvaux about a decade later.

Chrysogonus Waddell's edition of the early Cistercian narrative texts, published in 1999, offers a new understanding of these documents. Although Waddell assumed the Cistercian documents were honest efforts to describe the Cistercians' foundation, he presented them as layered compositions, repeatedly revised in conjunction with revisions to the Cistercians' customary. According to Waddell, Stephen Harding assembled the kernel of the *Exordium Parvum* around 1113: the initial document consisted of nine letters and charters issued by ecclesiastical officials, linked by short narratives describing the foundation of the new monastery. The earliest extant version of the Charter of Charity, the *Carta Caritatis prior*, was the charter that Calixtus II confirmed in 1119. The stylistic unity of the *Exordium Cistercii* and the *Summa Cartae Caritatis* suggested a single author: Waddell attributed them to Abbot Raynard de Bar of Cîteaux, dated their composition after the death of Stephen Harding in 1134 and posited that they were intended as an introduction to a revised Cistercian customary. When the Cistercians rewrote their customary again in 1147 after their liturgical reforms, they inserted a new historical introduction by revising the *Exordium Parvum*. At this point, they added chapters to give a detailed account of Cîteaux's foundation, its later growth and the early statutes of the General Chapter (chapters 3 and 15 to 18). The 1147 customary, however, was further revised after 1152 when Pope Eugenius III confirmed a new version of the Charter of Charity. The customaries from the second half of the century show more variation in the choice of the narrative accounts that prefaced them.[1]

Waddell's interpretation of these documents brings the early history of the Cistercians into sharper focus. Much of the traditional narrative remains in place but two interrelated characteristics of the Cistercian reform become clearer. One is that if the documents embedded in the *Exordium Parvum* are legitimate, as Waddell suggested, then the foundation of the community at Cîteaux and the negotiations over the return of Robert to Molesme was an international affair: it involved the papal legate and archbishop of Lyons, two popes, two cardinals, five local bishops and three abbots. This was not the establishment of an unstructured hermitage in the wilderness but a carefully planned undertaking whose instigators were accustomed to working with ecclesiastical officials and accepted their authority. Second, Cîteaux's founders did not question the basic assumptions of the monastic life they knew. They continued to exchange spiritual benefits for land, and even more importantly, they sought to find ways to preserve the observances they believed Benedict and his Rule had established. The bishops who described what Robert, Alberic and Stephen had proposed emphasised their desire to follow the Benedictine Rule 'more strictly', Stephen's prologue to the *Exordium Parvum* records the negotiations over Cîteaux's foundation so that the monks there could 'sweat and toil' in their observance of the Benedictine Rule, and the non-Cistercian monastic chroniclers from the 1120s, William of Malmesbury and Orderic Vitalis, noted the importance of the Benedictine Rule to this new community.[2] These early texts suggest that Cîteaux's founders started with structure – with the Rule, with the authority of the bishops and the pope – but then found within this structure the potential for a rich religious life.

The relationship between the Cistercians' organisation and their religious life quickly became apparent. When Stephen Harding composed the Charter of Charity that linked Cîteaux to affiliates, he changed the authority of the abbot and his relation to his community. Abbots of prominent monasteries such as Molesme often presided over numerous affiliated priories that sent agricultural and other revenues back to the central abbey. These abbots were also responsible for the spiritual care of the monks in these priories, no matter how distant, and they had the authority to establish how their communities interpreted the Rule. As a result many abbots spent much time on the road, travelling between priories, and they modified Benedict's regulations to take particular circumstances into consideration.[3]

Stephen Harding created a different administrative structure. The Charter of Charity established each abbey as independent, run by its own abbot and responsible for its own economic well-being. At the same time, it diminished the abbot's authority to modify monastic customs: what bound the abbeys into an Order was the uniform observance of customs and a set of annual meetings and visitations designed to ensure that these uniform observances were maintained. The Charter of Charity and the Cistercians' customary thus placed the abbot within his community of monks rather than emphasising his discretionary authority. By the time the monks created their customary of the 1130s, the abbot, like his monks, slept in the common dormitory; he, too, could be punished if late for prayers; and he and his monks viewed themselves as obedient to the Rule that Benedict had established. It is within this more egalitarian community structure that Cistercian monks articulated the more distinctive elements of their culture and theology.

BERNARD OF CLAIRVAUX AND THE
GROWTH OF THE ORDER

Although the traditional histories of the Cistercians impute the growth of the Order to the entrance of Bernard of Fontaines-lès-Dijon and his friends and relatives, it has long been recognised that Cîteaux started to expand before Bernard and his companions converted. As Constance Bouchard and others have argued, Cîteaux and its affiliates in Burgundy and Champagne appealed especially to the lesser nobility in the region who used their donations to these small, new communities to enhance their own status and assist their hopes for salvation. Nonetheless, Bernard of Clairvaux's fame and activity did much to foster the expansion of the Order in the years between 1130 and 1150. Bernard's prolific writings, his extensive travels and political activities, and the rapid growth of the monasteries associated with his abbey of Clairvaux have raised questions about the relationship of his ideas to those of the initial founders of the Order. Did Bernard reshape the Cistercian Order? Should he be considered the Cistercians' charismatic founder?

We now know not to put too much emphasis on foundation charters and filiation lists for dating Cistercian communities: such documents often present the incorporation of existing monasteries as if they were new foundations, and they ignore the existence of Cistercian women. Nonetheless, the filiation charts from the early thirteenth century that list abbeys associated with each of the first five Cistercian communities do demonstrate Clairvaux's distinctiveness. By Bernard of Clairvaux's death in 1153 there were nearly as many abbeys of men associated with Clairvaux as there were abbeys in the affiliations of the other 4 houses combined; 167 abbeys were associated with Clairvaux, while there were 187 in the rest of the Order.[4] Also, a large proportion of Clairvaux's affiliated monasteries were directly subject to Clairvaux itself, suggesting that communities wanted to claim Clairvaux as their 'mother house'. Finally, a number of Clairvaux's affiliates can be directly linked to Bernard's travels, political activity and contacts. These patterns suggest Bernard of Clairvaux's importance for the Order's expansion.

Bernard of Clairvaux also articulated and enacted ideas about monastic life that differed from those of the first Cistercian founders. Whereas Stephen Harding controlled the geographical location of Cîteaux's first affiliates, carefully locating them on relatively flat land and near streams, he left the planning of Clairvaux to Bernard, who placed his abbey in a narrow valley.[5] Whereas the monks at Cîteaux, under Stephen Harding's supervision, produced highly decorated manuscripts that are masterpieces of Romanesque imagination, Bernard complained about the distracting nature of images. Whereas Stephen Harding wrote few letters, appeared in few charters and confined his political activities to the region around Cîteaux, Bernard quickly became prominent throughout Europe by intervening in episcopal elections and helping heal schisms, preaching for crusades and against heretics and writing letters to correspondents spread across Christendom. And whereas the few extant hints of Stephen's religiosity suggest his emphasis on the model of Benedict, Bernard's extensive religious writings instead focus on the imitation of Christ through voluntary poverty, humility and love.[6]

It is less clear, however, that these differences demonstrate tension between Stephen Harding and Bernard of Clairvaux, or suggest, as has Berman, that the only real organisation of Cistercian houses before the 1160s consisted of those associated with Clairvaux. Stephen Harding's ideas about suitable locations for new houses prevailed even among abbeys in Clairvaux's filiation, but the Order adopted Bernard's ideas about manuscript decoration and architectural forms, creating manuscripts and buildings with a distinctive simplicity. By the 1130s Bernard's political involvement and preaching clearly overshadowed the influence of the abbot of Cîteaux, and his writings made him a spokesman for the Order, but his close relations with ecclesiastical officials followed the pattern set by Cîteaux's foundation. Bernard's writings demonstrate an awareness of the organisation that Stephen Harding had established. While never explicitly mentioning the Charter of Charity, he wrote of both the general and specific 'customs' and 'observances' of the Cistercian way of life: these included general meetings of abbots, visitations to other monasteries, manual labour and a strict observance of the Benedictine Rule. Rather than attesting to an opposition between Cîteaux and Clairvaux, or between Stephen and Bernard, Bernard's ideas developed within the structures that the Cistercian founders had established.

Bernard's presence, both in person and through the spread of his writings, made Cistercian life attractive to donors and potential monks, as the distinctive growth of Clairvaux's filiation suggests. Bernard articulated a particular form of *imitatio Christi*, a stress on the incarnation and an affective spirituality whose expressions of love and friendship, put in a religious key, encouraged personal repentance, contemplation and social reformation. His writings present an interplay between scriptural exegesis and what he called the 'book of experience', and he encouraged his audiences to use their sensory and somatic knowledge as a starting point in their progression toward the divine. These ideas were not Bernard's alone – he attracted like-minded men to the Order who brought their own concerns and backgrounds into the conversation – nor were these ideas only articulated by Cistercians. However, Bernard, together with figures such as William of Saint Thierry, Guerric of Igny, Aelred of Rievaulx and Isaac of Stella, took what was fundamentally a conservative movement, interested in returning to a strict observance of the Benedictine Rule, and transformed it into one whose spiritual ideals resonated with the religious aspirations of many in twelfth-century European society.

From the very beginning these Cistercian ideals had appealed to women as well as men. Stephen Harding helped establish a female community at Tart in the 1120s; by 1147 this monastery had received a papal confirmation of its tithe exemption and its customs that resembled those offered to Cistercian houses of men. By the thirteenth century Tart had established a structure of filiations and a meeting of abbesses over which the abbot of Cîteaux presided. Some of these affiliated communities may have been established by nuns from Tart but many others had been independent establishments or double houses that adopted Cistercian customs and then became affiliated with the Order. Another women's community, Jully, had close relations with Cistercian men and received Bernard of Clairvaux's female relatives. However, Jully never affiliated with the Cistercians: associated from its beginning with the monastery of Molesme, and guided by Stephen Harding's friend Peter, the community was formally placed under the guidance of the abbot of Molesme in 1145.[7] Still other houses of Cistercian women were established by reform-minded bishops; such for instance was the case of the women's community of Wechterswinkel, founded before 1144 by the bishop of Würzburg, and associated with the Cistercian men of Ebrach.

The diverse ways in which women's communities were established and their various associations with Cistercian monks once led scholars to doubt the existence of twelfth-century nuns. But more recently it has become clear that the incorporation of men's communities into the Cistercian Order followed a pattern similar to that of women: some communities were new foundations established by monks from other Cistercian houses, some were initiated by bishops or powerful lay patrons, while many others were already existing communities that gradually adopted Cistercian customs. Furthermore, while the early Charter of Charity did link the existing monasteries into an Order, we must be careful not to read late twelfth-century institutional structures back into the Order's earlier organisation. The Cistercians were initially bound by shared customs and regulations, but by the middle of the century they were also linked by a shared attraction to the religious ideas and examples articulated by their prominent abbots. The men's houses quickly settled on a process of General Chapters and visitations to ensure these commonalities. For the women, the supervision was more variable: in some cases, women's houses were formally affiliated with male abbeys and supervised by Cistercian abbots, but in other cases, they were associated through informal correspondence and shared customs. It was this mixture of administrative centralisation and common spirituality that made the Cistercian Order so attractive to Church leaders and to men and women seeking a religious life.

INSTITUTIONAL ORGANISATION AND LATE TWELFTH-CENTURY DIVERSITY

In the second half of the twelfth century the Cistercian Order encountered the effects of its rapid growth and prominence. On the one hand, the Order became less uniform, reflecting in part the political divisions and cultural differences of the territories in which the abbeys were located. On the other hand, it became more institutionalised as the General Chapter tried to speak for the Order and ensure conformity to its decisions. By the end of the twelfth century the Cistercians were celebrated as a model for the organisation of other monastic Orders but also criticised for losing track of their ideals.

The death of Bernard of Clairvaux and the Cistercians' twenty-year effort to secure his canonisation made some of the divisions apparent. The various reworkings of Bernard's *vita* suggest that even many of the men closest to Bernard were uncertain how to reconcile his political activities with his spiritual message, and whether to present him as a man of their Order or a man of the Church.[8] After Bernard's canonisation in 1174, as his saintly image began to coalesce in liturgical commemorations and the official *vita*, monks at Clairvaux also began to compose shorter exemplary stories that portrayed him as a monk within his community, caring for his brethren with often miraculous results. These stories, collected with *exempla* depicting other holy Cistercians, continued to encourage a shared monastic culture, one which, as the collections by Caesarius of Heisterbach and Engelhard of Langheim show, included religious women as well as men.

Some of the divisions within the Order resulted from the ecclesiastical disputes of the 1160s and 1170s. In the 1130s, during the papal schism that pitted Innocent II against Anacletus, the Cistercian expansion had just started, and the Cistercian abbeys had united with many other religious communities in support of Innocent II. The conflicts between Alexander III and Frederick Barbarossa, and between Henry II and Thomas Becket, in comparison, were more detrimental to the unity of the Order. Geoffrey of Auxerre's deposition as abbot of Clairvaux in 1165 probably resulted from his refusal to support Becket against Henry II, despite Becket's refuge at Pontigny.[9] Similarly, during the papal schism some German abbots were caught between loyalty to their diocesan bishop and loyalty to Alexander III. Both political disputes suggest that the Cistercians' vision of a unified Order within the body of the Church had become difficult to maintain. Furthermore, when Cistercian monks did try to create such unity, as through their preaching against the Cathars in southern France, their work exposed the changing religious ideals of the late twelfth century: they no longer seemed the poor of Christ when compared to the Cathar *perfecti*. Their evocation of a militant Christianity with which they encouraged officials to uncover secret threats to Christian unity contributed to both the Albigensian crusade and the formation of inquisitorial theory.

The Cistercians' economic practices present another area in which the Order became more varied. Much scholarship on the Cistercians' economy suggests that, by the late twelfth century, they had abandoned their early ideals. Yet, as I have suggested earlier, the first Cistercians were more interested in maintaining the precepts of the Benedictine Rule than they were in articulating more abstract ideals such as poverty. Many of their economic practices, such as their rejection of manorial revenues and their insistence on manual labour, stem from this desire to uphold the Rule. Language expressing ideas of poverty became more prevalent in the 1130s as Cistercian monks sought to explain their differences with other monks and to justify their tithe exemptions. This polemical language returned to haunt them by the end of the century when critics such as Walter Map and Gerald of Wales contrasted the Cistercians' claims of poverty with their now privileged economic condition.[10] Yet, while some monasteries had become very wealthy and profited from their participation in a new commercial economy, other houses struggled. These contrasts are particularly apparent among women's communities; by the thirteenth century a few women's abbeys possessed extensive endowments but the majority of Cistercian women's houses were small and survived off occasional donations and the women's own labour.[11]

By the second half of the twelfth century the lay brothers also posed problems for the Cistercians' claims of unity and uniformity. The monks had instituted their lay brotherhood so that their communities could fulfil obligations both to labour and to pray, but despite the monks' descriptions of the unity of their communities, the lay brothers lived distinct lives in which they worked more, prayed less and often ran estates and granges at a distance from the abbey. By the late twelfth century the tension in some monasteries between the lay brothers' subordinate status and their economic importance to their communities occasionally erupted into violence. These revolts were often triggered by abbots who reinforced observances that confirmed the distinctions between the two groups. The Cistercian General Chapter also attempted to enforce statutes regulating the lay brothers' subordinate position and practices but these efforts appear to have fostered still more resentment: some lay brothers, at times aided by monks, detained abbots from attending General Chapter while others refused to offer hospitality to abbots travelling to and from this assembly.[12]

The General Chapter's regulation of the behaviour of lay brothers was only a part of a broader effort by the assembled abbots in the late twelfth and early thirteenth centuries to enforce uniformity on an Order that had spread across political borders and encompassed cultural, geographical and economic differences. The General Chapter first codified its statutes in 1202, thereby making its collection of regulations accessible and useful to its abbots. Jean Leclercq criticised this effort as an unproductive focus on minutiae that lost sight of the spirit of early Cistercian life, but by the early thirteenth century such institutional decisions may have been the only way to reproduce the sense of 'being of one spirit' that the early twelfth-century Cistercians had created in a less formal fashion.[13] Certainly, ecclesiastical officials of the period still found much to admire in the Cistercian organisation: the Fourth Lateran Council required all monastic congregations to hold a General Chapter modelled on the Cistercian assemblies. The Cistercian Order of 1215 looked little like the initial foundation at Cîteaux in 1098, but even a century after its establishment, it continued to respond to prevailing ideas and concerns and incorporate them into its religious culture.

CONCLUSION

The Cistercians were one of the numerous new religious communities that formed in the last decades of the eleventh century and early decades of the twelfth. Many of these new groups coalesced around leaders who found inspiration in biblical models and stories of heroic saints; these charismatic individuals attracted groups of followers and eventually formed them into communities. By the middle of the twelfth century, some of these communities had disappeared, others had written their own rules and customs and still others had adopted Cistercian practices and become part of the Cistercian Order. But the foundation of Cîteaux and the initial establishment of the Cistercian Order did not follow this pattern. Robert of Molesme, Alberic and Stephen Harding were not at the vanguard of the period's religious movements, nor were they remembered as charismatic figures who explored forms of apostolic life. Rather, they were monastic administrators who worked within existing parameters of religious life. They developed a monastic organisation that preserved the observances of the Benedictine Rule but that remained flexible enough to elaborate and modify what the founders had established.

Yet the Cistercians contributed more to twelfth-century society than just the formation of the first religious Order. Cistercian monks articulated a language of contemplation, experience and religious longing that influenced the development of medieval mysticism, they worked toward a vision of ecclesiastical reform that shaped papal ideology, they encouraged a militant Christianity that was enacted in crusades against Muslims and Christian heretics and they managed estates that experimented with water technologies and commercial transactions. While we know little about the religious ideals of the founders of the Order other than their interest in the Benedictine Rule, we know that communities they established allowed for the incorporation of new ideas. By attracting some of the most ardent and articulate figures of the twelfth century, the Cistercian Order gradually developed a distinctive culture that became interwoven with its organisational structure. Its influence and popularity derived from the monks' ability to mix traditional assumptions of monastic life with a nascent institutional framework and new religious ideas, and from this to create a religious culture that was distinctively Cistercian.

Notes

1   For a critique of Waddell's argument that suggests Stephen Harding wrote the entire *Exordium Parvum*, see C. Holdsworth, 'Narrative and Legislative Texts from Early Cîteaux: A Review Article', *Cîteaux*, 51 (2000), 157–66.

2   William of Malmesbury, *De gestis regum Anglorum libri quinque* 4.366, ed. W. Stubbs, 2 vols. (London, 1887–89), vol. II, p. 383; Orderic Vitalis, *Historia aecclesiastica* 8.26, ed. M. Chibnall (Oxford, 1969–80), vol. IV (1973), pp. 312–27.

3 B. Rosenwein, 'Rules and the "Rule" at Tenth-Century Cluny', *Studia Monastica*, 19 (1977), 307–20.
4 A.H. Bredero, *Bernard of Clairvaux: Between Cult and History* (Grand Rapids, MI, 1996), pp. 250–51.
5 J.-B. Auberger, *L'unanimité cistercienne primitive: mythe ou réalité?*, Cîteaux: Studia et Documenta 3 (Achel, 1986), pp. 91–108.
6 See M. G. Newman, 'Text and Authority in the Formation of the Cistercian Order: The Early Cistercians Read Gregory the Great', in *Reforming the Church before Modernity: Patterns, Problems and Approaches*, ed. L. Hamilton and C. Belitto (Farnham, 2005), pp. 173–98.
7 C.H. Berman, 'Were There Twelfth-Century Cistercian Nuns?', *Church History*, 68 (1999), 824–64.
8 Bredero, *Bernard of Clairvaux*, pp. 23–90.
9 See *ibid.*, pp. 49–50 and Martha G. Newman, *The Boundaries of Charity: Cistercian Culture and Ecclesiastical Reform 1098–1180* (Stanford, CA, 1996), pp. 213–14.
10 Walter Map, *De nugis curialium* 1.25, ed. and trans. M.R. James, rev. C.N.L. Brooke and R.A.B. Mynors (Oxford, 1983), p. 93; Gerald of Wales, *Speculum ecclesiae* 2.12, ed. J.S. Brewer *et al.* (London, 1861–91), p. 54.
11 A. Lester, *Making Cistercian Nuns: Gender, Society and Religious Reform in Medieval Champagne* (Ithaca, NY, 2011).
12 B. Noell, 'Expectation and Unrest among Cistercian Lay Brothers in the Twelfth and Thirteenth Centuries', *Journal of Medieval History*, 32 (2006), 253–74; and J. France, *Separate but Equal: Cistercian Lay Brothers 1120–1350* (Collegeville, MN and Kalamazoo, MI), esp. chapter 7.
13 J. Leclercq, 'Aspects de la vie cistercienne au XIIIe siècle: à propos d'un livre récent', *Studia Monastica*, 20 (1978), 223–6.

Primary sources

Lucet, B. (ed.), *La codification cistercienne de 1202 et son évolution ultérieure* (Rome, 1964)
Matarasso, P. (ed.), *The Cistercian World: Monastic Writings of the Twelfth Century* (Harmondsworth, 1998)
Waddell, C. (ed.), *Narrative and Legislative Texts from Early Cîteaux*, Cîteaux: Studia et Documenta 9 (Brecht, 1999)
  Twelfth-Century Statutes from the Cistercian General Chapter, Cîteaux: Studia et Documenta 12 (Brecht, 2002)

2 The Cistercian Order 1200–1600

PETER KING

In his *Exordium Magnum*, composed between 1206 and 1221,[1] Conrad of Eberbach saw in the wonderful history of the Cistercian Order an example of the providence of God.[2] During the thirteenth century the Order was greatly admired. The Frankish lords of the new Latin Empire of Constantinople were generous benefactors,[3] though the hope of successful proselytism among the Orthodox proved illusory.[4] Ruling houses often chose Cistercian abbeys as burial places for their dynasties.[5] In 1228 King Louis IX of France founded the Cistercian abbey of Royaumont near one of his castles, for members of the royal family other than the kings themselves.[6] The remains of Pribislav, the first Christian ruler of Pomerania, were translated to the abbey of Doberan by his son Borwin around 1219.[7] Mariensee/Chorin was founded in 1258 as a burial place for the younger line of the Ascanian margraves of Brandenburg.[8] In 1291 King Wenceslas II of Bohemia founded the Cistercian abbey of Zbraslav (Aula Regia) as the necropolis of his dynasty.[9]

Most spectacular was the increase in houses for Cistercian women. 'The religious movement of women of the Cistercian Order', wrote Jacques de Vitry, a contemporary, 'increased to infinity like the stars of heaven.'[10] Local studies confirm Jacques's enthusiasm. In 1234, for instance, the archbishop of Cologne approved the foundation of a house of Cistercian nuns at Duissern near Duisburg. It was to be for thirteen nuns, a number which was not to be exceeded. Already in 1237 the archbishop agreed to twenty-five. In 1240, six years after its foundation, there were enough sisters in Duissern for the foundation of a daughter house.[11]

Competition with the mendicants made it imperative for the Order to modernise. As the Englishman Stephen of Lexington, successively abbot of Stanley, Savigny and, after 1243, Clairvaux, wrote, 'For the last thirteen years no prominent scholar, especially in biblical studies, has joined us. Those now in the Order are growing old, and advancing along the way of all flesh.'[12] The answer, Stephen was convinced, was for Cistercians to study at the universities.

Since 1224 the abbey of Clairvaux had possessed a little property in Paris. In 1237 the General Chapter sanctioned the residence there of some student monks from various abbeys.[13] In 1245 the General Chapter confirmed the *Studium* at Paris begun by the abbot of Clairvaux.[14] In 1247 a plot of land for more ample premises was acquired and the students were in place by 1250. There seems, however, to have been considerable opposition to this innovation within the Order. In 1256 Stephen was deposed, and ended his life in retirement at the abbey of Ourscamp.[15] The *Studium* survived, however. In 1320 it was sold to the abbey of Cîteaux[16] and became a recognised house of studies for the whole Order to which the larger abbeys were obliged to send their most promising subjects. Eventually houses for study were also opened in Toulouse, Montpellier, Salamanca, Metz, Bologna and Oxford.[17]

The adoption by the thirteenth-century Cistercians of the new Gothic style was another example of their determination to be up to date. The wide proportions, low vaults and shallow sanctuaries of their twelfth-century churches were abandoned. The change was spectacularly evident at Rievaulx in north Yorkshire, England, where a low twelfth-century nave, probably covered, like the aisles, by a barrel vault, led into soaring transepts and a chancel, seven bays long, covered by cross-vaulting.[18] In central Italy the three most spectacular Cistercian churches built in the French Gothic manner are Fossanova consecrated in 1208, Casamari, 1217, and San Galgano (now a ruin), which was being built throughout most of the thirteenth century.[19] In northern Europe churches were built in brick. Cistercian examples in Germany are Chorin in Brandenburg and Doberan in Pomerania.[20] The latter has an apse surrounded by an ambulatory with radiating chapels, like a French cathedral.

The thirteenth century began with a quarrel between the Order and Pope Innocent III.[21] Invoking their exemptions, the monks made difficulties about a financial contribution to the pope's planned crusade. Innocent threatened to revoke their privileges. By July 1201 a generous grant from the Order had mollified him. Thereafter it enjoyed papal favour. In 1215 the Fourth Lateran Council decreed that in each ecclesiastical province, Benedictine abbots who had no superiors should hold occasional General Chapters, and that initially two Cistercian abbots, experienced as they were in such meetings, might guide their proceedings.[22] Cistercians came to be regarded as experts in monasticism. Between 1220 and 1245 they took over twenty-five communities from other Orders. Most of these were affiliated to the line of Clairvaux.[23]

The General Chapter codified its binding legislation in 1202, 1237, 1257, 1316 and 1340.[24] The codes were efficiently arranged according to subjects or *distinctiones*, a list of which appeared at the beginning of each volume. The text of each *distinctio* was preceded by a list of contents. Modern editions have indices, but for most purposes the original arrangement remains the easiest to use.

The codifications are evidence of clear thinking at the centre of the Order, but the rivalry between the abbots of Cîteaux and Clairvaux always stood in the way of smooth government. The most serious crisis was in 1263–5.[25] The quarrel was about appointments to the *diffinitorium*, a steering committee of the General Chapter. Even Pope Clement IV's bull *Parvus fons* of 1265 did not quite settle the matter. It required the intervention of a papal legate to effect a compromise. The abbot of Cîteaux would appoint four abbots of his choice; each of the other four proto-abbots might nominate two abbots whom the abbot of Cîteaux could not veto. They could nominate three more, of whom the abbot of Cîteaux was to reject one.[26]

Finance was another source of friction within the Order. When the General Chapter met, the visiting abbots were accommodated at Cîteaux. To house several hundred abbots was a considerable burden for the mother house. In 1189 Richard I of England donated the church of Scarborough to help with the expenses.[27] There were also benefactions from other rulers, and annual pensions from some of the richer abbeys. None of this covered all the costs. Moreover the Order was burdened with other financial demands. The popes wanted support for their crusades against the Hohenstaufen. By the end of the thirteenth century kings were successful in exacting money from the religious Orders. To meet ever-increasing demands the Cistercians had to devise a system of taxation for all their abbeys. By the early fourteenth century each one had been assessed on a sliding scale according to its revenues and the needs of the Order. The collections remained an unpopular feature of Cistercian life for the rest of the Middle Ages, but until the end of the 1340s they were relatively successful.[28]

During the fourteenth century the General Chapter gradually lost authority and prestige. In 1340 it was prepared to excuse poor attendance 'because of the danger on the roads'; no doubt on account of the war between England and France. In 1349 the Black Death was recognised as a more than sufficient reason for absence.[29] The origins of the trouble, however, went further back. Abbots at a distance from Cîteaux were already excused attendance every year.[30] Such abbots, unfamiliar with procedures and personalities, might not find the long journey worth while. Domination by a steering committee of insiders would make things worse. In 1356 only twenty-three abbots attended the General Chapter; in the next year there were twenty-four. By this time the assembly had lost all authority. Already in 1341/2, to the dismay of the General Chapter, the English abbots had met to regulate their own affairs, an arrangement tacitly approved in 1357.[31] During the papal schism of 1378–1415 there were two General Chapters recognised by rival popes.[32]

The fourteenth century was a time of plague and wars. A certain loss of confidence in the religious life was noticeable. Many religious houses fell into troubles from which they never emerged.[33] Cistercian abbots began to live outside their monasteries. In 1342 seven of them, including the abbot of Cîteaux, were residing at the Order's college in Paris.[34] Even more damaging was the system of *commendam* whereby the pope, and later on local rulers, could appoint anyone, even a layman, to be an abbot.[35] With some exceptions, these absentee superiors were interested only in their revenues. Many communities decayed and eventually dwindled to almost nothing. In January 1532 Edme de Saulieu, abbot of Clairvaux, visited the abbey of Franquevaux in southern France. Its commendator, a canon of Nîmes, did not show up. The buildings were dilapidated. There were assorted fowls in the cloister, sheep in the chapter house, cows in the parlour and pigs in the noviciate. The community consisted of three irregular religious. On the morning of Dom Edme's visitation one of them had left early to hunt rabbits, another was out looking for eggs.[36]

The austere Cistercian pope Benedict XII (1334–42)[37] wanted to restore standards, especially in his own Order, but his plan, borrowed from the Dominicans, to allow representatives of each community to attend the General Chapter with the abbots met with vehement opposition from the latter and had to be withdrawn.[38] The bull *Fulgens* (1335)[39] made provisions about debt, finance, visitations and attendance at the General Chapter. It regulated studies in the Order, confirming the *Studia* in Paris and elsewhere. Known as the *statuta papalia*, the bulls *Parvus fons* and *Fulgens* replaced the older texts as the legal basis for Cistercian life during the later Middle Ages.[40]

Reform was more effective when it was localised and involved a smaller number of houses. The women showed the way. The expansion of women's houses in the thirteenth century had taken the Order by surprise. Abbots were afraid to take responsibility for so many new houses. The General Chapter often forbade the incorporation of houses for women into the Order, although at other times individual houses were recognised. The Order's policies were far from consistent.[41] By 1300 there were numerous monasteries for women which followed Cistercians customs but did not officially belong to the Order.

Whether incorporated or not, houses for women often acted together. The best-known association is the one dependent on the abbey of Tart (Côte-d'Or, France). The abbey was founded by Stephen Harding and it followed the Cistercian customs although it never formed part of the Order. Its eighteen daughter houses met for an annual General Chapter under the joint presidency of the abbess and the abbot of Cîteaux. The records of these meetings are sparse. All but one of the surviving statutes date from the thirteenth century. Tart and its daughters may be regarded as the earliest of the Cistercian congregations.[42]

In Castile a congregation of Cistercian women's houses came into being through the will of Alfonso VIII (1158–1214). In 1187 he had founded the abbey of Las Huelgas near Burgos, and ordained that its nuns should follow the Cistercian rule. At his request the General Chapter at Cîteaux agreed that the Cistercian abbesses of Leon and Castile should meet annually at Las Huelgas to discuss their common affairs and enforce discipline. Two such meetings took place in 1189 but some abbesses came only under pressure from the king and in later years they refused to attend.[43]

In Flanders the three houses for women founded by Bartholomew of Tienen: Bloemendaal (Florival) near Nivelles, Maagdendaal (Val-des-Vierges) near Tienen and its daughter house of Nazareth near Lierre, together with La Ramée near Tienen, appear to have worked closely together.[44] Bartholomew's daughter Beatrice (the future mystic, d. 1268) became a novice at Bloemendaal. Her superiors sent her to La Ramée to learn calligraphy. We next hear of her at Maagdendaal. From there she was sent to the newly founded house of Nazareth.[45] Abbess Gertrud of Hackeborn, superior of Helfta in Saxony during its golden age (1252–92), was also for a time abbess of the nearby house of St Gertrud in Hadersleben, and for most of the thirteenth century relations between the two houses remained close.[46]

Formal federations for the men came into being during the fifteenth century. The *Colligatio Galilaeensis* was a gathering of very strict Cistercian houses in the Netherlands strongly influenced by the *Devotio moderna*. Its constitutions were drawn up in 1418. Communities were small. The monks lived in poverty and isolation. To emphasise humility, superiors were known as priors not abbots. Communities avoided using the word 'chapter' for their meetings.[47] More controversial was the reform associated with Martin Vargas in Castile. A former confessor of Pope Martin V, he became a Cistercian and with papal permission founded some hermitages where the Cistercian customs were strictly observed. In 1437 papally approved statutes formed them into a congregation completely independent of the Cistercian General Chapter. The outraged Cistercian authorities excommunicated Vargas, who died in a monastic prison.[48] His congregation, however, survived and flourished.

It should not be supposed that only houses in these and similar congregations were observant. Exempt by papal privilege from the *commendam*, Cîteaux, Clairvaux and other great abbeys maintained their high standards.[49] During a long period of office Jean de Cirey, abbot of Cîteaux (1476–1501), made determined efforts to reform the Order, predictably hampered by a long-running feud with Pierre de Virey, abbot of Clairvaux (1471–96).[50] A number of late medieval Cistercians were involved in public affairs. Richard Stradell, abbot of Dore in Hertfordshire, England (1305–46), was sent by Edward III on embassies to Scotland and France.[51] In 1423 John of Hallis, abbot of Balmerino in Scotland, was a member of the embassy sent to England to negotiate the release of King James I. It was the beginning of a distinguished diplomatic and legal career.[52] In Florence Cistercians played a part in the administration of the city. After 1259 a monk of the abbey of Settimo was one of the officers who kept the communal accounts. In the fourteenth century a Cistercian and a *Humiliato* took charge of the city's seal. The chapel in the Palazzo Vecchio was dedicated to St Bernard.[53] Dante's veneration for the saint is well known:

> ... vidi un sene
> vestito con le genti gloriose.
> Diffuso era per gli occhi e per le gene
> di benigna letizia, in atto pio,
> quale a tenero padre si conviene.[54]

('I saw an old man clothed like those in glory, benign joy shone out of his eyes and features, his gestures were gentle, as befits a tender father.') It is Bernard who explains to the poet the different states of bliss in heaven and prepares him for the beatific vision.[55]

Cistercian charities were impressive. During the great European famine of 1315–17, according to a contemporary, Cistercian abbeys in France ruined themselves by giving relief to the crowds44 which flocked to them for help.[56] There were still traditional monasteries in which the spiritual life flourished. In the middle years of the fourteenth century Guillaume de Digulleville (c. 1295–after 1358), a monk of Chaalis, wrote the *Pèlerinage de la vie humaine*, in which he compared human life to the journey of a pilgrim to Jerusalem.[57] It was very influential and popular, as numerous manuscript copies and translations show.[58] Another much-read treatise was the *Malogranatum* ('The Pomegranate'), produced, most probably, in the Bohemian abbey of Zbraslav at the end of the fourteenth century. The author discussed the three traditional stages of union with God and advised frequent communion, as demanded by many of the Bohemian laity at the time.[59]

Among the nuns the traditional concept of Jesus as spouse was spectacularly developed.[60] A noteworthy feature of the women mystics was their pastoral concern. The charity of Ida of Leeuw (d. 1260) extended beyond the cloister.[61] Of Beatrice of Nazareth (d. 1268) we read that 'Persons of various ages, conditions, and professions were to be seen daily coming with their needs to the blessed woman.'[62] Gertrud of Helfta (1256–1302) translated portions of the Bible into the vernacular. She was always ready to interrupt her meditations to support someone prey to temptation, comfort the bereaved or help the needy.[63]

There were few ways for the women to make their writings and activities widely known. Their influence during the Middle Ages was very localised. This changed with the invention of printing. In 1536 the *Exercises* of Gertrud of Helfta were printed by the Carthusians of Cologne. Ten further editions of her works, some translated into Italian, French and German, followed in the sixteenth century, published in Cologne, Venice, Paris and Madrid. A Spanish translation was published in Salamanca in 1601. Further editions continued until the twentieth century.[64]

The Reformation deprived the Order of all its houses in northern Europe. Of those that remained many were demoralised, and the Council of Trent at first made little difference. In 1561 and 1579 visitations of Cistercian houses in central, southern and northern Italy revealed dilapidated buildings and monasteries with few or no inhabitants. The formation of congregations in Italy, Spain and Portugal brought about slow improvements. Characteristics of these organisations were: superiors elected for a limited term (to exclude commendators), annual General Chapters which appointed visitors and even moved monks from one house to the other, and common noviciates. Relations with Cîteaux were formal.[65]

A spectacular reform movement was that of Jean de la Barrière (1544–1600).[66] As a student in Paris he came under the influence of a devout priest. Since the age of eighteen he had been commendatory abbot of the Cistercian abbey of Feuillant near Toulouse, and in 1573 he decided to become a monk there and to introduce reform. He made a short retreat at a nearby abbey, took the monastic habit and was later ordained. At Feuillant resistance to his reforms was fierce, and in 1577 he was forced to leave for Toulouse, where he made his name as a preacher. A local bishop gave him the abbatial blessing. Thereupon he returned to Feuillant. The refractory monks were persuaded to leave and a new community came into being, marked by extraordinary penances which owed nothing to Cistercian tradition, of which Jean was largely ignorant. Papal approval came in 1581 and 1586. The Feuillants were freed from the authority of the Cistercian General Chapter and authorised to found new houses. A branch for women came into being in 1588. At a General Chapter of the new congregation held under papal auspices in 1590 the more bizarre penances were abandoned.

Near the end of his life Jacques de Thérines, the Cistercian abbot of Chaalis near Paris (1308–17), wrote to the pope about the life of the White Monks. They kept, he said, very exactly the threefold vows made by all Benedictines. They were strictly enclosed, their nourishment was sparse, they were devoted to prayer and devout reading. They were meticulous in celebrating the divine office. They found time during the day for manual labour. They were generous to the poor. They held study in high regard and had teachers at the major universities. Discipline was maintained by an efficient system of visitation.[67]

Jacques was no Bernard, but his was a noble vision. Very many religious houses in the late Middle Ages failed to live up to it. In the worst of times, however, there were still large Cistercian communities where it was a lived reality. It was a guide to men of the calibre of Stephen of Lexington, Pope Benedict XII and Jean de Cirey. It inspired visionaries like Beatrice of Nazareth and Gertrud of Helfta.

Notes

1   É. Brouette, A. Dimier and E. Manning (eds.), *Dictionnaire des auteurs cisterciens, la documentation Cistercienne 16* (Rochefort, 1975–9), vol. 1, p. 183.
2   B. Griesser (ed.), *Exordium Magnum ... auctore Conrado* (Rome, 1961), p. 73.
3   E. Brown, 'The Cistercians in the Latin Empire of Constantinople and Greece', *Traditio*, 14 (1958), 64–120; R. Clair, 'Les filles d'Hautecombe dans l'Empire latin de Constantinople', *ASOC*, 17 (1961), 261–77.
4   B. Bolton, 'A Mission to the Orthodox? The Cistercians in Romania', in *The Orthodox Churches and the West*, ed. D. Baker (Oxford, 1976), pp. 169–81.
5   J. Hall and C. Kratzke (eds.), *Sepulturae Cistercienses*, thematic issue of *Cîteaux*, 56 (2005).

6   G. Pelliccia and G. Rocca (eds.), *Dizionario degli Istituti di Perfezione*, 10 vols. (Rome, 1974–2003), vol. vii (1983), p. 2056.

7   *Sepulturae Cistercienses*, pp. 275–7.

8   G. Abb *et al.* (eds.), *Germania sacra: historisch-statistische Darstellung der deutschen Bistümer*, 5 vols. (Berlin and Leipzig, 1929–72), vol. i, *Das Bistum Brandenburg*, ed. G. Abb and G. Wentz (1929), p. 305.

9   K. Benešovskà, '*Aula regia* près de Prague et *Mons regalis* près de Paris', *Cîteaux*, 47 (1996), 233–4.

10   Jacques de Vitry, *Historia Occidentalis*; ed. J.F. Hinnebusch, *The Historia Occidentalis of Jacques de Vitry* (Fribourg, 1972), p. 117.

11   G. von Roden (ed.), *Die Zisterzienserinnenklöster Saarn, Duissern, Sterkrade*, Germania Sacra, NF 18 (Berlin, 1984), pp. 93, 103 and 153.

12   B. Griesser (ed.), 'Registrum Epistolarum Stephani de Lexington', *ASOC*, 3 (1947), p. 117; C.H. Lawrence, 'Lexington, Stephen of', *Oxford Dictionary of National Biography*, vol. xxxiii (Oxford, 2004), pp. 683–4.

13   Canivez, *Statuta*. The statutes are cited by year and number, here 1237:9. Papal bulls in the collection are cited by volume and page number. On the Study House see C.H. Lawrence, 'Stephen of Lexington and Cistercian University Studies in the Thirteenth Century', *Journal of Ecclesiastical History*, 11 (1960), 164–78.

14   Canivez, *Statuta* 1245:4.

15   Lawrence, 'Stephen of Lexington', pp. 170–78.

16   P. Dautrey, 'Croissance et adaptation chez les Cisterciens au treizième siècle', *Analecta Cisterciensia*, 32 (1976), 122–215 (p. 138 and n.72).

17   C. Obert, 'La promotion des études chez les Cisterciens', *Cîteaux*, 39 (1988), 65–77 (pp. 66–7).

18   N. Pevsner, *The Buildings of England: Yorkshire, the North Riding* (London, 1966), pp. 300–1.

19   L.F. de Longhi, *L'architettura delle chiese Cistercensi Italiane* (Milan, 1958), pp. 235–56.

20   W. Erdmann, *Zisterzienser-Abtei Chorin* (Königstein-in-Taunus, 1994) and *Zisterzienser-Abtei Doberan* (Königstein-in-Taunus, 1995).

21   Brown, 'The Cistercians in the Latin Empire', pp. 69–72.

22   N.P. Tanner (ed.), *Decrees of the Ecumenical Councils*, 2 vols. (Georgetown, Washington DC, 1990), vol. i, pp. 240–41.

23   Dautrey, 'Croissance et adaptation', p. 138 and n.72.

24   B. Lucet (ed.), *La codification cistercienne de 1202 et son évolution ultérieure* (Rome, 1964); B. Lucet (ed.), *Les codifications cisterciennes de 1237 et de 1257* (Paris, 1977); H. Séjalon (ed.), *Nomasticon Cisterciense* (Solesmes, 1892).

25   L.J. Lekai, *The Cistercians: Ideals and Reality* (Kent, OH, 1977), pp. 70–2.

26   Canivez, *Statuta*, 3, pp. 21–30 and 31–2.

27   C.H. Talbot, 'Cîteaux and Scarborough', *Studia Monastica*, 2 (1960), 95–158.

28   P. King, *The Finances of the Cistercian Order in the Fourteenth Century*, CS 85 (Kalamazoo, MI, 1985), pp. 30–52, 59–88 and 89–125.

29 Canivez, *Statuta* 1340:7 and 1349:1.
30 Lucet, *Les codifications*, pp. 109–10 and 261. See Emilia Jamroziak's chapter in this volume.
31 P. King, 'Attendance at the Cistercian Chapter General during the Fourteenth Century', in *Festskrift til Troels Dahlerup*, ed. A. Andersen *et al.* (Aarhus, 1985), pp. 55–63.
32 B. Griesser *et al.*, 'Generalkapitel ausserhalb Cîteaux', *Cistercienser Chronik*, 62 (1955), 65–83; 63 (1956), 7–11; 64 (1957), 21–2.
33 P. King, *Western Monasticism*, CS 185 (Kalamazoo, MI, 1999), pp. 229–35.
34 King, *The Finances*, pp. 184–5.
35 Lekai, *The Cistercians*, pp. 101–8.
36 *Frère Claude de Bronseval: Peregrinatio Hispanica 1531–1533*, ed. M. Cocheril, 2 vols. (Paris, 1970), pp. 126–31.
37 G. Mollat, *The Popes at Avignon* (London, 1963), pp. 26–36; B. Guillemain, *La cour pontificale d'Avignon* (Paris, 1966), pp. 134–6; B. Schimmelpfennig, 'Zisterzienserideal und Kirchenreform: Benedikt XII (1334–1342) als Reformpapst', *Zisterzienserstudien*, 3 (1976), 11–43.
38 J.B. Mahn, *Le pape Benoît XII et les Cisterciens* (Paris, 1949).
39 Canivez, *Statuta*, 3, pp. 410–36.
40 See, e.g., Canivez, *Statuta* 1340:6; 1341:6; 1343:6; 1346:2.
41 See the important article by E. Freeman, 'Houses of a Peculiar Order', *Cîteaux*, 55 (2004), 245–86. Though it deals mostly with England, it is relevant to the Continent also.
42 J. de la C. Bouton (ed.), *Les moniales Cisterciennes*, 4 vols. (Aiguebelle, 1986–9), vol. 1, pp. 47–54.
43 P. Feige, 'Filiation und Landeshoheit: die Entstehung der Zisterzienserkongregationen auf der Iberischen Halbinsel', *Zisterzienser-Studien*, 1 (1975), 37–48.
44 R. De Ganck, 'The Three Foundations of Bartholomew of Tienen', *Cîteaux*, 37 (1986), 49–75.
45 R. De Ganck and J.B. Hasbrouck (eds. and trans.), *The Life of Beatrice of Nazareth*, CF 50 (Kalamazoo, MI, 1991), pp. 59–61 and 269–71.
46 C. Oefelein, *Das Nonnenkloster St. Jacobi und seine Tochterklöster im Bistum Halberstadt* (Berlin, 2004), pp. 167–8. See E. Rozanne Elder's chapter in this volume.
47 K. Elm and P. Feige, 'Reformen und Kongregationsbildungen der Zisterzienser in Spätmittelalter und früher Neuzeit', in *Die Zisterzienser: Ordensleben zwischen Ideal und Wirklichkeit*, ed. K. Elm *et al.* (Cologne, 1981), pp. 243–54.
48 Feige, 'Filiation und Landeshoheit', pp. 48–62; Elm and Feige, 'Reformen und Kongregationsbildungen', pp. 249–52; D. Yanez, 'Los primeros usos de la congregación de Castilla', *Cîteaux*, 32 (1981), 1–16.
49 On these two abbeys during the fourteenth and fifteenth centuries see A. Manrique, *Annales Cistercienses, Lyons 1642–59*, 4 vols. (Westmead, 1970), vol. 1, pp. 480–8 and 522–77.
50 Lekai, *The Cistercians*, pp. 31, 105–6 and 110–12.

51   H. Shaw, 'Cistercian Abbots in the Service of British Monarchs (1135–1335)', *Cîteaux*, 58 (2007), 239–40.

52   J. Kerr, 'Balmerino Abbey: Cistercians on the East Coast of Fife', *Cîteaux*, 59 (2008), 37–60 (pp. 47–8).

53   M.K. Lesher, 'St. Bernard of Clairvaux and the Republic of Florence in the Later Middle Ages', *Cîteaux*, 34 (1984), 258–67.

54   *Paradiso* 31.59–63.

55   *Paradiso* 32.1–87; 33.1–39.

56   N. Valois, 'Un plaidoyer du XIVe siècle en faveur des cisterciens', *Bibliothèque de l'école des chartes*, 69 (1908), 352–68 (p. 366).

57   J.J. Stürzinger (ed.), *Pèlerinage de la vie humaine, Pèlerinage de Jésus Christ*, 3 vols. (London, 1893–7).

58   F. Duval and F. Pomal (eds.), *Guillaume de Digulleville: les pèlerinages allégoriques* (Rennes, 2008).

59   M. Gerwing, *Malogranatum oder der dreifache Weg zur Vollkommenheit* (Munich, 1986); H. Krmíčková, 'Le *Malogranatum* et la question de la communion fréquente', *Cîteaux*, 47 (1996), 135–43. There is no modern edition of the text.

60   See R. De Ganck, *Beatrice of Nazareth in Her Context*, 2 vols., CS 121 (Kalamazoo, MI, 1991); R. De Ganck (ed. and trans.), *The Life of Beatrice of Nazareth*, CF 50 (Kalamazoo, MI, 1991); M.J. Finnegan, *The Women of Helfta* (Athens, GA, 1991).

61   T. Renna, 'Hagiography and Feminine Spirituality in the Low Countries', *Cîteaux*, 39 (1988), 285–96 (p. 293).

62   *The Life of Beatrice of Nazareth*, p. 335.

63   J. Hourlier *et al.* (eds. and trans.), *Gertrude d'Helfta: oeuvres spirituelles*, 5 vols., SCh 127, 139, 143, 255 and 331 (Paris, 1967–86), vol. II, ed. P. Doyère (1968), pp. 152–4 and 144.

64   *Gertrude d'Helfta: oeuvres spirituelles*, vol. I, ed. J. Hourlier and A. Schmitt (1967), pp. 52–3. See also Elizabeth Freeman and E. Rozanne Elder's chapters in this volume.

65   Lekai, *The Cistercians*, pp. 106 and 126–30.

66   'Barrière', in *Dictionnaire d'histoire et de géographie ecclésiastiques*, ed. A. Baudrillart *et al.* (Paris, 1912–), vol. VI (1931), cols. 924–6; 'Feuillants et Feuillantines', in *Dictionnaire d'histoire et de géographie ecclésiastiques*, vol. XVI (1967), cols. 1338–44; 'Feuillants', in *Dictionnaire de spiritualité ascétique et mystique: doctrine et histoire*, ed. M. Viller *et al.*, 17 vols. (Paris, 1932–95), vol. V (1964), cols. 274–87; G. Crucifix-Bultingaire, *Feuillants et Feuillantines* (Paris, 1961); 'Barrière', *Dizionario degli istituti di perfezione*, vol. I (1969), pp. 1059–61; 'Foglianti', *Dizionario degli istituti di perfezione*, vol. IV (1973), pp. 93–4.

67   Valois, 'Un plaidoyer', pp. 352–68.

Primary sources

Beatrice of Nazareth, *Vita*, ed. R. De Ganck and J.B. Hasbrouck, *The Life of Beatrice of Nazareth, 1200–1268*, CF 50 (Kalamazoo, MI, 1991), Beatrice's life and teaching

Bronseval, Frère Claude de, *Peregrinatio Hispanica 1531–1533*, ed. M. Cocheril, 2 vols. (Paris, 1970), a day-to-day account of the abbot of Clairvaux's visitation of daughter houses in southern France, Spain and Portugal

Canivez, J.-M. (ed.), *Statuta capitulorum generalium ordinis cisterciensis*, 8 vols. (Louvain, 1933–41), the classic collection of the Order's statutes

Conrad of Eberbach, *Exordium Magnum Cisterciense*, ed. B. Griesser (Rome, 1961; repr. Turnhout, 1994), a history of the Order based on the sources, as seen from a thirteenth-century perspective

Cotheret, Nicolas, *Annales de Cîteaux*, ed. L. J. Lekai, 'Les *Annales de Cîteaux* de Nicholas Cotheret (1680–1753)', *Analecta Cisterciensia*, 40 (1984), 150–303; 41 (1985), 42–315; 42 (1986), 265–332; a reader-friendly version has been produced by L. J. Lekai, *Nicolas Cotheret's Annals of Cîteaux*, CS 57 (Kalamazoo, MI, 1982)

Gertrud of Helfta, *Exercitia spiritualia*, ed. and trans. J. Hourlier *et al.*, *Gertrude d'Helfta: oeuvres spirituelles*, 5 vols., SCh 127, 139, 143, 255 and 331 (Paris, 1967–86), Gertrud's life and theology, partly written by her, partly about her

Gertrud of Helfta *Exercitia spiritualia*, trans. G.J. Lewis and J. Lewis, *Gertrud the Great of Helfta: Spiritual Exercises*, CF 49 (Kalamazoo, MI, 1989)

Griesser, B. (ed.), 'Consuetudines Domus Cisterciensis', *ASOC*, 3 (1947), 138–46, a thirteenth-century version of the customs of Cîteaux

'Registrum epistolarum Stephani de Lexington abatis de Stanleio et de Savigniaco', *ASOC*, 2 (1946), 1–118; 8 (1952), 182–378. Official letters of the Order's ruthless moderniser before he became abbot of Clairvaux in 1243

Jacques de Vitry, *Historia Occidentalis*, ed. J.F. Hinnebusch, *The Historia Occidentalis of Jacques de Vitry* (Fribourg, 1972), chapter 15, *De monialibus cysterciensibus* (pp. 116–18), is the classic account of the expansion of Cistercian houses for women in the thirteenth century

Johnsen, A.O. and P. King (eds.), *The Tax Book of the Cistercian Order* (Oslo, 1979), a fourteenth-century guide to the Order's taxation system

Lucet, B. (ed.), *La codification cistercienne de 1202 et son évolution ultérieure* (Rome, 1964), a systematic codification of Cistercian legislation

Les codifications cisterciennes de 1237 et de 1257 (Paris, 1977), older compilations brought up to date

Manrique, A., *Annales Cistercienses, Lyons 1642–59*, 4 vols. (Westmead, 1970), compiled by a seventeenth-century Spanish Cistercian, based on documents, some of them inauthentic. For better or worse contains useful information about the later Middle Ages

Séjalon, H. (ed.), *Nomasticon Cisterciense* (Solesmes, 1892), a *de luxe* second edition of Cistercian legislation, first published by Julien Paris (1664). There are more modern editions of all the earlier legislation, but the codifications of 1316 and 1340 can be found only here

Talbot, C.H. (ed.), *Letters from the English Abbots to the Chapter at Cîteaux 1442–1521* (London, 1967), a vivid picture of Cistercian life in England and its problems on the eve of the Reformation

3 The Cistercian Order since 1600
MICHAEL CASEY OCSO

This chapter covers the history of the Cistercian Order from the time of Elizabeth I and Shakespeare up to the present. We begin with a survey of the state of the Order at the beginning of that period.

CISTERCIANS IN 1600

It is wise not to give too much credence to generalisations. Cistercian monasteries, although they belong to a centralised Order, are effectively autonomous. Despite protestations of unanimity, there has always been considerable variation among monasteries. Furthermore, monasteries in different regions formed different strategies to respond to different pressures. In the years leading up to 1600 the cohesion and uniformity envisaged by the foundational documents of the Order were no longer possible. There were several hundred Cistercian monasteries of monks and nuns, from Portugal to Scandinavia and from Ireland to Eastern Europe; there were more than 200 abbeys of monks in France alone. The political map of Europe had changed greatly since the twelfth century. With the rise of nation states, and as a result of hostilities and wars, the traditional structures of filiation and visitation were strained, and the practical jurisdiction of the General Chapter was considerably weakened.

The generally perceived decline in the fervour of Cistercian monks and nuns was not primarily a result of moral decadence, although the common practice whereby surplus sons of noble families became monks meant that many of those who lived in monasteries had neither the vocation nor the desire to lead a monastic life. Scandals and moral lapses appear only occasionally in the records of General Chapters. There was a loss of vitality, but this was due, initially, to several external factors, which affected different monasteries in varying degrees. In particular, reduction in numbers had an effect on the quality of lifestyle. Three factors were involved in this. Firstly, many monasteries never recovered from the ravages of the Black Death. In 1600 only a few monasteries had more than twenty members, and many had far fewer. As a result, appropriate standards for the admission of candidates were not observed, and often the mitigations necessitated by extraordinary circumstances were institutionalised. In particular, the right to dispense from perpetual abstinence from meat granted to the Order by Sixtus IV in 1475 became a major point of contention in later centuries. Secondly, with the multiplication of religious Orders, potential candidates had more options available and, inevitably, the more modern expressions of religious life seemed more in contact with the aspirations of the age. Thirdly, the Reformation further reduced the pool of candidates. Once-Catholic countries became hostile to monasticism; monasteries were closed, their inhabitants dispersed and the option of entering a monastery became more extreme.

Meanwhile, although the number of monks and nuns decreased, the extensive monastic domains formerly needed to support large communities remained substantially intact. Cîteaux, for example, owned nearly 10,000 ha of productive land. Monasteries were seen to be rich and became thereby objects of envy for secular and religious authorities, and potential plunder for ravaging soldiery during the many wars of the period.[1]

Partly because of this perceived wealth, the system of commendatory abbots had operated in some Cistercian abbeys since the fourteenth century, especially in France and Italy. This practice of imposing on a community a nominal superior from outside the Order led to many abuses, especially when the commendatory abbot was a lay person with little interest in monastic life whose only concern was to milk the monastery for as much income as possible. To maximise profit commendatory abbots often neglected the upkeep of the buildings, discouraged the reception of new candidates and sought to reduce monastic living expenses, especially concerning food and clothing. The results are listed in the records of General Chapters: disorder, demoralisation, violation of monastic enclosure, a widespread reliance by individual monks and nuns on private sources of income, the breakdown of the common life and, in the absence of an effective superior, a general tendency to mitigate observances. Commendatory abbacies were repeatedly resisted within the Order, but to no avail. The practice was enforced by secular authorities who regarded the monasteries as lucrative benefices to be bestowed on favoured followers.

MOVEMENTS OF REFORM

From the beginning the Cistercians were a reforming Order. They identified with the austere end of the Benedictine spectrum. As long as the Order had attractive and charismatic leadership such high ideals were relatively easy to realise. Moreover, in its absence, the Charter of Charity had provided supervision through an annual visitation of each monastery by its founding house, and an annual General Chapter of all abbots to review the state of each monastery and its governance. As the Order grew numerically and geographically, this yearly supervision became less effective. The necessity for adaptation to different places and ever-changing circumstances made practice less uniform and often led to less exigent observance. Attendance at General Chapters fell away. In many places the fading of the primitive ideals resulted in relaxation and occasional disorders.

The decline in standards provoked its own reaction. There were many attempts at revitalisation of the Order from both within and without. Clement IV in his bull *Parvus fons* (the 'Clementina' of 1265) and Benedict XII in his Apostolic Constitution *Fulgens sicut stella matutina* (the 'Benedictina' of 1335) insisted on reform; these official documents were often cited in the following centuries. Meanwhile, General Chapters from the fourteenth century consistently addressed situations of laxity and disorder and took measures to correct them, sometimes repeatedly, but these often had little direct effect on distant monasteries. From the fifteenth century various national and regional groupings of monasteries began meeting together, sometimes but not always with the approval of the General Chapter. In time these groups became distinct congregations, vicariates or provinces within the Cistercian Order, often with a degree of independence and with their own particular law.

The general movement to ongoing reform was given an impetus when, in 1563, the Council of Trent promulgated its decree *De regularibus et monialibus*, making provision for the reform of religious life. The abbot of Cîteaux and the four proto-abbots travelled widely in the years immediately following the Council, bringing its message of reform, but with mixed results. Thirteen plenary General Chapters were held in the following century in an attempt to implement the conciliar precepts.[2] In addition, the General Chapter of 1604 made provision for intermediary Chapters in which the abbot of Cîteaux and the four proto-abbots dealt with urgent matters. Besides dealing with routine and recurrent business, disputes between monasteries, liturgical matters and particular cases, the General Chapters sought to remedy irregularities in both male and female monasteries. There were occasional scandals to be dealt with, but these were not numerous. The concerns which were most often addressed included the following: the observance of enclosure, the maintenance of buildings, the abuse of keeping private funds and possessions, the wearing of the habit, absences from the common refectory and dormitory, care of monastery temporalities, the formation of novices.

An effort at systematic reform was initiated at the Chapter of 1601 under the leadership of Edmond de la Croix, abbot of Cîteaux. The work was taken up by Denis Largentier, abbot of Clairvaux, and others who, in 1604, produced an ample document based on the deliberations. The General Chapter of 1605, however, refused to confirm this text and pointedly reaffirmed the less demanding decisions of 1584. Wherever there was reforming zeal, resistance to it was also found.

As the seventeenth century advanced, several issues assumed more importance: the practice of perpetual abstinence from meat became symbolic of the struggle between those in favour of a stricter rule (the 'Abstinents') and the rest of the Order (the 'Common Observance'), who advocated a uniformity of discipline based on the acceptance of legitimate dispensations. Powering the controversy about observance, however, was a disedifying political struggle between the General Chapter and various regional and other groupings, and between reforming abbots of individual houses. Debates became acrimonious as each faction sought to win the support of either the French court or the papacy for their cause.

STRICT OBSERVANCE

The beginning of the Strict Observance movement is linked with Octave Arnolfini (1579–1641), at first the commendatory abbot of La Charmoye and later abbot of Châtillon. The Strict Observance was termed 'Étroite Observance' until the Revolution; afterwards it became 'Stricte Observance'. In Latin, papal documents named the observance as 'Strictae Observantiae' though the General Chapter usually designated it as 'Strictioris Observantiae'. Initially the Strict Observance merely advocated a more primitive lifestyle, including abstinence and a little manual labour, though buttressed by a wide range of contemporary devotional practices. It did not envisage separation from the rest of the Order. At the General Chapter of 1623 an attempt to establish the Reformed Congregation of St Bernard composed of fifty-eight abbeys attached to Clairvaux failed,[3] although, in an act of appeasement, communities were permitted to adopt the practice of perpetual abstinence.[4] In 1624 the Apostolic Visitor, Cardinal de La Rochefoucauld, permitted an intermediary gathering of the superiors of 10 Strict Observance abbeys (representing some 200 monks). They assembled at the monastery of

Vaux-de-Cernay and published their revised usages.[5] These represented a return to the ancient practices with certain adaptations to changed conditions. Perpetual abstinence from meat is taken for granted and not mentioned.

The monasteries of nuns were exposed to the same vicissitudes as the monks but were permitted no direct involvement in the General Chapters which legislated for them. Inconvenient daughters of the nobility found themselves deposited as reluctant nuns, and serious lapses in discipline resulted. Reforms were instituted sometimes by the parent monastery of monks and sometimes by local bishops. The French abbey of Port-Royal, considered by many to be tainted by Jansenism, became independent of the Order in 1627 and was eventually suppressed in 1709.

There was a general ferment of reform but no agreement about its details: the Order was divided as were individual monasteries. Both Clairvaux (1620) and Cîteaux (1625) experienced turbulent and contested abbatial elections and the juridical status of the Strict Observance remained uncertain. In 1632 there was a second Apostolic Visitation. In the absence of the Common Observance, Cardinal de La Rochefoucauld decided to restrict the powers of the abbot of Cîteaux, to introduce the Strict Observance into the principal houses of the Order and into the College of St Bernard in Paris, to allow only Strict Observance monasteries to admit novices and to choose a procurator general from among its adherents. These recommendations produced a flurry of protest on the part of the Common Observance which led, in 1634, to the choice of the First Minister of France, Cardinal Richelieu as arbitrator and then, in 1635, as abbot of Cîteaux.

Cardinal Richelieu died in 1642 and the 'war of observances' re-erupted with the disputed election of Claude Vaussin as abbot of Cîteaux. An inconclusive General Chapter in 1651 led to the matter being referred first to the parliament, then to the Council of State and thence, in 1661, to Rome. Since numerically the Common Observance was stronger, its voice was more influential. The response of Alexander VII was given in the bull *In suprema* of 19 April 1666.[6] This text was meant to put an end to all wrangling by an even-handed approach which professed respect for both forms of observance and called both to reformation. It framed its findings as declarations on chapters in the Rule of St Benedict, seeking a compromise that would be acceptable to all parties. Because Rome wanted to maintain the unity of the Order, it insisted on the existing forms of governance: the General Chapter, the abbot of Cîteaux, the four proto-abbots and the elected definitors.

The bull was not welcomed by the Strict Observance, and the General Chapter of 1667 was 'the stormiest ever recorded in Cistercian annals'.[7] A later Chapter in 1683, under Jean Petit, accorded a measure of internal autonomy to the Strict Observance, now numbering sixty houses. This paved the way, if not for reconciliation, at least for coexistence. General Chapters became rarer, with only seven plenary Chapters held in the period 1699–1786.[8] More positive steps 'by which the pristine unity of the Cistercian order might be reborn'[9] were mooted at the intermediary Chapter of 1784, and taken up again in 1786, but then the Revolution changed everything.

RANCÉ AND LA TRAPPE

Armand-Jean Bouthillier de Rancé (1626–1700), the godson of Cardinal Richelieu, became the commendatory abbot of La Trappe in 1637. In 1657 a series of events in his personal life triggered a conversion and, by 1662, he had taken the decrepit monastery of La Trappe in hand, asking for Strict Observance help to upgrade its manner of living and personally supervising the necessary repair of the buildings. On 13 June 1663 he took the novice's habit at Perseigne and, the following year, returned to La Trappe as its regular abbot. Almost immediately he found himself chosen to represent the Strict Observance at Rome. When his role as negotiator ended disappointingly with the publication of *In suprema* in 1666, he returned permanently to La Trappe.

Rancé gradually distanced himself from the Strict Observance movement, which he considered not strict enough, and from 1675 went his own way. Meanwhile, the austere life at La Trappe was attracting much public notoriety and many vocations. At the time of Rancé's death the community had ninety monks and lay brothers. Since the lifestyle at La Trappe went far beyond even the primitive level of austerity in the Order, the enthusiasm for Trappist life would be incomprehensible if it were true, as has been said, that the monastery was pervaded by the 'gloom of contemporary rigorism'.[10] On the contrary, the surviving testimonies indicate that the austere lifestyle created a haven of joyfulness and peace for those who had previously led troubled lives.[11] That this was a reality is confirmed by visitation reports of the period.[12]

Rancé's regulations for his community enjoined a more rigorous separation from the world, including the monk's family, near-continual silence, abstinence not only from meat, but also from fish, poultry and eggs. The use of milk-products was restricted. There were, moreover, three hours of daily work, a demanding practice of personal and corporate poverty, the curbing of self-will through obedience to superiors and to one another and, most controversially, the practice of public humiliation supposed to be a means of attaining humility.

The reforms at La Trappe were not, however, simply mindless austerity. They were supplemented by equally strong teaching. In 1683 Rancé published his work *On the Sanctity and Duties of Monastic Life* (*De la sainteté et des devoirs de la vie monastique*) and in 1688 his commentary on the Rule of St Benedict.[13] The reception given to these treatises was mixed but they had an ongoing influence with adherents of the Strict Observance. In addition, *lectio divina* was a communal exercise not easily avoided. The library was well stocked. Many monks were educated, knowledge of Latin was widespread; the invention of printing had made books more readily accessible. The monks were exhorted to read not only contemporary devotional literature, but also classical monastic sources, including the Desert Fathers, John Cassian, John Climacus and St Bernard, all of which had figured prominently in the formation of Rancé's own spirituality.

During the last decades of his life Rancé progressively withdrew from active association with either Observance, though his counsel was sought and followed in several communities. He was not the leader of an organised reform movement but, universally recognised as a man of great piety and zeal, he became a living symbol of the most austere form of the Cistercian charism – one that attracted and repelled in equal measure. He resigned in 1695 and died on 27 October 1700.

SUPPRESSION OF THE MONASTERIES

After the 1648 Peace of Westphalia had stabilised political structures in the Empire and allowed some measure of religious freedom, Cistercian life began to regenerate in Austria, Hungary, Poland and elsewhere. Churches were rebuilt in rich Baroque style, elaborate liturgies were staged. Monasteries became centres of high culture and the monks' standard of living approximated that of the aristocracy. Recruitment was good and often the personal level of monastic discipline was high, despite the grandiose environment.

From 1782 the Holy Roman Emperor Joseph II, although a practising Catholic, began a campaign to reorganise ecclesiastical life under the control of the state. This included the dissolution of those monasteries perceived as serving no useful purpose. The monasteries were obliged, therefore, to demonstrate their utility by accepting pastoral ministries and, more especially, by establishing educational institutions. Many monasteries in the Habsburg dominions were suppressed.

Events preceding and following the French Revolution led inexorably to the secularisation of monasteries. Monks prepared to take an oath of loyalty were given a pension; the monasteries were plundered and sold. Many monks were imprisoned or forced to seek refuge in foreign monasteries. Napoleon's conquest of much of Europe extended the process to the conquered lands: Piedmont and Lombardy (1797), Tuscany and Naples (1807), the Papal States (1809) and Parma (1810–11).

The process of dissolution continued throughout Europe with the suppression of Polish monasteries in 1795, the seizure of monastic property in Switzerland in 1798, the secularisation of the abbeys of the Upper German Congregation in 1803 and 1810 and the dwindling of monastic life in Lithuania until its final extinguishment in 1842. From 1814 Zirc in Hungary continued as an independent abbey, but was no longer able to follow a monastic timetable due to the pastoral and educational obligations which were the condition of its tolerance. Heiligenkreuz and other monasteries of the Austro-Hungarian Congregation survived.

The process of secularisation in the Iberian Peninsula was begun by the Napoleonic invasion. In Spain, after twenty years of alternating fortunes, the monasteries ceased to exist in 1835 and all monastic property was confiscated the following year. In Portugal the Congregation of St Bernard of Alcobaça was disbanded in 1834.

The destruction of monastic life meant the dispersal of libraries built up over centuries; some of the books and manuscripts found their way into public and private collections, others were mindlessly destroyed. The great monastery of Clairvaux became France's premier prison. The suppression of Cîteaux and the four proto-abbeys also meant that the traditional system of governance became impossible; residual authority was transferred to the Procurator General in Rome and to the abbot of Salem as president of the Upper German Congregation, but it seemed that the Cistercian Order was destined for extinction

BEGINNING OF TRAPPIST EXPANSION

The French Revolution caught most monasteries by surprise; they had failed to read the signs of the times and to formulate a coherent response to them. The novice master at La Trappe, Augustin de Lestrange (1754–1827), acted quickly. With more than twenty members of the community he took refuge in the abandoned Carthusian monastery of Valsainte in the Swiss canton of Fribourg. After winning approval from

Rome and becoming abbot, in 1794 Lestrange published his regulations. These went beyond what Rancé had prescribed, but should be seen as an expression of corporate fervour rather than authoritarian imposition. The young community desired, above all, perfect adherence to the Rule of St Benedict and to the primitive institutions of the Order, and the intensity of their lifestyle attracted many newcomers.

In 1795 the abbot of Valsainte was designated by the papal nuncio in Switzerland as the head of all the monasteries of the Order, taking the place of the abbot of Cîteaux and bypassing existing authorities. Lestrange was bubbling with new projects including several attempts at international foundations and the establishment of third Orders of male and female religious to teach in schools. In 1798, when the French invaded Switzerland, Lestrange gathered his monks and other religious together with the children in their charge and sought asylum in Russia under Tsar Paul I.[14]

Nothing came of this venture and the motley group wandered through Europe for two years before arriving back in Valsainte in 1802. Relative peace followed the treaties made by France with Germany at Lunéville (1801) and with England at Amiens (1802); in 1814 Napoleon abdicated. Valsainte was suppressed again in 1811 and reopened in 1815 but, that year, Lestrange returned to La Trappe. Within ten years there were eleven houses of monks and five of nuns following the same observances. By 1855 twenty-three abbeys belonged to this group, which had expanded to Belgium, England, Ireland, the United States and Algeria. By 1894 there were fifty-six Trappist monasteries stretching from Spain to the Middle East, to the Far East; from South Africa to Australia. Some 3,000 monks belonged to these houses.

In the Papal States Casamari was reopened in 1814 under Pius VII, and two Roman monasteries, Santa Croce in Gerusalemme (closed in 2011) and San Bernardo alla Terme followed suit in 1817. Eventually six houses were able to hold a General Chapter and elect a president general, considered by the Holy See to take the place of the abbot of Cîteaux. With the changed conditions in the Austro-Hungarian Empire following 1849, the abbots of the severely challenged monasteries in that region began to work towards the formations of their own congregation.[15]

UNION OF 1892

In 1867 the Common Observance included four congregations, with the Swiss-German Congregation to be added in 1891. A General Chapter was held in 1869 to which the Trappists were not invited, although nominally they remained under the authority of the Common Observance. At this Chapter it was decided to have an abbot general in Rome, charged with the visitation of all the abbeys once every ten years and with the summoning of a General Chapter once every ten years. Each congregation was permitted to maintain its own constitutions.

Meanwhile, the Trappists were divided among those who followed the regulations of Lestrange and those who reverted to Rancé's earlier version. In 1834 Pope Gregory XVI formed all the French monasteries into a single congregation with its own General Chapter, nominally under the Order of Cîteaux but with the abbot of La Trappe as vicar general. Most of the specific additions of Valsainte were abandoned by the General Chapter of 1835 in an effort 'to keep charity pure and whole in the Congregation, despite the diversity of observances'.[16] Divisions remained, however, and in 1847 Pius IX divided the 32 monasteries with nearly 2,500 monks and nuns into two Cistercian congregations, one grouped around La Trappe, the other around Sept-Fons. Westmalle and Saint-Sixte in Belgium had formed a separate congregation since 1836. After a failed attempt in 1878, the three congregations were finally united by a decree of Leo XIII in 1892. At this time, partly as a result of dispersion due to persecution, there were three Trappist monasteries in the United States (Gethsemani, New Melleray and Spencer), three in Canada (Oka, Prairies, Mistassini), two in Ireland (Mount Melleray and Roscrea) and one in England (Mount Saint Bernard). In 1902 the Reformed Cistercians purchased the abbey of Cîteaux. New constitutions for the separated Order were approved in 1894 and in 1926.

TWENTIETH-CENTURY CISTERCIANS

At the beginning of the twentieth century, despite a few nineteenth-century houses in North America, Asia and Africa, both Cistercian Orders existed mainly in Europe and were, therefore, subjected to the upheavals experienced on that continent during the twentieth century. These included two World Wars and their aftermaths, fascist and communist regimes, anti-clerical governments, a growing tide of secularism and, in the latter part of the century, the opening up of Eastern Europe and vast demographic and technological changes. Together these have created vastly different environments for monasticism, and have had an effect both on recruitment and on the way monks lived. Such changes were amplified as a result of the Second Vatican Council, especially in Strict Observance monasteries.

Both Observances have expanded geographically after the Second World War. This was particularly true of the Trappist monasteries in the United States, partly as a result of the writings of Thomas Merton (1914–1968). The three nineteenth-century monasteries of monks founded a further seven houses in the period 1944–55, plus three in South America and one in the Philippines in the period 1960–80. Five monasteries of nuns were established there from 1949 to 1987. Japan also enjoyed a post-war boom with two monasteries of monks and five of nuns by 1981; a foundation was made in Korea in 1987. In 2010 there were twelve monasteries of monks in Africa and nine of nuns. The five Common Observance monasteries in Vietnam are flourishing, despite severe restrictions imposed on them by the government.

The twentieth century has been marked by increasing pluralism. The Common Observance is a federation of thirteen independent congregations and thirteen monasteries (two male and eleven female) attached directly to the Order. As such it embraced a wide diversity of observances, often determined by local situations. The Strict Observance with its single General Chapter, however, had from its inception insisted on a high degree of uniformity, even in minor details. The expansion of the Order to different climates and hemispheres caused a softening in this rigidity. In 1969 the General Chapter published its *Statutes on Unity and Pluralism*, defining the essential observances of the Order and making room for local adaptation. This, in turn, led to greater recognition being given to Regional Conferences as appropriate agencies for dealing with more local issues and for facilitating discussion. This decentralising approach was embodied in the post-Conciliar constitutions finally approved in 1990. From 1970 the abbesses held their own General Chapter under the presidency of the abbot general. From 1987 to 2011 the male and female General Chapters, though remaining separate, met jointly. In 2011 the Holy See finally gave approval for abbots and abbesses to meet as a single General Chapter.

In developed countries both Observances declined numerically during the twentieth century. According to official statistics, in 2009 the Common Observance had 1,913 monks and nuns in 121 establishments, not including Vietnam. The Strict Observance, excluding China, had 2,127 monks and 1,772 nuns in 102 monasteries of men and 73 of women.

Notes

1   D. Beales, *Prosperity and Plunder: European Catholic Monasteries in the Age of Revolution, 1650–1815* (Cambridge, 2003).

2   1565, 1567, 1573, 1578, 1584, 1601, 1605, 1609, 1613, 1618, 1623, 1628 and 1651.
3   *Statuta* 1623:22; Canivez, *Statuta*, 7, p. 348; other texts in P. Zakar, *Histoire de la Stricte Observance de l'Ordre Cistercien depuis ses débuts jusqu'au Généralat du Cardinal Richelieu (1606–1635)* (Rome, 1966), pp. 158–65.
4   *Statuta* 1623:26; Canivez, *Statuta*, 7, p. 350.
5   The text is given in Zakar, *Histoire*, pp. 168–77.
6   Canivez, *Statuta*, 7, pp. 426–37; T. Nguyên-Dính-Tuyén, 'Histoire des controverses à Rome entre la Commune et l'Étroite Observance de 1662 à 1666', *Analecta Cisterciensia*, 26 (1970), 3–247 (pp. 223–41).
7   L.J. Lekai, *The Cistercians: Ideals and Reality* (Kent, OH, 1977), p. 149.
8   1699, 1738, 1765, 1768, 1771, 1783 and 1786.
9   *Statuta* 1784:10; Canivez, *Statuta*, 7, p. 788.
10 Lekai, *The Cistercians*, p. 151.
11 D.N. Bell, 'Armand-Jean de Rancé: A Conference of Spiritual Joy', *CSQ*, 37 (2002), 33–46, and 'Rancé's Joy', in *Understanding Rancé: The Spirituality of the Abbot of La Trappe in Context*, CS 205 (Kalamazoo, MI, 2005), pp. 97–117; J. Leclercq, 'La joie de Rancé', *COCR*, 25 (1963), 206–15.
12 A.J. Krailsheimer, 'Le rôle de Rancé et de La Trappe dans la Réforme de l'Ordre de Cîteaux', in *Réformes et continuité dans l'Ordre de Cîteaux: de l'Étroite Observance à la Stricte Observance*, ed. T. N. Kinder (Brecht and Cîteaux, 1995), pp. 59–68 (pp. 64–66).
13 For a full bibliographical history, see Bell, *Understanding Rancé*, pp. 263–8, 270–3.
14 M. de la Trinité Kervingant, *A Monastic Odyssey*, CS 171 (Kalamazoo, MI, 1999).
15 N. Konrad, *Die Entstehung der Österreichisch-Ungarischen Zisterzienserkongregation (1849–1869)* (Rome, 1967).
16 *Acta capituli generalis* 1835, n.42; ed. V. Hermans, *Actes des Chapitres Généraux des Congrégations Trappistes au XIXème siècle: 1835–1891* (Rome, 1975), p. 107.

Primary sources

Canivez, J.-M. (ed.), *Statuta Capitulorum Generalium Ordinis Cisterciensis ab anno 1116 ad annum 1786*, 8 vols. (Louvain, 1933–41), although there are some errors and omissions, this is the primary source for the official records of the Cistercian General Chapter up to the time of the French Revolution
Hermans, V. (ed.), *Actes des Chapitres Généraux des Congrégations Trappistes au XIXe siècle: 1835–1891* (Rome, 1975), more than a mere listing of the official decisions, this collection of the Acts of the Trappist General Chapters gives an abundance of detail concerning the internal affairs of the Trappist Congregations

Konrad, N. (ed.), *Die Entstehung der Österreichisch-Ungarischen Zisterzienserkongregation (1849–1869)* (Rome, 1967)

Leloczky, J.D. (ed.), *Constitutiones et Acta Capitulorum Strictioris Observantiae Ordinis Cisterciensis (1624–1687)* (Rome, 1967)

Tuyén, T. Nguyên-Dính-, 'Histoire des controverses à Rome entre la Commune et l'Étroite Observance de 1662 à 1666', *Analecta Cisterciensia*, 26 (1970), 3–247

Zakar, P., *Histoire de la Stricte Observance de l'Ordre Cistercien depuis ses débuts jusqu'au Généralat du Cardinal Richelieu (1606–1635)* (Rome, 1966)

These four last invaluable collections by Common Observance scholars are preceded by introductions which contextualise the documents. Readers should note that their objectivity is threatened by a lack of sympathy for the Strict Observance.

Websites

Useful information can be found on the official websites of both Orders: www.ocist.org and www.ocso.org. From the latter can be downloaded the document *Observantiae: Continuity and Reforms in the Cistercian Family*, which deals with the period discussed in this chapter.

Part II

Structure and materiality

4 Centres and peripheries

EMILIA JAMROZIAK

The history of the Cistercian Order in the Middle Ages encompasses the histories of its central structures, the General Chapter, the international networks and the experiences of individual monastic houses. We cannot isolate one from the other; if we want to explore the history of the White Monks as a whole, we have to consider both the centre and the periphery of the Order and their influence on each other.

In the course of the twelfth and thirteenth centuries the Cistercian movement spread from Burgundy to the very frontiers of Latin Christendom in Scandinavia, the Baltic region, Central-Eastern Europe, Iberia, the crusader states and Greece. Cistercian expansion in the 1120s and 1130s involved primarily the core of Western Europe – France, Germany, the British Isles and Christian territories in Iberia – whilst in the 1140s a wave of foundations emerged in Central-Eastern Europe (Poland, Bohemia and Hungary) and Scandinavia (Denmark, Sweden and Norway). The White Monks spread through the foundation of new monasteries from mother houses, but also through incorporation of other reformed communities and appropriation of existing monasteries. Proprietary patrons were often instrumental in this process. In Ireland Cistercian monasteries play an important part in bringing the Hibernian Church in line with the continental model of diocesan and monastic structures. Although the first Cistercian abbey in Ireland, Mellifont, was a direct foundation from Clairvaux, its many daughter houses were originally native monastic communities, which took up Cistercian customs to become incorporated into the Order. Their success was in no small part a result of Irish kings' support for the ideas of reform.[1] In Denmark the Hvides, a leading noble family in the region, transformed the Benedictine house at Sorø on Zealand (founded in the late 1140s) into a Cistercian monastery in 1161.[2] The founders of the oldest Polish Cistercian abbeys were predominantly bishops, whilst the arrival of White Monks in Scotland was closely connected with the implementation of Church reform there. Many lay founders were

ambitious noblemen, such as Fergus, lord of Galloway or Warcisław
Świętobrzyc, castellan of Szczecin in Western Pomerania. For the social
elites of the European frontiers the Cistercians represented aspirational
cultural and spiritual capital. Their acts of patronage were one way of
asserting their status as members of the Latin Christian nobility.

THE MYTH OF PIONEERS

The traditional narratives of the Cistercian success emphasise the
pioneering nature of Cistercian foundations on marginal lands, cutting
down forests and expanding cultivation. Moreover, the White Monks
have been credited with introducing more effective agricultural methods and new varieties of plants and animals to improve the yields. Older
historiography, especially in the field of economic history, emphasises
these features as the central reasons for founders to establish Cistercian
communities on their land, because the improved local economy
brought 'civilisation' to 'undeveloped' parts of Europe. This explanation
fitted well with much twentieth-century thinking which did not perceive religion as a sufficient reason for such large-scale endeavours as
the foundation of religious houses. The investments made by laity in
the monasteries needed more 'rational' motivations. The major problem of this interpretation of the Cistercian success is the juxtaposition
of a rational – economic – motivation with an irrational – religious –
drive. In the medieval context they were not seen as separate or mutually contradictory forces. In the last few decades the motivations for
founding monasteries have been perceived in a more subtle way, as a
combination of spiritual, material and social factors.

In the heartland of Europe Cistercians were yet another wave
of monastic foundations, whilst in some frontier regions, recently
converted to Christianity, they formed the first layer of ecclesiastical structures and marked, by their presence, the advancements of
Christianity. There is also compelling evidence of their involvement
in missionary activities. We find Cistercian presence in all areas of
the 'expanding Europe' of the twelfth and thirteenth centuries. The
first Cistercian houses in the Holy Land were established in 1157 in
Belmont (southwest of Tripoli) and in 1161 in Salvatio (in the kingdom
of Jerusalem), both foundations from Morimond. The former seemed
to survive only until 1174, but Salvatio continued until the early thirteenth century, when a Cistercian monk from La Ferté, Peter of Ivrea,
became the patriarch of Antioch (1209) and made vigorous attempts to
extend the Cistercian network in the crusader states. He persuaded an

independent Benedictine community in Jubin (on the Black Mountain near Antioch) to join the Order. Later thirteenth-century attempts to establish Cistercian communities involved primarily refoundations of abandoned or impoverished houses. After the fall of Antioch in 1268 the Cistercians of Jubin followed other retreating Latin Orders and moved to Beaulieu in Cyprus.[3]

The emergence of Cistercian monasteries in Byzantine Greece, conquered by crusaders in 1204, was a part of papal efforts to strengthen the Latin Church in the Orthodox world. In 1205 Innocent III asked prelates in France to send capable Cistercian and Cluniac monks to Greece. Although it was not expressed openly, it appears that the Cistercians were to be missionaries to some degree. The foundations of Cistercian monasteries were primarily a matter of taking over abandoned or dispossessed Orthodox abbeys. The whole experiment was largely a failure and almost all foundations had collapsed by the time of Greek resurgence in 1276. The reason was not the monks' inability to follow the prescribed norms of Cistercian life, as older literature has suggested, but the political situation; when the influence of the Franks declined in the 1260s and was replaced by Venetian domination, the Cistercian houses lost their supporters.[4]

Cistercians were also active on the northern and north-eastern edges of Christendom. A string of Cistercian abbeys appeared on the southern coast of the Baltic Sea from Mecklenburg to Livonia (in present-day Estonia and Latvia) from the second half of the twelfth century and in Prussia in the 1220s and 1230s. Already in 1155 a Cistercian monk, Berno from Amelungsborn Abbey (Lower Saxony), was appointed missionary bishop to the pagan Obodrites, and in 1168 he took part in the military conquest of the pagan island of Rügen by King Valdemar of Denmark. Berno cooperated closely with Duke Henry, the Lion of Saxony, who appointed him to a newly created bishopric. As bishop, Berno was instrumental in persuading the recently Christianised local ruler Pribislav to found the first Cistercian abbey in Mecklenburg – Doberan in 1171 – as a daughter house of his home community in Amelungsborn.[5]

At the turn of the twelfth and thirteenth centuries the south-eastern Baltic was still a pagan region, which attracted the attention of German territorial princes and knights. The Baltic crusades turned into several campaigns of conquest, and Cistercian monks continued to be involved in the missions. The first missionary bishop of Estonia, the Cistercian monk Fulco from La Celle (Provence), was appointed in 1162, but it is unclear whether he ever made it to the Baltic coast. The Cistercians also played a major role in the later stages of Christian conquest in the 1180s and 1190s. Before and during his activities in Livonia as missionary bishop (1188), Meynardus, an Augustinian canon from Segeberg (Schleswig-Holstein), had Cistercian monks 'on his team', including Theodoricus (Dietrich) from Loccum (Lower Saxony), who baptised the Livonian chieftain Kaupo. Meynardus and his Cistercian monks' conversion methods were peaceful at this stage. The second bishop of Livonia, Berthold (1196–8), was also a Cistercian monk and abbot from Loccum. He was not only involved in the mission, but also instrumental in bringing crusaders to the region, primarily from northern Germany. This marked a turn for the Cistercians in the Baltic from engagement in peaceful mission to support of violent crusades. The bishop himself took part in the military expedition, sword in hand, and was killed in a battle against pagans.[6] Berthold's successor, Bishop Albert of Buxhövden (formerly a canon in Bremen), founded a Cistercian abbey in Dünamünde and continued to employ Cistercians as missionaries.[7] In Prussia, from 1206, a peaceful mission was conducted by the monk Christian from Kołbacz Abbey leading a group of Cistercians from Łekno Abbey with the explicit backing of Pope Innocent III but with limited success.[8] The neighbouring Christian rulers wanted protection from Prussian raids, and plans for a crusade were made. When the Teutonic Knights invited by Duke Conrad of Mazovia began a brutal war of conquest, any effect of the Cistercian mission was wiped out.[9] Cistercians who wanted to further missionary work were prevented from setting up a monastery in Prussia, and Christian's plans to found an 'episcopal' state in Prussia came to nothing, largely because of opposition from the Teutonic Knights.[10] For them, the Cistercians were simply an obstacle to their plans for their own territorial rule.

The emergence of Cistercian foundations on the peripheries of the Western Latin world was an important element of the 'making of Europe': the spread of Western social and cultural norms among the lay elites beyond the geographical core. This provided an important stimulus for numerous foundations. The founders of Rievaulx in Yorkshire (Walter Espec), Dundrennan in Galloway (Fergus, lord of Galloway), Łekno in Greater Poland (Zbyluta), Osek in Bohemia (Slávek) and countless others thus marked their ascent in the social status, and gained access to a particularly effective intercession. These monasteries commemorated their founders, acted as prestigious necropoleis and built their material well-being on very diverse economic bases which reflected regional specificities. Yet all were embodiments of Cistercianness.

THE ROLE OF THE FILIATION SYSTEM

One of the clearly innovative developments in the organisation of the Cistercian Order was the central governing body, the General Chapter, and filiations linking individual houses.[11] Although Cluny introduced a system of hierarchical links between the abbey and houses reformed by it, the centre of the Cluniac family was a single monastery and not a collective body. Many new early twelfth-century reform movements formed groupings of communities, but these tended to be fairly amorphous. The White Monks were the first to introduce a coherent network structure and a central representative body.

The shape, remits and character of the General Chapter evolved over a long period. In the early stages it was a type of working group whose main focus was on the spiritual and moral development of the growing Cistercian family. It did not have legislative power in the modern sense. In practice, the membership of the General Chapter was restricted to the abbots from houses relatively near Cîteaux. There are no surviving records of the General Chapter meetings before 1147, and the dating of the twelfth-century documentation is much debated by the historians.[12] The function of the General Chapter was described in the *Carta Caritatis*: controlling the proper observance of the Rule, making decisions, preserving good relations between the abbots and giving participants the opportunity to 'discuss the salvation of their own souls'.[13] Only from the early thirteenth century onwards was the General Chapter concerned with formulating rules and regulations and not simply with discussing individual cases.[14] From 1221 Cîteaux became the central archive, collecting all the documents pertinent to the Order but not those of individual houses.[15]

The precise structure of the meetings was set in the early thirteenth century. The gatherings lasted five days and 'business sections' were interspaced with masses and prayers and readings from the martyrologies, the Rule, *Carta Caritatis* and sermons.[16] Although the General Chapter was intended as a gathering of abbots from all the Cistercian houses, in practice it was always a selection. The abbots of French houses were far more numerous than those of the distant northern and north-eastern ones. In 1199, to eradicate absenteeism of abbots from the peripheries of the Order, the abbots of the proto-monasteries La Ferté, Pontigny, Clairvaux and Morimond were obliged to report, during their yearly visitation to Cîteaux, which abbeys of their filiations were due to send their abbots in which year. From about 1179 Scottish abbots were allowed to attend every fourth year; this was granted to the Irish in

1190.[17] Regulations of exemptions were codified only in 1202, repeated in 1237 and 1257. The *Libellus antiquarum definitionum* (1289) specified that abbots from Ireland, Scotland, Sicily, Galicia and Portugal could attend every fourth year, whilst the most distant houses in Syria and Cyprus were obliged only every seventh year. Abbots from Greece, Norway and Livonia should come every fifth year. Permission to attend every third year was given to Hungary, Leon, Castile, Frisia and Styria. Finally, biennial attendance was permitted to the abbots from Aragon, Navarre and Catalonia. The coordination of attendance from within particular regions and kingdoms was organised so as to ensure that two abbots from each area were in attendance to guarantee that the decisions from the General Chapter were transmitted to their fellow monasteries.[18]

The statutes of the General Chapter are central to our understanding of the relationships between different houses, the geographical spread of new foundations and the concerns of the abbots and their responses to internal and external difficulties affecting their communities. The statutes follow a strict formula for recording information, decisions and pronouncement of the General Chapter. Matters were brought to the attention of the General Chapter only if reported by the abbots of either the houses concerned or daughter houses or monasteries in their region. A large proportion of the cases discussed at the meeting involved matters of internal discipline and conflicts between neighbouring monasteries. In addition to the statutes of the General Chapter, the Order also produced several codifications of the regulations known as *Libelli diffinitionum* (1202, 1220, 1237, 1257 and 1288/9), *Libellus antiquarum definitionum* (1316) and *Libellus novellarum definitionum* (1350). These collections reflect concerns with the Order's authority over observance and internal control and the diverse problems that communities encountered.

The Cistercian Order was constituted not only by the General Chapter and the power of the proto-abbeys and Cîteaux, but also by the network of connections between individual houses. *Carta Caritatis* formalised the crucial bond between mother and daughter houses. Father abbots were obliged to make yearly visitations to the daughter houses in order to maintain uniformity of practice and discipline and to oversee the election of abbots. From the thirteenth century onwards admonishing of abbots who did not fulfil their duties was fairly frequent in the statutes. Meanwhile, interfering father abbots were much dreaded and their arbitrary interventions much disliked. The abbot of Rievaulx deposed the abbot of its daughter house of Melrose in 1261.

It took place in the chapter house of the mother house, clearly indicating the subordinate position of the daughter house.[19] The community of Melrose considered this action unjust not only because the monks regarded Abbot Matthew as an excellent leader, but also because the deposition was done *in absentia*. It is clear that the monastic community felt that this was an arbitrary decision on the part of the abbot of Rievaulx, but the monastic chronicle had to maintain a respectful tone towards the mother house. At first the Melrose chronicle noted, between 21 January 1264 and mid 1264, that Matthew resigned due to infirmity. Two decades later, between 14 April 1286 and May 1291, the removal of the abbot was described as a deposition enacted by the abbot of Rievaulx, who made it 'without counsel or knowledge of any living soul in Scotland' and in spite of the strong support of the community at Melrose for its abbot.[20]

The framework of the visitation was based on the Order's legal structure specified in the *Instituta* and repeated in the ruling of the General Chapter of 1193.[21] The visitations were vital for maintaining personal connections and for communication between monasteries. The abbot father's commitment to the control of the spiritual and economic prosperity of the filiation was essential for the effectiveness of the visitation. The visitations were also crucial for the transfer of knowledge of problems in the Order's chain of command to the General Chapter.[22] In 1202 the General Chapter ruled that the written report should contain the exact information given to the community undergoing inspection at the chapter meeting with the inspectoral abbot. The cantor kept this document until the next visitation.[23] From the thirteenth century onwards the Order developed a number of formula books explaining and regulating all aspects of the visitation: types of questions and issues to investigate as well as models of visitation reports.[24] Such works are particularly useful for our understanding of the internal working of the monastic communities and the problems encountered by visitors. There seemed to be a fear of 'conspiracies' against abbots and of fragmentation of the community into opposing cliques, but instances of possible favouritism were also investigated. The communal welfare was above the wants of individuals, hence the monks who were particularly rebellious or unwilling to change could be expelled to prevent 'infection' of the rest of the community.

The filiation system was hierarchical. The hierarchy between abbeys was organised according to 'generations' from each proto-monastery in Burgundy, its direct daughter houses, their daughters and so on. Within each group the date of foundations determined the abbatial precedence.

The meetings of the General Chapter were organised according to this structure. A special list was maintained by the cantor at Cîteaux with day and year of each foundation in order to establish the order of the abbots' precedence, but the accuracy of that list was much contested by abbots who wanted to improve their standing.[25] The idea of the Cistercian family was frequently represented visually as a genealogical tree with branches showing filiations.[26] The widespread presence of lists and genealogical tables of Cistercian abbeys kept in numerous monasteries and produced throughout the Middle Ages, often included in cartularies, is an important testimony to the vitality of the idea of the transnational network.

Regular links were also maintained through the movement of personnel, especially through the career structure of monastic promotions. Monks moving between monasteries to take up offices helped to transfer not only information, but also ideas, practices, views and expectations between mother and daughter houses and within the immediate filiation. Most commonly the pattern of promotion involved a period in one of the lesser offices such as prior or novice master followed by the office of abbot in a smaller house finally leading to taking up the abbacy in the larger house. This pattern can be observed for several houses belonging to the Rievaulx–Melrose filiation. In the twelfth century Silvanus first held the abbacy of Dundrennan, from which he resigned in 1167 to take up the abbacy at Rievaulx, which he held until 1188.[27] Ernald was abbot of Melrose from 1179 and followed Silvanus in the abbacy of Rievaulx between 1189 and 1199.[28] In the following century William de Courcy was the head of three monasteries; first Holme Cultram, in 1215 Melrose and a year later Rievaulx, where he was abbot until his death. Leonius started his career as a monk of Melrose; in 1239 he was promoted to the abbacy of Dundrennan and in 1240 elected as abbot of Rievaulx.[29] These people had strong loyalties to their mother house and promoted the version of Cistercian life they had been acculturated in.

Promotions from the abbacy of a smaller to a major abbey were fairly common, but were not the only pattern possible. Transfers to lesser offices in larger houses offered an attractive stepping-stone. In 1233 Abbot Gilbert of Glenluce resigned in order to become a novice master at Melrose. His later career included the bishopric of Whithorn.[30] Some careers might have been accelerated by connections to patrons. In 1165 the prior of Dundrennan was Walter, formerly sacristan of Rievaulx and chaplain to the abbey's founder, Walter Espec.[31]

But there was no guarantee that monks sent by the mother house to a filial monastery would be good at their job or even welcomed by their new community. In 1235 Prior Hugh of Melrose was elected as abbot of its granddaughter Deer Abbey in Aberdeenshire, but he resigned and returned to his old community after only a year as he could not cope with the harsh climate. In 1267 the sacristan of Melrose, Adam of Smailholm, resigned after five years in the abbatial office at Deer. The official version of events recorded in the chronicle after Easter 1286 states that he preferred the 'sweetness of Melrose' to the 'hovel' of Deer. The unofficial account, written in the lower margin in or soon after 1267 and later erased, noted that the monks of Deer opposed Abbot Adam 'as one'.[32]

On both the regional and the international level, the filiation networks were central for the transfer of information and ideas, upholding common observance and for sustaining an effective 'career structure'. Whilst General Chapters were held in Cîteaux and the proto-abbeys remained important reference points, from the thirteenth century onwards we can observe the increased significance of regional centres, which became a more proximate authority than distant Burgundy. Many of these regionally or nationally important Cistercian monasteries were the oldest foundations and headed large local and national families of daughter houses. This role was clearly exercised by Altenberg for Rhineland, Kołbacz for Pomerania and Melrose for Scotland. The cultural influences emanating from these mother houses gave a sense of identity to their family of abbeys, but these identities were neither politically nor linguistically universal.

THE REGIONALISATION IN THE LATE MIDDLE AGES

The regionalisation was the result of many external pressures weakening the international networks such as wars, financial demands of kings and papacy, the papal schism and the development of more rigid national borders. Also the increasing significance of vernacular languages changed the Cistercian family.

The Great Schism (1378–1417) was one of the most damaging developments, affecting the Order's international network and forcing the creation of alternative structures as the proto-abbeys were cut off. The Roman popes Urban VI and Boniface IX forbade Cistercian monasteries under their jurisdiction any contact with fellow houses in regions loyal to the Avignon papacy. Meetings of the General Chapter were impossible for decades. Instead, the Roman papacy encouraged 'reduced' General Chapters within the territories under its control – primarily to facilitate the collection of papal taxation from the Order.

Italian abbots met in Rome, abbots from the Empire in Vienna, smaller
regional chapters were held in Nuremberg, Worms and Heilsbronn.
Some of these gatherings became 'national' Chapters. For example,
English abbots met in 1394 and 1400 at St Mary Graces Abbey in
London.

One of the clear manifestations that international bonds were
eroded and displaced by territorial bonds was the General Chapter's
introduction of provincial visitations in 1433. The traditional system
of visitation was not abolished, but in practice it became defunct in
many areas, especially across hostile political borders.[33] In order to preserve connections between the centre and the individual monasteries,
the General Chapter frequently replaced the father abbot of a distant
mother house who neglected his visitation duties with an abbot of a
locally important Cistercian house. For example, the abbot of Fountains
was criticised by the General Chapter in 1213 for neglecting his duties
towards the Norwegian daughter house in Lysa.[34]

The issue of language as a unifying or dissipative element of
Cistercian communication surfaced relatively early – especially so in
the periphery. Already during Stephen of Lexington's reforming mission
to Ireland in the 1220s one of the major problems he observed was the
lack of knowledge of French – the main language of communication
within the Order – in the Irish Cistercian houses. Stephen's plans for
establishing a higher level of education within the Order aimed specifically at establishing common standards and language among the
monks. He wanted to make fluency in French and Latin a prerequisite
for admission into the Order and proposed that all Cistercian Chapters
be conducted in either French or Latin. Stephen recommended the recitation of the Rule of St Benedict in French to improve active knowledge
of that language.[35]

Language issues became particularly intense in the frontier
areas between different ethnic, linguistic and political orientations.
Wągrowiec in Greater Poland was a daughter house of Altenberg
(Rhineland) and was founded (on another site in Łekno) in 1142. The
community continued to have German abbots and monks well into the
fifteenth century, when Wągrowiec became part of the Polish Cistercian
province, which caused contention. In 1487 the German community
of Wągrowiec refused obedience to the abbot of Mogiła, the head of
the Polish Cistercian province; it continued to recruit monks from
Rhineland and refused to accept Polish entrants. The issue became so
politicised that Polish kings issued decrees in 1538 and 1550 that only
Polish noblemen could be elected to the abbatial position in Wągrowiec

and two other houses in Greater Poland. The conflict lasted until 1580, when Polish monks took over the control of Wągrowiec.[36]

Vernacular language was not only a source of fragmentation. In the fourteenth and fifteenth centuries a majority of the texts in Cistercian libraries were still in Latin, but the later part of the period saw a growth of vernacular texts. In the late thirteenth and first half of the four-teenth century pious noblewomen, who populated southern German Cistercian houses, were a 'target group' for translations of spiritual works by Bernard of Clairvaux and other early Cistercian authors. The library of the wealthy nunnery of Kirchheim (northern Bavaria) has 122 German-language manuscripts from the fifteenth and sixteenth centur-ies and only twenty in Latin (excluding liturgical books) from the same period.[37] The process of 'vernacularisation' of Cistercian libraries was, however, a regional issue, and in northern Germany Latin texts contin-ued to dominate much longer than in the south.

CONCLUSION

What is so remarkable about the spread of Cistercian foundations is the adaptability of the communities to local conditions; their ability to take advantage of diverse conditions and respond to the expectations of the local laity whilst maintaining the core Cistercian qualities.

The bond between mother and daughter houses was central for the Cistercians – and far stronger than the Order-wide connection that hinged on the General Chapter. The filiation was a channel for infor-mation and appointments to monastic offices, and the authority of the father abbot often loomed large over the daughter houses. In the end, Cistercian history is constituted by the experiences of individual houses as much as by the international networks and central structures of the General Chapter and French proto-abbeys. The traditional view, and historiography, has been that religious Orders go through cycles of development – rise, decline and reform. If we abandon this centrally orientated approach and focus on the regional aspects of the Order's history, a different image will emerge. If we study surviving chroni-cles and cartularies of houses belonging to different Orders, local and regional affairs overshadow the wider perspective of the institutional network.[38] The ability to respond to local expectations whilst main-taining what outsiders perceived as a Cistercian 'brand' and keeping internal observance was crucial not just for the international struc-ture of the Order. The connections to the lay world can be seen as a fairly cynical mechanism for securing donations and protection, but on the spiritual level it was an expression of a love that binds monks to God and unites the community. It was the concept of the love of one's neighbour which secured the network of institutions, benefactors, patrons and neighbours.

The regionalisation of the Cistercian Order in the fourteenth and fifteenth centuries was parallel to processes of fragmentation within the Church as a whole. The papacy – the traditional source of support at the highest level – no longer fulfilled its role, and predatory taxation as well as the appointment of commendatory abbots weakened the viability of the General Chapter and the finances of many French and Italian houses.[39] On the macro-scale the Order was affected by external forces such as the development of effective state taxation as well as rigid borders upheld through wars. On the micro-scale internal centrifugal forces such as linguistic and cultural changes also affected its unity. Nevertheless, the late medieval Cistercian world was still full of abbeys which provided important spiritual focal points for their benefactors and friends, established significant libraries and continued to express corporate confidence through extensive building projects. We cannot separate a centrally focused perspective on the Order from regional variations, problems and successes. All these perspectives constitute Cistercian history, and there is no single one which is more 'authentically Cistercian' than the rest.

Notes

1   M.T. Flanagan, 'Irish Royal Charters and the Cistercian Order', in *Charters and Charter Scholarship in Britain and Ireland*, ed. M.T. Flanagan and J.A. Green (Basingstoke, 2005), pp. 122–5.

2   K. Esmark, 'Religious Patronage and Family Consciousness: Sorø Abbey and the "Hvide Family", *c.*1150–1250', in *Religious and Laity in Western Europe 1000–1400: Interaction, Negotiation and Power*, ed. E. Jamroziak and J. Burton (Turnhout, 2006), pp. 93–110 (pp. 97–8).

3   A. Jotischky, *The Perfection of Solitude: Hermits and Monks in the Crusader States* (University Park, PA, 1995), pp. 58–62 and 133.

4   N. Tsougarakis, 'Religious Patronage in Medieval Greece', in *Monasteries on the Borders of Medieval Europe*, ed. E. Jamroziak and K. Stöber (Turnhout, in press)

5   T. Nyberg, *Monasticism in North-Western Europe, 800–1200* (Aldershot, 2000), pp. 232–8; S. Rosik and P. Urbańczyk, 'Polabia and Pomerania between Paganism and Christianity', in *Christianisation and the Rise of Christian Monarchy: Scandinavia, Central Europe and Rus c. 900–1200*, ed. N. Berend (Cambridge, 2007), pp. 300–8.

6 C. Krötzl, 'Die Cistercienser und die Mission "ad pagano" 1150–1250', *Analecta Cisterciensia*, 62 (2012), pp. 278–98.

7 P. Raudkivi, 'Cistercians and Livonia: Problems and Perspectives', in *L'espace cistercien*, ed. L. Pressouyre (Paris, 1994), p. 350.

8 K. Conrad (ed.), *Pommersches Urkundenbuch*, vol. 1 (Cologne, 1970), no. 5.

9 L. Pósán, 'The Invitation of the Teutonic Order into Kulmerland', in *The Crusades and the Military Orders: Expanding the Frontiers of Medieval Latin Christianity*, ed. Z. Hunyadi and J. Laszlovszky (Budapest, 2001), pp. 430–5.

10 K. Zielińska-Mlekowska, 'Św Chrystian – misyjny biskup Prus', *Nasza Przeszłość*, 83 (1994), 46.

11 See Brian P. McGuire's chapter in this volume.

12 D. N. Bell, 'From Molesme to Cîteaux: The Earliest "Cistercian Spirituality"', *CSQ*, 34 (1999), 469–82 (p. 479); L.J. Lekai, 'Ideals and Reality in Early Cistercian Life and Legislation', in *Cistercian Ideals and Reality*, ed. J.R. Sommerfeldt, CS 60 (Kalamazoo, MI, 1978), pp. 4–29 (p. 7); a new edition of the oldest fragmentary series between 1157 and 1161 is found in Waddell, *Statutes*, pp. 65–75.

13 Bell, 'From Molesme to Cîteaux', p. 479.

14 B.P. McGuire, 'Norm and Practice in Early Cistercian Life', in *Norm und Praxis in Alltag des Mittelalters und der frühen Neuzeit*, ed. G. Jaritz (Vienna, 1997), pp. 107–24 (p. 111).

15 E. Goez, *Pragmatische Schriftlichkeit und Archivpflege der Zisterzienser: Ordenszentralismus und regionale Vielfalt, namentlich in Franken und Altbayern (1098–1525)* (Münster, 2003), pp. 139–40.

16 Waddell, *Statutes*, pp. 37–8.

17 *Ibid.*, pp. 38–9.

18 *Ibid.*, p. 39.

19 'Chronicle of Melrose'; ed. and trans. J. Stevenson, *The Church Historians of England*, vol. IV. 1 (London, 1856), pp. 79–242 (p. 214).

20 D. Broun, 'Melrose Abbey and Its World', in *Chronicle of Melrose Abbey: A Stratigraphic Edition*, ed. D. Broun and J. Harrison, vol. 1 (Woodbridge, 2007), pp. 1–12 (pp. 3–4).

21 Waddell, *Statutes*, 1193:1.

22 J. Oberste, *Visitation und Ordensorganisation: Formen sozialer Normierung, Kontrolle und Kommunikation bei Cisterziensern, Prämonstratensern und Cluniazensern (12.–frühes 14. Jahrhundert)* (Münster, 1995), p. 117.

23 J. Oberste, *Die Dokumente der Klösterlichen Visitationen*, Typologie des sources du moyen âge occidental 80 (Turnhout, 1999), p. 34.

24 J. Oberste, 'Normierung und Pragmatik des Schriftgebrauchs im Cisterziensischen Visitationsverfahren bis zum beginnenden 14. Jahrhundert', *Historisches Jahrbuch*, 114 (1994), 327–34.

25 P. King, *The Finance of the Cistercian Order in the Fourteenth Century*, CS 85 (Kalamazoo, MI, 1985), pp. 14–15; F.R. Swietek, '*Et Inter Abbates de Majoribus unus*: The Abbot of Savigny in the Cistercian Constitution,

1147–1243', in *Truth as Gift: Studies in Medieval Cistercian History in Honor of John R. Sommerfeldt*, ed. M.L. Dutton *et al.*, CS 204 (Kalamazoo, MI, 2004), pp. 89–118 (p. 98).

26   R. Locatelli, 'Les Cisterciens dans l'espace français: filiations et réseaux', in *Unanimité et diversité cisterciennes: filiations, réseaux, relectures du XIIe au XVIIe siècle*, ed. N. Bouter (Saint-Etienne, 2000), pp. 51–85 (p. 58).

27   P.C. Ferguson, *Medieval Papal Representatives in Scotland: Legates, Nuncios, and Judges-Delegate, 1125–1286* (Edinburgh, 1997), p. 61.

28   'Chronicle of Melrose', pp. 147–8; ed. G.W.S. Barrow, *The Acts of Malcolm IV, King of Scots, 1153–1165* (Edinburgh, 1960), p. 22.

29   D. Knowles *et al.* (eds.), *The Heads of Religious Houses: England and Wales*, 3 vols. (Cambridge, 1972), vol. I, p. 140; vol. II, p. 302.

30   'Chronicle of Melrose', pp. 177–8 and 61; K. Stringer, 'Reform Monasticism and Celtic Scotland', in *Alba: Celtic Scotland in the Middle Ages*, ed. E.J. Cowan and R.A. McDonald (East Linton, 2000), pp. 127–65 (p. 155).

31   Stringer, 'Reform Monasticism and Celtic Scotland', p. 152.

32   Broun, 'Melrose Abbey and Its World', p. 5, n.24; A. Orr Anderson and M. Ogilvie Anderson (eds.), *Chronicle of Melrose: From the Cottonian Manuscript, Faustina B. IX in the British Museum. A Complete and Full-Size Facsimile in Collotype* (London, 1936), p. 129, lxiv; 'Chronicle of Melrose', p. 220.

33   Oberste, *Die Dokumente*, p. 35.

34   J. France, *The Cistercians in Scandinavia*, CS 131 (Kalamazoo, MI, 1992), p. 321.

35   D.M. La Corte, 'Pope Innocent IV's Role in the Establishment and Early Success of the College of Saint Bernard in Paris', *Cîteaux*, 46 (1995), 289–303 (pp. 292–3); B. Griesser, 'Registrum Epistolarum Stephani de Lexington', *ASOC*, 2 (1946), 1–118 (pp. 93, 102).

36   L. Grajkowska, 'Polonizacja klasztoru cystersów w Wągrowcu', in *Cystersi w kulturze średniowiecznej Europy*, ed. J. Strzelczyk (Poznań, 1992), pp. 113–21.

37   N.F. Palmer, 'Deutschsprachige Literatur im Zisterzienserorden: Versuch einer Darstellung am Beispiel der ostschwäbischen Zisterzienser- und Zisterzienserinnenliteratur im Umkreis von Kloster Kaisheim im 13. und 14. Jahrhundert', in *Zisterziensisches Schreiben im Mittelalter: Das Skriptorium der Reiner Mönche*, ed. A. Schwob and K. Kranich-Hofbauer (Bern, 2005), pp. 231–66 (pp. 242–4).

38   J. Röhrkasten, 'Regionalism and Locality as a Factor in the Study of Religious Orders', in *Mittelalterliche Orden und Klöster im Vergleich: Methodische Ansätze und Perspektiven*, ed. G. Melville and A. Müller (Berlin, 2007), pp. 243–68 (p. 255).

39   W. Telesca, 'The Order of Cîteaux during the Council of Basel, 1431–1449', *Cîteaux*, 32 (1981), 17–36 (p. 35).

Primary sources

Broun, D. and J. Harrison (eds.), *Chronicle of Melrose Abbey: A Stratigraphic Edition*, 2 vols. (Woodbridge, 2007–)

Górecki, P. (ed.), *A Local Society in Transition: The Henryków Book and Related Documents* (Toronto, 2007)

Waddell, C. (ed.), *Twelfth-Century Statutes from the Cistercian General Chapter*, Cîteaux: Studia et Documenta 12 (Brecht, 2002)

5 The Cistercian community

JAMES FRANCE

According to tradition the New Monastery, later known as Cîteaux, was founded on 21 March 1098. The choice of day was no coincidence as on that day the feast of St Benedict was celebrated. It was also apt, for on moving from Molesme the twenty-one monks under their abbot Robert had left behind the 'old' ways of traditional monachism with its emphasis on the elaborate and time-consuming celebration of the Divine Office in order to embrace a 'new' interpretation of the Rule, one in which the balance between the three constituent parts of the monastic horarium – prayer, study and work – had been restored. The Rule and its revised implementation were basic to the Cistercian reform and were commented upon both in all early Cistercian texts as well as by a number of contemporary outside observers. The Premonstratensian abbot Philip of Harvengt claimed that with the foundation of Cîteaux the 'monastic Order, formerly dead, was revived ... and the Rule of St Benedict recovered in our times the truth of the letter'. Even some of the Cistercians' severest critics acknowledged their achievement. The chronicler William of Malmesbury refers to their distress that they were not able to follow 'the purity of the Rule' to which he states that they attached great importance by saying, 'So intent are they on their Rule, that they think not a jot or tittle of it should be disregarded.' The Norman Benedictine Orderic Vitalis described them as endeavouring 'to carry out a literal observance of the Rule of Saint Benedict'.

Although the Cistercians did away with many of the accretions to the liturgy that had been introduced over the centuries, the *opus Dei* – the Work of God – still remained their primary and distinctive occupation, constituting the very *raison d'être* of monasticism. St Benedict devoted twelve chapters in the Rule to its composition and the manner of celebrating the seven daytime canonical Hours of Lauds, Prime, Terce, Sext, None, Vespers and Compline, plus the Night Office. The primacy of the Office was endorsed by Bernard of Clairvaux in these words: 'By our Rule we must put nothing before the Work of God.'

Lectio divina – Sacred Reading – follows the Rule's opening statement, 'Listen carefully … to the precepts of the master', and was the bedrock upon which the community was formed into 'a school of the Lord's service' (*RB* Prologue). It differs fundamentally from profane reading. Derived from the Latin verb '*lego*', *lectio* does not so much mean to 'read' as 'to gather' or 'to collect'; a slow process, originally carried out aloud, with Scripture and the works of the Fathers at its core. It is traditionally likened to 'ruminating' or 'chewing', almost in the sense of chewing the cud.

Following the rejection of the traditional income from rents, tithes and the possession of churches, the restoration of manual labour – *labor manuum* – to the monastic horarium was one of the main planks of the Cistercian reform and was binding on all members of the community, even the abbot. By their compliance the Cistercians conformed to what St Benedict had enjoined: 'Idleness is the enemy of the soul. The brethren, therefore, must be occupied at stated hours in manual labour' (*RB* 48).

Obedience is the monastic virtue par excellence, chosen by those 'not living by their own will, and obeying their own desires and passions, but walking by another's judgement and orders, they dwell in monasteries, and desire to have an abbot over them' (*RB* 5). The responsibility of the abbot was awesome and Benedict devoted four chapters to the office in his Rule (*RB* 2, 27, 56 and 64). Immediately after his definition of the four kinds of monks Benedict describes the kind of man the abbot should be. He is 'the representative of Christ in the monastery'. He is to teach 'by deeds and by words, but by deeds rather than by words'. Although he should love all in his care equally:

> One he must humour, another rebuke, another persuade, according to each one's disposition and understanding, and thus adapt and accommodate himself to all in such a way, that he may not only suffer no loss in the sheep committed to him, but may even rejoice in the increase of a good flock. (*RB* 2)

Human frailty inevitably meant that the ideal envisaged by Benedict was not always achieved, but by the two main provisions of the Charter of Charity, the visitation of daughter houses by father abbots and the annual meeting at Cîteaux of abbots in General Chapter, the Cistercians had devised a mechanism whereby autocratic excesses could be curbed. They provided a restraint on the arbitrary rule of abbots – hitherto unknown among the Black Monks, whose abbeys were entirely autonomous – and ensured a degree of uniformity which they deemed essential.

The Rule assumed that an abbot held office for life, and among the Black Monks voluntary resignations were almost unknown, but among the Cistercians resignations were recognised practice from the first and were relatively common. In some cases the gift of spiritual leadership was not matched by the necessary administrative ability; in others, resignations were due to feelings of unworthiness or nostalgia for the house of profession to which they wished to return. Although depositions were rare, the Charter of Charity provided for the removal of abbots who showed 'contempt for the Rule or the Order' and who, after being warned four times, failed to emend.

The pastoral nature of the abbatial office was symbolised by the staff or crosier with which abbots were invested and which represented their authority over the monks in their care. The change from the simple shepherd's crook to the elaborate gilt crosiers with carvings and set with precious stones marked the emergence in the later Middle Ages of abbots as powerful prelates almost on a par with bishops. Abbots gradually withdrew from the common dormitory to a separate house where they could entertain distinguished guests in the same style they experienced when fêted by them. In the fourteenth century their social position was recognised by grants of *pontificalia*, whereby they were given the right to the use of a number of episcopal *insignia*, including the mitre.

One of the abbot's responsibilities was the appointment to all offices in the monastery. First was that of his deputy, the prior, who was in charge during the abbot's absence (*RB* 65). According to Benedict, 'the more he is set above the rest, the more scrupulously should he observe the precepts of the Rule', but if he failed he should be deposed.

Of crucial importance was the cellarer, who was responsible for the economy of the monastery and its estates and granges. The material well-being of the community, upon which its spiritual health rested, depended on his stewardship. He was therefore to be 'prudent, of mature character, temperate, not a great eater, not proud, not headstrong, not rough-spoken, not lazy, not wasteful, but a God-fearing man who may be like a father to the whole community' (*RB* 31). There are many examples of a successful term as cellarer leading to election as abbot, and the importance Bernard attached to the office may be seen by the choice of his brother, Gerard, as his cellarer at Clairvaux. In his lament upon his brother's death in Sermon 26 on the Song of Songs, Bernard outlined the duties of the office when he asked:

> Did anything ever escape the skilled eye of Gerard in the buildings, in the fields, in gardening, in the water systems, in all the arts

and crafts of the people of the countryside? With masterly competence he supervised the masons, the smiths, the farm workers, the
gardeners, the shoemakers and the weavers.

The porter or gate keeper is the only other official named by Benedict in
a chapter heading (*RB* 66). A 'wise old man' living near the gate was the
ideal person to scrutinise the coming and going, to ensure that no one
entered who did not have legitimate business and that monks did not
wander outside as 'all necessary things, such as water, mill, garden and
various crafts be within the enclosure'.

Two office holders, the guest master and the novice master, are not
mentioned in the Rule's chapter headings, but their all-important duties
are outlined in its text. The guest house was 'to be assigned to a brother
whose soul was full of the fear of God'. His responsibility it was to
ensure that the paramount Benedictine obligation that 'all guests that
come be received like Christ' was fulfilled (*RB* 53).

The novices were placed in the charge of one of the senior monks
'skilled in winning souls that he may watch over them with the utmost
care' (*RB* 58). He was responsible for their formation and for discerning
their suitability. Earlier in his career Aelred of Rievaulx is said by his
biographer, Walter Daniel, to have excelled as novice master, making
good monks of his novices as 'worthy vessels of God and acceptable to
the Order and even examples of perfection to those who truly yearn to
excel as patterns of goodness'. Another distinguished novice master was
Caesarius of Heisterbach, who in the early thirteenth century wrote the
Dialogue on Miracles – the *Dialogus miraculorum* – which takes the
form of a dialogue between him and one of his novices.

Benedict outlines the procedure for the reception of novices (*RB* 58).
He insists that only those who are persistent in their attempts to enter
a monastery be admitted and that they should spend four days in the
guest house before being taken to the chapter house. Here the abbot
would point out the severity of the Rule and only after the candidate
had three times freely consented to keeping it all would he be taken to
the noviciate – the *cella novitiorum* – there to spend his year of proba-
tion. At the end of this he made the three monastic vows of stability,
conversion of life and obedience, confirmed in a written petition which
he placed on the altar. Having disposed of all his property, the novice
was stripped of his own clothes and put on the cowl. He was now a full
member of the community with a vote in abbatial elections. Sometime
in the second half of the twelfth century novices were given their own
habit. According to the *Ecclesiastica Officia*, in which Cistercian life

was regulated in the minutest detail, novices were required to wear 'the same habit as the monks except for what is the special monastic item', in other words excepting the cowl, instead of which they had a sleeveless mantle.

Compliance with the precepts of the Rule, dedication to a life of humility and obedience lived in accordance with the three elements of prayer, study and work under the three monastic vows and its transmission to future generations by the formation of novices was the stated aim of the early Cistercians. As we have seen, a strict interpretation of the Rule constituted their very *raison d'être*, which was mentioned over and over again in their early texts. And yet, paradoxically, they chose to deviate from the Rule in two fundamental respects, one of them by omission, the other by addition. As a result of this change the Cistercian community was to become radically different from the earlier Benedictine model.

The omission from the Rule consisted of doing away with the *oblati* – youngsters offered by their parents to be reared in the monastery, also known as *nutriti*, that is, those given board in the monastery. According to the Rule, upon the reception of young boys, the petition which was normally written by the novices themselves was drawn up by their parents and placed on the altar (*RB* 59). They were to be corrected according to their age with 'an appropriate measure of discipline' (*RB* 30). In future admission was to be a matter of free choice and limited to adults, what today would be defined as a 'vocation'. According to an early statute the minimum age of the reception of Cistercian novices was set at fifteen, but sometime around the middle of the twelfth century it was raised to eighteen.

The addition to the Rule was the introduction of lay brothers, also known as *conversi* or *fratres laici*. They represented a new form of religious life, now for the first time open to the broad populace. Although the vast majority of lay brothers were recruited from the rural poor, out of humility a number of knights and scholars chose to become lay brothers in preference to joining as monks. The obligation of manual labour rested on all members of the community, but the Cistercians soon found that they were not able, by the work of their own hands alone, to fulfil their primary occupation, the *opus Dei*, and their obligation of residing in the cloister (*RB* 66). In announcing the institution of lay brothers the *Exordium Parvum* states that 'lay brothers, and not monks, should be in charge of those dwellings [granges], because, according to the Rule, monks should reside in their own cloister'. The grange formed the basis of the Cistercian agrarian economy, and early evidence shows the connection between the introduction of lay brothers and the establishment of the earliest granges, both thought to be around 1120. The institution of the lay brotherhood was not original to the Cistercians, having already been introduced as a distinctive feature of the monastic reform of the second half of the eleventh century, but they developed it to its fullest extent. In some cases lay brothers outnumbered monks by two to one or even by three to one. While monks were clean-shaven and distinguished by the clerical tonsure and the wearing of the monastic cowl, the *conversi* were, as the name implies, lay. They were bearded – and therefore also known as *barbati* – and wore a sleeveless mantle. Being lay, they were nevertheless religious, having, after a year's noviciate, made the same three vows as monks. Separate architectural provision was made within the monastery: they were housed in the west range, where a lane, separated by a wall from the monks' cloister, served as their own cloister. They had their own choir in the western part of the nave, separated from the monks by a screen. Although separate, the lay brothers enjoyed the same spiritual and temporal status as monks, but in practice they were frequently patronised. Their inferiority vis-à-vis the monks in a servant–master relationship was a flaw which, together with economic, agrarian, demographic and cultural factors, contributed to their sharp decline in numbers in the fourteenth century.

Like most of their medieval contemporaries lay brothers were 'ignorant of letters' (*illiterati*), in other words lacking in knowledge of Latin, a skill required only for the *opus Dei* and *lectio divina*. The crucial part lay brothers played in the early material success of the Order was based on other skills and contributed substantially to the phenomenal growth of the monastic estates. Later evidence in the form of General Chapter statutes highlights the disciplinary problems partially caused by the large numbers who joined out of necessity, in the words of Caesarius of Heisterbach 'driven to enter by the furnace of poverty'. The moralising stories of visions and revelations contained in the *exemplum* literature are an invaluable source in telling us a great deal about the daily lives and mentality of lay brothers as well as about the monk-authors who wrote them. Towards the end of the twelfth century the earlier more heroic age had come to an end, and stories of exceptional lay brothers were used to show disapproval of the increasing clericalisation of monks and distrust of secular learning as well as being a spur to recapturing some of the simplicity of earlier times. The spiritual as well as material contribution of lay brothers to Cistercian history was immense.

In spite of the importance the Cistercians attached to a strict adherence to the Rule, their insistence on limiting their intake to adults and their introduction of lay brothers were to fundamentally change the composition of all their communities.

Primary sources

Caesarius of Heisterbach, *Dialogus miraculorum*, ed. J. Strange, *Caesarii Heisterbacensis monachi Ordinis Cisterciensis Dialogus miraculorum*, 2 vols. (Cologne, 1851); trans. H. von Essen Scott and C.C. Swinton Bland, *Dialogue on Miracles by Caesarius of Heisterbach* (London and New York, 1929)

Canivez, J.-M. (ed.), *Statuta Capitulorum Generalium Ordinis Cisterciensis ab anno 1116 ad annum 1786*, 8 vols. (Louvain, 1933–41)

Conrad of Eberbach, *Exordium Magnum Cisterciense*, ed. B. Griesser (Rome, 1961); trans. B. Ward and P. Savage, *The Great Beginning of Cîteaux*, ed. E.R. Elder, CS 72 (Collegeville, MN, 2012)

Griesser, B., 'Die *Ecclesiastica Officia Cisterciensis Ordinis* des Cod. 1711 von Trient', *ASOC*, 12 (1956), 153–288

The Rule of Saint Benedict, trans. J. McCann (London, 1976; first pub. 1921)

Waddell, C. (ed.), *Cistercian Lay Brothers: Twelfth-Century Usages with Related Texts*, Cîteaux: Studia et Documenta 10 (Brecht, 2000)

   Narrative and Legislative Texts from Early Cîteaux, Cîteaux: Studia et Documenta 9 (Brecht, 1999)

   Twelfth-Century Statutes from the Cistercian General Chapter, Cîteaux: Studia et Documenta 12 (Brecht, 2002)

6 Constitutions and the General Chapter

BRIAN PATRICK MCGUIRE

The Cistercians created in the course of the twelfth century the first monastic Order in the Western Church. By 'monastic Order' I mean an institution with regularised contacts among the monasteries, following common statutes and identifying itself in a separate tradition from other monastic traditions. Since the time of Emperor Louis the Pious (d. 840) virtually all monasteries had followed the Rule of Benedict, but its provisions deal solely with the individual monastery and provide no constitutional structure for regular contacts among monastic houses.

After the foundation of Cluny in 910, however, there did appear groups of monasteries bound to each other by tradition or by singular personalities, but until the Cistercians one can speak only of monastic congregations, not of Orders. If we use the term *ordo monasticus*, before the twelfth century, it means the entire monastic body pure and simple; those monasteries that had chosen to follow Benedict's Rule.

The Cistercians changed everything, and so their constitutions and especially the institution of the General Chapter deserve close attention. For the monks who in 1098 left behind Molesme in Burgundy and established what they called the 'New Monastery' (*Novum monasterium*), which later took the name Cîteaux, there was no intention of starting a new monastic Order. Under Robert, who had been abbot at Molesme, the New Monastery's monks intended to follow the Rule of St Benedict more faithfully and perfectly. Their departure from Molesme, however, led to a complaint by the monks who stayed behind. They appealed to the pope, an unusual step for any Church institution at the time. He recalled Robert to Molesme. The abbot returned, together with some of the monks who had accompanied him, but a number remained in the new foundation, headed by the former prior, Alberic.

On Alberic's death in 1109 his prior, Stephen Harding, became abbot. During the years until his resignation from the abbacy in 1133, Stephen formulated the essentials of what became the Cistercian Order: a constitution known as the Charter of Charity, the annual General

Chapter and yearly visitations by father abbots of daughter houses. If the Cistercians have any founder, it is Stephen, though today Trappist-Cistercians celebrate the feast of their founders by including Robert, Alberic and Stephen.

THE FIRST GENERAL CHAPTER

On 23 December 1119 Pope Calixtus II confirmed the decisions of Stephen Harding 'and his brethren'. The pope accepted 'certain articles concerning the observance of the Rule of the blessed Benedict, and concerning some other things which seemed necessary to your Order and place'.[1] By using the term *ordini vestro*, however, Calixtus promulgated the idea of a separate and discrete monastic Order for those monasteries affiliated with Cîteaux (*Cisterciensis monasterii*), no longer called the 'New Monastery'. The bull can be considered the founding document of the Order, whose monks from this point onwards are called Cistercians.[2]

Probably this same year one of the first General Chapters was held at Cîteaux. We have no contemporary record, but William of Saint Thierry, the first biographer of Bernard of Clairvaux's *Vita Prima*, wrote in the 1140s of how Bishop William of Champeaux went 'to the Cistercian chapter' (*ad capitulum cisterciense*) and there, in the presence of 'the few abbots who were present there', asked that Bernard be handed over to him for a year. The idea was that the bishop would have control of Bernard's diet and lifestyle, in order to improve his health after the ascetic regime that had destroyed his digestion. Bernard would have to avoid 'the strictness of the Order' (*ordinis districtionem*), a clear indication of his belonging to a well-organised institution that considered itself a discrete monastic Order.[3]

The 'few abbots' present at this General Chapter would have included the first daughters of Cîteaux, La Ferté and Pontigny, while Clairvaux was absent because of Bernard's ill health. At this time the abbots would have drawn up an early version of the Charter of Charity (*Carta Caritatis*), which became the constitution of the Cistercian Order. It is virtually impossible to get back to the moment of creation at Cîteaux and to find this text in its original form. The fact that all Cistercian documents are from later in the twelfth century has persuaded one historian, Constance Berman, to claim that there was no Cistercian Order until after the death of Bernard of Clairvaux.[4] I think Professor Berman overstates her case and misconstrues contemporary evidence showing an awareness of the Cistercians as a separate monastic

Order.[5] The letters of Bernard of Clairvaux, especially, provide a sense of the language and concept of the Cistercian Order.[6] Constance Berman is correct, however, that the Cistercian filiation based on the foundation of daughter houses by mother abbeys is not the only way the Order grew. The Cistercians took over many extant houses.

Here what emerged was allegiance to a constitution and an Order that distinguished itself from other monastic traditions. The Cistercians knew who they were and what was required of them, as shown in the stories collected at the end of their first century in the *Exordium Magnum Cisterciense*. This source shows how the Cistercians understood the development of their Order: they returned to stories of their origins, reshaping them and reforming them, in order to maintain a regulated and coordinated way of life in belonging to a monastic Order.

THE EARLIEST DOCUMENTS: THE BEGINNINGS OF THE ORDER

Probably early in the abbacy of Stephen's successor at Cîteaux, Raynard de Bar (1134–50), a customary was made, a collection of documents concerning the beginnings of the Cistercian Order. These include the *Exordium Cistercii*, the story of how the Cistercians began; the *Summa Cartae Caritatis*, an abridged version of the Order's constitution, and a number of *Capitula*, the first collection of statutes for the Order, dating from the time of Stephen Harding.

The *Exordium Cistercii* tells how the monastery at what became Cîteaux was established, 'at that time a place of horror and vast solitude'.[7] Here the brothers were citing Deuteronomy (32.10) and perhaps exaggerating the desolation of their new home, but the Cistercians were wonderful storytellers, aware of their past and eager to maintain the traditions that they considered essential for the maintenance of their identity as a body of monks devoted to the Rule of St Benedict.

The *Exordium* especially mentions the Charter of Charity, called such 'because its every article is redolent of only what pertains to charity'.[8] This constitution is said to have been drawn up by Stephen Harding and confirmed by twenty abbots. After the narrative of the *Exordium Cistercii* comes the text of the *Summa Cartae Caritatis*. The very first provision, and one that is often ignored in histories of the Cistercian Order, emphasises that bonds between monasteries were not to have any financial element: 'mother abbeys can impose upon the daughters no material contribution'.[9] This provision can be looked upon as a response to Cluny, whose lord abbot did collect money from daughter priories. In the Cistercian constitution bonds would be based on charity and not on economy. At the same time, however, it is made clear that there were 'mother abbeys' and 'daughters', and that the 'father abbot' would hold visitations of the daughters.

This 'general statute between abbeys', as it is titled, makes it clear that the Cistercians were different from their predecessors. The statute takes for granted a filiation of mother and daughter houses, and it is clear that the father abbot was expected to make sure that all was well in the daughter houses he visited. But he does not have unlimited powers to intervene in the affairs of the daughter house, unless 'he discover in the same place anything contrary to the Rule or the Order'. This visitation takes place 'at least once a year'. Later it was made clear that the father abbot can hand over the task of visitation to another abbot, something that must have been the case for an abbot such as Bernard, whose many activities would have prevented him from visiting Clairvaux's myriad daughters.[10]

The next article in the *Summa Cartae Caritatis* concerns the General Chapter: 'once a year all abbots come together to visit with each other, to re-establish good order, to confirm peace, and by grace to safeguard charity'.[11] This description is worth noting, for it indicates that the annual meeting in Cîteaux, which took place in mid September, after the harvest and before the winter made travels difficult, had as its central purpose to encourage the abbots in their lives and to create an atmosphere of cooperation and even charity. Thus the term 'Charter of Charity' is not mere Cistercian propaganda but an expression of the idea that contacts among abbots and monasteries were for the furthering of charity, and not for the sake of power or finance.

The publication of the statutes of the General Chapter in the 1930s and 1940s provided researchers with a relatively easily accessible compilation of decisions made at Cîteaux.[12] This edition has now been partially replaced,[13] but the impression still remains that the General Chapter was a legislative body. This was the case by about 1200, but until that time the annual meeting was more a forum for discussing common problems and for the abbots to give each other good advice. It was also a centre for storytelling, as can be seen in some of the miracle narratives collected by the Cistercian Caesarius of Heisterbach Abbey on the Rhine. Time and again, Caesarius remarked that he was telling a story that had been brought back from the General Chapter.

Already in the *Summa Cartae Caritatis* it is made clear that abbots are allowed to remain absent from the Chapter only in special circumstances. Later decisions indicate that many abbots often did absent themselves and were meant to be disciplined for their negligence. Eventually it was decided that abbots of houses that were very distant, such as Sweden and Scotland, did not have to come every year.[14]

Everywhere in the early sources for the Cistercian Order it is made clear that there was to be a system of what later could be called checks and balances in order to make sure that no abbot, not even the abbot of Cîteaux, could avoid the scrutiny of others. If there was any question of his transgressing the Rule or the constitutions of the Order, then the abbots of the first daughters of Cîteaux – La Ferté, Pontigny and Clairvaux, and later Morimond – were obliged to discipline and even remove him. If the latter happened, then the abbot of La Ferté was to take charge of Cîteaux until a new abbot could be elected.[15]

The *Summa Cartae Caritatis* envisioned the bonds among monasteries in terms of filiations: each abbey which founded a daughter house became thereby the mother house and had a special responsibility for annual visitations and for intervention when disciplinary problems might arise. Otherwise the *Summa* and its *Capitula* were mainly concerned with the asceticism of monastic life and its separation from secular society: 'No monasteries of ours are to be built in cities, walled settlements or rural domains.' Clothing was to be 'simple and ordinary, no fur garments and undergarments of wool or linen'. No one was to eat meat or lard in the monastery, a departure from the Rule of Benedict. Monks were to work with their own hands, preferably in farming, and especially were to have granges, 'supervised and administered by lay brothers'.[16] This brief phrase indicates that the Cistercians lived off the land, thanks to the recruitment of lay brothers, who in the words of one researcher were 'separate but equal'.[17] One of the constitutions, however, insisted that 'we hold them as brothers and, equally with the monks, as sharers in our goods, spiritual as well as temporal'.[18]

Women were to be kept at a distance: 'It is absolutely forbidden for us and our lay brothers to have women living under the same roof as ourselves.' Nor were they allowed inside the gate of the monastery or the grange enclosure.[19] Recent research has indicated that many women's houses imitated the Cistercian way of life and had contacts with abbots from Cistercian monasteries, but until the end of the twelfth century the Order did what it could to keep women at a distance.

The Cistercians as they defined themselves in these early constitutions did their best to keep themselves apart from secular society. They also tried to live simply, not only in terms of food and housing, but also in relation to sacred art: 'All the ornaments, vessels and utensils of the monastery are to be without gold, silver, and precious stone.'[20] They were not to have sculptures but could have paintings on crosses, which were to be made of wood.

MID-TWELFTH-CENTURY NORMATIVE SOURCES

A new recension of the early sources came in about 1147. This included the *Exordium Parvum*, a more complete narrative of the beginnings of Cîteaux than the *Exordium Cistercii*, the *Carta Caritatis prior*, a fuller edition of the Cistercian constitution, and the *Instituta Generalis Capituli apud Cistercium*. These Institutes provide the decisions of the General Chapter and in the edition of Chrysogonus Waddell they continue until about 1179.[21]

The *Exordium Parvum* repeats a great deal already found in the *Exordium Cistercii*, but it opens with a preamble that reveals a fuller sense of identity than is apparent in the older document, which had bent over backwards to be kind to Molesme and its tradition. Instead we have now the term *cistercienses*, Cistercians, as a self-aware type of monks who intended to show that their origins were legitimate and laudable: 'We Cistercians, the first founders of this church, by the present document are notifying our successors how canonically, with what great authority, and also by whom and by what stages their monastery and tenor of life took their beginning.'[22]

The *Exordium Parvum* reviews the 'whole affair' (*toto negotio*), dealing with the return of monks with Robert to Molesme and the survival of Cîteaux under Alberic. Much of the narrative consists of documents from popes and bishops legitimising what the first monks did. Eventually, however, there is a statement about the way of life of these men: 'Having spurned this world's riches, behold! The new soldiers of Christ, poor with the poor Christ, began discussing by what device ... they would be able to support themselves in this life.'[23] Here is mentioned the reception of lay brothers as a means of maintaining a contemplative way of life and earning an income. But the first monks are said to have been sad 'that only rarely did anyone come there in those days to imitate them'.

The turning point seems to have been the abbacy of Stephen Harding, who is revered for his 'love of the Rule and of the place'.[24] This description would become an apt point of departure for Cistercian identity, attached not only to the Rule of St Benedict but also to the places chosen by the monks as their home. Thus Cistercian names of monasteries, emphasising fruitful valleys and the presence of light, were deliberately chosen to celebrate what was meant to be a beloved heritage.

The *Carta Caritatis prior* has a new preface that points to how Stephen Harding did his best to avoid controversies between bishop and monks. Thus before an abbey was to be founded in a diocese, its bishop would be asked for his approval. The same opening paragraph emphasises the Order's initial decision: 'averting the burdensome levying of all exactions, its statute pursues only charity'.[25]

The *Instituta Generalis Capituli* provide a detailed overview of the norms of Cistercian life as they had developed by mid-century or in the succeeding decades. Their provisions repeat decisions found in the earlier sources, but often with further detail. The second institute, for example, states that uniformity of way of life is to be a landmark of the Cistercians: 'So that an indissoluble unity between abbeys may perpetually endure, it has been established ... that the Rule of the blessed Benedict be understood by all in one way alone.'[26] Food, clothing and observances were to be 'everywhere the same'. Nothing could better express the Cistercian desire to establish a monastic Order in which faithfulness to a common way of life was a primary goal. Benedict's Rule was a foundation, but it needed to be interpreted so that all monasteries kept the same observances.

Cistercian uniformity applied to small details of everyday life, as in the fifteenth institute, 'of cowls and shoes': 'The day shoes are not to be of goat-skin or Cordoba leather, but of cow-hide.'[27] The eighteenth institute repeats an ordinance that had apparently existed from the beginning of the century. Molesme had been dedicated to Mary, and so was Cîteaux: all monasteries were to 'be founded and dedicated in memory of the same Queen of heaven and earth, Saint Mary'. The Cistercians would do their utmost to spread the cult of the Virgin, as we find in many stories in which monks and nuns gain her assistance, as well as in the tale of the Madonna who protects the Cistercians whom she keeps neatly beneath her cape.

The thirtieth institute describes how new abbeys were to be founded. It is required that an abbot first should look around for a suitable location for a new monastery. When he thinks he has found a place, he should show it to two of his neighbouring abbots, 'and let him do whatever they advise him'.[28] Thus the foundation of a daughter house does not rest solely on the shoulders of the father abbot: he is to take counsel. The intention is to avoid sending monks abroad who cannot cope, with the result that 'they be forced, driven by necessity, to beg shamefully'.

The *Instituta* provided detailed information on how visitations should be made (section 33). The abbot of the house being visited should show due respect and even obedience to the visiting abbot. The abbot is to encourage his monks to speak out about what needed to be corrected, and he is to avoid 'retaliation, reproaches, or expressions of indignation against any of the brethren'. The abbot of the house being visited is to show patience and understanding with critical monks, also after the visitor has departed: there are to be no recriminations!

The Institutes of the mid-century also required that mother houses be visited at least once a year by the abbots of daughter houses (section 34). This was a reversal of hierarchy that made it possible for daughter abbots to return to the houses from which many of them once had come in order to make sure that their father abbots were not behaving in an arbitrary manner. In the thirteenth century the Dominicans and Franciscans would find inspiration in the Cistercian General Chapter and visitations.

The remainder of the Institutes, which show some variations in the surviving manuscripts, reveal a continuing desire for uniformity, even in what might seem like small matters, such as whether one is allowed to travel with a mattress (section 43); abbots at the General Chapter are always to stand when they speak (section 47); younger brethren are to take their mixt (breakfast) at a given time (section 52); monks or lay brothers are not to sell wine at taverns (section 54). There is special concern about attendance at the General Chapter (section 55), the bringing of guests there (section 57) and the withdrawal of Cîteaux's own monks from this meeting at a given time, when the abbots were left to be alone with one other (section 50).

These provisions might seem chaotic and badly organised, and there is no doubt that they reflect the fact that each new General Chapter added new decisions according to the needs of the moment and not in harmony with any grand plan. But the early Cistercian documents in general reveal a sense of the identity of a monastic Order that sought clarity of observance and regularity of life. The phrase *'nos cistercienses'* (we Cistercians) emphasises the confidence the monks felt about their common origin and development in a constitution based not on hierarchy but on shared stories and a regular way of life that applied to every monastery belonging to the many filiations which ultimately traced their origin to Cîteaux.[29]

DARLINGS OF THE CHURCH

At the Fourth Lateran Council in 1215 it was decreed that all monasteries would be obliged once every three years to attend a General

Chapter. The first time this was done, the Cistercians were to be called
in for expert advice 'to furnish appropriate counsel and assistance, as
they have long been accustomed to holding such chapters and are very
knowledgeable'.[30] The decision could hardly have been more flattering
to the Cistercian way: the Chapter was to be held for 'several consecu-
tive days, as is Cistercian practice' in considering 'the reform of the
Order and the observance of the Rule'.

In this way was founded the Benedictine Order, almost as an afterthought to the Cistercian Order. Until this time there had been only
limited constitutional bonds among monasteries that followed the Rule
of St Benedict but did not identify themselves as Cistercian. Now these
houses had to be in regular contact with each other, to discuss common
problems and reach solutions that would provide a common ordinance
for all the monasteries. We can see attempts to implement this reform,
for example in the archdiocese of Lund in what today is Sweden. Here
Archbishop Anders Sunesen, who had attended the Council, loyally followed its statutes.[31]

In this manner the Cistercians can be seen as a great success story
in the twelfth- and thirteenth-century Church. Thanks to the administrative genius of Stephen Harding and the propaganda of Bernard of
Clairvaux, the Order spread to all corners of Europe, from Norway
to Sicily and Portugal. The General Chapter remained the centre
and focus of efforts to maintain order and discipline, as can be seen
from a statute drawn up in 1181. It warns against abbots coming to
or returning from the General Chapter and stopping at the nearby
city of Dijon. On these occasions 'they are not to hold hands with
each other or in any noticeable manner walk down the street'.[32] The
Cistercians distinguished themselves in the twelfth century with a
new language of affectivity, especially in terms of friendship, but the
General Chapter did not want to scandalise the population of Dijon
with monastic demonstrations of tenderness! In another decision
from the same year, it was said to be 'indecent' that in some abbeys
when abbots returned from travels, 'even after not long absences',
they seek the 'kiss of peace' from their monks. The General Chapter
seems again to have been concerned about demonstrative manifestations of affection.[33]

Even if the Cistercians were the darlings of the Church at the turn
of the century, there seems to have been a growing concern that the
monasteries were not maintaining the standards found in their constitutions and narrative literature. In 1202 and again in 1220, 1237

and 1257 the decisions of the General Chapter were grouped together according to subject and thus made more accessible and rational.[34] The fact that it was found necessary to provide a handy guide to decisions indicates a sense of unease about how the Order was developing, an awareness also manifested in the decision in the 1230s to found a house of studies at Paris, the College of St Bernard, where the intellectually brightest monks were to be sent to follow a course of studies. This 'scholasticisation' of the Cistercian Order was a far cry from its original direction 'far from the madding crowd' and emphasising the monastery's distance from society. The ideal of the contemplative monk was being replaced by the schooled monk, and in this manner the Cistercians were coming to resemble other Orders, including the Franciscans and Dominicans.

Years ago Jean Leclercq, probably the leading monastic scholar of the twentieth century, reviewed the edition of the Cistercian codifications of 1237 and 1257 and virtually threw up his hands in disgust.[35] He found that the Order had become bogged down in minutiae, which must have distracted from the monks' praising God in choir and doing manual labour. These decisions, nevertheless, show a sense of mission and purpose. The first distinction covers the building of monasteries and their decoration or lack of it; the second deals with dedications of churches, ordinations of priests and blessings given. The third alone is devoted to the divine office, the fourth to immunities, privileges and indulgences. The fifth covers the General Chapter; the sixth the daily chapter held in the individual monastery and the correction of faults there. The seventh distinction has to do with visitations, elections and degradations from office; the eighth with the various officials of the monastery. The ninth distinction concerns brothers who are travelling and how they are to act; the tenth covers those who are to be allowed into the monastery, especially women. Five more distinctions follow, the last two covering the lay brothers and nuns, almost as an afterthought. These decisions can almost all be traced back to individual General Chapters, but now they were organised according to subject, and so an abbot in doubt about how to punish a miscreant monk could easily check the latest codification. For the historian interested in everyday life, these sources are rich in material. The penalties at times seem relatively mild, at least in view of the harshness of the age. A monk 'taken in manifest abuse of the flesh is to be sent to another house' and cannot return to his own monastery for ten years, unless the General Chapter gives permission. The opportunity for remaining in the Order in spite of a blatant sexual act seems generous. But this literature needs further study and awaits a new generation of scholars.

PERENNIAL CISTERCIAN REFORMATIONS

At conferences discussing Cistercian and monastic history one of the common questions is: when did the Order begin to go into decline? Some scholars date the slide downwards from the decision to send brothers to Paris, while others think that the best days were over once Bernard died in 1153. Today for the first time since before the French Revolution it is possible to visit the great Gothic room of the College of St Bernard in Paris and to see how much the Order must have invested in its reformation through learning. In the fourteenth century a Cistercian abbot, Jacques Fournier, became pope and took the name of Benedict XII. He did his best to reform his own Order as well as others. His success was limited, but his bull for the Cistercians, *Fulgens sicut stella matutina* (Shining like the Morning Star), expresses his idealism and hope.

Every institution in history is bound to die, but the Cistercians through their history have shown a remarkable ability to refashion themselves and to offer their contemplative monasticism to new generations. One possible explanation for Cistercian vitality lies in the constitutions of its first century, which provided a foundation based on love of place and love of the Order. In spite of all the controversies that shook the Order from the thirteenth century onwards, it managed time and again to reform and renew itself. The successors of the monks at the New Monastery inspired their successors to maintain regular institutional contacts with one another and to return time and again to a shared past.

Notes

1   Waddell, *Narrative*, p. 451.
2   *Ibid.*, p. 452.
3   B.P. McGuire, 'Charity and Unanimity: The Invention of the Cistercian Order. A Review Article', *Cîteaux*, 51 (2000), 285–97 (p. 293). For the original reference see *PL* 185:246.
4   C.H. Berman, *The Cistercian Evolution: The Invention of a Religious Order in Twelfth-Century Europe* (Philadelphia, PA, 1999).
5   McGuire, 'Charity and Unanimity'. See also C. Waddell, 'The Myth of Cistercian Origins: C.H. Berman and the Manuscript Sources', *Cîteaux*, 51 (1999), 299–360.

6 B.P. McGuire, 'Bernard's Concept of a Cistercian Order: Vocabulary and Context', *Cîteaux*, 54 (2003), 225–49.
7 Waddell, *Narrative*, p. 400.
8 *Ibid.*, p. 402.
9 *Ibid.*, p. 404.
10 C. Holdsworth, 'Bernard as Father Abbot', in *A Companion to Bernard of Clairvaux*, ed. B.P. McGuire (Leiden, 2011), pp. 169–219, esp. p. 203.
11 Waddell, *Narrative*, p. 405.
12 Canivez, *Statuta*.
13 Waddell, *Statutes*.
14 See Emilia Jamroziak's chapter in this volume.
15 Waddell, *Narrative*, p. 406: 'Of the faults of abbots'.
16 *Ibid.*, pp. 408–10 for the statutes given here.
17 J. France, *Separate but Equal: Cistercian Lay Brothers 1120–1350* (Collegeville, MN and Kalamazoo, MI, 2012).
18 Waddell, *Narrative*, p. 411.
19 *Ibid.*
20 *Ibid.*, p. 413.
21 *Ibid.*, pp. 415–16.
22 *Ibid.*, p. 417.
23 *Ibid.*, p. 434.
24 *Ibid.*, p. 438.
25 *Ibid.*, p. 442.
26 *Ibid.*, p. 458.
27 *Ibid.*, p. 462.
28 *Ibid.*, p. 468.
29 See 'From Twelfth-Century Cistercians to Twentieth-Century Americans: Myths of "The Valley of Fruitfulness" and "The City on the Hill"', in B.P. McGuire, *The Difficult Saint: Bernard of Clairvaux and His Tradition*, CS 126 (Kalamazoo, MI, 1991), pp. 279–302.
30 Statute 12; trans. P. Geary, *Readings in Medieval History* (Peterborough, Ontario, 1989), pp. 466–7.
31 B.P. McGuire, 'Anders Sunesen og klostervæsenet: Kontinuitet eller brud?', in *Anders Sunesen: Stormand, teolog, administrator, digter*, ed. S. Ebbesen (Copenhagen, 1985), pp. 27–41.
32 Waddell, *Statutes*, p. 94.
33 *Ibid.*, p. 95.
34 B. Lucet (ed.), *La codification cistercienne de 1202 et son évolution ultérieure* (Rome, 1964) and Lucet (ed.), *Les codifications cisterciennes de 1237 et de 1257* (Paris, 1977).
35 J. Leclercq, 'Aspects de la vie cistercienne au XIIIe siècle: à propos d'un livre récent', *Studia Monastica*, 20 (1978), 223–6.

Primary sources

Canivez, J.-M. (ed.), *Statuta capitulorum generalium ordinis cisterciensis ab anno 1116 ad annum 1786*, 8 vols. (Louvain, 1933–41)

Lucet, B. (ed.), *La codification cistercienne de 1202 et son évolution ultérieure* (Rome, 1964)
   Les codifications cisterciennes de 1237 et de 1257 (Paris, 1977)
Waddell, C. (ed.), *Narrative and Legislative Texts from Early Cîteaux*, Cîteaux: Studia et Documenta 9 (Brecht, 1999)
   Twelfth-Century Statutes from the Cistercian General Chapter, Cîteaux: Studia et Documenta 12 (Brecht, 2002)

7 Nuns

ELIZABETH FREEMAN

What do we mean when we refer to a medieval Cistercian nun? How many houses of Cistercian nuns were there in the Middle Ages? The answers to these questions are not clear-cut. Ever since the nineteenth century, when Leopold Janauschek produced his influential listing of Cistercian abbeys, the study of medieval Cistercian nuns has been a study of inconsistencies, confusions and omissions.[1] Janauschek intended to produce a survey of Cistercian women's houses but, in fact, never published this work. His influential *Originum Cisterciensium* therefore includes male abbeys only, and thereby paved the way for a modern scholarly tradition which tended to treat medieval Cistercian nuns as peripheral players in the wider Cistercian story. One of the great editorial projects of twentieth-century Cistercian scholarship, Canivez's publication of the General Chapter's statutes, had the unintended consequence of confusing the study of Cistercian nuns even further.[2] Many Cistercian nunneries are absent from the statutes, despite having existed for centuries. With modern scholars paying such close attention to the statutes, and with the statutes referring rarely or never to a certain female house, for many years it was easy to believe that the Cistercian Order's approach to the religious lives of women was one of neglect (at best) or suspicion and rejection (at worst). The first statute reference to nuns being 'incorporated' (formally accepted into the Order) was in 1213. Despite the fact that the 1213 statute refers to nuns 'already' incorporated, the inference has often been drawn that the Order refused to admit women as members until the early thirteenth century. Likewise, the statutes for 1228 state that no monasteries of nuns were to be built in the name or under the jurisdiction of the Order, nor were female houses to be united to the Order. The same statute mentions that nuns were free to emulate Cistercian customs, but that the General Chapter would take no responsibility for their spiritual care or visitation. For many scholars, this statute seemed to sum up perfectly an Order which, in its foundational medieval period, was reluctant to include nuns within its fold.

But such conclusions have since been reassessed. Ground-breaking research of the last three decades has changed our understanding of the first two centuries of Cistercian women's history. New research proposes that, far from being signs of General Chapter resistance towards the *cura monialium* (the care of nuns), the statutes concerning nuns in fact indicate an Order which took the religious aspirations of women seriously, even if the Order was sometimes unsure how best to meet these aspirations. According to this interpretation, statutes which seemed to place restrictions on nuns were, rather, designed to ensure that nunneries had sufficient finances to prosper and that there were systems in place for nuns to receive adequate pastoral care and access to the sacraments.[3] Also, the statutes reveal only part of the picture, and there is much that we can learn from other sources.[4] Following this newer approach, the picture we gain of Cistercian nuns' histories in the Middle Ages is an exciting one of variety, flexibility and fluidity.

The eleventh and twelfth centuries witnessed much experimentation in corporate religious life in Latin Christendom. Monasteries were often founded spontaneously; some survived and thrived, while others did not. It is unsurprising that the early years of many Cistercian nuns' communities are unclear and confusing. (We often forget that the early decades of Cistercian male houses can also be shadowy.) The first fifty or more years of the Cistercian Order were years of experimentation – legislative texts were written and rewritten, the liturgy was revised and efforts were expended in the basic administrative and physical labour of acquiring land for monasteries and then building these monasteries. It is little wonder that communities of women who were impressed by the Cistercian experiment should have engaged in differing forms of Cistercian life; there were, after all, no clear guidelines in the early decades of the twelfth century, and certainly no guarantee that those texts which had been produced were disseminated to all the groups throughout Europe that were forming new monastic communities. Nonetheless, it is clear that, at a local level, medieval Europe was beginning to acknowledge that there were nuns in its midst who followed the Cistercian *ordo* (way of life). In 1139, in England, the bishop of Lincoln reported that some local nuns followed the life of the Cistercian monks as far as the condition of their sex allowed.[5] In the mid twelfth century the Cistercian Idung of Prüfening praised women who he said emulated 'our order',[6] and Idung's contemporary, Herman of Tournai, wrote that the women of Montreuil monastery were living according to the *ordo* of Cîteaux, specifically via their focus on manual labour and silence.[7]

Cistercian nunneries founded in the twelfth century often benefited from the experimental nature of monastic life at this time, and were granted freedoms that later houses did not experience once the Cistercian Order, and the papacy, began paying closer attention to the administration of women's religious houses in the thirteenth century. The French abbey of Tart is a key example. Founded in around 1120, Tart is traditionally seen as the first Cistercian nunnery. Tart had a rare level of autonomy, and by around 1200 it had eighteen nunneries 'belonging to it'.[8] The abbey of Las Huelgas, a twelfth-century royal foundation in Castile, also enjoyed unusual independence. By the 1180s, both Tart and Las Huelgas abbeys were permitted their own annual general chapters (something otherwise not allowed for Cistercian nunneries), which were attended by abbesses from nunneries affiliated to each respective house.[9] In twelfth-century England some houses of nuns received documentation from the papacy stating that their communities followed Cistercian practices. Little by little, in different parts of Europe, communities of twelfth-century women were following the new Cistercian *ordo* and were sometimes gaining written evidence to confirm this.

By the early thirteenth century the pace of new Cistercian foundations for women quickened, although if one reads the *Exordium Magnum Cisterciense*, composed at this time, one could be forgiven for thinking that the Cistercian Order was an Order of men only. On the other hand, in the early 1220s Bishop Jacques de Vitry certainly knew about the popularity of the Cistercian Order for women: he wrote that the observance of the nuns of the Cistercian Order had multiplied like the stars of heaven, and that nuns were transferring from other monasteries in order to lead the better life of the Cistercians.[10] By this stage, the Cistercian Order had gained administrative efficiency, and it is no coincidence that this is when Cistercian nuns and nunneries begin appearing in the General Chapter's statutes. The statutes concerning Cistercian nunneries in the 1210s–1250s indicate both that the number of Cistercian nunneries seeking a relationship with the Order was growing and, also, that the Cistercian Order was unsure how to deal with this influx. These statutes are notable for their inconsistency; circumstances were clearly changing quickly. The 1228 prohibition against incorporations of nunneries was soon a dead letter, and incorporations continued. The thirteenth-century codifications of Cistercian legislation also show a growing attention to nuns.[11] While nuns did not warrant any reference in the 1202 or 1220 collections, they do appear (as the last item!) in the issues of 1237 and 1257.

Between 1200 and 1240 more than forty Cistercian nunneries were founded or incorporated in the Southern Low Countries (roughly equivalent to modern Belgium). Many of the new thirteenth-century foundations were initiated by royal and noble women. But even though the statutes mention the incorporation of many houses, other female houses being accepted as Cistercian did so thanks to other mechanisms of support. Evidence for this is most readily found in local administrative sources such as charters, in papal and episcopal documents, in records from local Cistercian monks' houses and, of course, in surviving documentation from the nunneries themselves. This means that we can rarely point to one single piece of evidence which can demonstrate that a medieval nunnery was a Cistercian nunnery. We are better served if we accept the lack of homogeneity in Cistercian nunnery affairs, and examine various pieces of evidence and criteria in order to establish that a nunnery was a member of the Cistercian Order. Scandinavia, Switzerland and England all provide examples of the usefulness of this approach.

The bulk of a nun's life did not involve interactions with the General Chapter or with officialdom. The life of a nun was centred around the liturgy. Eight times a day, every day, a nun would join with her fellow sisters in Christ to chant the prayers of praise which were the Divine Office. Other liturgical activities included the mass, of course, as well as processions and the Office of the Dead. It is surely significant that the earliest medieval image we have of Cistercian nuns appears in an antiphonary, a key communal book needed for the recitation of the Divine Office. The illustration in this late twelfth-century manuscript (probably from a Flemish Cistercian nunnery) depicts a group of nuns in the presence of Bernard of Clairvaux, all of whom are linked both pictorially and in their shared commitment to the Office.[12]

Learning about nuns' spiritual lives is not easy, but it can be done. Strangely, very few customaries (compilations of key Cistercian sources, including the *Ecclesiastica Officia* [*Liturgical Duties*]) survive from medieval Cistercian nunneries – this may mean that nunneries were permitted some independence when it came to following Cistercian practices. But in the mid thirteenth century a man called 'poor Martin' translated a customary into French for an unknown community of Cistercian nuns.[13] Another manuscript with interesting liturgical material survives from the French nunnery at Saint-Just.[14] Famous today as the only surviving copy of the primitive Cistercian breviary (i.e. it was written before the Cistercian liturgical reform of 1147), this manuscript was given by the Cistercian monks of La Bussière to Saint-Just at the nunnery's foundation in the 1340s. In other words, when La Bussière's monks donated the manuscript, they donated a liturgical book which had been superseded 200 years earlier! Perhaps the monks did not believe that differences in liturgical practice mattered for nuns, and perhaps the nuns themselves did not mind? Certainly, the monks' donation of a breviary to a new nunnery shows that La Bussière made some effort to provide for nuns' spiritual needs.

Another way to learn about nuns' liturgies and broad spiritual practices is by examining biographical and autobiographical writings, a number of which were produced in the Southern Low Countries in the thirteenth century. The writings by and about the Cistercians Gertrud of Helfta (Saxony), Mechtild of Hackeborn (also a nun at Helfta) and Beatrice of Nazareth Abbey (Belgium) are today well known.[15] These writings not only provide insights into the individual women's relationships with God and Christ, but also give a flavour of life in the monasteries more generally. Indeed, Gertrud's *Herald of God's Loving-Kindness* and Mechtild's *Book of Special Grace* were not composed solely by the nuns in question but, rather, by a collaborative effort from a number of the community's nuns. From these works we learn about the daily round of prayer engaged in by the whole community (Mechtild was cantor at Helfta, and the work attributed to her shows an immersion in the liturgy), and we also learn about nuns' devotion to the incarnate Christ. Beatrice of Nazareth tied some parchment to her arm on which the cross was painted. This parchment reminded Beatrice of the crucifixion and the passion, and it can remind modern readers that there were many other Cistercian nuns who shared Beatrice's Christocentric devotional focus. At the Polish nunnery of Chełmno, for example, every time the nuns went into the upper choir of their church they would have seen, and ideally reflected on, the mural of Christ's passion which was painted there.[16]

The literary skills of Cistercian nuns would have varied greatly. The Belgian abbey of La Ramée was a centre of learning – the nun Ida the Gentle of Gorseleeuw (or Lewis/Léau) copied and corrected church books there, and Beatrice of Nazareth was sent there specifically to learn the art of writing. At Nazareth Abbey, two nuns produced an antiphonary, under Beatrice's supervision. German nuns also had a well-developed literary culture. From around 1300 onwards, the nuns at St-Thomas an der Kyll, near Trier, possessed a prayer book, in Latin and German, which included rosary devotions to read and perform.[17] In the fifteenth century a Rhineland nun recorded an Easter procession in her prayer book.[18] Devotional writings, and some of the wonderful illuminated manuscripts written in such nunneries as Medingen, as well as beautiful devotional objects from nunneries such as Wienhausen and Heilig-Kreuz (all three communities in Germany), indicate that Cistercian nuns engaged in much personal spirituality which was performed in private, outside formal Church services. But nuns also interacted with the Church in formal ceremonies, such as at mass and confession, and here the attendance of priests was required. How did Cistercian nuns interact with male clergy?

While the *Carta Caritatis* (Charter of Charity) states that a Cistercian monastery was to be visited annually by the abbot of the founding house, such a plan did not work for nunneries. Nunneries were rarely founded directly from an earlier house. Equally, if they did gain official incorporation, nunneries might be incorporated some years after their foundation and so would already have formed other, local, links of obedience. Local links were also strong for nunneries which were never formally incorporated; most English nunneries fall into this category, and they usually relied on local bishops to conduct visitations. Also, while monks' abbeys existed under a system of filiation, this was not the case for most nunneries. In theory there were female filiations of Clairvaux and Cîteaux, but what this meant in practice is unclear.

Nunneries whose incorporations appear in the statutes (for example, many in the Southern Low Countries) generally had a specified father abbot, but of course many nunneries are not recorded in the statutes and so it is not always clear whether they too had a father abbot. The duties of the father abbot included the provision of pastoral care (or the delegation of such care) and the general oversight of the nunnery. In many instances it was the 'visitor' who provided the actual care – the two roles could overlap, and the visitor may or may not have been the same as the father abbot. Stephen of Lexington, abbot of Savigny, left a record of his visitations in the 1230s, including his visitations of nunneries in north-western France.[19] He was particularly interested in ensuring that nunneries were economically self-sufficient, although the nuns often ignored his instructions since this would have meant abandoning their own commitment to providing charity. The 1243 statutes show that nuns sometimes resisted visitation; one community of nuns threatened and assaulted the visitors and refused to acknowledge their authority, while the abbess of another house would not open the gates to the visitors. Some Cistercian nunneries clearly preferred to keep representatives of the Order at arm's length. Even at the best of

times, the administrative systems for visitations were variable, hark-
ing back to the ad hoc ways in which nunneries had joined the Order
in the first place. The codifications of 1237 and 1257 stated that some
abbesses were conducting visitations – the codifications proceeded to
ban this practice but, at the same time, left scope for abbesses to provide
correction to their nuns after the relevant abbots had completed their
visitations. Interestingly, the French-language customary translated by
'poor Martin' does not include the chapter from the *Instituta Generalis
Capituli* which deals with visitations, perhaps a recognition that, in
practice, the pastoral care provided by visitations was supplied to nuns
in informal and changeable ways.

In other instances Cistercian monks provided general support of
local nunneries, even when this was nowhere legislated. The Belgian
abbeys of Villers and Cambron enthusiastically supported new
female foundations. Villers's abbot was sufficiently impressed by the
thirteenth-century Cistercian Ida of Nivelles (a nun at La Ramée) that
he ordered one of his monks to write her *Vita* (Life).[20] The writing of
treatises was a pivotal way for Cistercian monks to provide pastoral
care to nuns. This would have been particularly welcome since, in 1237,
abbesses and nuns were specifically forbidden from attending General
Chapters and so would have needed other ways to learn about Cistercian
practice. In around 1250 the abbot of Newenham in England wrote a
treatise of spiritual advice for the abbess of the nearby Cistercian house
of Tarrant.[21] Also in the thirteenth century, Thomas of Villers wrote
letters (some of which survive) to his sister, the Cistercian nun Alice of
Parc-aux-Dames, and gave advice on such things as the Divine Office,[22]
while in the late twelfth century Engelhard of Langheim wrote a book of
exempla (edifying moral stories) and dedicated it to the abbess and nuns
of the Franconian Cistercian nunnery of Wechterswinkel.[23] Monks also
provided an invaluable service to nunneries by giving manuscripts to
their libraries. Relationships of pastoral care worked both ways; Thomas
of Villers begged his sister Alice to send him her prayers, and in the thirteenth century the English Cistercian Simon of Waverley wrote a poem
in which he asked the nuns of the nearby Cistercian house of Wintney
to pray for him and to receive him into confraternity with them.[24]

Cistercian nuns were concentrated in modern-day France, Belgium,
the Netherlands and Germany. There were also nunneries in Switzerland,
Austria and Central and Eastern Europe. The Iberian peninsula, Italy,
Britain, Scandinavia and possibly Ireland also had Cistercian nunneries, not to mention the few communities in Constantinople, Cyprus
and the Holy Land mentioned by Jacques de Vitry. Naturally there were

variations in monastic life over this geography. English nunneries were in rural locations. On the other hand, many nunneries in the Southern Low Countries were on town edges, and this brought interactions with the urban communities of lay religious women known as Beguines. Indeed, many Cistercian nuns in the Southern Low Countries started their religious journeys as Beguines before transferring to Cistercian houses. In terms of well-known medieval Cistercian nuns and surviving manuscripts from medieval nunneries, the Southern Low Countries and the German-speaking lands provide the stand-out examples, as does France to a lesser extent. But this provides only one perspective. Administrative documents (charters, cartularies, inventories) survive in solid numbers for nunneries of other countries, and these can teach us about nunneries' interactions with their local regions. If we can predict one area where future scholarship may gain further insights, it will be by combining our knowledge of wider Cistercian trends with evidence drawn from individual local studies.

Discussion of administrative documents leads to economics. A nunnery had to support itself economically. Some nunneries were very wealthy, although this was the exception. Agricultural work was an intrinsic part of the Cistercian Order from its origins, and this applied to nuns as well as monks. When Herman of Tournai described the twelfth-century nuns of Montreuil, he praised them for working in the fields. But work differed in different times and places. Even the people who performed the work varied, with references to *conversi* (lay brothers) and *conversae* (lay sisters) appearing inconsistently in the records concerning nunneries. General Chapter statute evidence from the 1220s indicates that nunneries had their own lay brothers who made their profession kneeling before the abbess, but it is hard to know the details of lay brothers' lives in female houses. Father abbots, visitors, priors (also known as procurators) and the chaplains who are recorded in statutes, charters and other documents played a role in ensuring that the houses were supplied with able workers, in addition to their saying of mass and other liturgical duties. As the Middle Ages wore on, paid workers were increasingly employed.

Regardless of who performed the work, we know that convents engaged in varied economic practices. Wintney and Wienhausen are examples of nunneries which sold their sewing work. In Flanders and Hainaut nuns did more than simply support themselves; they were entrepreneurs involved in land-reclamations, keen to turn marshes into pasture that could provide wool, meat and associated income with minimal manual labour.[25] Nunneries in England were also wool producers and exporters. Overall, the economic practices of Cistercian monks and nuns had many features in common,[26] although it appears that, in some parts of Europe, nunneries tended to receive more urban properties and rents as endowments, whereas monks received more agricultural land. The nuns of Rifreddo in Italy provide a sobering example of economic conflict, as they came into dispute (over property and land boundaries) with the monks' abbey which provided their father abbot. Importantly, work was more than a means of survival. Many Cistercian nunneries in Champagne began as hospices, providing charity and medical care to lepers and others in need. For these women, working with their hands was a means for them to live out their dedication to the apostolic spirit of poverty and charity. These French nuns did not believe that Cistercians should spend all their time enclosed but, rather, believed that they should engage with the world.

While the basic division of the day into communal prayer, private prayer/reading and work remained constant throughout the centuries, other changes were afoot as the Middle Ages progressed, not least the effects of plague and warfare. The 1335 papal bull promoting internal Cistercian reform, *Fulgens sicut stella matutina* (Shining like the Morning Star), had little direct effect on nuns, although nuns were incidentally affected by the bull's focus on financial management. More influential were the changes of the fifteenth century. In 1399 the General Chapter declared that monasteries which could not support twelve monks or nuns should be combined with other communities. In France the fifteenth century saw nunneries closed down, taken over by monks or moved from rural locations into towns. Statute references from the early fifteenth century regularly call for reform of monasteries, 'male as well as female', and, for better or worse, fifteenth-century abbots made renewed efforts to visit Cistercian nunneries. The visitations continued in the sixteenth century. When Clairvaux's abbot visited nuns in Italy and France in 1520, he found that the reception varied. One community, which had an absentee abbess, begged him to spend time in their house, while at Rifreddo the community hid documentation from him.[27] In 1533, on the eve of the Reformation in England, the General Chapter ordered English Cistercian abbots to visit local Cistercian nunneries. We do not know if these visitations ever took place.

Outside the Cistercian Order, wider religious reform movements were in train in the late Middle Ages, with the *Devotio moderna* (Modern Devotion) being one example. In Spain, France and the German-speaking lands, male religious took female communities under their wings (whether willingly or not, from the nuns' perspectives), under various programmes of *reformatio* (reformation). Monarchs were also involved in reform. In around 1500 Las Huelgas was targeted by the Spanish monarchs Isabel and Ferdinand, as part of their broader programme of nationalising institutional religious life. Continuing into the sixteenth century, the religious histories of different parts of Europe began to diverge greatly, and the Reformation saw the closure of many monasteries. In England, in 1535 there were about thirty-five Cistercian nunneries. Within five years, all these communities had been dissolved and their inhabitants forced to return to lay life. In France the Wars of Religion seriously threatened monastic life. At this time Saint-Just was raided by Huguenot forces and its library, with its 400-year-old primitive Cistercian breviary, was pillaged. The Scandinavian nunneries were extinguished in the sixteenth century, as the Reformation spread. In Germany the Reformation saw most nunneries close, although some, such as Egeln near Magdeburg, survived. Overall, the changes experienced in the early modern period thanks to the Reformation, Counter-Reformation and warfare were too many to discuss comprehensively here.[28] Surviving nunneries made changes in order to continue, and so the varied and complex histories of Cistercian nuns continued to evolve.

It is notable that no one has succeeded in counting the number of medieval Cistercian nunneries. Given the ways in which nunneries moved in and out of relationship with the Order, and given that the few surviving medieval lists of nunneries are incomplete, it is not surprising that the task has proved elusive. About 650 to 700 communities seems a reasonable estimate. Cistercian nunneries were at times marginal, appearing and then disappearing from the official records. But we can learn much from studying the varied histories of Cistercian nuns, and in the process we can gain a deeper appreciation of the Cistercian Order in its full nature, both female and male.

Notes

1   L. Janauschek, *Originum Cisterciensium Tomus I* (Vienna, 1877).

2   Canivez, *Statuta*.

3   For example, B. Degler-Spengler, 'The Incorporation of Cistercian Nuns into the Order in the Twelfth and Thirteenth Century', in *Hidden Springs: Cistercian Monastic Women*, ed. J.A. Nichols and L.T. Shank, 2 vols., CS 113 (Kalamazoo, MI, 1995), vol. I, pp. 85–134.

4   For example, C.H. Berman, 'Were There Twelfth-Century Cistercian Nuns?', *Church History*, 68 (1999), 824–64; A.E. Lester, 'Cares beyond the Walls: Cistercian Nuns and the Care of Lepers in Twelfth- and Thirteenth-Century Northern France', in *Religious and Laity in*

Western Europe 1000–1400: Interaction, Negotiation, and Power, ed.
E. Jamroziak and J. Burton (Turnhout, 2006), pp. 197–224.

5   D.M. Smith (ed.), *English Episcopal Acta I* (London, 1980), pp. 24–5.

6   Idung of Prüfening, 'A Dialogue between Two Monks', in J. O'Sullivan
et al. (trans.), *Cistercians and Cluniacs: The Case for Cîteaux*, CF 33
(Kalamazoo, MI, 1977), p. 115.

7   C.H. Berman (trans.), *Women and Monasticism in Medieval Europe:
Sisters and Patrons of the Cistercian Reform* (Kalamazoo, MI, 2002), pp.
117–18.

8   E.R. Elder (ed.), *The New Monastery: Texts and Studies on the Earliest
Cistercians*, CF 60 (Kalamazoo, MI, 1998), p. 214.

9   'Statuts de chapitres généraux tenus à l'abbaye de N. D. de Tart.
(Archives de la Côte-d'Or, H. 78.1042', in P. Guignard (ed.), *Les monu-
ments primitifs de la règle cistercienne, publiés d'après les manucrits
de l' abbaye de Cîteaux* (Dijon, 1878), pp. lxxxviii–xc, 643–9; E. Connor,
'The Royal Abbey of Las Huelgas and the Jurisdiction of Its Abbesses',
Cistercian Studies, 23 (1988), 128–55. The general chapters of Tart
and Las Huelgas were quite separate from the Order's annual General
Chapters at Cîteaux.

10 J.F. Hinnebusch (ed.), *The Historia Occidentalis of Jacques de Vitry*
(Fribourg, 1972), pp. 116–18.

11 B. Lucet (ed.), *La codification cistercienne de 1202 et son évolution
ultérieure* (Rome, 1964); Lucet (ed.), *Les codifications cisterciennes de
1237 et de 1257* (Paris, 1977).

12 J. France, *Medieval Images of Saint Bernard of Clairvaux*, CS 210
(Kalamazoo, MI, 2007), pp. 158, 166.

13 'Ancienne traduction française des *Ecclesiastica officia, Instituta generalis Capituli, Usus conversorum et Regula sancti Benedicti*, publiée
d'après le manuscrit 352¹ de la Bibliothèque Publique de Dijon', in
Documents inédits pour servir à l'histoire de France, pp. lxxiv–lxxxviii,
407–642.

14 C. Waddell (ed.), *The Primitive Cistercian Breviary* (Fribourg, 2007).

15 R. De Ganck and J.B. Hasbrouck (trans.), *The Life of Beatrice of Nazareth,
1220–1268*, CF 50 (Kalamazoo, MI, 1991); G.J. Lewis and J. Lewis (trans.),
Gertrude the Great of Helfta: Spiritual Exercises, CF 49 (Kalamazoo,
MI, 1989); A. Barratt, *The Herald of God's Loving-Kindness, Books 1
and 2*, CF 35 (Kalamazoo, MI, 1991); A. Barratt, *The Herald of God's
Loving-Kindness, Book 3*, CF 63 (Kalamazoo, MI, 1999); A. Harrison,
'"I Am Wholly Your Own": Liturgical Piety and Community among the
Nuns of Helfta', *Church History*, 78 (2009), 549–83. See also E. Rozanne
Elder's chapter in this volume.

16 R. Bartal, '"Where Has Your Beloved Gone?": The Staging of the *Quarere
Deum* on the Murals of the Cistercian Convent of Chełmno', *Word and
Image*, 16 (2000), 270–88.

17 A. Heinz, 'Une forme ancienne du Rosaire au moyen âge chez les
Cisterciennes de Saint-Thomas-sur-Kyll', *Collectanea Cisterciensia*,
66 (2004), 140–52.

18   C. Waddell, 'The *Vidi aquam* and the Easter Morning Procession: Pages from the Prayerbook of a Fifteenth-Century Cistercian Nun', *Liturgy O.C.S.O.*, 21:3 (1987), 3–56.

19   B. Griesser, 'Registrum Epistolarum Stephani de Lexinton abbatis de Stanlegia et de Savigniaco. Pars Altera', *ASOC*, 8 (1952), 181–378.

20   M. Cawley (trans.), *Send Me God: The Lives of Ida the Compassionate of Nivelles, Nun of La Ramée, Arnulf, Lay Brother of Villers, and Abundus, Monk of Villers* (Turnhout, 2003).

21   E. Freeman, 'A Cistercian Monk Writes to a Cistercian Nun: John Godard's Treatise for the Abbess of Tarrant, England, *c.*1250', *CSQ*, 45 (2010), 331–51.

22   E. Mikkers, 'Deux lettres inédites de Thomas, chantre de Villers', *COCR*, 10 (1948), 161–73; partial translation in Cawley (trans.), *Send Me God*, pp. 255–8.

23   B. Griesser, 'Engelhard von Langheim und sein Exempelbuch für die Nonnen von Wechterswinkel', *Cistercienser Chronik*, 70 (1963), 55–73.

24   P. Meyer, 'Bribes de littérature anglo-normande', *Jahrbuch für romanische und englische Literatur*, 7 (1866), 37–57 (pp. 45–7).

25   E. Jordan, 'Patronage, Prayers and Polders: Assessing Cistercian Foundations in Thirteenth-Century Flanders and Hainaut', *Cîteaux*, 53 (2002), 99–125.

26   C.H. Berman, 'New Light on the Economic Practices of Cistercian Women's Communities', *Medieval Feminist Forum*, 41 (2006), 75–87.

27   Harmand, 'Relation d'un voyage à Rome, commencé le XXIII du mois d'août 1520, et terminé le XIV du mois d'avril 1521, par Révérend père en Dieu Monseigneur Dom Edme, XLIe abbé de Clairvaux', *Mémoires de la société d'agriculture, des sciences, arts et belles-lettres du département de l'Aube*, second series, 2 (1849), 143–235 (pp. 169–71, 230).

28   See L.J. Lekai, *The Cistercians: Ideals and Reality* (Kent, OH, 1977), chapter 22; A. Bonis, S. Dechavanne and M. Wabont (eds.), *Cîteaux et les femmes* (Paris, 2001); J.A. Nichols and L.T. Shank (eds.), *Hidden Springs: Cistercian Monastic Women*, 2 vols., CS 113 (Kalamazoo, MI, 1995), vol. ii.

8 Agriculture and economies
CONSTANCE HOFFMAN BERMAN

Like many new religious groups of the central Middle Ages the Cistercians had origins in the late eleventh-century eremitical reformers who questioned the comfortable lives of those earlier monastic communities that had held lordship over villages, rights to tithes, churches and other revenues. Instead, these Cistercian reformers embraced a reputation for foundations 'far from cities, castles and human habitation'.[1] Taking literally such self-descriptions by the Order's monks, earlier economic historians saw them as twelfth-century 'pioneers' whose clearing and draining of new lands led to an enormous acquisition of wealth derived from 'bumper crops' on 'never-before cultivated lands'.[2] More recent studies have shown that although many Cistercian abbeys became wealthy, they were not the pioneers once imagined. Cistercian wealth derived from providing meat, cheese and other animal products along with the usual agricultural products to neighbouring towns where they were sold free of tithes, tolls and market dues. Their pastoralism became famous especially in Britain, where they produced wool for export. Their attempts to revive the early simplicity of the Rule of Benedict included a reduced liturgical practice that allowed time for manual labour in the production of their own food and the gradual introduction of lay brothers and lay sisters as labourers.

While the earliest Cistercian communities may have lived on the produce of their little gardens, Cistercian grange agriculture would be based on large, compacted granges or farms created by reconstituting fragmented holdings of previously cultivated lands into large compact ones. Although Cistercian abbeys and granges might be sited on recently cleared lands (*assarts* or, in southern France, *artigues*), such land coming into Cistercian hands was almost entirely already settled and cultivated. It was extremely rare for Cistercian abbeys to clear and drain land. Although abbey and grange sites might give the appearance of recent wilderness, such land had features of earlier development such as roads, pathways, mills, farm buildings and established place-names.[3]

Acquisitions often had as their core the land given them by early donors and patrons, but large sums were needed to consolidate land rights into granges, using hundreds of contracts. These contracts were sometimes recorded in monastic charter books or cartularies that still survive. Such charters constitute a major source for our knowledge of the early Cistercians and their agricultural practices. Such contracts show both the hard work of reassembling rights and the cash needed to pay off peasant owners who were moving to villages or towns, or lords amassing cash in preparation for crusade and reconquest.

The Order's success derived from several trends. Cistercians reaped the benefits of changes in the rural landscape that saw lords in the eleventh and twelfth centuries gathering peasants from isolated hamlets and farmsteads into nucleated villages near castles and churches.[4] As a consequence, land at the edges of parishes became available for monastic sites. Such lands were often those that peasants were particularly anxious to sell: distant from new villages, they involved time-consuming travel for cultivation; if located in river beds, they were lands at risk of flooding, on the marginal and fragile soils of mountainsides, and after producing initial high yields, they quickly lost fertility and so forth. At this time, as well, Benedictine communities were granting or selling distant holdings and cells in order to consolidate lands closer to home. Cistercians often acquired such cells and communities, which sometimes became daughter houses, but could also be absorbed as granges. Often the initiative came from those living at such cells. We see this for the monks at Morin, a cell belonging to Saint-Bénigne of Dijon; its monks transformed their cell and lands into a grange of Clairvaux and, bringing the documents with them, entered that abbey as '*conversi*' c.1176.[5]

Cistercians also incorporated newly founded communities like Savigny and Obazine. These oft-cited incorporations, however, were part of more widespread absorption of earlier, independent reform communities by Cîteaux, Clairvaux and their daughter houses. Indeed it was primarily by such affiliation, rather than by colonisation from mother houses, that the Cistercian congregation grew. Such affiliation brought independent communities a 'package' of Cistercian practices – from a simplified liturgy to treatises on lay-brother labourers. An increasingly text-based practice evolved to communicate Cistercian practices to affiliated communities. Such communication needs led to the creation of the religious Order as the governing institution with its General Chapter. Such smaller communities in turn contributed to the rapid accumulation of Cistercian wealth and power, for they brought with them established patrons, lands and recruits.[6]

The effects of such transfers of wealth and land to the Cistercians through purchase and incorporation reflect the managerial prowess of early Cistercian administrators. While the expansion of most men's houses occurred primarily in the twelfth century, by the early thirteenth century it was the turn of the nuns, whose houses expanded enormously between 1200 and 1250. Abundant records show thirteenth-century abbesses creating systems of granges, pasturelands and other properties to support their abbeys over the next centuries.[7] Such evidence for Cistercian nuns belies earlier assumptions that their communities were invariably poor, powerless, under-endowed, unable to administer land because of enclosure and were consequently short-lived.[8] Nuns, like the monks of the Order, caused considerable change in the late medieval rural landscape as they vied for endowment with earlier ecclesiastical and secular owners. Still acquisitions by nuns were often made slowly and patiently, as we see even for the foundation of the house of Cistercian nuns at Maubuisson begun in 1236 by Louis IX's mother, Blanche of Castile.[9]

It was unusual, but sometimes entire villages or granges were acquired in single thirteenth-century purchases, as we see for the nuns at Rifreddo at their foundation.[10] Similar acquisitions by purchase using cash brought by a bourgeois entrant were made by the nuns of Saint-Antoine at the village of Champagnes near Beaumont-sur-Oise.[11] In the 1230s Louis IX did the same for the new abbey of monks at Royaumont founded for his father's soul. Among other such acquisitions, including an existing grange purchased for the abbey site, was the king's purchase in June 1231 of the grange of Belleéglise for 1,050 livres parisis paid to the knight Thibaut of Beaumont, lord of Luzarches, and his wife Ermengard. The conveyance included seven livres annual rent in the village there, three muids (wagonloads) of oats annually, all the vendors' vineyards, two winepresses and whatever other rights the vendors had within its boundaries or over its vineyards and tenants. Belleéglise included 50 arpents (each arpent about 85 per cent of an acre), the farmstead, barns and appurtenances, rights in the common fields, marshes, watercourses and a water-mill, and rights to feed animals in the common pasturelands along with the villagers' animals. The tenants of Belleéglise and other nearby villages who were accustomed to grinding their grain at the village mill could continue to do so.[12] These new granges, created by a single purchase, would have resembled very closely those that had been consolidated over many decades by earlier communities.

Cistercian agriculture benefited from being tithe-exempt. Indeed early claims to exemption from tithes were part of the larger programme of monastic reform, which included a refusal to live on income from tithes, altars and traditional estates worked by tenant labourers, but for Cistercians this also included a refusal to pay tithes on their own manual labour in the fields or on their animal husbandry.

Although Innocent II had granted tithe exemption for all the houses associated with Bernard of Clairvaux's congregation in 1132, it was only by the 1180s that such tithe exemptions were extended to the entire Order.[13] Earlier tithe privileges had been granted on a case by case basis to individual monastic communities by bishops and popes. Such privileges appear premised on the assumption that such grants to new semi-eremitical groups posed no conflict with existing owners of tithes.[14] This, in fact, was rarely the case, however. Indeed to exercise their tithe exemption Cistercians had to purchase tithes from earlier owners. Compromises over such tithe exemption might lead to innovative solutions such as that in which the monks of Silvanès granted the Hospitallers a tenth of the lands held by the abbey in the parish of Prugnes in return for tithe exemption on the other nine-tenths of their holdings there.[15] Yet the record of tithe purchases of this kind has caused consternation among historians of the Order who assumed that such tithes were those abjured by the Order's founders.[16] Most often they were not.

The importance of such tithe exemption for Cistercian agricultural success is obvious. It eliminated payment of 10 per cent of gross yields for field crops along with payment of every tenth lamb or calf. This certainly allowed rural economies to grow more quickly. Not surprisingly, although Cistercians almost always exercised their tithe exemption by repurchase, exemption became the focus of complaints about the Order's wealth. In 1215 the Fourth Lateran Council limited Cistercian tithe exemption to properties held before that Council and to its gardening, animal husbandry and 'noval' cultivation.[17] The issue was most difficult for thirteenth-century foundations of nuns (most monks had acquired properties before the Council and were 'grandfathered-in'). Moreover, some patrons of nuns at the time, like Bishop Manasses II of Orléans, founder of the abbey for Cistercian women at Voisins, appear to have preached the return of tithes to the Church by soliciting gifts to 'his dear daughters, the nuns of Voisins'. While such tithe acquisitions were quite early, eventually Voisins's granges were in the same parishes.[18] This is true too for the Cistercian nuns of Port-Royal, who argued at the beginning of the thirteenth century that they were tithe-exempt because they were Cistercians, but in this case at issue were *novales* that they had brought under cultivation (*ad culturam redidi faciunt*).[19]

In the earliest years cash for land purchases came not from agricultural surpluses or savings from ascetic lifestyles, but from the revenues of pastoralism, and possibly mills, iron and forges and saltworks.
Indeed Cistercian communities in their earliest guise often supported
themselves from pastoralism rather than agriculture. Such pastoral
economies were well suited to the economic needs of new reform communities intent on living 'by the labour of their own hands', but having
limited available labour. The earliest surviving Cistercian lay-brother
treatise (found in a manuscript from Clairvaux) makes no mention
of agriculture at all.[20] The earliest lay-brother and lay-sister labourers
among the Cistercians were probably those who acted as animal herders
or dairy-maids on pastoral properties. We see Nonenque's lay brothers
and lay sisters described thus in a dispute settlement over pasture on
the Causse de Larzac in southern France.[21] In the late 1150s monks from
Valmagne recruited such pastoralists at the same time that the community was acquiring land at Canvern. Recruits from that village included
two brothers settled there with three pair of oxen, three cows and two
calves, sixty sheep, money to buy eleven pigs, some fleeces, two cheeses
and three sets of clothing; in another case a recruit was set up in a shepherd's hut to make cheese.[22]

Shared pasture rights led to ties among reform communities, such
as those that linked houses in southern France associated with the
abbeys of Mazan and Bonnevaux even before their family of abbeys was
absorbed by the Cistercians. In a maximisation of seasonally available
pasture called transhumance these abbeys moved sheep and cattle from
the vicinity of abbeys near summer pastures in the high Massif Central
down to the verdant winter pastures of the Rhone valley where other
abbeys were located.[23] Such movement of Cistercian animals between
winter and summer pasture is documented by contracts reporting reso-
lution of disputes over access to intermediate areas through which animals could graze, drink water and rest for several days in coming and
going from the summer pastures in the Alps, Pyrenees and elsewhere.[24]

In early charters of land acquisition, access to pasture was granted
as an afterthought, but there came to be extensive grants by territorial rulers as well. Thus pasture rights were given along with vineyards, mills, a bathhouse and saltworks to the newly founded abbey
of Cistercian nuns at Las Huelgas in Burgos by Alfonso and Eleanor of
Castile in 1187:

> The animals belonging to that community and its abbey site or
> its granges will have free pasture rights in all the woods and other
> places in which the King's animals have pasture. The nuns will

pay no tax for their animals going up or coming down from the mountain pastures. Furthermore the nuns' shepherds' huts will all have the same protection as do those of the King.[25]

Closely related were woodland rights, as we see in the same document:

> The nuns may cut wood, beams and other building materials for the needs of construction of the monastery, its conventual buildings and its granges in all the woods and places where those materials are cut for purposes of the King's construction.[26]

There were similar forest concessions near Sens made to the nuns of Le Lys by Louis IX.[27] Monks at nearby Vauluissant and Pontigny east of Sens, too, seem to have benefited from access to the great forest of Othe on the boundary between Champagne and France, where clearance and reclamation came late because the forest marked that boundary.[28] In the mountainous, forested region of the Italian Piedmont, Rifreddo's nuns similarly appear to have acquired holdings paying rent in different varieties of chestnuts.[29]

The actual practice of agriculture on Cistercian granges developed more slowly than pastoralism, but in many locations can be documented by the mid twelfth century. Generally, the surviving documents provide relatively little information on what was planted and how lands once acquired were used. Still we glean occasional details; for instance in the charters for Chaalis, north-east of Paris, there is evidence for a three-year, three-field rotation.[30] As production moved away from the abbey itself, granges developed with different emphases; some devoted to a particular type of animal, others to cultivation of grain, still others to viticulture or olive groves. Usually, however, all granges retained in part the mixed agricultural/pastoral regime typical of all medieval agricultural production, drawing in the earliest years on the manual labour of monks and nuns themselves.

Such consolidated granges had efficiencies in terms of large-scale cultivation in contrast to the earlier fragmented holdings from which they were assembled. The repurchase of rights from all claimants to the land meant that crops did not rot in the fields while the harvest awaited an owner or tithe collector to take his share. Similarly, having no rents of particular kinds to pay, Cistercians could concentrate on the most appropriate cereals, introduce new spring (often nitrogen-fixing) crops, vary rotations to allow soil to rest, pasture their animals on them as needed and convert low-yielding or hard-to-cultivate fields to other uses.

That considerable investment was made in the most effective tools and techniques in Cistercian agriculture is confirmed indirectly

by the widespread acquisition, repair and expansion of the Order's
water-powered mills – which provided considerable labour savings in
grinding grain and other uses. The water-channels or aqueducts leading into an abbey complex were almost invariably used to power mills
for grinding grain, as seen in descriptions of Clairvaux and today at
Fontenay. The charters of acquisition of such mills and their accoutre-
ments – dams, rights to flood upstream and so forth – document large
numbers of Cistercian mills and mill sites acquired throughout Europe.
Usually they were of the Vetruvian (vertical-wheel) type and located
most often on smaller streams, but occasionally on major rivers. Such
mills are often documented because disputes arose as limits on water
resources were reached or because farmlands were flooded in spring.
There is also evidence for Cistercian tidal mills, for instance at Stratford
Langthorne near London, and for Cistercian windmills such as that at
Thame Abbey by *c.* 1237, which would have had similar labour-saving
advantages.[31]

Was mill ownership an abrogation of Cistercian ideals about not
being dependent on rents paid by peasants? The issue is complicated.
In 1953 Georges Duby, remarking on the numerous mills held by early
Cistercians, suggested that the income on flour-grinding at their mills
in Burgundy, like animal husbandry elsewhere, may have supported
those reformers before they had acquired their large granges.[32] Certainly,
by the thirteenth century it was accepted that mills acquired by the
Order's monks and nuns would continue to be used by earlier tenants
on what became Cistercian lands. Thus a contract in which the monks
of Royaumont paid the knight Thibaut of Beaumont 500 livres parisis
for the mill of Gien in July 1259 included the stipulation that those
tenants who had once paid the knight to use the mill would henceforth
make payments to Royaumont.[33] At Pont-aux-Dames, the nuns' mills
were closely associated with the village ovens over which the abbey
appeared to have exercised monopoly control of bakers.[34]

Whatever the case, given the labour-saving capacity of all these pow-
ered mills contracts may often have stipulated that monastic acquisition should not deprive neighbours and existing tenants (often removed
only slowly from Cistercian lands) of access to such mills.[35]

Mills also had industrial uses and the Order appears to have introduced the earliest documented fulling mill, described *c.* 1160 as having
two mills under one roof – one for fulling cloth, the other for grinding grain; there were also references to irrigating a meadow nearby.[36]
Waterworks might be more important than mills themselves, as they
were for Cistercian nuns at Manerbio near Brescia, who from the 1140s

were involved in canalisation of water to drain their fields.[37] Similarly, although the rights to fish in streams and behind mills have been little studied, artificial fishponds, like those adjoining Maubuisson, must have supplemented the resources of natural fishing in streams.[38] Such emphasis on mills, which invariably produced documentation, suggests that Cistercians invested as well in good ploughs, harrows and draught animals.

Cistercian viticulture is also somewhat problematic, for viticulture is very labour intensive. Medieval texts recommended extensive pruning and removing every other grape to improve size and yields, and explained how to graft or plant new vines. Cistercians certainly did receive gifts of vineyards, and often they were made with stipulations about using the wine produced for mass, and never alienating such gifts of wine given for commemoration of souls. Yet Cîteaux's vineyard and grange at Le Clos Vougeot in Burgundy were acquired early and would become one of the great viticultural centres of the world.[39] The growing importance of wine production and the profitability of vineyards in the Paris region is suggested by gifts and purchases made by Port-Royal. These include a gift of four arpents of vines in her vineyard of Sevres made in 1228 for the soul of the deceased Ingorrent of Sevres by his widow Odeline (their daughter was a nun there); the widow kept a rent of two deniers per arpent paid on the feast of Saint-Rémy and required the nuns to use her winepress unless they built their own.[40]

The house of Cistercian nuns founded by Blanche of Castile at Le Lys near Melun acquired existing vineyards and lands for planting more, along with wine-cellars and winepresses. Its abbesses created vineyards by letting out land in contracts called *medium vestum*, in which tenants would plant vineyards, pay nominal rents for a term of years and then split full ownership with the abbey which had granted the land.[41]

Early Cistercian agriculture benefited most from the innovations in labour already indicated – the devotion of time in the fields by monks and nuns themselves and the introduction of peasant labourers as lay brothers and lay sisters. Even before their granges were located too distant from the abbey, the Order began recruiting peasant labourers. Such recruits entered abbeys almost entirely along with land acquisitions. We see this in promises made to sellers that the abbey would accept a donor, a son or a daughter into the community – sometimes stipulating that they be healthy and that they not wait too long. In the early years such peasant recruits must have come with enthusiasm for working the land they knew well. Moreover, having taken vows of celibacy like monks and nuns, they worked without the dependency costs associated

with the labour of peasants and their families in villages. Their efficiency and hard work were critical to the success of Cistercian grange
agriculture.

At first equality reigned. These recruits entered as brothers and sisters of the community and were treated as equal to monks and nuns
except in so far as their participation in the Divine Office was more limited.[42] Although spending a greater amount of their time on agricultural
duties, such peasant recruits were called brothers and sisters, just like
those who devoted more time to the Divine Office. Lay brothers and lay
sisters were joined by monks and nuns in the harvest, as for example at
Elne near Perpignan, where Cistercian monks from Grandselve joined
the lay brothers for the olive harvest.[43] Eventually they would return to
the abbey from the granges only for weekly mass.

Difficulties about labour arose once grange acquisition stopped and
the automatic recruiting of new labourers with land acquisitions ceased.
By the 1180s some Cistercian houses had begun to make social distinctions in which men and women from the knightly class were expected to
become monks and nuns.[44] Eventually it would be the *conversi/ae* alone
who did the farm labour, with the choir monks and nuns only exceptionally leaving their enclosure to assist in the harvest. It was when this
happened that lay brothers and lay sisters had become a second class of
monks and nuns. Conditions worsened, lay-brother revolts increased
and eventually some abbeys would have to lease out lands or transform
granges into villages. This is seen in Gascony, for instance, where the
creation of such villages or towns (*bastides*) was made in equal shares
(*pariage*) between abbeys and the king or his officers.[45]

Cistercian agriculture was closely tied to town markets, and
Cistercians gradually acquired hospices, warehouses and even rental
properties in the growing cities. For nuns, whose abbey sites were often
closer to cities than those for monks had been, such urban properties
provided a place of retreat during warfare. The nuns of Saint-Antoine des
Champs, located just outside the city of Paris, went further than most.
By c. 1300 its nuns held more than 300 rental properties in Paris, often
a number on a single street. Their tenants ranged from great ecclesiastics and feudal lords to prosperous Parisian citizens and poor artisans.
Saint-Antoine made its urban endowment particularly inflation-proof
by frequent augmentations of rent – possibly in return for loans that
allowed tenants to make improvements.[46]

By the end of the thirteenth century Cistercian grange agriculture
was in place. Its benefits were shared by numerous Cistercian abbeys
for nuns, some of which rivalled in size and endowment those of the

Order's monks. Clearly, moreover, patrons did not hesitate to entrust those nuns with properties in support of their daughters, their elders and their anniversary masses, for which houses of nuns were as likely to be chosen as those for the Order's monks. In fact, patrons (many of them female) seem to have convinced themselves that women's prayers were possibly even more efficacious than men's for they speak often of their admiration and support of those poor nuns at a time when the Order's monks were dismissed as wealthy and arrogant. Despite the fact that the nuns would need to hire priests to celebrate masses for souls, it was deemed appropriate, possibly even best, to make contributions to 'poor Cistercian nuns' who might even build chapels for the anniversary masses for their patrons.[47] Cistercian nuns, like all religious women, did face institutional pressure that they remain enclosed, manage property in accordance with resources and not beg, but such nuns also took their charitable activities seriously – ignoring injunctions to prudence from father-visitors whether in giving alms to the poor at their gates or in admitting nuns in excess of established population maxima.[48]

Those nuns also defended their rights. Saint-Antoine's nuns showed their expertise in disputing an earlier contract for purchase of extensive woodlands from the Premonstratensians, as being too high with regard to 'the just price'.[49] Citing the volatility of prices and a decline in the purchasing power of cash, *c.* 1300, the nuns of Le Lys near Melun successfully challenged royal officials who had attempted to pay them in cash rather than grain. Presenting the documents for their foundation by Louis IX and Blanche of Castile, which included promises of annual rents in kind from the royal granaries, the nuns received a reissue of the royal grant of payments in kind.[50] In this and in many other ways, those nuns practised their agriculture and their almsgiving in ways that by the thirteenth and later centuries may even have seemed more effective than those of the monks.[51]

Notes

1   Canivez, *Statuta*, 1, p. 12, 'prima collectio', no. 1, attributed to the 1130s.

2   J.W. Thompson, 'The Cistercian Order and Colonization in Mediaeval Germany', *American Journal of Theology*, 24 (1920), 67–93.

3   C.H. Berman, *Medieval Agriculture, the Southern-French Countryside, and the Early Cistercians: A Study of Forty-Three Monasteries* (Philadelphia, PA, 1986).

4   P. Toubert, *Les structures du Latium médiéval: le Latium méridional et la Sabine du IXe siècle à la fin du XIIe siècle*, 2 vols. (Rome, 1973);

M. Bourin, *Villages médiévaux en Bas-Languedoc: genèse d'une asso-ciabilité, Xe–XIVe siècle*, 2 vols. (Paris, 1987).

5 J. Waquet *et al.* (eds.), *Recueil des chartes de l'abbaye de Clairvaux au XIIe siècle* (Paris, 2004), nos. 164–5 (*c.* 1176).

6 C.H. Berman, *The Cistercian Evolution: The Invention of a Religious Order in Twelfth-Century Europe* (Philadelphia, PA, 2000).

7 A. Bondéelle-Souchier, 'Les moniales cisterciennes et leurs livres man-uscrits dans la France d'ancien régime', *Cîteaux*, 45 (1994), 193–336, shows that only about a fifth of the abbeys of nuns did not survive to the French Revolution.

8 B. Barrière and M.-É. Henneau (eds.), *Cîteaux et les femmes: rencon-tres à Royaumont* (Paris, 2001), or E. Jordan, 'Prayers, Patronage, and Polders: Assessing Cistercian Foundations in Flanders', *Cîteaux*, 53 (2002), 99–125.

9 Pontoise, A.D. Val d'Oise, 72H12; selections were published by H. de l'Épinois, 'Comptes relatifs à la fondation de l'abbaye de Maubuisson, d'après les originaux des archives de Versailles', *Bibliothèque de l'école de chartes*, 19 (1858), 550–69.

10 C.E. Boyd, *A Cistercian Nunnery in Medieval Italy: The Story of Rifreddo in Saluzzo, 1220–1300* (Cambridge, MA, 1943).

11 Paris, A.N. LL1595 and S⋆4386, 'Cartulaires de Saint-Antoine'.

12 Paris, B.N. Latin MSS 9166–9, 'Cartulaire de Royaumont', fols. 872ff.

13 Berman, *The Cistercian Evolution*.

14 G. Constable, *Monastic Tithes from Their Origins to the Twelfth Century* (Cambridge, 1964); Berman, *Medieval Agriculture*.

15 *Cartulaire de l'abbaye de Silvanès*, ed. P.-A. Verlaguet (Rodez, 1910), nos. 170 (1154) and 174 (1165).

16 B.D. Hill, *English Cistercian Monasteries and Their Patrons in the Twelfth Century* (Urbana, IL, 1968).

17 J.S. Donnelly, *The Decline of the Medieval Cistercian Laybrotherhood* (New York, 1949).

18 J. Doinel (ed.), *Cartulaire de Notre-Dame de Voisins* (Orléans, 1887), nos. 49 (1207), 44 (1215), 46 (1217), 55 (1218), etc.

19 C.H. Berman, 'Cistercian Women and Tithes', *Cîteaux*, 49 (1998), 95–128; A. de Dion (ed.), *Cartulaire de l'abbaye de Porrois, au diocèse de Paris plus connue sous son nom mystique Port-Royal* (Paris, 1903), no. 4 (1206).

20 Montpellier, Bibl. École de Médicine, MS H322, *De usibus conver-sorum*; fols. 83v–84r; see C.H. Berman, 'Distinguishing between the Humble Peasant Lay Brother and Sister and the Converted Knight in Medieval Southern France', in *Religious and Laity in Northern Europe*, ed. J. Burton and E. Jamroziak (Turnhout, 2006), pp. 263–83.

21 C. Couderc and J.-L. Rigal (eds.), *Cartulaire et documents de l'abbaye de Nonenque* (Rodez, 1955), nos. 8 (1167–8), 21 (1173) and 26 (1177).

22 Montpellier, A.D. Hérault, 'Cartulaire de Valmagne' 1, fols. 76r–77r, 78r (1160–1).

23 Berman, *The Cistercian Evolution*, map, p. 119.

24 Berman, *Medieval Agriculture*.

25 J.M. Lizoain Garrido (ed.), *Documentacion del Monasterio de Las Huelgas de Burgos (1116–1230)*, 6 vols. (Burgos, 1985), vol. I, no. 11 (1187).
26 *Ibid.*
27 Paris, B.N. Latin 13892, 'Cartulaire du Lys'.
28 W.O. Duba (ed.), 'Cartulary of Vauluisant' (University of Iowa, MA thesis, 1994); C. Higounet, *Défrichements et Villeneuves du Bassin Parisien (XIe–XIVe siècles)* (Paris, 1990).
29 Boyd, *A Cistercian Nunnery*.
30 C. Higounet, *La Grange de Vaulerent: structure et exploitation d'un terroir cistercienne de la plaine de France* (Paris, 1965).
31 R.A. Donkin, *The Cistercians: Studies in the Geography of Medieval England and Wales* (Toronto, 1978), p. 138.
32 G. Duby (ed.), *Recueil des pancartes de l'abbaye de la Ferté-sur-Grosne: 1113–1178* (Gap, 1953).
33 Paris, B.N. Latin MSS 9166–9, 'Cartulaire de Royaumont', fols. 1441–3 (1259).
34 C.-H. Berthaut (ed.), *L'abbaye du Pont-aux-Dames, assise en la paroisse de Couilly (1226–1790)* (Meaux, 1878).
35 C.H. Berman, 'Women's Work in Family, Village, and Town after AD 1000: Contributions to Economic Growth?', *Journal of Women's History*, 19 (2007), 10–32.
36 A.-M. Bautier, 'Les plus anciennes mentions de moulins hydraulique industriels et de moulins à vent', *Bulletin philologique et historique*, 2 (1960), 567–626; *Cartulaire de Silvanès*, nos. 210 (1159), 145 (1164) and 227 (1164).
37 F. Menant, *Campagnes Lombardes du moyen âge* (Rome, 1993), p. 191.
38 R. Hoffmann, 'Mediaeval Cistercian Fisheries: Natural and Artificial', in *L'espace Cistercien*, ed. L. Pressouyre (Paris, 1994), pp. 401–14.
39 J.-M. Marilier (ed.), *Chartes et documents concernant l'Abbaye de Cîteaux: 1098–1182* (Rome, 1961).
40 de Dion (ed.), *Cartulaire de Port-Royal*, no. 98 (1228).
41 Paris, B.N. Latin 13892, 'Cartulaire du Lys'.
42 Recruitment of such lay brothers along with the land their families had once held is apparent at Silvanès by 1150; Berman, *Medieval Agriculture*.
43 Paris, B.N. Latin MS 9994, 'Cartulaire de Grandselve', fols. 223r–225v, and no. 752 (1157).
44 *Statuta* 1188:8; Canivez, *Statuta*, I, p. 108.
45 C. Higounet, 'Cisterciens et Bastides', *Le Moyen Âge*, 56 (1950), 69–84.
46 Paris, A.N. LL1595, fols. 19r–20v (1216).
47 *Ibid.*, fol. 41v (1228).
48 E. Makowski, *Canon Law and Cloistered Women: Periculoso and Its Commentators, 1298–1545* (Washington, DC, 1997), on how slowly Boniface VIII's 'Periculoso' was enforced.
49 Paris, A.N. S*4386, 'Cartulaire de Saint-Antoine'.
50 Paris, B.N. Latin 13892, 'Cartulaire du Lys'.

51   R. Gilchrist, *Gender and Material Culture: The Archaeology of Religious Women* (London, 1994); B. Barrière, 'The Cistercian Monastery of Coyroux in the Province of Limousin in Southern France, in the 12th–13th Centuries', *Gesta*, 31 (1992), 76–82, on nuns making less solid buildings than did monks; indeed when houses of nuns began to be suppressed, it was frequently to solve crises of debt among their father-visitors; see C.H. Berman, 'The Labors of Hercules, the Cartulary, Church and Abbey for Nuns of La Cour-Notre-Dame-de-Michery', *Journal of Medieval History*, 26 (2000), 33–70.

9 Art

DIANE J. REILLY

The Cistercian Order has sometimes been unfairly disparaged as hostile to art, or as embracing an aesthetic so profoundly plain that the interiors of their monasteries would have seemed oases of visual repose, free from distracting artistic ornament. The legislation promulgated by many of the earliest generations of Cistercians, and the shells of surviving Cistercian abbeys, might reinforce this impression. Nonetheless, despite legislative prohibitions against colourful, figurative decorations in glass, manuscripts or sculpture which were enacted by the middle of the twelfth century, Cistercian monks lived and worshipped in a visually lush environment. Their churches, typically emptied of original furniture, windows and pavements after the Reformation or the French Revolution, would once have been carpeted with patterned tiles and the windows filled with decorative glass. Their liturgical readings were furnished by colourful illuminated manuscripts, the texts of which were highlighted with giant painted initials, and their charters were guaranteed with delicately wrought figurative seals. Monasteries sometimes received manuscripts enhanced with complex painted figural scenes from wealthy non-Cistercian patrons, or noble postulants to the Order. Furthermore, by two centuries after the Order's foundation, enthusiasm for strict aesthetic asceticism had waned in many houses, where monks and nuns installed elaborate representational stained-glass panels, embroidered lavish figurative vestments and commissioned luxurious liturgical manuscripts for personal use. Thus while the Cistercians' artistic legislation may have set the Order apart from the mainstream, by and large the art which characterised it did not.

As with Cistercian architecture, Cistercian art is typified by a certain degree of uniformity engendered by the Order's well-developed bureaucracy, the lively exchange of monks, manuscripts and correspondence between houses and the artistic legislation intended to delimit some artistic production. Yet from the earliest days of the Order, the pioneer monks of Cîteaux embraced the artistic models provided by their local environment and the aesthetic heritage of the individual monks attracted to its houses from all over Europe. They also, by choice or necessity, bought and were given artworks made by artists who were not Cistercians. Both phenomena led to such artistic diversity that it is difficult to identify a 'Cistercian' type or style of art.

This combination of variety and uniformity is exhibited in the very first surviving artworks commissioned by the founding monks of the New Monastery. Faced with the immediate need to provide for choir worship and the education of converts, they promptly set about both acquiring and copying the manuscripts typical of a monastic library. The early Cistercian Institutes of the General Chapter mandated that each Cistercian foundation must possess a given set of liturgical manuscripts, as David Bell has explained.[1] Surprisingly, an example of only one of these, a Psalter Breviary, survives from early Cîteaux, and that was probably imported by the founding monks from northern France. Instead, the manuscripts that survive from the hands of the first scribes and artists at Cîteaux, and at its first daughter house, La Ferté-sur-Grosne, are patristic manuscripts: commentaries on the Bible, collections of epistles and disquisitions on Christian doctrine by Augustine, Gregory, Jerome, Bede, John Cassian and Ambrose.[2] Very large in format, carefully written and often copiously illustrated, these manuscripts would have perfectly suited both the private *lectio divina* and the public *lectio continua*, or cycle of oral reading, that took place in most monasteries that followed the Benedictine Rule.

At both Cîteaux and La Ferté, for instance, monks copied multi-volume versions of Gregory the Great's commentary on the book of Job, the *Moralia in Job*. At Cîteaux the largest of the four volumes was 46 cm tall, while at La Ferté all three were 45 cm tall. At Cîteaux the *Moralia* were copied beginning around 1111 by five different scribes, and outfitted by one artist (and possibly a less-skilled assistant) with colourful initials in a style inspired by that popular just a few years earlier in England, the home of Stephen Harding (abbot 1108/9–34).[3] The illuminations include leaves and tendrils that entangle flailing men bearing swords and axes, knights, monks at work and prayer, hybrid beasts and workers harvesting grapes, among other subjects, all keyed to the interpretative texts they accompany (Figure 9.1). Around 1134 the monks of La Ferté borrowed the manuscripts so that they could copy the text.[4] Their version was decorated with an equally lavish, but much less violent, series of colourful tendril initials inhabited with standing figures and narrative scenes. Rather than borrowing the English-influenced style of the Cîteaux *Moralia*, they were inspired by the regional Burgundian

Figure 9.1 Gregory the Great, Moralia in Job (Dijon, BM MS 173, fol. 29),
© Dijon, Bibliothèque municipale.

style by then in use at Cîteaux, featuring sober figures with heavy green
or brown shadows on their frowning faces and nested v-folds in their
drapery. In the meantime, Cîteaux had continued to fashion very large
manuscripts with dramatically coloured miniatures, sometimes highlighted with gold. The earliest Cistercians apparently saw no contradiction between their reformist mandate and the manufacture and use of
luxurious books.

These manuscripts seem to stand in vivid contrast to the first
reliably dated statement on art written within the Order. Bernard of
Clairvaux's *Apologia* to Abbot William of Saint Thierry can be assumed
to summarise the critical attitude towards excess and ostentatious display that characterised the early Cistercians. Drafted between 1124 and
1125, it was conceived, apparently in answer to a request from Abbot
William, as a comprehensive condemnation of the lifestyle of Cluniac
monks. Bernard explained:

> I am amazed that such intemperance in matters of food, drink,
> clothing, bedding, retinue, and the construction of buildings is
> possible to grow among monks to the extent that wherever these
> things are the more diligently, joyfully, and extravagantly done,

there the better is order said to be kept, there the greater is religious life thought to be.[5]

Bernard devoted considerable space to all of these perceived lapses, but the most to his chapter on paintings, sculpture, silver and gold as it was presumably found in Cluniac monasteries. Particularly disturbed by the money wasted in decorating sacred spaces, Bernard railed against costly candelabras, jewelled hanging fixtures, colourful images of saints and figured pavements. He observed:

> Why is it that we do not at least show respect for the images of the saints, which the very pavement which one tramples underfoot gushes forth? Frequently people spit on the countenance of an angel. Often the face of one of the saints is pounded by the heels of those passing by. And if one does not spare the sacred images, why does one not at any rate spare the beautiful colours? Why do you decorate what is soon to be disfigured?

Of fantastic cloister sculptures, he writes:

> But apart from this, in this cloisters, before the eyes of the brothers while they read – what is that ridiculous monstrosity doing, an amazing kind of deformed beauty and yet a beautiful deformity? What are the filthy apes doing there? The fierce lions? The monstrous centaurs? The creatures, part man and part beast? The striped tigers? The fighting soldiers? The hunters blowing horns? You may see many bodies under one head, and conversely many heads on one body. On one side the tail of a serpent is seen on a quadruped, on the other side the head of a quadruped is on the body of a fish. Over there an animal has a horse for the front half and a goat for the back; here a creature which is horned in front is equine behind. In short, everywhere so plentiful and astonishing a variety of contradictory forms is seen that one would rather read in the marble than in books, and spend the whole day wondering at every single one of them than meditating on the law of God. If one is not ashamed of the absurdity, why is one not at least troubled at the expense?

Principal among his concerns seems to have been the vice of avarice, which he felt enticed the Church to 'serve the eyes of the rich at the expense of the poor'. As he reasoned, 'Money is sown with such skill that it may be multiplied.'[6]

Whether he himself nurtured this attitude within the Order, or absorbed it from mentors such as Abbot Stephen Harding, is difficult to establish now, because all surviving descriptions of the original objectives of the founding monks were either written or revised after Bernard drafted the *Apologia* to Abbot William. Legislation eventually addressed many of Bernard's concerns, by limiting the colours, materials and contents of art produced by and for Cistercians. Conversely, no limits on monetary investment in art were ever specified, and while Bernard later resisted rebuilding Clairvaux in stone because of the expense, the excuse he gave was not that money would be taken from the mouths of the hungry, but rather that observers would think ill of the Clairvaux monks for the expenditure.[7]

Tracing the development of the artistic legislation through which Cistercian leaders sought to regulate the ornamentation of manuscripts, liturgical plate, stained glass and vestments is no easy task. The foundation documents of the Order are famously difficult to date and the early regulations on art exist in different versions using variant wordings. For our purposes, it is less important to pin down the exact date when a rule was established than to define the general principles behind the artistic legislation, and the period and order in which these rules were instituted. The earliest statutes, enacted most likely by the 1130s and perhaps originally drafted decades earlier,[8] appear to be those that addressed liturgical altar furnishings and monumental art. The first banned silken altar clothes and vestments, except for the maniple and stola, while chasubles were to be of only one colour. Further, it instructed that the metal altar utensils were to be without gold, silver or gems, except for the chalice and the fistula (a liturgical straw), both of which could be silver or silver gilt, but never gold.[9] A second statute banned sculptures and pictures, both from the church and the other rooms of the monastery, because of their potential to distract the monks from their meditations, but specified that figured crucifixes were allowed.[10] Finally, by 1152 a third statute had been enacted, this one explaining that 'letters' were to be made of only one colour, and not depictive, while windows were to be of 'white' glass, with no figures or crosses.[11] Thus, already in the early years of the Order the Cistercian monks had established that certain types of art must be created according to specific guidelines. However, these early rules did not mandate that art already owned by the monks be eliminated, nor did they specify a decorative aesthetic for the Order.

As the Order grew and its statutes multiplied in the later twelfth and thirteenth centuries, guidelines were generated for all sorts of decorative elements, including tile floors, painted doors and curtains, and earlier statutes were reiterated with more force, including admonitions to specific monasteries that offending art should be removed, although exceptions were sometimes made for houses that had previously belonged to a less stringent Order.[12]

In reaction to these statutes, the art of Cistercian illumination, for a time at least, changed dramatically. Manuscripts were decorated with what has been termed by modern scholars a 'monochrome' style. Monochrome letters, in fact, could feature highlighting in contrasting colours, or a single folio of a manuscript could be littered with letters of many different colours, each elaborated with scrolls, leaves, flourishes and buds. While beasts, humans and hybrids disappeared from the page, ornament did not, and Cistercian artists seem to have achieved a high degree of luxuriousness through the application of a non-figurative decorative repertoire. At Bernard's home monastery of Clairvaux, the monks read aloud from the magnificent, six-volume Clairvaux Bible (Troyes, BM MS 27, Figure 9.2), 49 cm high, and embellished with dozens of painted initials, carefully modelled with delicate white highlights or a paler version of the main colour. The Clairvaux monks also used a bible that was probably given to them by Prince Henry, son of Louis VI, when he entered the monastery in 1145. Much smaller and of only two volumes, its initials harbour beasts and narrative scenes, and are accented with gold.[13] Moreover, some texts could only be understood with their illustrations. In the early thirteenth century Clairvaux scribes illustrated copies of the *Speculum Virginum* and Richard of Saint Victor's commentary on Ezekiel with full-page pen drawings.[14] By 1200 most Cistercian artists had relaxed their observance of the 1152 statute, and were again producing manuscripts ornamented with multi-coloured decorative initials, although gold did not reappear in most Cistercian scriptoria for another century.

Under the feet of the monks as they consulted these manuscripts were the most common artworks in a Cistercian abbey: its tiled floors.[15] Despite the fact that Bernard of Clairvaux had condemned colourful church floors or those animated with holy subjects in his *Apologia*, the first General Chapter statutes intended to ensure the 'simplicity' of floors appeared only in the early thirteenth century, and no specific subjects or designs were ever forbidden. Interestingly, one statute chastised an abbot of Beaubec (Normandy) for allowing one of his monks to manufacture diverting pavements for non-Cistercians, but allowed him to continue to work for other Cistercians.[16] Archaeological evidence indicates that tile kilns operated within the walls of a number of Cistercian monasteries, and the remains of elaborate tile floors have been found in several. As with other forms of art found in Cistercian environments, floors demonstrate both a certain amount of uniformity engendered by the Cistercian bureaucracy and the travel of the monks between houses, and conformity to regional traditions.

Cistercian monasteries were furnished with several different types of tile floors. In the early houses of Normandy and Poitou, artisans

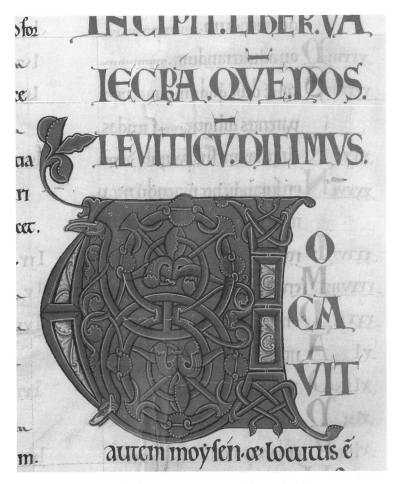

Figure 9.2 Clairvaux Bible (Troyes, BM MS 27, fol. 104v), © Troyes, Bibliothèque municipale.

sometimes used the same style as found in non-Cistercian contexts, where tiles of a variety of shapes, each of a single colour such as green, red, brown, yellow or black, were assembled into complex decorative patterns including shadowboxes, interlaced grids with embedded flowers and dodecagons. Elsewhere, plain square tiles in black and yellow were arranged in woven trellis patterns. A specifically Cistercian type found in many early houses is the glazed greenish-black or brown counter-relief or hand-incised tile, exhibiting sometimes quite complex foliate, fish-scale, interlace or geometric designs either stamped or drawn with the aid of a compass. Tiles from different houses differed in

Figure 9.3 Tile floor from Byland Abbey, © Emma Johnson.

size and were made of local clay, but typically displayed the same types of decorative motifs. By the 1240s tiles with foliate, geometric and animal designs inlaid in a contrasting colour were being used throughout Europe in Cistercian and non-Cistercian churches, and each Cistercian house seems to have chosen its tiles from a repertoire available from a local tiler. When laid, sometimes as multi-tile units, these tiles would have created continuously patterned decorative floors. Tiles with projecting relief designs of scrolls, fleur-de-lis, heraldic devices and even lions, leopards and dragons have also been found, mimicking those that would have been common in non-Cistercian contexts.

Most striking are the mosaic floors once found in northern English and Scottish abbeys such as Byland or Meaux, which featured panels assembled from hundreds of tiles fired in specialised shapes to create two-dimensional designs such as rose window patterns, chequerboards, interlaced panels, trellises of foliage and overlapping arcades of pointed arches (Fig. 9.3). Though the technique was probably imported from Norman Cistercian houses, the surviving British examples are the most complex of the type created, and undoubtedly would have been very expensive to manufacture and install.[17] The resulting riot of pattern and colour, usually concentrated at the liturgically most significant points in the church, was intended specifically for the eyes of the monks.

Although statutes had forbidden the insertion of coloured glass windows into Cistercian buildings by the middle of the twelfth century, from the second half of the twelfth century artists nonetheless developed a sophisticated repertoire of geometric and organic patterns rendered with glass panels held in place by lead cames, and, by the end of the twelfth century, painted in grey or black in a technique known as 'grisaille'. The twelfth-century abbey church of Obazine, for example, was outfitted with windows displaying all-over patterns of palmettes, lilies, strap- and knotwork (Figure 9.4). At other churches glazers employed lozenge patterns, fleur-de-lis, lattices or interlaced circles and squares, and patterns of such density that the distinction between figure and ground disappears. These designs may have been inspired by the bases of columns or by tile floors, or by the practice of filling window voids with patterned screens carved from soft stone, as seen in Visigothic, Islamic and some western French structures.[18] This style of glass was apparently compelling enough to be adopted by non-Cistercian foundations during the thirteenth century, so clearly it was not considered aesthetically bereft by its contemporaries. In a Cistercian abbey, these windows may have complemented a floor made of tile either inlaid with or assembled in a similar pattern, and indeed one may have inspired the other.[19]

The French abbey of Pontigny, one of Cîteaux's first daughter houses, by the early thirteenth century possessed a complement of artworks typical of early Cistercian houses. Its architecturally ambitious church was repeatedly damaged, and its glass and tile almost entirely destroyed, including by the explosion nearby of a munitions train in 1943. Nonetheless, nineteenth-century records and more recent archaeological finds allow us to reconstruct some of the elaborate 'white' glass panels of palmettes, lattices, shadow-boxes and clambering organic interlace, which were inserted in the church windows either when the church was first rebuilt in the mid twelfth century, or when the choir was rebuilt around 1200. At that time, tilers installed a multicoloured, mosaic tile floor whose interlace, shadow-box and dodecagon patterns were so eye-catching that the General Chapter promulgated a statute in 1205 ordering them to remove it.[20] This floor complemented the hand-etched and counter-relief tiles of the mid-twelfth-century nave and transepts.

Pontigny's library was confiscated after the French Revolution. Nonetheless, from its many surviving manuscripts we know that monks around 1200 may have employed, in the choir, refectory and cloister, manuscripts typical of twelfth-century Cistercian production. Some older

Figure 9.4 Knotwork window from Obazine Abbey, © MOSSOT.

manuscripts, such as a group of Augustine's sermons now in Cambridge
(Fitzwilliam, McClean MS 104), were decorated in the third quarter of
the twelfth century with single-colour painted initials embellished
with palmettes dangling into the margin and springy penwork. Others
had multicoloured foliate initials. A now dismembered bible (with surviving fragments in Paris and Cambridge, MA) from between 1195 and
1205 included an elaborate figural Genesis initial very similar in style

to art found in the Manerius Bible (Paris, Bibliothèque Sainte-Geneviève MSS 8–10), which was painted by a lay scribe in the Champagne region. Surrounding the interlocking circles containing scenes of the first six days of creation are layers of multicoloured enmeshed palmettes, interlaced tendrils and budding acanthus, patterns of similar complexity to Pontigny's new windows and pavement. The bible's New Testament decorations were instead painted in what is often termed the 'Channel Style', hinting that the scriptorium was open to a wide variety of influences.[21]

By the fourteenth century Cistercian stained glass, particularly in present-day Germany, could include small, coloured accent pieces and painted grotesques such as beast heads nestled in the foliage. Standing figures and narrative scenes also began to appear, such as at the Austrian abbey of Heiligenkreuz, particularly in the privacy of the monks' cloister.[22] Thus, as with manuscripts, statutes banning figured or multicoloured imagery appear not to have been enforced after the end of the thirteenth century, though some abbeys continued to observe their principles.

The triumph of colourful and figural imagery in what had formerly been an artistically restrictive Order can be seen at the Cistercian-guided nunnery of Wienhausen, founded in Germany around 1230 by a pious noblewoman. By the 1280s nuns erected a small chapel for their private devotions attached to the lower level of the two-storey cloister. They decorated it with narrative stained-glass windows and wall and vault frescoes depicting scenes from the passion, St Michael trampling the dragon and Christ in Majesty, and an altar statue of the Virgin and Child.[23] In the 1300s they acquired an elaborate programme of figurative stained-glass windows for their cloister and in the fourteenth and fifteenth centuries embroidered a rich cycle of wool on linen wall hangings and rugs for their convent, depicting the lives of saints, martyrs and chivalric heroes, along with others which they sold. Worked in vibrant wool thread, the embroideries could even incorporate freshwater pearls.[24] Also between the thirteenth and fifteenth centuries the nuns acquired wooden sculptures of the Crucified and Resurrected Christ, and in the early sixteenth century the latter was replaced with an elaborately wrought, multi-level altarpiece, which was set into the nuns' chapel, itself covered floor to ceiling in the early fourteenth century with over a hundred Old and New Testament scenes. During this time they also produced hundreds of small devotional images of Christ of the Veronica, or recording the images that surrounded them.[25] While the nuns may have been governed only indirectly by the Cistercian General Chapter, their art patronage, and the breadth and luxuriousness of the art they procured and produced, are typical of many Cistercian houses by the fourteenth century.

For instance, by the early fourteenth century the abbey of Wienhausen had a collection of three seals, one each for the abbess, the provost and the convent, which would have been used to authenticate their communications and contracts with outsiders. The most effective way in which a Cistercian monastery could have communicated its artistic ideals with the outside world was through texts, especially letters, and the images attached to them. Each abbey or abbot would, of necessity, have possessed a seal. Despite Bernard's avowed disapproval of figurative art on architectural sculpture, he himself commissioned at least two figurative seal matrices, and the resulting seals would have served as impressive visual markers of Bernard's presence in the text. The first depicted a cowled arm holding a crosier, and once that seal had been copied by a forger, its replacement depicted an 'effigy' of Bernard holding a crosier and included his name (Figure 9.5).[26] These two formats became the accepted types for a Cistercian abbatial seal, as confirmed by the General Chapter in 1200.[27] In the early years of the Order each Cistercian abbot sealed institutional charters with the same abbatial seal he may have used for his own letters. These seals, round or oval and between 3 cm and 5 cm long, were often less than half the size of seals used by Benedictine houses. This perhaps signified a conscious desire to broadcast, through these images designed to circulate in the world outside the monastery, the Cistercian monks' comparative artistic restraint. Nonetheless, because seal matrices were designed by professional seal makers, not monks, they typically followed local artistic conventions for shape, style and iconography from outside the Cistercian house where the seal was to be used, rather than a format mandated by a mother house.

Seals were also frequently replaced, either because they had been forged or to accord with the current fashion. When an abbot died, was deposed for misconduct or judged to have used his seal inappropriately, his seal matrix was smashed. Seals gradually grew in size and variety, though they still remained smaller than the often massive examples made for contemporary non-Cistercian foundations and bishops. The back could also be stamped with a counter-seal, rendering the resulting seal two-sided. By 1335 Pope Benedict XII ruled that a uniform conventual seal, round and featuring an image of the Virgin Mary, was to be used by each Cistercian house.[28] Already popular before this regulation

Figure 9.5 Seal of St Bernard, © Can Stock Photo Inc./Morphart.

was implemented, seals featuring a Gothic architectural canopy over a standing Virgin or Virgin and Christ Child, enthroned Virgin and Child or Virgin Protectrix proliferated.[29] These seals testify to the Order's departure from the relative austerity they had originally expressed through their small, simple seals. Just as stained glass, manuscripts and floors produced by late medieval Cistercians became indistinguishable in appearance from those commissioned by Benedictines or bishops, their late medieval seals feature layered, decorative architectural framing, diapered backgrounds and elegant seated or standing Virgins swathed in drapery, sometimes flanked by abbots, bishops or supplicant monks. As elaborate as those used by non-Cistercian religious and nobles, they signalled that the Cistercian Order had definitively joined the artistic mainstream.

Notes

1 See David N. Bell's chapter in this volume.
2 Y. Załuska, *L'enluminure et le scriptorium de Cîteaux au XIIe siècle* (Nuits-Saint-Georges, 1989), pp. 63–147.

3   C. Rudolph, *Violence and Daily Life: Reading, Art and Polemics in the Cîteaux 'Moralia in Job'* (Princeton, NJ, 1997), pp. 15–25.
4   Załuska, *L'enluminure*, p. 260.
5   C. Rudolph, *The 'Things of Greater Importance': Bernard of Clairvaux's 'Apologia' and the Medieval Attitude toward Art* (Philadelphia, PA, 1990), p. 261.
6   *Ibid.*, pp. 281–3.
7   William of Saint Thierry, *St. Bernard of Clairvaux: The Story of His Life as Recorded in the Vita Prima Bernardi*, trans. G. Webb and A. Walker (London, 1960), p. 87.
8   Waddell, *Narrative*, pp. 148–9.
9   *Exordium Cistercii* 25 and *Exordium Parvum* 10; Waddell, *Narrative*, pp. 413, 460.
10 *Exordium Cistercii* 26 and *Exordium Parvum* 20; Waddell, *Narrative*, pp. 413, 464.
11 *Instituta generalis capituli* 82; Waddell, *Narrative*, p. 491.
12 C. Norton, 'Table of Cistercian Legislation on Art and Architecture', in *Cistercian Art and Architecture in the British Isles*, ed. C. Norton and D. Park (Cambridge, 1986), pp. 317–93.
13 W. Cahn, 'The Rule and the Book: Cistercian Book Illumination in Burgundy and Champagne', in *Monasticism and the Arts*, ed. T. Vernon (Syracuse, NY, 1984), pp. 139–72 (p. 161).
14 *Ibid.*, pp. 147–51.
15 C. Norton, '*Varietates Pavimentorum*: contribution à l'étude de l'art cistercien in France', *Cahiers archéologiques*, 31 (1983), 68–113.
16 *Ibid.*, pp. 71–2.
17 C. Norton, 'Early Cistercian Tile Pavements', in *Cistercian Art and Architecture*, ed. Norton and Park, pp. 228–55 (p. 249).
18 C. Brisac, 'Grisailles from the Former Abbey Churches of Obazine and Bonlieu', in *Studies in Cistercian Art and Architecture*, 1, ed. M.P. Lillich, CS 66 (Kalamazoo, MI, 1982), pp. 130–9 (pp. 134–6).
19 Norton, '*Varitates*', pp. 88–94.
20 T. N. Kinder, 'Medieval Tiles and Bricks at Pontigny', in *Studies in Cistercian Art and Architecture*, 4, ed. M.P. Lillich, CS 134 (Kalamazoo, MI, 1993), pp. 15–44.
21 M. Peyrafort-Huin, *La bibliothèque médiévale de l'abbaye de Pontigny (XIIe–XIXe siècles)* (Paris, 2001), pp. 55–75.
22 J. Hayward, 'Glazed Cloisters and Their Development in the Houses of the Cistercian Order', *Gesta*, 12 (1973), 93–109 (p. 97).
23 *Ibid.*, p. 100.
24 V.J. Moessner, 'The Medieval Embroideries of Convent Wienhausen', in *Studies in Cistercian Art and Architecture*, 3, ed. M.P. Lillich, CS 89 (Kalamazoo, MI, 1987), pp. 161–77.
25 J.F. Hamburger, 'Art, Enclosure and the Cura Monialium: Prolegomena in the Guise of a Postscript', *Gesta*, 31 (1992), 108–34 (pp. 117–26).
26 J. France, *Medieval Images of Saint Bernard of Clairvaux*, CS 210 (Kalamazoo, MI, 2007), pp. 56–61.

27 T.A. Heslop, 'Cistercian Seals in England and Wales', in *Cistercian Art and Architecture*, ed. Norton and Park, pp. 266–83 (p. 266).

28 *Ibid.*, p. 278.

29 P. Bony, 'An Introduction to the Study of Cistercian Seals: The Virgin as Mediatrix, then Protectrix on the Seals of Cistercian Abbeys', in *Studies in Cistercian Art and Architecture*, 3, ed. Lillich, pp. 213–29.

10 Libraries and scriptoria

DAVID N. BELL

Some fifty years after Robert of Molesme and his twenty-one companions had founded the New Monastery in 1098 – the *Novum Monasterium* which would become the abbey of Cîteaux – the Order enacted legislation which specified the minimum number and nature of the books which each abbey was required to possess. The list appears in the Institutes of the General Chapter (*Instituta Generalis Capituli*), dating from about 1147, and the list is brief: apart from the Rule of St Benedict (the fundamental guide to Cistercian life), it includes only liturgical volumes necessary for the daily worship of God, the *opus Dei*: Missal, Epistolary (Epistle Book), Evangeliary (Gospel Book), Collectary (which contained the collects and other formulae for the celebration of the Divine Office), Gradual (containing the mass chants), Antiphonary (containing the Office chants), Hymnal, Psalter, Night-Office Lectionary and Martyrology. A little later, as part of the process of updating, the Book of Usages (*Liber usuum*) was added to the list.[1]

This is not to say, however, that these were the only books required in any Cistercian monastery. Chapter 48 of the Rule of St Benedict stipulates that every religious – monk or nun – should be given a book from the common collection at the start of Lent and read it through from beginning to end, and it follows from this that any monastery must have had in its collection at least as many books as there were religious. From the foundation of the Order until about the end of the twelfth century, a library of sixty to eighty books would not have been uncommon.

A good example is the collection of the small English abbey of Flaxley in Gloucestershire, whose early thirteenth-century book list records seventy-three entries in eighty volumes.[2] It is a conservative collection, almost entirely theological or ecclesiastical, and, save for three books in English (including one on medicine) and two in French (lives of St Godric and Thomas Becket), entirely in Latin. There is a bible in three volumes, standard glosses and biblical commentaries by well-known authorities and good holdings of Augustine, Gregory the

Great, Peter Lombard, the Victorines and (understandably) Bernard of Clairvaux. There are also two treatises on canon law, collections of sermons and a few less common works. All in all, it is a collection well suited to *lectio divina*, and is probably representative of a large number of smaller Cistercian houses whose catalogues (alas) have not survived.

The books were to be housed between the monastic church and the chapter room, and a visitor to almost any Cistercian site where walls are still standing will find the remains of an *armarium* or book-cupboard in just this location. Such *armaria* were simple and plain, and ranged from small cupboards to recessed arches considerably taller than a tall person. The interior was lined with wood (books do not like damp), there were wooden shelves (books at this time were shelved flat, not on their edges) and they had doors which could be securely locked. If the *armarium* proved too small, the extra volumes were stored in free-standing cupboards or book chests. Books were valuable items, and at this time a monastic 'library' was no more than a glorified safe providing secure and dry storage for the monastic collection. It was not a space for reading or writing.

Towards the end of the twelfth century collections began to expand rapidly, primarily as a result of donations and bequests, but also from copying in monastic scriptoria. By this time the Order was well established and well known, and (to the medieval mind) the prayers of holy monks and nuns were of sure assistance in securing a place in paradise. Donations, therefore, were of first importance for one's own personal salvation, and became of ever-increasing importance as the Middle Ages progressed. By the time we reach the brothers' library at Bridgettine Syon – the catalogue dates from the early sixteenth century – almost 86 per cent of its contents was the result of bequests and donations.

The problem with donations, however, is that one has no control over what is donated, and the contents of a donation may tell us more about the interests of the donor than about the needs of the recipient. In May 1306, for example, the Cistercian abbey of Bordesley in Worcestershire received a donation of twenty-seven fine books from Guy de Beauchamp, earl of Warwick.[3] They were all in French, and although a few of them might have been useful for members of the community, the great majority were not. On the one hand there was a copy of the Gospels, some lives of saints, a Psalter and an Apocalypse, but on the other there was a collection of French romances – *Lancelot*, the *Chanson d'Aspremont*, *Gui de Nanteuil*, the *Roman de Joseph d'Arimathie*, *Amadas et Ydoine* and the like – and such romances formed no part of the *lectio divina* of a Cistercian monk. What happened to the books is unknown, but it is possible that they were sold (they would have brought a considerable sum) and the money redirected to some other, more appropriate, purpose. As Dom David Knowles has said, 'The monastic library, even the greatest, had something of the appearance of a heap ... at the best, it was the sum of many collections, great and small, rather than a planned, articulated unit.'[4]

Books were also being produced in monastic scriptoria or writing-rooms, and would continue to be so until monastic book production was slowly superseded by secular workshops. By the end of the thirteenth century book production was almost entirely in the hands of the professional book trade, and although monastic book production did not cease – there was more of it in the later Middle Ages than has hitherto been supposed – it was certainly limited. Individual houses might have produced their own service-books, local hagiographical collections, cartularies and domestic histories, but by this time the great majority of the books in monastic collections were almost certainly acquired by purchase or (as we have seen) by donation.

Visitors to monastic sites will often be shown a room described as the scriptorium, but there is rarely clear evidence to substantiate the identification. For the copying of manuscripts two things are essential: light (you cannot copy in the dark) and warmth (you cannot copy if your fingers and/or ink are frozen). One would also prefer a location which was not damp and in which there was no too much of a draught. We must remember, too, that the apparatus required by scribes for their work was entirely portable and could be moved from place to place without difficulty. What seems to have been the case, therefore, was that in the heyday of the monastic scriptoria, the writing-rooms were, so to speak, peripatetic. In Cistercian houses we have clear evidence for the copying of manuscripts in the north aisle of the cloister (most probably within wooden carrels to provide necessary shelter), the chapter room, the warming-house and a room adjacent to the warming-house. There is no doubt, too, that, when necessary, artificial light was used, and, as to heat, the scribes were permitted access to the kitchen to smooth their wax, liquefy their ink and dry their parchment. The evidence from Rievaulx, however, indicates that, on some occasions at least, they simply moved themselves and their equipment bodily into the warming-house. How long the copyists wrote was determined by their Rule – about six hours in summer; less in winter – but these hours could be varied by the abbot if circumstances demanded it; but wherever they wrote, it had to be within the monastic precinct, and exercising their skills *extra terminos* was strictly forbidden.

In Cistercian houses, the person in charge of books and copying was the *precentor* (*precentrix* in women's abbeys), though in other houses he appears under other names. Part of his task was to provide the scribes with all the equipment they needed, but neither he nor an abbatially appointed delegate could actually enter the writing-rooms. They could go just as far as the entrance, and there use sign language to indicate what they needed. The scribes were not to be disturbed.

The consequences of donations and copying were immediate and obvious: too many books and too little space in which to house them. The claustral *armaria* were almost immediately outgrown, and in the course of the twelfth century book collections overflowed into the neighbouring sacristy. In the vast majority of cases, the sacristy was then partitioned off into two rooms, one for the vesting of the priests and the other for the secure storage of the books. The latter opened out onto the cloister; the former into the church. Yet even this solution sometimes proved inadequate, and we find some Cistercian houses storing their books under the night-stairs which led down from the monks' dormitory into the church. In other houses, the book collection expanded into part of the adjoining chapter room, though this was rare. Rare, too, save in certain German and Scandinavian abbeys, was the construction of a separate book-room, and Cistercian libraries as separate and independent buildings do not make their appearance until the very end of the fifteenth century.

In the course of the thirteenth century the monastic scriptoria were still active and donations continually increased. More and more men and woman were happy to have their way to heaven – or at least, their way out of purgatory – paved by the prayers of holy monks and nuns. But it is also at this time that another factor came into play which would have a profound impact on the library holdings of some, though not all, Cistercian abbeys: the foundation of the College of St Bernard in Paris in 1245, and, in subsequent years, the other Cistercian colleges. It is true that the General Chapter was not especially happy with this development, but it recognised the fact that, if the Cistercians were to keep up with the other Orders (especially the Franciscans and Dominicans), there was really no other choice. The foundation of the Parisian college was only one part of what, in the second half of the thirteenth century, was a true intellectual revolution, though not all abbots welcomed it. In England, for example, the abbey and *studium* of Rewley was founded in 1282, and in the same year the General Chapter ordained that all English monasteries with twenty or more monks had to send one of their number to Oxford with an allowance of sixty shillings a year – a considerable amount.[5] To this there was strong opposition from the English abbots. Some houses, of course, were simply too small to be affected by the ordinance, and some had no young monks who could profit from a university education. Some abbots, however, feared (with justice) the contaminating influence of the university world; some thought that the monk-scholars would become proud and conceited (which many undoubtedly did); and all, without exception, objected to the expense.

But although the impact of the universities could not be withstood, the immediate impetus they gave to the intellectual life of Europe was not to last. The beginning of the fourteenth century ushered in a period of stagnation which lasted for about a century to a century and a half. It tended to be shorter for those houses more involved with university studies, and longer for those which were not. Thus, if we examine the numerous fourteenth- and fifteenth-century library catalogues from France, Belgium, England and Germany, we see that, in the great majority of cases, the collections effectively come to an end at the beginning of the fourteenth century. This is not to say that books were not added after that date – they were – but the writers and works they represent usually belong to an earlier age.

The book-loving Richard d'Aungerville of Bury, writing in the 1340s, noted that 'long lifeless books, once most dainty' had now become 'corrupt and loathsome, covered with litters of mice and pierced with the gnawings of the worms',[6] and although he was referring specifically to England, his sad comments could be applied to much of Europe. Indeed, as Geneva Drinkwater has said, monastic libraries throughout Europe 'were sinking into decay, interested neither in taking care of the books they had nor in increasing their number'.[7] There were, of course, exceptions to this trend, especially in Austria and Germany, but they were few in number.

The late fourteenth-century catalogue of the library of Meaux in the north of England may be seen to illustrate this trend.[8] It was compiled by a former abbot of the house, Thomas de Burton, and dates from 1396. There are 363 entries in the catalogue, though most of them list more than one work, and they reveal a library very much larger, though just as conservative, than that of Flaxley which we discussed earlier. The catalogue begins, as usual, with bibles and glosses, followed by standard patristic and medieval authorities. Among the latter, as we might expect in a Cistercian house, are a large number of the works of Bernard of Clairvaux. There are plenty of fourteenth-century *distinctiones*, the usual concordances and *tabulae* and lots of collections of sermons, a typical feature of later catalogues. There is little in the way of law, either civil or ecclesiastical, but the Cistercians did not approve of their monks either studying or having access to legal materials.

Grammatical works are few and old-fashioned, but we must again bear in mind that Meaux was a Cistercian house, and at this time Cistercian monasteries did not operate as schools. Nor was there much in the way of classical authors. Cicero, Lucan, Ovid, Sallust and Seneca all make an appearance – there is nothing unusual in that – but there is no Horace or Virgil. There was, however, a copy of Martial's Epigrams, which might be thought odd reading for a Cistercian monk. The scholastic writers, like the grammatical works, are also few and old-fashioned. There were volumes of Aquinas, Bonaventure, Richard of Middleton and Henry of Ghent, but that is all, and the latest of them – Richard of Middleton – was dead by about 1305, some ninety years before the catalogue was compiled. There is rather more in the way of history and chronicles (nearly 4 per cent of the total), but the English Cistercians always had a marked interest in English history.

The dominant feature of the Meaux library is Latin theology, which comprises more than 80 per cent of the total, and that may be significant. It is true (as we have said) that the collection effectively stops about a century before the compilation of the catalogue, but the proportion of 80 per cent is markedly higher than the percentage of similar volumes is the libraries of similar date of almost any other Order. There is also a dearth of university textbooks. It may be that this is no accident, and the singularly high proportion of theological texts at Meaux may reflect a determined effort on the part of at least some Cistercians to limit the effects of academic scholasticism, to reduce the impact of the universities and to retain the emphasis on *lectio divina* and spirituality which had been established by Bernard and the other great lights of the twelfth century.

Other monasteries seem to have been less conservative. Buckfast, for example, far down in Devon, may have had much closer links to the university world, for when John Leland visited the house in the 1530s he saw two works by William Slade, abbot of Buckfast from sometime after 1398 to his death in about 1415, which clearly reflected a university setting: *Quaestiones de anima* and *Quaestiones* on the four books of Peter Lombard's *Sentences*. A third book by the same author, *Flores Moralium*, may have reflected a more monastic milieu.[9] But there were also *lectura* on the fourth book of the *Sentences* by one Blencot (Blaincothus Britannus, a writer of unknown date), Robert Kilwardby's (d. 1279) *De conscientia et synderesi*, the *Quaestiones subtiles* of the Franciscan William Gainsborough (d. 1307), the *Quaestiones theologicae* and *Quodlibeta* of Gilbert Seagrave (d. 1312), the *Quaestiones* on Aristotle's *Physica* of John Sharpe (d. after 1403) and the *Quaestiones* and *Quodlibeta* of the Carthusian John Sutton (d. 1473). Most of these works have not survived. On the other hand, Leland also noted works by Bede, Stephen Langton, Robert Grosseteste and the Cistercian John of Forde, and without a library catalogue (which we do not have) it is impossible to say anything of relative proportions. Nevertheless, it remains possible that, as Christopher Cheney has suggested, some Cistercian houses did try to restrict their libraries to a narrower range of topics than was generally the case with other Orders.[10]

This period of stagnation, which was also a period of wars, political and social unrest, famine, plague, murrain and climate change, came to an end in the first half of the fifteenth century, when we see a second intellectual revival. There were a number of factors which contributed to this, not least a significant decrease in the price of books, a significant increase in vernacular literacy and the intellectual stimulus provided by the Councils of Constance (1414–18) and Basle (1431–49) as well as from certain pre-Reformation reform movements. The effects of the revival were manifest throughout Europe, and the Cistercian General Chapter responded to this new awakening with a series of demands for more and better learning in Cistercian houses. Thus, in 1443, the Chapter stated unequivocally that the 'honour of the Order' depended principally on its graduates,[11] and two years later, in 1445, it lamented that the Order was sorely deficient in 'men of letters'.[12] Nine years after this, in 1454, the General Chapter took the English abbots to task for their neglect of their books and promulgated a most important statute which demanded immediate repairs and which referred to the monastic library as a *thesaurus monachorum*, 'a treasure-house for monks'.[13]

Two decades later, in 1473, the Chapter turned its attention to the Scandinavian houses, again pointing out the importance of men of letters and the Order's reputation,[14] but it is clear that these dictates were not always welcomed and not always heeded. Many houses could not, or would not, afford to send students to university, and in 1488 the General Chapter was forced to reiterate its exhortation: 'All the glory and growth of our Order', said the assembled abbots, 'is seen to depend to the greatest extent on increasing [the numbers] of men of letters.'[15]

Yet the size of collections was everywhere increasing – 500 books at Zwettl in 1451; 1,000 at Lehnin in 1450; 2,000 at Himmerod in 1453; 1,200 at Cîteaux, and so on – but, once again, the problem was space. The old sacristy/book-rooms had long outgrown their capacities, and fifteenth-century records from a number of monasteries in England,

Germany, Italy and France reveal collections of books scattered throughout the houses. At Cîteaux in 1472 they were to be found in no less than seventeen different locations.

Such a situation was clearly unsatisfactory, and the most dramatic evidence for the impact of this second intellectual revival is the building of new libraries or the relocation of older libraries to newer and larger premises. In this matter the monastic and secular cathedrals led the way, but monasteries, including those of the Cistercians, soon followed suit. Nor were these new libraries mere storage spaces: they were also places for study, and study demanded space and light. The new library at Clairvaux dated from 1495 to 1503, and Jacques de Pontaillier's splendid new building at the mother house of Cîteaux was completed in 1509. In Germany alone, new libraries were built or rebuilt, or old libraries relocated, at Altenberg, Altzella, Bronnbach, Doberan, Eberbach, Heiligengrabe, Kaisheim, Kamp, Loccum, Marienfeld, Riddagshausen, Salem, Schöntal and Waldsassen. The fifteenth century was indeed, as one writer has called it, 'the age of libraries'.[16]

On the other hand, it was also a time of war, pillage and grave unrest, and books were often in danger. In 1459, therefore, the General Chapter demanded that the superiors of all Cistercian houses should compile an inventory of 'each and every book and precious object in the monasteries of either sex which are subject to them',[17] though how many did so is unknown. Monastic librarians were also busy during these unstable years, and books in many abbeys were being repaired, rebound, recatalogued and rearranged. In France, for example, we have evidence for this from (at least) Cîteaux, Fontenay, Signy and Clairvaux (where the library was catalogued and recatalogued three times between 1410 and 1472), and, in England, at Fountains and Holme Cultram. Further examples may be adduced from other areas of Europe.

It was also at this time that printing with movable type was introduced into Europe, though it took some decades for it to have a real impact. As Lawrence McCrank has said, the effect of printing on medieval library development was evolutionary rather than revolutionary.[18] Not everyone liked or appreciated the newfangled printed volumes, and, in any case, until about 1470–80 printed books were still very expensive and not vastly cheaper than manuscripts, which had been diminishing in price since about 1400. Books were still being copied by hand, though the days of the old claustral scriptoria were long past. From the early thirteenth century we see the development of private chambers in Cistercian monasteries, and although the General Chapter regularly fulminated against them, the trend towards privacy was inexorable. By the fifteenth century such chambers had doors and locks (the Chapter objected to both), and even (*proh dolor!*) stoves or fireplaces. Again the General Chapter objected, and again it was ignored. There is no doubt, however, that by this time whatever writing was to be done was done in these chambers, and there is equally no doubt that books were kept there. A statute of 1601 specifically mentions book-chests (*scrinia*) in private chambers,[19] but books were there long before that. Such books could not be regarded as private possessions – that was contrary to the Rule of St Benedict – but we have clear evidence that monks and nuns possessed them *ad terminum vitae*. After that *terminus* the volumes were to be returned to and remain within the convent.

The new printing technology seems to have appealed to the Cistercians, and they were not slow to adopt it. A printing-press was established in the abbey of Zinna in Brandenburg in the early 1490s, and the earliest incunable from the abbey press which still survives, the quarto *Novum Psalterium Beatae Virginis Mariae*, was printed in about 1493. At Baumgarten, between 1484 and 1487, Abbot Nicolas Wydenbosch or Weidenbusch (Nicolaus Salicetus in Latin) was printing Missals, Breviaries, Diurnals and Psalters, and the General Chapter was so impressed with his work that it instructed all monastic superiors to provide their religious with copies of the said books, and directed that the other service-books in their houses were to be corrected in accordance with the new printed editions.[20] Wydenbosch, however, did not install a press in the abbey: he used commercial printers in Basle and Strasburg.

From the early sixteenth century books were obtainable more easily and cheaply than they had ever been before, and once the printing trickle had become a flood, nothing could withstand it. Many abbeys began to accumulate books in vast numbers, though there is evidence that the books accumulated at this time were, on the whole, fairly conservative. To some extent this is a reflection of the conservative nature of much early printing, for apart from the classics and the sciences, a great deal of fifteenth- and early sixteenth-century printing looked to the past rather than what was, for them, the present. But an examination of Cistercian library catalogues and surviving printed books reveals a general disinclination to accumulate novel material. That there were exceptions is only to be expected, but a glance at the book list of Les Écharlis in northern Burgundy, compiled by the Revolutionary authorities in 1789, reveals a collection which could provide any eighteenth-century monk with a sound basis for his education and his spirituality. Almost 60% (57% to be precise) of the holdings may be classed as generally 'religious', and the other 43% are divided among history (13%), a variety of sciences (14%), *belles-lettres* (6%), classics (5%) and law (5%).[21] At the great abbey of Pontigny the catalogue of printed books compiled by its bibliophilic librarian (and afterwards abbot), Jean Depaquy, in 1778, just about half (49%) of the titles are theological, and the other half include history (21%), humanities (12%), jurisprudence (9%) and sciences and arts (9%).[22]

Depaquy's catalogue lists 2,193 titles in 3,832 volumes, but this was not large for the library of a major house in the eighteenth century. By the middle of the sixteenth century many Cistercian libraries had become vast repositories of printed materials, and splendid new libraries were built to house them. Few could rival the huge and magnificent neo-classical library at Vaucelles – a glorious achievement – built by Abbot Jacques-Christophe Ruffin in 1760 to house his collection of more than 40,000 carefully selected books and manuscripts.

And the tradition continues. Many contemporary Cistercian abbeys in Europe and the Americas have large and well-chosen book collections, suitable both for study and for *lectio divina*, and, as in previous centuries, it is sometimes difficult to know where to house them. Just as in the past, libraries have been relocated and new libraries built, and the Cistercian tradition, which is a living and creative tradition, still seeks to retain, in its book collections as in its way of life, that essential spiritual integrity so dear to the hearts of its founding fathers.

Notes

1 Waddell, *Narrative*, pp. 326, 330, 458 and 461.
2 D.N. Bell (ed.), *The Libraries of the Cistercians, Gilbertines, and Premonstratensians* (London, 1992), pp. 15–26 (Z7).
3 *Ibid.*, pp. 4–10 (Z2).
4 D. Knowles, *The Religious Orders in England*, 3 vols. (Cambridge, 1948–59), vol. II (1955), p. 332.
5 A.G. Little, 'Cistercian Students at Oxford in the Thirteenth Century', *English Historical Review*, 8 (1893), 84–5.
6 *The Love of Books, being the 'Philobiblon' of Richard de Bury, Bishop of Durham* (St. Louis, [s.d.]), p. 55.
7 G. Drinkwater, 'French Libraries in the Fourteenth and Fifteenth Centuries', in *The Medieval Library*, ed. J.W. Thomson (New York and Chicago, IL, 1939; repr. 1957), p. 414.
8 Bell, *The Libraries of the Cistercians*, pp. 34–82 (Z14).
9 *Ibid.*, pp. 10–12 (Z3).
10 C.R. Cheney, 'English Cistercian Libraries: the First Century', in *Medieval Texts and Studies* (Oxford, 1973), pp. 328–45 (p. 344).

11   Canivez, *Statuta*, 4, p. 539 (1443:71).
12   *Statuta* 1445:9; Canivez, *Statuta*, 4, p. 562.
13   *Statuta* 1454:95; Canivez, *Statuta*, 4, p. 714.
14   *Statuta* 1473:45; Canivez, *Statuta*, 5, pp. 326–7.
15   *Statuta* 1488:7; Canivez, *Statuta*, 5, p. 630.
16   C.L. Kingsford, *Prejudice and Promise in Fifteenth Century England* (Oxford, 1925; repr. London, 1962), p. 42.
17   *Statuta* 1459:41; Canivez, *Statuta*, 5, p. 33.
18   L.J. McCrank, 'Libraries', in *Dictionary of the Middle Ages*, ed. J.R. Strayer, 13 vols. (New York, 1982–9), vol. vii (1986), p. 563.
19   *Statuta* 1601:xv.2; Canivez, *Statuta*, 7, p. 217.
20   *Statuta* 1487:14; Canivez, *Statuta*, 5, pp. 572–3.
21   D.N. Bell, 'Reading Revolutionary Catalogues: The Case of Les Écharlis', in *Truth as Gift: Studies in Medieval Cistercian History in Honor of John R. Sommerfeldt*, ed. M. Dutton *et al.*, CS 204 (Kalamazoo, MI, 2004), pp. 237–63.
22   D.N. Bell, 'Abbot Jean Depaquy and the Printed Books of Pontigny, 1778–1794', *Cîteaux*, 51 (2000), 117–48 (p. 121).

11 Cistercian architecture or architecture of the Cistercians?

THOMAS COOMANS

Architecture is, without a doubt, the most tangible witness to the medieval Cistercian legacy. Not only standing churches and cloisters, but abbey ruins and rural granges also attract several million visitors yearly; special routes and networks of Cistercian abbeys may be found across Europe, and no less than five abbeys have been inscribed on the UNESCO World Heritage list.[1] Cistercian architecture is a popular subject – attractive to tourists, fascinating to scholars and a niche for publishers. This chapter contains four complementary approaches to the subject. After sketching the main historiographical steps of past and present research, I shall examine the central issue of the architectural specificity or identity of medieval Cistercian abbeys, then consider the abbey buildings as a material source for monastic life and finally define major research perspectives.

HISTORIOGRAPHY

In his famous *Dictionnaire* (1854) Eugène Viollet-le-Duc, as one of the first scholars, stressed the specificity of Cistercian architecture by analysing the plans of Clairvaux and Cîteaux, the churches of Fontenay and Pontigny, the cloisters of Thoronet and Fontfroide and the infirmary of Ourscamp.[2] This was the source for a long line of scholars who were to consider Cistercian architecture in the first instance as a product of the Romanesque period, originating in Burgundy, intimately related to Bernard of Clairvaux, spreading internationally through the network of the Order and controlled by its General Chapter. Edmund Sharpe, author of the first book dedicated entirely to Cistercian architecture (1874),[3] focused on the buildings of the White Monks in an international and comparative perspective. Contemporaneous authors considered it as part of a national style. In the increasingly nationalistic climate preceding the First World War, authors such as Camille Enlart depicted the medieval Cistercians as 'missionaries' of an early Gothic canon to Italy,

Scandinavia, Poland and other countries.[4] Inversely, British and German scholars, refusing the theory of a pure French export, tried to prove how Cistercian architecture was indigenous to their respective countries. To this end they employed different rational and positivist methods. Art historians made architectural parallels, comparing series of church plans on the same scale to show similarities and differences, and to define evolution and geographic groups.[5] In parallel fashion, archaeologists began to study buildings and to excavate ruined sites, bringing to light material evidence of abbey layouts and publishing the first series of monographs. The outstanding work done by William St John Hope from the 1870s can be considered the birth of monastic archaeology, an expertise that remains prominent in British scholarship.[6]

The monastic revival that developed in Europe from the last decades of the nineteenth century attempted to restore authentic monastic life on the basis of new knowledge of both liturgy and architecture. From then on several generations of French, Belgian, German and Italian Cistercian 'monk-scholars' were particularly active and produced high-level scholarship until the 1970s.[7] During the period between the two World Wars lay scholars had other priorities. Two volumes on Cistercian architecture in France (1943) by Marcel Aubert and the marquise de Maillé are a milestone, not only because they provide a synthesis, but also because they include monastic and ancillary buildings as well as abbeys of Cistercian women.[8] After the Second World War, the commemorations of the death of Bernard of Clairvaux (1153) gave a boost to the study of Cistercian architecture. French and German scholars accepted the concept of 'Bernardine' church layout as defined by Karl-Heinz Esser,[9] and the standard works by Father Anselme Dimier and Georges Duby greatly contributed to the diffusion of the so-called Bernadine paradigm.[10] Literary fictions and illustrated publications popularised this architectural stereotype.[11]

The 1980s and 1990s could be considered the 'golden age' of Cistercian architectural studies. Important exhibitions in Aachen (1980) and Paris (1990),[12] international Cistercian celebrations in 1990 and 1998, numerous conferences and workshops, the promotion of five abbeys to World Heritage status, the multiplication of excavation campaigns and other studies considerably broadened the field of research in time and space. New series were launched, such as Studies in Cistercian Art and Architecture,[13] and special sessions on Cistercian architecture organised at the annual congresses for medieval studies at Kalamazoo and Leeds. Scholars began working on Cistercian Gothic architecture,[14] granges and rural space,[15] mills and hydraulic works[16] and decorative arts related to architecture (grisaille windows, patterned floor tiles, wall paintings and so forth). The British tradition of monastic archaeology, combined with building as well as landscape archaeology, reached high levels at Fountains and Bordesley and generated several excellent synthetic publications.[17] Elsewhere, high-quality architectural monographs integrated a broad range of sources and combining different methods.[18] After 1989 the Cistercian heritage of central Europe received new attention and regional studies began to appear, such as brick architecture of the abbeys in the Baltic area.[19]

After the proliferation of publications leading up to the nine-hundredth anniversary of the foundation of Cîteaux Abbey in 1998, the acquisition of new information and acknowledgement of the complexity and diversity of Cistercian architecture led to synthetic works, the best amongst which are those by Terryl N. Kinder and Matthias Untermann.[20] The most recent developments look at Cistercian architecture through the lenses of anthropology, gender, funerary spaces and the environment.[21] These are part of the current interest in the Order and try to overcome the earlier tendency of isolating the Cistercian contribution from the broader field of monastic (and non-monastic) architecture.

ARCHITECTURE AND CISTERCIAN IDENTITY

The Cistercian Order was not created *ex nihilo* but developed as a reform of the Benedictine Cluniacs, motivated by the desire to return to the original spirit of austerity and poverty of the Rule of Benedict. Cistercians thus never rejected the monastic tradition but did reform the components of monastic life according to what they called the *forma Ordinis*, a general term referring to the exterior forms of Cistercian practice such as behaviour, habits, diet and buildings. There is, however, no written explanation that defines an architectural norm, only some decisions made by the General Chapter which condemned buildings that did not conform to the *forma Ordinis*.[22] The statutes do nevertheless specify that 'all unnecessary new things and notable curiosities' (*omnes superfluae novitates et notabiles curiositates*) were to be rejected, and this interdiction included towers, ornate pavements, coloured glass windows, figurative paintings, sculpture, bells, images (except that of Christ) and ornaments. Since the legislation repeated these interdictions until the end of the thirteenth century, it would appear that the norm was not always respected.

The most important sources are the buildings themselves. Despite the destruction of many pivotal abbey churches – including those of the

Figure 11.1 Eberbach (Germany), interior of the abbey church to the choir,
photo: Thomas Coomans, © THOC-SOFAM.

mother houses of Cîteaux, Clairvaux, Morimond and La Ferté – as well
as the difficulty of dating most medieval buildings with accuracy, it is
only possible to understand the meaning of *forma Ordinis* by comparing
Cistercian churches to architecture outside the Order, especially that of
twelfth-century Benedictine monasteries. For Cistercians austerity meant
simplicity of design, structure and decoration, reduced to the functional
and the essence. The character of Cistercian churches results from a combination of geometric proportions, pure forms, high-quality stone carv-
ing, good acoustics and light (Figure 11.1). This material harmony framed
an equally simplified liturgy and sought to trace a path leading without
distraction to contemplation and ultimately to God. The *forma Ordinis*
is certainly not a style but rather a spirit that can be found in buildings of different periods, locations, scales, functions, materials, details
and even styles. Contextualisation is therefore indispensable in order to
understand Cistercian architecture and to appreciate the differences and
similarities inherent in the formula 'unity and diversity' exemplified in
the contemporaneous twelfth-century abbey churches of Fontenay and
Pontigny, both in Burgundy (Figure 11.2 and Figure 11.3); the twelfth-
and thirteenth-century building campaigns of the churches at Fountains
and Ourscamp; or the Romanesque ashlar masonry at Sénanque and the
Gothic brick architecture at Løgum. Just as with illumination and music,

Figure 11.2 Pontigny (France), abbey church seen from the south,
photo: Thomas Coomans, © THOC-SOFAM.

Figure 11.3 Fontenay (France), façade of the church from the west,
photo: Thomas Coomans, © THOC-SOFAM.

the radical architectural norms of the Cistercians did not stifle creativity;
they generated unique compositions such as the choir of Rievaulx, the
rose window of Huerta, the oculus windows of Villers (Figure 11.4), the
gable of Kołbacz and the apse of Heisterbach.

Figure 11.4 Villers (Belgium), northern transept of the church,
photo: Thomas Coomans, © THOC-SOFAM.

In the first generations of the Order's existence a rather strict architectural church design was implemented: a nave with or without aisles, square east end and transept with two, four or more rectangular eastern chapels. This design was 'anti-Cluniac' because it lacked towers, a lantern at the crossing, crypt, rounded apses, ambulatory and radiating chapels, and was based on a square. In his famous sketchbook of around 1235, Villard de Honnecourt drew the plan of a church with the caption: 'this is a church of squares as is usually made by the Order of Cîteaux'.[23] In the 1950s this angular design was associated with Bernard of Clairvaux because most twelfth-century churches of the Clairvaux branch did use a square east end. This plan came to be called

'Bernardine', and the church of Fontenay (usually dated 1139–47,[24] thus before Bernard's death in 1153) was seen to exemplify the 'Bernardine' prototype (Figure 11.3). Even though Bernard never wrote a word on architecture, this hypothesis was attractive because of its direct connection to Bernard, as well as the institutional links that existed between a mother house and its daughter houses as defined by the *Carta Caritatis*. Some abbey chronicles mention converse-'architects' (lay brothers) being sent from Clairvaux to a daughter house in order to supervise the first phases of building works. As we will see, the angular or 'Bernardine' basic design could be developed on various scales and combined with different elevations and other vaulting systems as contexts and influences dictated. The angular plan did not, however, originate with the Cistercians, but it did influence the early generations of White Monks and they certainly preferred it during the twelfth century, and not only in the Clairvaux filiation. In some places it was employed as late as the thirteenth century. Such late examples, like the abbey church of Magerau in Switzerland (built in the 1260s), should not be considered as anachronisms but as explicit references with a precise meaning.[25]

The spectacular growth of the Cistercian Order in the twelfth century not only meant the creation of 'families' of churches throughout Europe; it also motivated translations of abbeys to more appropriate sites as well as the construction of larger churches. The first abbey confronted with the need for a larger church was Clairvaux, the most powerful of the five Cistercian mother houses. Founded in 1115 by Bernard, the first abbey was soon too small and in 1135 a new abbey was built on another site further down the valley. After Bernard's death in 1153 the community transformed the church by building a new choir with ambulatory and radiating chapels around his tomb. Little material evidence has been preserved for any of the three churches of Clairvaux. In order to distinguish successive phases, architectural historians have used numbers; the case of Cluny I, II and III is famous, and a similar numbering system is used to distinguish the successive rebuilding of Cistercian abbey churches. Clairvaux I designates the earliest settlement, with primitive buildings and a square wooden church; Clairvaux II is the great church built under Bernard, which is considered to have included the prototypical 'Bernardine' plan; Clairvaux III is the church as transformed soon after Bernard's death. At Cîteaux, Pontigny, Fountains, Rievaulx, Vaucelles, Ourscamp in France, Villers in Belgium, Tintern in Wales and other major abbeys such phases are also distinguished by numbers (Figure 11.2. and Figure 11.5).

Figure 11.5 Rievaulx (England), choir and transept of the abbey church,
photo: Thomas Coomans, © THOC-SOFAM.

From the thirteenth century on, some great abbeys adopted Gothic
cathedral plans and elevations with ambulatories and radiating chapels; among the most famous are Royaumont and Longpont in France,
Alcobaça in Portugal, Beaulieu in England, Altenberg in Rhineland,
Sedlec in Bohemia and Doberan in northern Germany. However, other
important abbeys developed original Gothic choir designs belonging
to the Gothic 'avant-garde' of their time, such as the famous Chapel
of Nine Altars at Fountains Abbey, the choirs of Rievaulx (Figure
11.5) and Tintern resembling huge glass shrines, or the hall-choir of
Heiligenkreuz. Modifying the eastern part of the church – its light,
form, scale and acoustics – had fundamental consequences for the daily
liturgy, as well as for the identity of the community that was facing the
choir during day and night offices, masses and other events in the most
spiritually charged part of the abbey.

The Cistercian Order would not have been as successful as it was
without the support of the highest aristocracy. Not only emperors
and kings, but also most dynasties of territorial princes granted the
White Monks lands, privileges, exemptions, endowments and other
advantages. In exchange for these material gifts, the donors expected
non-material gifts from the community such as prayers for their souls
and in their memory. In this context lay burial in abbey churches

became a crucial issue, and the General Chapter had to regulate it in order to avoid an excessive increase in the number of such tombs.[26] In the beginning, burials in Cistercian churches were prohibited; abbots were interred in the chapter house and other religious in the cemetery. From 1157, exceptions would gradually be made for the burial of founders in the church and, from 1180, for the tombs of kings, queens and bishops in the church and cloister galleries. The General Chapter repeated this rule and sanctioned burials of dukes, counts and other aristocrats during the thirteenth century. Nevertheless, many abbey churches had become funerary churches, some of them developing specific architectural designs with crossing towers, decorated gables, westworks, ambulatories and other embellishments because of the presence of tombs and relics, for example at Poblet, Hailes, Royaumont, Chorin, Sedlec and Heiligenkreuz. From the early thirteenth century Cistercian nuns were reputed to provide the purest memorial prayers, and some of their churches – Las Huelgas Reales at Burgos, Maubuisson near Paris, Flines in Flanders, Roermond in Guelders and others – became princely necropoleis. Such buildings expressed their aristocratic status with towers, chapels and rich decoration that definitely did not conform to the *forma Ordinis*. From the last quarter of the thirteenth century the Cistercians opened their churches to lay burials as a consequence of a financial crisis as well as competition with the mendicants, who accepted revenues from burials in their churches. Funerary chapels with Gothic windows, stained glass and rich furnishings were erected along the sides of the nave or transept.

Around 1100 the Cistercians had begun as a reform of the Benedictines, but two centuries later it had become necessary to reform the reform. Despite the papal endeavours of 1335 Cistercian unity weakened and its identity changed. The development of regional groups of abbeys and specific congregations meant that the central authority gradually weakened. The wealthiest abbots expressed their status and autonomy with rich transformations of their churches, including bell towers (Fountains *c.* 1500); some abbeys built elaborate Gothic towers at the crossing (Poblet *c.* 1330 and Bebenhausen in 1407). Other abbots tried to reform their own houses. Because the two are often linked, it is not always easy to define whether late medieval modernisations are a matter of pure prestige or expressions of reform. Changing the shape of the choir or enlarging windows, building new stalls and erecting an elaborate high altar seem to have been common methods used to reform a community, or at least to mobilise the monks around a project and so develop a new dynamic. A well-preserved example can be seen at Maulbronn, where, in the middle of the fifteenth century, the Romanesque eastern wall of the sanctuary was pierced with a window of Gothic tracery and new stalls were built in the choir. In other cases the whole eastern end was rebuilt, such as at Melrose in 1390 and Furness in the late fifteenth century.

Some authors check individual Cistercian buildings against the 'Bernardine' canon in order to see how they conform to it and thus how 'Cistercian' they are. If the building does not fit in with the expected *forma Ordinis*, it is considered less valuable or even 'decadent'. Such interpretations are misguided because they are not driven by an interest in unravelling the cultural and historical meaning of individual buildings in their unique contexts. Even though the striving for an architectural identity was evident during the first century, right from the beginning the expressions were diverse, depending on the evolving geographical and historical contexts.

The permanent tensions between the strong centralised structure of the General Chapter – a guarantor of tradition and unity – and the diversity of local conditions generated an original dynamic that explains both the common identity and the multiple specificities of Cistercian architecture.[27] The buildings, especially churches, should be understood as having been shaped by the interaction between three different levels at a precise moment. The first, or international, level is the Cistercian Order with its norms, legislation, liturgy and *forma Ordinis*, including an aesthetic dimension. This level is common to all Cistercian abbeys and expresses the identity of the Order as an institution. The second level is regional; the patrons or decision makers: the abbot with his community, his mother house and the regional networks supporting the abbey, including the nobility and the bishops. Some abbots had previously lived in another abbey and therefore chose that as their model. The influence of the burial of founders and other benefactors on the design of the abbey also belongs to this level. The third level is local: the builders, masons, carpenters and other workers and craftsmen using local building materials to give physical form to the project. It should be said here that the legends of monks building their own church and transmitting building secrets is a Romantic myth. As explained above, there were sometimes teams of specialised lay brothers acting as master masons or foremen who gave directions to lay workers, but monks were expected to pray and not carve stone or make mortar. Monk or layman, the master or 'architect' had to synthesise the influences of these three levels when he designed a project and translated the complex identity of a group into form, matter and structure.

ARCHITECTURE AS MATERIAL SOURCE
FOR MONASTIC LIFE

Abbeys are much more than churches; they are enclosed building complexes organised around cloisters and courtyards. Community life according to a religious belief, a rule and vows implied strict organisation. Centuries of experience defined the daily life of the monk or nun as well as all other religious and lay people living in specific parts of the abbey (*conversi*, novices, sick and elderly monks, guests, servants, farmers and seasonal workers). Again, the Cistercians followed a long tradition, modifying some aspects as appropriate to their time and location. The *Ecclesiastica officia*, a Cistercian book of customs from the twelfth century,[28] contains 121 chapters with precise information on the way in which behaviour, liturgy, rituals, feasts and work were to be performed in the church, cloister, chapter house, dormitory and other common rooms. This exceptional source defined the theoretical and spiritual aspects of the services that monks practised in the gate house, refectory, kitchen, infirmary, guest house, storeroom, sacristy and the novices' house.

Scholars have combined material evidence from the monastic buildings surrounding the cloister with written and visual sources – including the instructions in the *Ecclesiastica officia* – to define a 'Cistercian model plan' that became commonplace in most publications about the White Monks. The symbolically and liturgically charged east–west orientation of the church determined the development of the rest of the complex. The cloister forms a central square (Figure 11.6), surrounded by four galleries flanking the church to the north, the monks' wing to the east, the lay-brothers' wing to the west and the refectory wing to the south. In each wing the rooms follow a predictable succession. The monks' range to the east included the sacristy, book cupboard (*armarium*), chapter house, parlour, monks' room (sometimes *scriptorium*) and the day-stairs leading to the monks' dormitory on the first floor (Figures 11.7 and 11.8). The building opposite the church consists of a warming room (*calefactorium*) and kitchen, each with chimneys, flanking the refectory; close to the entrance of the latter in the cloister garth is the fountain (*lavatorium*). The lay brothers' range is sometimes, but not systematically, separated from the cloister by an open space called a 'lay brothers' lane'; the building contains a storeroom and lay brothers' refectory on the ground floor and a dormitory on the upper floor. The dormitories of both monks and lay brothers are connected to the church to facilitate access for night prayers; on the opposite side they are connected with a latrine block (the 'reredorter').

Figure 11.6 Sénanque (France), cloister and church,
photo: Thomas Coomans, © THOC-SOFAM.

Figure 11.7 Fountains (England), chapter house and southern transept of the
church, photo: Thomas Coomans, © THOC-SOFAM.

Figure 11.8 Le Thoronet (France), eastern gallery of the cloister, photo: Thomas Coomans, © THOC-SOFAM.

This functional model has been enhanced by nineteenth-century rationalism that defined standardised designs for all building types, especially for communities (schools, prisons, barracks, convents and so on). Recent developments in archaeology, construction history, hydrology, landscape history and other aspects of material culture seriously challenge this theory and invite something more nuanced than the simplistic idea of a 'model Cistercian plan'. The first consideration is the influence of the topography on the choice of site and general design of the abbey. Most abbeys are situated in valleys, with the church at the highest point and the water supply close to the kitchen and refectory, but they also needed ponds, mills and other workshops. Hydraulic systems were created to include ingenious networks of pipes and sewers which differ from abbey to abbey according to location, the size of the community and its economic activity. The second consideration is that an abbey cannot be reduced to a church and monastic buildings around the cloister. Abbeys were self-sustaining institutions that also needed areas for production and storage. The 'model plan' ignores indispensable structures such as the abbot's house, infirmaries for monks and lay brothers, guest house, ancillary buildings and the home grange and stables. Pioneering work by Glyn Coppack on the abbey precincts of Rievaulx and Fountains in Yorkshire has distinguished inner and outer courts for specific activities, accessible to specific groups of people whose circulation was controlled by several inner and outer gate houses.[29] This complex spatial organisation was adapted to each abbey, as has been shown in other case studies.[30] The third consideration is that abbeys had to modify their buildings in response to constantly evolving factors which differed from abbey to abbey and resulted in a variety of architectural solutions. For example, the reduction or disappearance of the *conversi* from the mid thirteenth century led to the reuse of their buildings; the development of privacy from the fourteenth century resulted in the partition of common dormitories and infirmary halls into individual cubicles and later into separate rooms;[31] the size of some communities as well as their income was sometimes so dramatically reduced that whole buildings, including unused parts of churches, were demolished. Yet another consideration is that each abbey was the centre of a domain, sometimes tens of thousands of acres in extent, that developed a wide range of types of forestry as well as agro-pastoral and pre-industrial economies. Buildings were spread over the domain, organised in specialised units or granges, with barns, mills, stables and forges, and also urban cellars for selling goods at markets.[32]

The confrontation of the theoretical monastic 'model plan' with several hundred preserved or excavated abbeys does reveal some similarities, at least enough to allow us to recognise a 'family resemblance'. Once again, however, a huge gap between 'ideal and reality' becomes evident, all the more since the 'ideal' in question comes from nineteenth-century scholars rather than medieval monks. Since current archaeology not only brings walls to light and follows them in order to reveal plans – as in William St John Hope's time – but also analyses contexts, material traces and artefacts with the help of natural science, the reality is much more complex than the theory and may perhaps be more human than the ideal(s).

RESEARCH PERSPECTIVES

The current challenge to Cistercian studies – including architecture, which comprises the best material evidence – is to extend the scope of the enquiry by looking beyond medieval Cistercian life. This challenge implies multidisciplinary investigation combined with other historical sciences and methods. Three main research perspectives are beginning to broaden the field: Cistercian architecture after the Middle Ages, Cistercian women's houses and monasteries of other religious Orders.

Because the twelfth and thirteenth centuries are the most spectacular phase of Cistercian history, development and institutional unity, these centuries unfairly eclipse the rest of the Order's history, including the present. The changes in administration after 1335, attempts at reform in the fifteenth century, suppression of all abbeys in Protestant countries (England, Holland, Scandinavia, northern Germany) during the sixteenth century, systematic imposition of commendatory abbots, the Strict Observance reform in the seventeenth century, massive suppressions of abbeys during the French Revolution (France, Belgium, Germany, Italy) or under early nineteenth-century liberal governments (Portugal, Spain, Switzerland) and then monastic revival and world-wide expansion in the twentieth century are fascinating chapters of Western monastic history that also include architectural transformations. Some abbeys were destroyed; others received new architectural layers in the dominant style of the time: late Gothic (Figure 11.9), Renaissance, Baroque, Rococo, Classical, Gothic revival or modern. Where monastic life was abandoned, abbeys (or parts of them) were recycled as prisons, factories or mansions; other monastic ruins were restored and maintained, and sometimes abbeys were even refounded on old sites – though none of this is unique to the Cistercians. In any case, one might ask how Cistercians redefined their architectural identity and transformed their monasteries? Were the White Monks aware of architectural specificity or symbolism inherent in the buildings? From this point of view, the nineteenth century is a crucial period because architecture was not a major issue for the (Cistercian) Trappists. Only when scholars began to define medieval Cistercian architecture as a 'style' would modern Cistercians claim it as a part of their legacy.[33] From the early twentieth century, this 'rediscovered architectural identity' became a reference for foundations such as Orval (1926).

Because the female branch of the Cistercian Order was not part of the original project and did not develop significantly before the thirteenth century, its history was long ignored or neglected. Compared with the architecture of the men's abbeys, nunneries were often considered 'simple' and therefore less relevant, ignoring the conditions under which the women often struggled to achieve and maintain Cistercian identity in a male-dominated culture. Architectural and historical interest in women's houses is recent and still limited to the Middle Ages.[34] Pioneering archaeological work of Roberta Gilchrist on houses of religious women developed a gender approach to space, enclosure, architecture and other aspects of material culture, without positing a difference between Cistercian women and those of other Orders.[35] From an art historical point of view, recent work coordinated by Jeffrey Hamburger and Suzan Marti questions the relationship between objects and liturgical space in medieval women's monasteries.[36] In this regard, the exceptionally well-preserved medieval interiors of the Cistercian

Figure 11.9 Caduin (France), late medieval cloister gallery, photo: Thomas Coomans, © THOC-SOFAM.

nunneries of Wienhausen and Magerau provide fascinating evidence. Such approaches should be expanded to post-medieval times, especially the seventeenth-century Counter-Reformation and the monastic revival of the nineteenth century (Figure 11.10).

Only the combination of a diachronic approach to Cistercian architecture through the centuries and a synchronic approach which juxtaposes contemporaneous components of monasticism is able to reveal the variety and the identity of the Order's architecture. Therefore it would be more appropriate to speak about the architecture of the Cistercians than about Cistercian architecture. It is true that there seems to have been an architectural canon in the twelfth century, defined as *forma*

Figure 11.10 Herkenrode (Belgium), gate house of the nunnery (1531), photo: Thomas Coomans, © THOC-SOFAM.

Ordinis. Yet the idea that there was a 'Cistercian architecture' rests on the assumption that all Cistercian buildings had to follow a standardised programme with strict rules about style, whereas 'the architecture of the Cistercians' insists, more correctly, on the diverse and evolving architectural identity of the White Monks across more than nine centuries.

Notes

1 Fontenay (1981), Fountains (1986), Alcobaça (1989), Poblet (1991) and Maulbronn (1993).
2 E.E. Viollet-le-Duc, *Dictionnaire raisonné de l'architecture française du XIe au XVIe siècle*, 10 vols. (Paris, 1854–68).
3 E. Sharpe, *The Architecture of the Cistercians*, 2 vols. (London, 1874).
4 C. Enlart, *Origines françaises de l'architecture gothique en Italie* (Paris, 1894).
5 G. Dehio and G. von Bezold, *Kirchliche Baukunst des Abendlandes*, 2 vols. (Stuttgart, 1887–1901).
6 G. Coppack, *Book of Abbeys and Priories* (London, 1990), pp. 22–31.
7 Most Cistercian journals were begun by monks and supported by abbeys: *Cistercienser Chronik* 1889; *Collectanea Cisterciensia* 1934; *Analecta Cisterciensia* 1945; *Cistercium: Revista monastica cisterciense* 1948; *Cîteaux: Commentarii cistercienses* 1950; *Cistercian Studies Quarterly* 1966; *Rivista Cisterciense* 1984.
8 M. Aubert and A. de Maillé, *L'architecture cistercienne en France*, 2 vols. (Paris, 1943).

9   K.-H. Esser, 'Les fouilles à Himmerod et le plan bernardin', *Mélanges Saint Bernard* (Dijon, 1953), pp. 311–15; H.-P. Eydoux, 'Les fouilles de l'abbatiale d'Himmerod et la notion d'un plan bernardin', *Bulletin monumental*, 111 (1953), 29–36; H. Hahn, *Die frühe Kirchenbaukunst der Zisterzienser: Untersuchungen zur Baugeschichte von Kloster Eberbach im Rheingau und ihren europäischen Analogien im 12. Jahrhundert* (Berlin, 1957).

10 A. Dimier, *Recueil de plans d'églises cisterciennes*, 2 vols. (Grignan and Paris, 1949–67); A. Dimier, *L'art cistercien* (Saint-Léger-Vauban, 1962); A. Dimier, *L'art cistercien hors de France* (Saint-Léger-Vauban, 1971); G. Duby, *Saint Bernard: l'art cistercien* (Paris, 1976).

11 F. Pouillon, *Les pierres sauvages* (Paris, 1964); F. van der Meer, *Atlas de l'ordre cistercien* (Paris and Brussels, 1965); F. Cali, *L'ordre cistercien d'après les trois sœurs provençales, Sénanque, Silvacane, le Thoronet* (Paris, 1972).

12 K. Elm, P. Joerissen and H.J. Roth (eds.), *Die Zisterzienser: Ordensleben zwischen Ideal und Wirklichkeit*, 2 vols. (Cologne, 1980–2); L. Pressouyre and T. N. Kinder (eds.), *Saint Bernard et le monde cistercien* (Paris, 1990).

13 By Cistercian Publications (Kalamazoo, MI), 6 vols. (1982–2005), ed. M.P. Lillich.

14 C.A. Bruzelius, 'Cistercian High Gothic: The Abbey Church of Longpont and the Architecture of the Cistercians in the Early Thirteenth Century', *Analecta Cisterciensia*, 35 (1979), 3–204.

15 L. Pressouyre (ed.), *L'espace cistercien* (Paris, 1994).

16 L. Pressouyre and P. Benoit (eds.), *L'hydraulique monastique: milieu, réseaux, usages* (Paris, 1996).

17 C. Norton and D. Park (eds.), *Cistercian Art and Architecture in the British Isles* (Cambridge, 1986); P. Fergusson, *Architecture of Solitude: Cistercian Abbeys in Twelfth-Century England* (Princeton, NJ, 1984); R. Stalley, *Cistercian Monasteries of Ireland* (New Haven, CT and London, 1987); G. Coppack, *The White Monks: The Cistercians in Britain 1128–1540* (Stroud, 1998); G.G. Astill, 'The Bordesley Abbey Granges Project', in *L'espace cistercien*, ed. Pressouyre, pp. 537–53; D. Robinson, *The Cistercians in Wales: Architecture and Archaeology, 1130–1540* (London, 2005).

18 For example M. Plouvier and A. Saint-Denis (eds.), *Pour une histoire monumentale de l'abbaye de Cîteaux 1098–1998*, Cîteaux: Studia et Documenta 8 (Vitreux, 1998); G. Coppack, *Book of Fountains Abbey* (London, 1993); P. Fergusson and S. Harrison, *Rievaulx Abbey: Community, Architecture, Memory* (New Haven, CT and London, 1999); T. Coomans, *L'abbaye de Villers-en-Brabant: construction, configuration et signification d'une abbaye cistercienne gothique* (Brussels, 2000); C. Kratzke, *Das Zisterzienserkloster Dargun in Mecklenburg-Vorpommern: Studien zur Bau- und Kunstgeschichte* (Petersberg, 2004).

19 M. Hörsch, 'Tendenzen der Zisterzienser-Literatur der letzten zehn Jahre unter besonderer Berücksichtigung kunsthistorischer Studien zu den Ordensklöstern in Mitteleuropa', *Cîteaux*, 58 (2007), 131–70.

20 T.N. Kinder, *Cistercian Europe: Architecture of Contemplation* (Grand Rapids, MI, 2002); M. Untermann, *Forma Ordinis: Die mittelalterliche Baukunst der Zisterzienser* (Munich and Berlin, 2001).

21 M. Cassidy-Welch, *Monastic Spaces and Their Meanings: Thirteenth-Century English Cistercian Monasteries* (Turnhout, 2001).

22 C. Norton, 'Table of Cistercian Legislation on Art and Architecture', in *Cistercian Art and Architecture in the British Isles*, ed. Norton and Park, pp. 315–93.

23 Paris, B. N., MS fr. 19093, fol. 14v: 'vesci une glize desquarie ki fu esgardee a faire en lordene de cistiaus'.

24 This dating has been contested recently. The church seems to have been completed in the 1160s, after Bernard's death; S. Harrison, 'Dating the Abbey Church of Fontenay: A Reassessment of the Evidence', *Cîteaux*, 61 (2010), 99–124.

25 S. Gasser, 'Die Zisterzienserinnenkirche in der Magerau: Retrospektive Architektur als Trägerin ordenspolitischer Intentionen', *Zeitschrift für Schweizerische Archäologie und Kunstgeschichte*, 54 (2001), 259–66.

26 J. Hall and C. Kratzke (eds.), *Sepulturae cistercienses: Burial, Memorial and Patronage in Medieval Cistercian Monasteries*, thematic issue of *Cîteaux*, 56 (2005).

27 Untermann, *Forma Ordinis*.

28 Choisselet/Vernet.

29 Coppack, *Book of Fountains Abbey*, pp. 81–128.

30 Coomans, *L'abbaye de Villers-en-Brabant*, pp. 431–542.

31 D.N. Bell, 'Chambers, Cells, and Cubicles: The Cistercian General Chapter and the Development of the Private Room', in *Perspectives for an Architecture of Solitude: Essays on Cistercians, Art and Architecture in Honour of Peter Fergusson*, ed. T.N. Kinder (Turnhout, 2004), pp. 187–98.

32 F. Blary, *Le domaine de Chaalis, approches archéologiques des établissements agricoles et industriels d'une abbaye cistercienne* (Paris, 1989).

33 T. Coomans, 'La ricerca di una nuova identità nell'architettura cisterciense del XIX secolo', in *Arte Cisterciense*, ed. T.N. Kinder and R. Cassanelli (Milan, in press).

34 For example, M.P. Lillich (ed.), *Cistercian Nuns and Their World*, Studies in Cistercian Art and Architecture 6 (Kalamazoo, MI, 2005).

35 R. Gilchrist, *Gender and Material Culture: The Archaeology of Religious Women* (London, 1994).

36 J.F. Hamburger and S. Marti (eds.), *Crown and Veil: The Art of Female Monasticism in the Middle Ages* (Columbia, NY, 2008).

Part III

Religious mentality

12 Bernard of Clairvaux: his first and greatest miracle was himself

CHRISTOPHER HOLDSWORTH

The earliest surviving reaction to the news of Bernard's death on 20 August 1153 was written by Gilbert Foliot, bishop of Hereford, who had met Bernard in northern France, during 1147 and 1148. He wrote to congratulate a friend, William de Hinet, who had recently joined Bernard's Order, and possibly even his own monastery, and then to sympathise with him on Bernard's death and to praise the qualities of the dead man. He began those praises by expressing his inability for the task, using the rhetorical device of *praeteritio* (literally: a passing over): 'O who am I that I might worthily commemorate that holy pastor and that most famous and fecund abbey of Clairvaux?' and then doing just that.[1]

One sentence reflects the impression that Bernard, then in his late forties and already, by that day's standards, an old man, had made on him. 'He was a man horrible with filthiness, whose shrivelled flesh stuck everywhere to his bones, whose body never tasted too much wine, nor mouth any delicacies save for spiritual ones.' Yet although he looked so appalling, he was 'celebrated for his knowledge. Most well-known for holiness, most holy without deceit, a famous writer, eminent preacher, the mirror of his order, and enlarger of the church.'[2] That shrunken figure was produced largely by having strained his physical resources by long periods at prayer, often at night. As early as 1119 his physical condition was such that his fellow abbots allowed the bishop William of Champeaux to take him away from the monastery for twelve months to convalesce.[3] Another picture of Bernard at an earlier stage of his life, by Geoffrey of Auxerre, who had first met Bernard in 1140, scarcely hints at how Bernard was ageing, except when he wrote 'his body was very thin, and he seemed gaunt'.[4]

Appearance was not, however, how popes measured holiness: rather they looked for more concrete evidence. So Alexander III in 1174, as he informed the archbishops and bishops and abbots 'in the French kingdom' that he had discerned Bernard to be a saint, mentioned three sides of his life which he had considered:

How supported by tokens of special grace he shone forth not only in sanctity and way of life ... in the whole church of God through the light of his faith and teaching ... that he had transferred the institutions of a holy way of life as far as the furthest parts and barbarous peoples ... that he had supported the most holy church of Rome ... when it suffered, through his virtuous life ... and through his divinely bestowed wisdom.[5]

Such words bring us nearer to what Bernard had done so here we will first consider Bernard as a Cistercian, then look at his work for the Church in the wider world and lastly at what the pope may have included among 'those tokens of special grace' (*singularis gratiae praerogativa*).

BERNARD THE CISTERCIAN

When Bernard met Foliot, he had been a Cistercian for over thirty years, having entered Cîteaux in 1113, when he was probably twenty-three years old. Two years later, the abbot, Stephen Harding, chose him as abbot for a new foundation at Clairvaux, placed close to the borders of Champagne and Burgundy, some 100 km to the north of Cîteaux, a position he held until his death.[6]

Bernard was born into a noble family at their castle at Fontaines, now within the suburbs of Dijon in Burgundy. He, the third of six brothers, was probably destined for an ecclesiastical career since he would have stood little chance of inheriting sufficient land to support himself in secular society. He was sent for schooling to Châtillon-sur-Seine, where his family had property, and where the teaching must have been good, judging from the quality of Bernard's writings. Following his mother's death, he underwent a conversion experience towards the monastic life, which seems to have been connected with the fact that he was aware of his attractiveness to women, and of theirs to him, which could have made a Church career difficult, since by then marriage and the priest-hood were coming to be held incompatible. He chose to join the recently founded monastery at Cîteaux, known for its poverty and strenuous attempt to follow the old monastic Rule of Benedict, rather than join other members of his family in an older house, like Saint-Bénigne in Dijon. Some years later Bernard explained that his choice reflected his sense of needing 'stronger medicine' than was available elsewhere.[7] It was, however, typical that he persuaded all of his brothers, bar the youngest, an uncle, a cousin and numerous friends to become monks with him, around thirty men in all. Cîteaux was only just beginning to attract recruits, and so becoming capable of establishing new monasteries attached to itself. Bernard's conviction that the Cistercian way was best emerges in a letter he sent to a bishop of Lincoln after one of his canons had set off for Jerusalem, but had found when he visited Clairvaux that he could go no further, since Clairvaux had become for him the real Jerusalem, where he would stay for ever.[8] It was this kind of 'discovery' which drew men from many parts of the Latin West into this new monastery.

When Bernard died, Clairvaux had around 200 monks and 500 lay brothers, while its archives contained nearly 900 statements of profession made by novices there, which had enabled it to establish over 60 or so foundations of its own, from Portugal to Denmark and Sweden, or from Scotland and Ireland to southern France and central Italy.[9] Over a third of them were not new monasteries, but rather, to use a modern term, take-overs, of communities of monks, canons or hermits. In such places a small group would be sufficient, who, once they had passed on Cistercian customs, might be able to return home. Even so, to staff 39 new houses over 500 monks would have to have been recruited at Clairvaux: say, on average, around a recruit for every month of Bernard's abbacy. There is clear evidence too that Clairvaux had grown so large that it was forced to move to a more spacious site with larger buildings during the 1130s.[10] In 1130, as Bernard's work beyond Clairvaux was growing rapidly, there were in all thirty-nine Cistercian monasteries, of which the mother house, Cîteaux, had the largest family, twelve, followed by Clairvaux and Morimond (both founded in 1115), with eight each. Twenty-three years later at Bernard's death, the total was about 340 houses, of which almost half, 160, were in Clairvaux's family, while Cîteaux, the earliest monastery, had 57, and Morimond, 87.[11]

Clairvaux differed from other Cistercian houses in two, related respects: that Bernard was its abbot, and that he led a community which included many of his relations. Bernard's absences grew sharply in the 1130s, as he dealt with problems which he claimed he had been 'dragged into', but that, of course, made him known to a wide range of potential founders and supporters, as well as potential monks and lay brothers.[12] That Clairvaux contained for some years a significant number of his relatives affected how the community worked, as we shall see.

BERNARD BEYOND CLAIRVAUX

Writing diaries was not a typical activity in the twelfth century, but there is one period, the three months between November 1146 and

February 1147, when some of Bernard's companions kept such records as they journeyed with him in the empire and north-eastern France to preach the crusade.[13] One may calculate that from 1130 until his death he was away from Clairvaux for at least a third of the time, a significant proportion when one considers the weight of responsibility that the Rule places upon an abbot's shoulders. His letters, more than any of his other writings, show that he felt torn by these absences and lamented the nets of obedience (*oboedientiae retibus*), which we, in a more sociological mode, might call networks, that drew him away from the quiet of his monastery into the cities.[14] At Clairvaux stories were recorded showing how some of the community tried to reassure themselves about his continuing care for them during his absences, expressed in the form of 'visions' in which he was 'seen' present in choir, or while monks were engaged in other tasks.[15] Bernard himself described how he felt while away from home, in various ways, of which the most poignant comes from around 1150 when he called himself 'a sort of modern chimaera, neither cleric nor layman', who 'had kept the habit of a monk, but ... long ago abandoned the life'.[16] The chimaera was to him monstrous because it combined parts of distinct species, and over twenty years earlier in what is now his best known work, his *Apology*, he railed against those monasteries whose cloisters contained carvings of such unnatural animals. Such 'ridiculous monstrosities', he claimed, had no place within parts of a monastery only used by monks: now he lamented that he had become just such a one himself.[17] The point was not lost upon some of his contemporaries, most interestingly Peter Abelard, master of the cathedral school in Paris, who fiercely attacked abbots who busied themselves by attending councils and synods and interfering in business which did not directly concern them.[18] One could spend much time understanding the relations between these two extraordinary men, here I can only observe, as Michael Clanchy did in his great book on Abelard, that they were much more like one another than it was comfortable for either to recognise.[19] Once Bernard attacked Abelard as someone who retained only the habit to show that he was a monk – the very criticism which he applied to himself.[20]

The event which pulled Bernard out of Clairvaux and launched him into the wider world was the schism which broke out following the death in Rome of Honorius II on 13 (or 14) February 1130.[21] The cardinals divided over the merits of two candidates, Gregory cardinal priest of Sant'Angelo and Peter cardinal priest of Santa Maria in Trastevere, who on election took the names of Innocent and Anacletus, being second popes with those names. Neither party was strong enough to oust the other, largely because neither could persuade all the significant rulers in the West to support them. Broadly speaking, Italy, particularly Sicily, remained faithful to Anacletus, while most of Europe north of the Alps came into Innocent's camp, creating a division which lasted eight years, the longest schism in the Latin Church until the so-called Great Schism of the later Middle Ages. Bernard was drawn into Innocent's party through his friendship going back some years with the Burgundian Haimeric, Innocent's campaign manager and chancellor. So in 1131 and 1132 Bernard spent months travelling with Innocent in northern France and the empire, and went to Italy to be with him in 1133, 1135 and, lastly, 1137 and 1138, when he was away continuously for about eighteen months. But why, one must ask, did Innocent want to have Bernard with him?

Fundamentally Innocent wanted him because he was already such a persuasive speaker and writer. His rhetorical skills enabled Bernard to build what the pope hailed in a privilege he awarded to the abbot and his monastery as early as 1132 as 'an impregnable wall around the Church'.[22] Although those who wrote the so-called *Vita Prima* (*First Life*, so called to distinguish it from later lives) may have overemphasised just what he achieved for Innocent, there can be little doubt that his contribution was significant, but even so, there were others who aided Innocent considerably, among whom Norbert of Xanten and Peter the Venerable stand out. The former, founder of a successful Order of canons centred upon the northern French monastery of Prémontré, ended his career as archbishop of Magdeburg, and became close to the ruler of Germany. Innocent hailed him with the same 'wall' metaphor, a year after he had used it for Bernard. Peter, abbot of the great monastery of Cluny, possessed a large family of monasteries spread wide over the West, and he plumped for Innocent as soon as he heard the news of the schism. The *Vita Prima* also claimed that Bernard's oratory tipped the scales of opinion in favour of Innocent at a council summoned by Louis VI at Étampes, yet an overlooked letter from Louis to cardinals in Rome makes it clear he had decided for Innocent before he summoned the Council, and planned for it to merely confirm his decision.[23] When Bernard visited Italy in 1135, he was sent by Innocent to Milan and other former strongholds of Anacletus, to reconcile them with Innocent, a process which included spectacular exorcisms believed to drive out the devil.[24] When the schism ended in 1138, Bernard never again left Clairvaux for such long periods, but there were many calls for his intervention, of which the most significant was his preaching of the Second Crusade, already mentioned.

Two things happened to Bernard during the years he worked in the public eye: he became known for his skill as a peacemaker between factions in and around a number of cities, and he was offered election to two archbishoprics and at least two bishoprics. These are worth brief consideration.

The cities involved were Milan (1135), Reims (1139), Metz (1153) and Langres (?), and in all of them his success as peacemaker was assisted by his healing powers, which at Milan and Langres was linked with encouragement which came to him through dreams.[25] Geoffrey gives a long account of events at Metz during Bernard's last spring, when the dying abbot responded to a heartfelt appeal from the archbishop of Trier, who had travelled to Clairvaux and prostrated himself before Bernard to emphasise the need for his help.

The places where he was offered promotion were Milan (1135) and Reims (1139–40), both archbishoprics, and certainly two bishoprics, Châlons-sur-Marne (1131–9), Langres (1138) and possibly Genoa (1130). He refused all these opportunities, arguing, in words originally used by Jesus, 'That he came not to be served, but to serve' (Mark 10.45).[26] The second author of the *Vita Prima* makes it clear that Bernard's own community did not wish to lose him, and got some assurance from Innocent II that he would not press Bernard to leave. William of Saint Thierry, on the other hand, comments that Bernard could never be persuaded to do anything against his will.[27] How successful a bishop he might have been cannot be known, but one might expect that without the regular presence of his own brothers, he might have become isolated and remote. Monastic life probably suited him better, and fortunately for him and the wider Church, there, despite his absences, he stayed.

BERNARD AND MIRACLES

Now we turn to an aspect of Bernard's activity to which most modern scholars have paid little attention, namely his numerous miracles, which, then, for many people, indicated that he had a close relationship with God. When Alexander III, as we have already seen, claimed in 1174 that Bernard's life had been 'supported by tokens of special grace', it seems likely that he would have included miracles among them, since by then popes were stressing that miracles were a necessary qualification for sanctification. Now we must consider the evidence about them in the *Vita Prima*.

This was the work of three men, all of whom had known Bernard. William of Saint Thierry met Bernard around 1119 when himself a

Benedictine, remaining in touch with Bernard until his own death in 1148. He concentrated on Bernard as monk, mainly on his home ground. Ernald of Bonneval, a Benedictine house in the diocese of Chartres, possibly chosen because he knew well two of those who had been close to Bernard in the 1130s, Geoffrey, bishop of Chartres, and Theobald, count of Blois, focused on Bernard away from Clairvaux during the Anacletan schism.[28] The last three books were written by Geoffrey of Auxerre, who became Bernard's secretary soon after he had left the schools in Paris in 1140. He seems to have initiated the writing of the Life, since he wrote notes about Bernard's life up to 1145 which both William and Geoffrey used. The five books were largely written while Bernard was alive, and probably finished by 1155–6, within three years after Bernard's death.

But what counted as a miracle for Bernard and for those who wrote about him? He himself provides evidence in his Life of the Irish bishop Malachy, who died at Clairvaux in 1148, written not long before his own death. Bernard lists six different kinds of 'ancient' miracles which Malachy had performed: prophecy, revelations (by which he meant meaningful night dreams and waking ones), revenge on the ungodly, healing, changing people's minds and raising the dead.[29] He also wrote that 'these are not the times for signs' because there were no prophets, and rejoiced that Malachy was 'so rich in signs'. Gerhoh of Reichersberg, a German Augustinian canon, writing in 1148, attacked fraudulent miracle-workers, but excepted Bernard, and him alone, from that category, praising his thundering sermons and sparkling miracles.[30] Sixteen years later, about ten years after Bernard's death, John of Salisbury expressed himself somewhat sceptically: 'he was a man mighty in deed and word with God, so some would believe, and with men as we all know'.[31]

How large a part do signs or miracles, these general terms are used interchangeably, play in the *Vita Prima*? The surprising answer is that they occur on nearly every page, and although many accounts are quite short, others, particularly in Ernald's book, last for several pages. Even so, the modern scholarly world paid this substantial evidence little attention, until a Canadian Trappist, André Picard, published his master's thesis from the University of Montréal in 1991. By coincidence, I published my own, much slighter, essay in 1990, the year he presented his thesis, each of us ignorant of the other's work.[32] Since then, Picard and his former supervisor, Pierre Boglioni, published a joint article in 1993, and I another in 2006.[33] Both of us tried to understand the extent and chronology of miracles in the *Vita Prima* and to assess how Bernard saw this side of his life, and how others saw it. The fact that no response has, as far as I know, been published probably indicates the influence of views expressed by two scholars now dead who dominated Bernardine studies since the 1950s, namely Dom Jean Leclercq and Professor Adriaan Bredero. The former never discussed the miracles in his voluminous writings, while the other analysed those who recorded the miracles, rather than the meaning of the miracles themselves, which he dismissed as part of the traditions found in hagiographical writings.[34] The *Vita Prima* contains 337 miraculous events (of which two-thirds are various kinds of healing), increased to 840 when other contemporary sources are included.[35] Such a number is far larger than those attributed to well-known contemporaries of Bernard's, Anselm of Canterbury and Norbert of Magdeburg.[36]

Twenty years ago, I thought I could distinguish in the *Vita Prima*, particularly in the early parts of William's book, episodes concerning Bernard's own growth and development, from others which reassured his community that he was capable of fulfilling his responsibilities as abbot.[37] For example, when Bernard joined the monks harvesting, he found it hard to wield his scythe, something that as a young noble, he would not have been expected to learn, just like Levin in Tolstoy's *Anna Karenina*. He was ordered to sit down and rest, and then prayed that God might help him. When he rejoined the labouring monks, he found that now he could work quite easily, and one can suppose that just by watching them he had found what to do.[38] The other group can be illustrated with the occasion when his brother Gerard complained that he had no money to meet various pressing needs. Then Bernard reassured him, went off to pray, and almost immediately someone arrived with just the sum of money required.[39] Now I find the distinctions not so clear, since in both the examples, both Bernard and the community could have been affected. Knowing that he could work effectively on the farm could encourage the community, and knowing that his prayer could have such quick effect could have encouraged Bernard.

Much more significant to his work as abbot was giving sermons and hearing confessions, both duties which William explains Bernard found extremely difficult, while to his monks his sermons were unintelligible, and his advice to penitents unsympathetic.[40] Here William makes clear that he felt he was portraying an imperfect abbot, indeed these apparent failures in Bernard's holiness become an integral part of it, something which Bredero, I suspect, would have found shocking.[41] Part of the trouble seems to have been that Bernard had formed a low view of the monks, especially because of their moral failures, those 'fragilities of the human condition and ... the temptations and filthiness of such thoughts'.⁴² But as he realised that his community, which included many older than he, was trying to take his sermons and directions seriously, he was, as it were, opened up to a new approach, after he had experienced a period when he felt that his monks would do better to meditate in silence than listen to him, and wished that he was not obliged to preach regularly. That new direction appeared one night in a vision, when he saw a young man standing beside him, who told him 'with great authority' that he should speak faithfully whatever came to him, since it was not he who would speak, but the Holy Spirit (Matt. 10.20). After this Bernard's sermons changed,

> the Holy Spirit spoke more clearly in him, through his mouth came more eloquent words and more abundant thoughts on the Bible, and grace (gave) him more credit and power with his hearers, and a more wholesome understanding of the poor and needy, and of the repentant sinner who demands forgiveness.⁴³

It was apparently after this that there is evidence that some of Bernard's relatives began to belittle his healing powers.⁴⁴ This first happened when his uncle Gaudry and younger brother Gerard accompanied Bernard, who had been summoned by the family of the local landowner, Josbert de la Ferté, who could not speak and appeared to be dying; they feared that if he died without making a full confession, his eternal destiny would be jeopardised. Bernard promised that if his family returned all the property which he had taken from the Church and from the poor, Josbert would be able to speak and make a confession. Everyone who heard Bernard's promise, but particularly Gaudry and Gerard, were horrified because they had no experience of how much grace God had given him. Indeed the *Vita* goes on to recount how his relatives, now named as Gaudry and brother Gui, belittled all the good things that Bernard had done, denying that he had done any miracles, and hurt Bernard so much that he wept. They seem to have been worried about his youth and short experience as a monk. The sequel, some years later, shows Bernard with a sense of humour. Uncle Gaudry fell ill with a fever and, in distress, asked his nephew to do as he had done for others and heal him. Bernard then reminded him of the disparaging remarks he had made years before, and it was only after some time that he agreed to lay his hand upon him, and the fever disappeared.⁴⁵

Much later, in the summer of 1145, when Bernard was travelling with bishop Geoffrey of Chartres in Aquitaine to combat the heretical teaching of Peter de Bruys and his pupil Henry, Bernard talked about his own miracles with some of his monks who were with him in a way that he had never done before:

> I ask myself with deep astonishment what these miracles mean, and why God has found it good to do such things and through such a person. I think I have never read in the pages of Holy Scripture about this type of signs. In truth, signs have sometimes been done by holy and perfect men [*per sanctos homines et perfectos*] and sometimes also by impostors [*et facta sunt per fictos*]. I know that I am not perfect, nor an imposter [*Ego mihi non perfectionis conscius sum, nec fictionis*]. I know that I do not possess the merits of saints who were lit up by miracles, and am confident that I do not belong to that class of men who do many good things in the name of the Lord, 'and yet are not known by him' [Matt. 7.23].[46]

Here one may deduce that he had become more cautious over the years, since his uncle and brother had been worried about him becoming over-confident, even though so many signs had, according to authors of the *Vita Prima*, been done by him. Geoffrey went on to say that he often talked in private about such matters with 'spiritual men', and included a passage of equal length to the one just considered, when Bernard developed similar ideas not long before he died.[47] There he stressed that the marvels which had occurred were not done to magnify his own attainments, or to suggest that he was more holy than others, but rather to help others to have more love and zeal for holiness, ending that his miracles happened 'not to commend me, but to warn others'.

CONCLUSION

This attempt to give some impression of the life of a very active person, many of whose acts were recorded during his lifetime, or soon afterwards, has, inevitably, omitted a number of sides of his life which were important for him, and which affected many of Bernard's contemporaries. Concentration on three aspects, his work as a monk, his work in wider society and his miracles, has left a great deal unsaid: for example the links which enabled him to found monasteries over much of Western Europe, or how he appealed for men to fight in Palestine and how he felt when the Second Crusade failed. But all this is but to draw attention to the obvious: Bernard was an extraordinary man who affected many different sorts of people. Thanks to his travels, he was actually seen by more individuals than anyone else, and while many only glimpsed him at a distance, during a great service in a church, or passing him closer on the road, others, like Gilbert Foliot, saw his face clearly or noticed how he held or touched a sick person. The abbot, leader of a large community, healer of wounds in the Church or wider society, was also a man whose lesser and mighty acts of healing, and other signs of another world impending on our own, must have left many impressions. And it was the combination he had found between caring for his community and the wider world that left many feeling that he was a special person. One can understand to some degree why Geoffrey chose to apply to Bernard a phrase which Bernard had coined for Malachy: 'In addition', as he commended Malachy, 'the first and greatest miracle that he did, to my judgement, was himself.'[48]

Notes

1 *Ep* 108; ed. A. Morey and C.N.L. Brooke, *The Letters and Charters of Gilbert Foliot* (Cambridge, 1967), pp. 146–9.

2 Compare Foliot's address to Bernard in *Ep* 72 of c. 1147–8, 'Adiutori Domini fidelissimo', 'most faithful helper of the Lord'; *Letters and Charters*, p. 106.

3 C. Holdsworth, 'The Early Writings of Bernard of Clairvaux', *Cîteaux*, 45 (1994), 21–60 (pp. 36–9, 58 for the date).

4 J. France, *Medieval Images of Saint Bernard of Clairvaux*, CS 210 (Kalamazoo, MI, 2007), p. 2, citing *Vita Prima* iii.3.1; *PL* 185:303.

5 A.H. Bredero, 'St Bernard and the Historians', in *Saint Bernard of Clairvaux: Studies Commemorating the Eighth Centenary of His Canonization*, ed. M.B. Pennington, CS 28 (Kalamazoo, MI, 1977), pp. 27–62; quotation from appendix, *Saint Bernard of Clairvaux*, pp. 269–71, followed by three other translated privileges of same date.

6 This paragraph and the next follow L.J. Lekai, *The Cistercians: Ideal and Reality* (Kent, OH, 1989), pp. 33–4.

7 *Apo* iv.7; ed. M.B. Pennington, *The Works of Bernard of Clairvaux: Treatises*, vol. i, CF 1 (Shannon, 1970), p. 42 has 'remedy'.

8 *Ep* 67; *The Letters of St Bernard of Clairvaux*, intro. B.M. Kienzle, trans. B. Scott James (Stroud and Kalamazoo, MI, 1998), pp. 90–2.

9 A.H. Bredero, 'Un brouillon du XIIe siècle: l'autographe de Geoffrey d'Auxerre', *Scriptorium*, 13 (1959), 27–60 (p. 44).

10 T.N. Kinder, 'Les églises médiévales de Clairvaux: probabilités et fiction', in *Histoire de Clairvaux: actes du colloque*, ed. J.F. Leroux (Bar-sur-Aube, 1992), pp. 205–29 (pp. 209–10).

11 R. Locatelli, 'L'expansion de l'ordre cistercien', in *Bernard de Clairvaux, histoire, mentalités, spiritualité*, ed. D. Bertrand and G. Lobrichon, SCh 380 (Paris, 1992), pp. 103–40.

12 *Ep* 51.2 and *Ep* 146.4; *Letters*, pp. 80 and 215.

13 The *Historia miraculorum in itinere Germanico patratorum*; *PL* 185:373–410.

14   *Ep* 22; *Letters*, p. 55, dated end 1127–beginning 1128.

15   *VP* IV.1.3; *PL* 185:323, *Ep* 143; *Letters*, pp. 212–13, *VP* II.5.28; *PL* 185:284.

16   *Ep* 326.4; *Letters*, p. 402.

17   *Apo* XII.29; *Treatises*, vol. I, p. 66.

18   M.T. Clanchy, *Abelard, a Medieval Life* (Oxford, 1997), p. 244. See also Wim Verbaal's chapter in this volume.

19   Clanchy, *Abelard*, p. 9.

20   *Ep* 241; *Letters*, p. 321.

21   C. Morris, *The Papal Monarchy: The Western Church from 1050 to 1250* (Oxford, 1989), pp. 182–8.

22   P. Dinzelbacher, *Bernhard von Clairvaux: Leben und Werk des berühmten Zisterziensers* (Darmstadt, 1998), pp. 148–9.

23   T. Reuter, 'Zur Annerkennung Papst Innocenz II', *Deutsches Archiv für Erforschung des Mittelalters*, 39 (1983), 395–416.

24   C. Holdsworth, 'Saint Bernard: What Kind of Saint?', in *Monastic Studies: The Continuity of Tradition*, ed. J. Loades (Bangor, 1990), pp. 86–101 (pp. 94–6); A. Picard, *La thaumaturgie de Bernard de Clairvaux d'après les 'Vitae'* (Montréal, 1991), pp. 100–7.

25   *VP* II.2–4.8–24; *PL* 185:273–83; Landulfo de S. Paulo, *Historia Mediolanensis*, ed. I. Bethmann and P. Jaffé, MGH SS 20 (Hannover, 1868), pp. 46–7; *VP* I.14.67; *PL* 185:264; *VP* v.1.3–6; *PL* 185:352–5; *VP* IV.8.46; *PL* 185:348. The date of the Langres episode is not clear.

26   Two lists of offers: *VP* I.14.69; *PL* 185:265 and II.4.26; *PL* 185:283; F. Gastaldelli, 'Le piu antiche testimonianze biografiche su san Bernardo', *Analecta Cisterciensia*, 44 (1989), 3–80 (pp. 26–9). For words from Mark, *VP* II.4.27; *PL* 185:283.

27   *VP* I.14.69; *PL* 185:265.

28   About Ernald's status: A.H. Bredero, *Études sur la 'Vita Prima' de Saint Bernard* (Rome, 1960), pp. 109–12; D. Farkasfalvy, 'The Authenticity of Saint Bernard's Letter from His Deathbed', *ASOC*, 36 (1980), 263–8.

29   *V Mal*; trans. R.T. Meyer, *Bernard of Clairvaux: The Life and Death of Saint Malachy the Irishman*, CF 10 (Kalamazoo, MI, 1978), paragraphs 66, 84.

30   'Praedicantibus contonantibus et miraculis nonnullis coruscantibus', *In Ps. XXXIX*, MGH, *Libelli de Lite Imperatorum et Pontificium*, 3 vols., ed. E. Bernheim *et al.* (Berlin, 1892–7), vol. III, p. 436.

31   *John of Salisbury: Historia Pontificalis*, ed. M. Chibnall (London, 1956), pp. 20 and xxiv–xxx.

32   Holdsworth, 'Saint Bernard: What Kind of Saint?'.

33   A. Picard and P. Boglioni, 'Miracle et thaumaturgie dans la vie de saint Bernard', in *Vies et légendes de saint Bernard de Clairvaux: création, diffusion, réception (XIIe–XXe siècles)*, ed. P. Arabeyre *et al.* (Brecht and Cîteaux, 1993), pp. 36–59; C. Holdsworth, 'Reading the Signs, Bernard of Clairvaux and His Miracles', in *Writing Medieval Biography 750–1250: Essays in Honour of Professor Frank Barlow*, ed. D. Bates *et al.* (Woodbridge, 2006), pp. 161–72.

34 J. Leclercq, *Nouveau visage de Bernard de Clairvaux* (Paris, 1976), pp. 11–34; *VP* I reveals more about the author than Bernard: Bredero, *Études sur la 'Vita Prima'*, pp. 73, 104, 142–4 and 151.
35 Picard and Boglioni, 'Miracle et thaumaturgie', pp. 41–2.
36 Holdsworth, 'Reading the Signs', pp. 164–5.
37 Holdsworth, 'What kind of Saint?', pp. 90–91.
38 *VP* 1.4.24; *PL* 185:240.
39 *VP* 1.6.27; *PL* 185:242.
40 *VP* 1.6.28–9; *PL* 185:243–4.
41 A. Piazzoni, 'Le premier biographie de saint Bernard: Guillaume de Saint-Thierry. Le premier partie de la *Vita Prima*, comme œuvre théologique et spirituelle', in *Vies et légendes*, ed. Arabeyre *et al.*, pp. 4–18.
42 *VP* 1.6.28; *PL* 185:243.
43 *VP* 1.6.29; *PL* 185:244.
44 *VP* 1.9.43 and 45; *PL* 185:252–3.
45 *VP* 1.10.46; *PL* 185:253–4.
46 *VP* III.7.20; *PL* 185:314–15; for Bernard's typical play with *perfectos* and *per fictos*, see C.S. Jaeger, *The Envy of Angels: Cathedral Schools and Social Ideas in Medieval Europe 950–1200* (Philadelphia, PA, 1994), p. 276.
47 *VP* III.7.20; *PL* 185:315.
48 *VP* III.1.1; *PL* 185:303; *Life of Malachy*, paragraph 43.

Primary sources

Vita Prima; PL 185:225–368; references are to this version. It can be accessed without charge at www.binetii.ru/bernardus. A modern scholarly version, including the *Fragmenta Gaufridi*, has been published in *Guillelmi a sancto Theodorico Opera Omnia* VI, ed. P. Verdeyen and C. Vande Veire, CCCM 89 (Turnhout, 2011)

Book I; trans. M. Cawley, *Bernard of Clairvaux: Early Biographies*, vol. I, *William of Saint Thierry* (Lafayette, OR, 2000)

Excerpts, mainly from *Book I*; trans. P. Matarasso, *The Cistercian World: Monastic Writings of the Twelfth Century* (London, 1993), pp. 15–41

Bernard's letters have been published in SBOp 7 and 8. Notes there are fairly sparse, and much more information is in the Italian edition, *Opere di san Bernardo*, ed. F. Gastaldelli, vols. VI.I and VI.I.II (Milan, 1986–7). Those notes are translated en bloc in the German edition, *Bernhard von Clairvaux: Sämtliche Werke*, ed. G.B. Winkler, vols. II and III (Innsbruck, 1992)

The Letters of St Bernard of Clairvaux, intro. B.M. Kienzle, trans. B. Scott James (Stroud and Kalamazoo, MI, 1998; orig. pub. 1953); my references are to the 1998 edition.

13 Bernard of Clairvaux: work and self

M.B. PRANGER

LIFE AND WORK

There is no doubt that Bernard of Clairvaux (1090–1153) is the most famous Cistercian, so much so that he is often mistakenly considered to be the Order's founder. It is Bernard who expanded the modest beginnings of the Order under Robert of Molesme (1098) into universal fame. After a brief spell in the monastery of Cîteaux, Bernard moved to Clairvaux in Champagne, whence he organised and supervised, in the shape of an amalgam of intra- and extramural activities, both his own life and the life of the Cistercian Order.[1] In themselves those activities amount to an ecclesiastic-political career that, in theory, does not betray any need of monastic underpinnings. Thus Bernard's (in)famous interventions in the world of (Church) politics such as his manoeuvrings on behalf of Innocent II during the papal schism of 1130, his meddling in the theological controversy surrounding Abelard at the Council of Sens in 1140 and his preaching of the Second Crusade in 1147 could all have been the work of any politically minded cleric whosoever. His activist behaviour certainly does not seem to owe anything to a particular brand of Cistercian spirituality. At the same time, ever since founding Clairvaux Bernard held but one position: the abbacy of his monastery. Whether attending to his duties as an abbot inside that monastery or hitting the road on Church business, he acted on the assumption that his authority did not exceed the limits of his profession, even though, unsurprisingly, his opponents took a different view on this claim. As such there was nothing abnormal about an abbot reaching out beyond the walls of his monastery in matters political and ecclesiastical. In the case of the freshly established Cistercian Order, however, with its ambition of return to the letter of the Benedictine Rule – that is, to poverty, withdrawal and *stabilitas loci* – things looked different. In fact, no one was more vociferous than Bernard in denouncing monastic exhibitionism both intra- and extramurally. In criticising the splendour of Cluny (as well as the political and architectural power play of the abbot of Saint-Denis, Suger) Bernard has drawn a line in the sand separating the politics-prone existence of prelates and bishops from 'us' monks 'who have withdrawn from the people, we who have left behind all that is precious and beautiful in this world for the sake of Christ'.[2]

As Bernard has left us an extensive literary oeuvre, it would be interesting to know to what extent this life hovering between monastic contemplation and extramural activities is reflected in his work. As a matter of fact, in describing, in this chapter, Bernard's writings, I shall focus on this particular aspect. Before doing so, let me first take a look at the nature and scope of his literary production. Taking pride of place are the *Sermones super Cantica canticorum*, the Sermons on the Song of Songs, a work that has been highly influential in the history of Western Christian devotion. This *chef d'oeuvre* is supplemented by a vast body of sermons. Thus we have sermons following the rhythm of the liturgical year from Christmas to Ascension, sermons on feast days of saints and on a variety of incidental subjects. Next there are the treatises, some of which have become highly popular: on the Benedictine theme of the degrees of pride and humility, on love, on grace and free will, the so-called *Apologia*, a diatribe against the luxurious excesses of Cluny. Another work that has become immensely popular is *De consideratione*, dedicated to Bernard's pupil-become-pope, Eugenius III. Designed as a handbook for papal behaviour, both spiritual and political, it deals with topics ranging from practical instructions to the pope to mystical contemplation. Finally, there is a collection of parables and an extensive letter collection dealing with a variety of topics, most famously the controversy between Bernard and Abelard.

LITERARY REPUTATION

Paradoxically, Bernard's reputation as an ecclesiastical power broker and as a devout mystic has got in the way of his being appreciated as a writer. Admittedly, the epithet *mellifluus* (honey-dropping) testifies to his eloquence. In addition to Bernard's political reputation, it was on the intensity and the personal touch of his devotion, however, that his fame became founded rather than on his stylistic merits. As for those merits, it should be pointed out that post-medieval Roman Catholic literary taste tended to share the humanistic criteria dominated by a preference for moderation and classicist form. Thus it became possible to extol the authenticity of Bernard's devotion while voicing one's reservation with regard to his style. Bernard's nineteenth-century biographer

Vacandard is a case in point. Emphasising Bernard's 'originality' he feels obliged to point to the danger of excess resulting in a loss of control with regard to style: 'There is, therefore, no lack of originality in the abbot of Clairvaux. However, one serious criticism that can be made with regard to his style is that it is not always in accordance with the standards of literary tradition. Bernard's was an age in which taste was neither predominant in literature nor in the arts.'[3] Although Vacandard wrote before the revaluation of twelfth-century art and literature – to begin with Charles Homer Haskin's seminal *The Renaissance of the Twelfth Century* of 1927 – his views echo through in Henri de Lubac's characterisation of Cistercian and, in particular, Bernardine devotional style:

> Under the hands of the Cistercian monks it looks sometimes as though traditional doctrine particularises towards an inner experi- ence of increasing richness and subtlety which, however, is no longer, can no longer simply be, the experience of the Church itself, that is of the entire community of the faithful. A culture of the hothouse, ardent meditation on liturgical texts rather than on the Bible for its own sake.[4]

This intra-Catholic criticism of Bernard's subjectivism testifies to some uneasiness with regard to the literary liberties he apparently took com- pared to a more objective and more organised method of reading, and meditating on, the Bible 'for its own sake'. Paradoxically, Bernard him- self has become notorious for accusing others like Abelard of impos- ing their own 'subjective' standards and 'overstepping the boundaries set by the Fathers'.[5] By trespassing those supposedly fixed boundaries of orthodoxy, Abelard is to be seen as the pinnacle of egotistical sub- jectivism: 'There is nothing he does not know of all things in heaven and on earth except his own self.'[6] Admittedly, Christianity was famil- iar with a long tradition in which heretical views were condemned as the aberrations of *singular* minds incapable of adhering to what was believed and upheld by all, always and everywhere. The twelfth cen- tury, however, saw the rise of the singular mind as a more independ- ent and self-conscious individual, which is why the era is dubbed by some as that of 'the discovery of the individual'.[7] Although slightly over-the-top, this characterisation is correct in so far as Bernard did indeed initiate a devotion in which the intimate relationship between the adoring subject and the objects of adoration such as God, Christ and Mary took pride of place. Highly influenced by Bernard, this intimacy was further processed in Franciscan and other late medieval thought and went on to become the standard expression of Catholic as well as pietistic Protestant faith (Mary excluded, of course). What remained unsolved in the process is the freedom of movement this devotional subject was allowed vis-à-vis Church doctrine and rules. At which point were boundaries overstepped? It is clear that the late Middle Ages and the early modern era witnessed an increase in Church authority proportionate to the intensification of subjective devotion, both looking as if entangled in an iron embrace. Inside that embrace it is hard to detect an independent human subject or individual operating for its own sake.

Now if we want to assess Bernard's work, devotional subjectivity and individuality as they have emerged out of the Cistercian and, more generally, the twelfth-century mindset are squarely in the way. In order to get a less anachronistic glimpse of Bernard's notion of the self as a key to understanding his literary work, we should realise that his subjectivity originates in the monastic community and its tradition of living the repetitious and communal life of the liturgical Hours. This in itself would suffice to prevent Bernard's self from acting as a merely private individual. His is a monastic *persona* representing its community. What is new about this representation is the highly privatised way in which Abbot Bernard's 'self' claims to speak on behalf of that community as if there is only place for one person qua person – the abbot – whilst the listening community serves as the silent audience for the latter's rhetorical performance.

Talking about 'rhetoric' we are back at Vacandard's and Lubac's characterisation of Bernard's style as a little wild and out of control. In voicing their concerns, those two authors conflate, as it were, two turning points in twelfth-century thought. The first is the one described above, the rise of the individual (devotional) subject, which runs the risk, feared in retrospect by Catholic historians and theologians, of running counter to the sound exteriority of Church authority and rules. Underlying this first turning point is a second one, the fear of a loss of control over the fixed rhetorical genres in use ever since the birth of Christian literature, in which an authorial self, or, for that matter, a self *tout court*, is always embedded in the rules and games imposed by rhetoric. Shaped by the history of devotion as well as by its sequel, the Romantic subject, the modern reader has to cleanse his mind of notions of personal and psychological directness. When tackling texts such as Bernard's that seem to overflow with precisely that, our reader should honour the fact that they can only be accessed indirectly, by following and decoding the rules of rhetoric.

A MISERABLE LIFE

Let us turn to a conspicuous example of what seems to be a *cri de coeur*, and nothing but that, Bernard's famous outcry about his tormented self in his Letter 250:

> It is time for me to think of myself. My monstrous existence, my tormented conscience beg for your pity because I have, so to speak, become the chimaera of my century. I am living neither as a cleric nor as a layman. Long ago I abandoned, if not the monastic habit, then, at least the monastic way of life.[8]

Generally, this outcry has been taken to represent Bernard's frustration about the disproportionate amount of time he spent, willy-nilly, outside his monastery. Thus we would have an example here of quasi-modern, psychological introspection dealing with the troubles of a divided self. Meanwhile it may be worth remembering that being tormented by a divided self was part of the monastic profession just as it was the monk's duty to lament the sinful state of the human condition regardless of the specifics of his own sinful behaviour: the so-called *officium flendi*, the office of weeping. Here we are confronted with the opposite of what British prime minister Harold Macmillan once described, over and against all attempts at long-term planning, as the inevitable core business of politics: 'events, dear boy, events'.[9] In Bernard's case, this would come down to acknowledging the fact that his extramural dealings with short-term projects would always be overruled by the *longue durée* of monastic rituality. In that light it is not surprising to find another version of the 'short-term' personal outcry in one of the Sermons on the Song of Songs as part of the routine of monastic self-accusation and contrition:

> I have been living miserably because I have been wasting my time. All I know is that you, O God, will not reject a contrite and humble heart.[10]

This 'outcry' could have been uttered by any monk anywhere and at any time. In fact, 'at any time' means 'always'. Hard though it may be for the modern reader to understand individuality in terms of ritual and repetition, this is exactly what is required in order to get access to Bernard's texts. Perhaps the counter-intuitive nature of this approach is sweetened a bit if one realises, first, that the premise that our *ordre du discours* with regard to individuality always moves from the singular to the general may be less self-evident than it seems (take, for instance, the expressions of singularity in classified advertisements, mostly in terms of one comprehensive *uomo universale*) and, second, that, then as now, expressions of the self are intrinsically rhetorical. Thus Bernard's *'perdite vixi* / I have lived miserably' tries to say something, not about the psychological state of his mind, but, rather, about the performance of life – *his* life, that is – as exemplary. In that respect the difference between a medieval saint's life and Bernard's personal account of his sinful existence is one of genre rather than of essence. Both are concerned with sin and perfection. If to the modern ear 'exemplary' primarily rings a moralistic bell, the notion of *imitatio* is what comes first and foremost to the fore in the medieval context of *exemplum*.

THE AUTHOR AS ABBOT, FATHER AND BROTHER

With notions such as imitation and *exemplum* we have at our disposal the principal tools that go into the making of Bernard's literary oeuvre, albeit on the condition that here too the difference with later use of those notions should be taken into account. This difference mainly lies in the fact that late medieval *imitatio* such as Thomas à Kempis's *Imitation of Christ*, although deeply influenced by Bernard, is much more of a one-way affair than the original. In Thomas we find, for instance, Christ vis-à-vis the believer, the one to be 'imitated' by the other, the one superior and, in a sense, immovable to be approached by the other, the inferior sinner. What has gone in the historical process is the performative aspect which makes the relationship between Bernard and his 'example' reciprocal, and sometimes even interchangeable to the extent that the one is absorbed by the other.

The framework set for this literary performance is the office of the abbacy itself – which means that, just as in his political activities so also in his writings, Bernard, whether extending or diminishing his personal position, speaks *ex officio*. In accordance with the Rule of Benedict this position comes down to being, within the monastic space, the vicar of Christ. 'For the abbot is thought to perform the offices of Christ, which why he is called by His name, as the Apostle says: "You have received the spirit of adoption of sons, whereby we cry: Abba, Father".'[11] Now, in spite of the fact that humility is the benchmark of the Benedictine/ Cistercian life, in exercising his function the abbot is not asked to hold himself in low esteem but, rather, to follow the firmness of the divine person(s) he represents. Characteristically, Bernard can be seen to take this prescription from the Rule with regard to the abbot one step further and adorn it with biblical, literary embellishments that hitherto had seemed to be the privileged domain of God and Christ themselves. A spectacular example of this theatrical technique of crossing borders in which divine firmness and human vulnerability merge, can be found in Bernard's famous lament over the death of his brother Gerard (in Sermon 26 of the Sermons on the Song of Songs). In that sermon Bernard, while commenting on the Canticle text about 'the tents of Cedar', breaks down into tears, suppressed so far; he has to interrupt his ongoing commentary on the Canticle and tells the story of his personal grief. One border is crossed here already, that of the sermonic genre which yields to the genre of the lament.[12] Inevitably, we come across a lot of 'self' in this sermon-alias-lament, the more so since the commonplace of having one's life divided into halves when losing a friend is further 'personalised' because Bernard has not only lost a friend but also a brother. At the same time, at no point does Bernard lose sight of the fact that his brother is, however special, his monastic brother, like a Martha of sorts taking care of the practical affairs of the monastery in order to unburden his more Mary-like, contemplative brother, the abbot. But inside the monastery, family ties are even more complicated than that, since for Bernard being his brother's brother is preceded by being his brother's Father as well. In the end – that is, at the moment Gerard dies – this fatherhood is enacted by the one and only representative of fatherhood on the spot: the abbot. Staying his brother's brother, he makes his appearance in the deathbed scene somehow disguised as God the Father:

> And he [Gerard] repeated those words: 'Father, into thy hands I commend my spirit' and he sighed frequently. *And turning himself to me* he said with a happy look on his face: 'Father, Father, what great good it is that God deigns to be the Father of mankind! What glory for men to be sons of God, God's heirs. For if they are sons, they are also heirs.'[13]

Vacandard's verdict notwithstanding, literary taste reigns supreme in this passage. Perhaps this can be illustrated when we first pay attention to the surface level of this text and dissect the various elements from Scripture and actual facts and experience glued together in accordance with medieval reading techniques. Thus we have the quotation from the Psalms ('Father, into thy hands ...') that had in turn been adopted by Christ on the cross. 'Father' being the key word here also triggers memory by calling to mind passages from Paul about the Father of mankind. Next we notice the unbreakable bond between fatherhood and sonship which includes the right of inheritance, so tight indeed that no explicit

mention of brotherhood is made. The effect of this semantic (contrary
to factual) absence makes itself felt if we compare this passage as it is
repeated, almost to the letter, in the *Exordium Magnum*, a later, hagiographic account of Bernard's life and work by Conrad of Eberbach:

> And repeating this phrase: 'Father, into thy hands I commend my
> spirit', sighing frequently, he said: 'Father, Father', turning himself
> to the holy abbot, his brother, 'what great good it is that God in his
> dignity is willing to be the Father of mankind.'[14]

Inevitably, there is the shift from the first to the third person singular,
which tends to objectify the story a bit. More dramatically, there is
also a change of word order. Instead of 'turning to me [or, turning to
the holy abbot, his brother], he said: "Father"', a clear distinction is
established between Father and brother by having 'turning himself to
the holy abbot, his brother' moved to a safer position, much closer to
the 'facts', after 'Father' has been evoked and an unmistakable shift
to the brother is made. With that shift the author of the *Exordium*
appears to ignore the specifically Bernardine suggestion of ambiguity with regard to the question of who exactly is being addressed as
'Father'. Of course, it is God, the Father, but Bernard himself does
not exclude himself from being part of that picture. By 'specifically
Bernardine' I do not mean the use of well-known exegetical techniques such as typology (the establishing of links between biblical
figures extended to the writer/believer: David, Christ, Bernard and,
in this case, quite audaciously between God and Bernard in their capacity as father) without denying that such a technique is somehow in
place here. It is the suspense that counts, the very fact that no fixed
scheme is visibly applied. Instead we see the hand of the author draw
a picture in which Bernard is hovering between his various roles of
brother, abbot and Father without either firmly denying or affirming
the distinctness of any one of them.

So far the embedding of Bernard's authorship in his abbacy has produced two seemingly contradictory results. On the one hand, in order
to be effective his 'personal' exclamations have to be assessed against
the backdrop of ritual. On the other hand, once seen as part and parcel
of the monastic Order, as yet unknown vistas became visible, paving
the way for the primordial functionary inside that Order to claim literary freedom and flexibility of movement for his devotional and literary self. The simultaneous functioning of both dimensions seems to go
against the grain of general suppositions about exegetical writing in the
high Middle Ages as being primarily technical, objective, schematic,

exemplary and depersonalised and, conversely, once personalised, *really* personal over and against the impositions of schemes and ritual.

In what follows I will give two more examples of this symbiosis of form and flexibility as a literary principle set out on a scale of increasing intensity and audacity: Bernard addressing the Virgin Mary and his intrusion into, and fusion of, the scenes of Christ's birth and passion.

THE AUTHOR AND THE VIRGIN MARY

It is a well-known fact that Bernard played a major part in developing both the devotion to the Virgin Mary and a sensitivity for the religious importance of the major aspects of Christ's life on earth, his birth and suffering. Now the iconic presence of such images has become so familiar a part of the Western mindset as to make us forget that once upon a time they were coined and established. As with the origins of so many such devotions the initial picture is more complicated than the eventual, more simplified images of Mary and Christ. Let us have a look at such a constitutive text in which Bernard evokes the scene of the Annunciation by dramatically beseeching the Virgin to consent to the Angel's proposal of sacred conception:

> You heard that you will conceive and that you will give birth to a son. You heard that it will happen, not through a man but through the Holy Ghost. The Angel is awaiting an answer. For the time has come for him to return to the one who sent him. It is in the same manner that we, O Mistress, are waiting for the word of mercy in a state in which we are miserably held down by the sentence of damnation ... And, behold, to you is offered the price of our salvation. If you consent, we will be freed at once ... Blessed Virgin, open your heart to faith, your lips to confession, your body to the Creator. Look, he for whom all nations have been longing is standing outside, knocking on your door [Rev. 3.20; S. of S. 5.2]. O, do not let your hesitation cause him to pass by! Then your soul would start to wander again, looking for him whom your soul loves [S. of S. 3.1–4]. Rise, run and open! Rise in faith, run in devotion and open your heart in confession![15]

Again, if we look at this passage from the viewpoint of the tradition at whose origin it lies, we recognise the iconic features as we know them from medieval art in the guise of a static and almost frozen rendering of biblical scenes, including the presence of the adorer(s). What we are not presented with in those iconic settings is the restlessness, not only of the adoring soul but also of the adored object. In this particular scene that restlessness is distilled by Bernard the author from the biblical text in a highly theatricalised manner. Rather than offering the reader an explanatory reading of the text, Bernard creeps into it, so to speak; he makes himself part of the biblical scene both as observer and participant-alias-vocal supporter of the Angel's message and request. Once again it is his position as abbot that authorises him to enter into the conversation between the Angel and the Virgin. Whilst in Gerard's death scene Bernard acted on behalf of – even, in a sense, *as* – God the Father, he now represents the human race, lending voice to the latter's urgent need of redemption. In either case borders are being blurred between the human and the divine, between the voice of the Virgin and the voice of the abbot. Thus Bernard's own restlessness is in a sense transferred from the longings of the sinful and unquiet soul to the oxymoronic possibility of the Virgin herself turning into a wandering ghost due to her having been too late in consenting when her lover passed by. The very fact that the relationship between Christ's incarnation and his virginal mother is expressed in terms of the Song of Songs, although deriving from an older tradition, is also vintage Bernard. In using Song of Songs texts, Bernard does not hold back from drawing erotic imagery into virginal scenes ('rise, run and open'). But to highlight the 'erotic' and isolate it from its context would be anachronistic. The text is more complex and multilayered than that. First and foremost it reveals the suspenseful existence of Christ's representative, the abbot, more specifically, the abbot's self. What follows, in terms of reading and explanation of sacred scenes, is but an extension of that nucleus out of which the literary universe of a virginal existence can be seen to spring.

Surprisingly, Bernard's mentioning of Song of Songs fragments does not betray any trace of allegory or the fourfold meaning of Scripture (literal, allegorical, moral, mystical). That very device can be held responsible for producing a fixed and stable reading method which has contributed to the impression, right or wrong, of medieval exegesis having become a semi-automatic affair. Elsewhere, as in the Sermons on the Song of Songs, Bernard did indeed move from the historical to the mystical, for instance when discussing the various meanings of the 'kiss' from the opening line of Song of Songs: 'Let Him kiss me with the kiss of his mouth.' However, rather than producing fixed meanings of scriptural words and texts, Bernard, also when using a common device such as allegory, prefers to blur borders and to keep moving without pinning down one singular and static meaning. His work is littered with striking examples of this flexible way of reading. I conclude this chapter with one such display of rhetorical cunningness which – seemingly – covers its technical tracks.

THE AUTHOR'S STAGING OF THE NATIVITY AND THE PASSION

In the third Sermon on the Nativity of the Lord we find Bernard once more in proximity to sacred events. Musing about the miracle of Christ's birth, the paradox of God's son shrinking down to the size of a child in the manger, he reflects on the fact that this entire scene is produced for his benefit:

> And I recognise for my own the time and the place of this birth. Tender infant frame, wailing screaming child, and then the poverty and the wakefulness of those to whom the birth of the saving God is first announced, the shepherds. These things are mine. They happen for me. They are laid down before me to imitate. At night time, in winter time is when Christ was born. By chance? Winter, summer, day, night are his for the choosing. And was it by chance he was born in this unkind season, at dead of night?[16]

Measured against Bernardine standards this passage is fairly routine. A picture is painted of Christ wailing in the crib; a scene which is subsequently appropriated by the observer as being 'his'. The self that is thus brought out does, however, keep a certain distance. No ambiguous use of fatherhood here. Nor does Bernard intrude as unashamedly into the scene as when taking up the role of participant in the Annunciation. Before long, however, the writing abbot enters the scene, not only by taking up a part in it but, once more, by developing various roles out of his very own 'self':

> Brethren, Christ's tears bring on in me at once shame and agony. There was I playing outside in the square, while in the secrecy of the royal bedroom a sentence of death was brought against me. His Only Begotten got to hear of it. He came out. He had put down his diadem. He was wearing sackcloth, and his head was spattered with ash. He was barefoot, and weeping and wailing, because his little slave-boy had been condemned to die. Quite suddenly, I see him coming out. I am struck dumb. New thing. I am told the reason why. What am I to do? Play on, make play of his tears? If I have taken leave of my senses, if I am not of sound mind, I will not follow him, will not weep with the weeping.[17]

Due to its kaleidoscopic composition, this text makes heavy demands on the reader. In terms of medieval exegesis, the only fixed element the reader can go by is the moral meaning to be distilled from the picture of the wailing Christmas child in the crib, that those tears cause shame and agony to the extent of making our reader weep as well. In other respects the passage is utterly confusing. Take the biblical references. They are scattered all over the text but none of them constitutes an identifiable quotation. 'Playing on the square' may allude to Zech. 98.5: 'And the streets of the city shall be full of boys and girls playing in the streets thereof' but can also refer to Matt. 11.16: 'What shall I compare this generation with? It is like boys sitting in the square.' Next there is the 'bedroom' of the king, clearly from the Song of Songs, but in this place primarily meaning 'a courtroom'. This is quite unlike the standard approaches to scriptural allusions, which are somehow meant to ring a bell with the monastic audience. Here that ring only causes confusion with regard to any mnemonic technique; a confusion that is next extended to another one underlying all this dreamlike vagueness: the question of who exactly is talking. Where Bernard's line of exposition started with the tears of the Christmas child versus the tears to be elicited from the stony heart of the believer, the expositor's self and baby Christ change places: Bernard turns into an innocent child playing in the square whilst his master hears about the deliberations inside the royal bedroom that lead to his 'little slave-boy' being sentenced to death. Clearly, no distinct narrative and expository lines can be drawn. What does 'the royal bedroom' mean and what does it contribute semantically to the grimness of this tearful episode? Do love and tenderness absorb doom and death, and do monastic wailing and weeping come down to enacting precisely that? Maybe, but this much is clear: what is being expressed here moves beyond the parameters of a distinct and prosaic reading of the text and has meanwhile turned into poetry of a kind. Of course, this entire procedure is rooted in the establishment of a self, the self of the Father abbot whose reading authority includes the playing out of different roles, Father, Son, brother, lover and child.

All this seems to justify Lubac's suspicion that what we have here is a 'culture of the hothouse, ardent meditation on liturgical texts rather than on the Bible for its own sake'. As a Jesuit trained in the classical tradition but also steeped in modern literature, Lubac sensed that Bernard's writings, rather than being governed by austere rules of faith and genre, testified to a freedom of literary movement springing from the mnemonic overflow of a literary self. The display of such freedom may have been hard to swallow for those for whom the exteriority of Church authority prevailed, always and everywhere. If one looks at Bernard from the perspective of a different and less anachronistic time line, however – one that takes its starting point in the beginnings of Christianity rather than in its late- and post-medieval outlook – Bernard's daringness in absorbing and reproducing biblical and liturgical texts processed through his very own, literary self is in a league with the way the Apostle Paul handled *his* self by reading it into *his* holy writ as did, in turn, Church Fathers such as Origen and Augustine. Not for nothing, besides being called *Doctor mellifluus* (honey-dropping doctor), has Bernard's official epithet always been *ultimus inter patres*, 'the last of the Fathers'.

Notes

1   See Christopher Holdsworth's chapter in this volume.
2   *Apo* XII.28; C. Rudolph, *The 'Things of Greater Importance': Bernard of Clairvaux's 'Apologia' and the Medieval Attitude toward Art* (Philadelphia, PA, 1990).
3   E. Vacandard, *Vie de Saint Bernard, abbé de Clairvaux* (Paris, 1920; first pub. 1895).
4   H. de Lubac, *Exégèse médiévale: les quatre sens de l'Écriture*, 4 vols. (Paris, 1959–63), vol. II (1959), p. 582.
5   *Ep* 193; SBOp 7, pp. 44–5.
6   *Ep* 193; SBOp 7, p. 45.
7   C. Morris, *The Discovery of the Individual, 1050–1200* (New York, 1972).
8   *Ep* 250.4; SBOp 7, p. 147.
9   Like many famous quotations, this one is unsourced.
10   *SC* 20.1.1; SBOp 1, p. 114.
11   *Rule of Benedict*, ed. P. Schmitz (Maredsous, 1955; first pub. 1946), chapter 2, p. 49; Rom. 8.15.
12   In an ironic attack, Abelard's student Berengar accused Bernard of trespassing the laws of rhetoric by mixing up his commentary on a bridal song (the Song of Songs) with a lament. See Berengar, *Apologeticus, PL* 178:1863–4.
13   *SC* 26; SBOp 1, pp. 170–81; Rom. 8.16–17.
14   Conrad of Eberbach, *Exordium magnum cisterciense sive narratio de initio ordinis cisterciensis*, ed. B. Griesser (Rome, 1961), 154, dist. 3.
15   *Miss* 4.IV.8; SBOp 4, p. 54.
16   *Nat* 3.1; SBOp 4, pp. 257–8, translated by P. Cramer in M.B. Pranger, *Bernard of Clairvaux and the Shape of Monastic Thought: Broken Dreams* (Leiden, 1994), p. 240.
17   *Nat* 3.4; Pranger, *Bernard of Clairvaux*, p. 242.

14 Early Cistercian writers

E. ROZANNE ELDER

The *Dictionnaire des auteurs cisterciens* published in the 1970s[1] lists some fifteen Cistercian writers active in the formative early twelfth century, a staggering one hundred thirty-eight for the full twelfth century, and another one hundred seventy-nine who lived on into the thirteenth century. Even allowing for some duplication in this count, readers will understand that a short article cannot introduce all of them. Only the best known Cistercian writers, and of them those whose works have been critically edited and/or are available in English, are presented here.

THE 'FIRST FOUNDERS OF THIS CHURCH': THE CISTERCIAN AUTHORS OF THE FORMATIVE YEARS[2]

Stephen Harding[3] (third abbot of Cîteaux, 1108/9–33, d. 1134) deserves pride of place in any list of Cistercian writers, even though his literary legacy is slight. It was Stephen who established the constitution, the *Carta Caritatis*[4] and formed the character of what became the Cistercian Order.

An oblate at Sherborne Abbey in Dorset, the young Anglo-Saxon Harding left cloister and country in the aftermath of the Norman Conquest, perhaps prey to 'worldly nettles' or perhaps wary of his new overlords. After studying and travelling through Europe, he re-entered monastic life at Molesme, recently founded by the Benedictine Robert and the hermit Alberic. In community discussions of Abbot Robert's plans for a another new foundation, as imaginatively depicted by William of Malmesbury, Stephen defended stricter fidelity to the Rule of Benedict as being in accord with reason.[5] As the third abbot of Cîteaux – following Robert's return to Molesme and Alberic's death – he sent monks out to make the first Cistercian foundations (La Ferté, in Cîteaux's diocese of Châlons-sur-Saône in 1113 and Pontigny in Auxerre diocese in 1114) and received Bernard of Fontaines and his thirty companions into the noviciate.[6] In addition to *The Charter of Charity* which regulates relationships between the mother house and its new daughters, there survive from his pen a letter to the monks of Sherborne, the homily he likely preached at the funeral of his predecessor and his preface to the reformed Cistercian hymnal.[7]

Bernard of Clairvaux (1090–1153), the most eloquent and best known of all Cistercian writers, is treated elsewhere in this volume. His prodigious literary output displays his mastery of every literary genre of the day, and his nearly 500 surviving letters testify to the breadth of his contacts with 'the world'. So great was his reputation that a number of works by other Cistercians came to be misattributed to him in the late Middle Ages.

William of Saint Thierry[8] (1080?–1148), Bernard's friend and first hagiographer, was rescued from obscurity in the twentieth century, and the works of this brilliant theologian and spiritual writer were restored to him after being attributed for centuries to other, better-known, writers when a listing of them by his own hand was published in 1924 by Dom André Wilmart.[9] Of the sixteen works William mentions, only one, called simply *Sententiae*, has been lost. The other fifteen have been increasingly the subject of scholarly attention. Some he wrote as abbot of the Benedictine monastery of Saint Thierry, near Reims, and some after he retired in 1135 to the Cistercian abbey of Signy in the Ardennes; some before he raised the alarm against the theologies of Peter Abelard (1139 or 1140) and some afterwards.

The Benedictine works, *De natura et dignitate amoris* (*On the Nature and Dignity of Love*), *De contemplando deo* (*On Contemplating God*) and *Meditativae orationes* (*Meditations*), manifest his growing desire for the personal experience of God he saw in Bernard. His correction in *De sacramento altaris* (*On the Sacrament of the Altar*) of a small 'blemish' in the *De divinis officiis* of the Rhineland abbot Rupert of Deutz presages the theological acuity he later displayed against Abelard.

His Cistercian works include scriptural commentaries written during his first four or five years as an abbot-guest at Signy: the *Brevis Commentatio* on the Song of Songs (sometimes attributed to William and sometimes considered a collaborative effort between William and Bernard); his verse-by-verse commentary on Paul's Letter to the Romans (*Expositio in epistolam ad Romanos*); two *florilegia* he created from commentaries on the Song of Songs by Ambrose and Gregory the Great (*Commentarius in Cantica canticorum e scriptis Sancti Ambrosii* and *Excerpta ex libris Sancti Gregorii Papae super Cantica canticorum*) and his own unfinished *Expositio super Cantica canticorum* (*Exposition on the Song of Songs*). A long treatise *On the Nature of the Body and the Soul* (*De natura corporis et animae*) reveals his interest in medicine and in the 'psychology' of the spiritual life. Reading the *Theologia*[10] of Peter Abelard so alarmed him that he alerted Bernard and the papal legate by letter[11] and a detailed analytic *Disputation*. He then tackled what he considered Abelard's errors and reconsidered his own earlier opinions in *Speculum fidei* (*The Mirror of Faith*) and *Aenigma fidei* (*The Enigma of Faith*). A second tocsin to Bernard against William of Conches went unheeded. His two final, and best-known, works were his *Epistola ad Fratres de Monte Dei* (*Letter to the Brothers of Mont-Dieu*), long attributed to Guigo the Carthusian, and Book One of the First Life of Bernard (*Vita Prima*), written to secure Bernard's official canonisation by Rome. In 1148, William preceded Bernard in death, and the final canonisation dossier was left to others.

Aelred of Rievaulx[12] (1110–67), born to a family of hereditary priests,[13] was perhaps educated at Durham's cathedral school. Barred by Gregorian legislation from following his forebears' clerical career,[14] he entered the service of David I of Scotland. In that capacity he travelled to Yorkshire in 1134 and, prompted by its proud patron, Walter Espec, visited the newly founded monastery at Rievaulx, where, according to Walter Daniel (*Life of Aelred* 7), he was greeted with suspicious warmth. After a single night's reflection, he abandoned royal service for monastic austerity. Permitted as a monk to be ordained, he served successively as novice master at Rievaulx, abbot of its third daughter house, at Revesby (1143–7) and finally as abbot of Rievaulx (1147–78). Despite the civil war raging in England, he doubled 'lands, dwellings, wealth, and church ornaments'[15] and drew men to the monastery in extraordinary numbers as monks and *conversi* (lay brothers). All this suggests he was both a good manager and a warm person. He also 'trebled the intensity of the monastic life and its charity'[16] in the words of his posthumous biographer, Walter Daniel. While at Revesby he carried the reform message to clergy by preaching at synods, and became 'greatly beloved by all in the province' of York.[17] Aelred rejoiced in human relationships and believed that true friendship begins in Christ, grows through Christ and reaches perfection in Christ,[18] and that in the company of a friend the Lord Jesus is always present. A historian, a hagiographer and a spiritual writer, Aelred left an impressive literary legacy, yet more than once protested his lack of schooling.

His historical and hagiographical works focus on events outside the cloister: *Eulogium Davidis regis Scotorum* (*Eulogy of King David* of Scotland), Genealogia regum Anglorum (Genealogy of the Kings of England), an account of the 1138 Battle of the Standard between English and Scottish troops (De bello Standardii), the curious tale of the Nun of Watton (De sanctimoniali de Wattun) and The Life of Saint Edward the Confessor (Vita sancti Edwardi regis et confessoris), a melding of history and hagiography. He celebrated the pioneering saints of the north: Ninian, the 'apostle of the north' (Vita Niniani Pictorum australium apostoli) and the founders of Hexham, his father's church (De sanctis Hagulstaldensis ecclesiae).

His spiritual works stress the vital role of friendship in learning to love God and the human need to grow by love, human and divine, to perfection. 'Amor is the central term in Aelred's vocabulary', declares Bernard McGinn.[19] Aelred seems to have understood natural human love (amor) and divine love (caritas) not as sequential stages, as William did, but as distinguished by their objects. In speculum caritatis (The Mirror of Charity) and De spirituali amicitia (On Spiritual Friendship) he linked human and divine love in the soul's devotion to the God who is caritas, and who in love became human, suffered, died and left for human strengthening his eucharistic body and blood. His dialogue Dialogus de anima (On the Soul) manifests both his Augustinian traditionalism and his love of human relationships. This and his devotion to the human Jesus are reflected in his treatises De Iesu puero duodenni (On Jesus at the Age of Twelve), De institutione inclusarum (On the Institution of Recluses) and his intensely personal Oratio pastoralis (Pastoral Prayer). His Liturgical Sermons connect the imitation of Christ with the liturgical year, and his reflections On the Burdens of Isaiah (Homeliae de oneribus propheticis Isaiae) examine the obstacles, innate and external, to spiritual development.

Guerric of Igny[20] (d. 1157), whose life is as little documented as his surviving works are few, was very likely born and educated at Tournai.[21] Highly thought of by contemporaries,[22] he entered monastic life probably at Clairvaux under Bernard.[23] In 1138, at Bernard's prompting,[24] he was elected to be the second abbot of Igny[25] near Reims. There he preached the fifty-four Liturgical Sermons which constitute his surviving literary legacy. Not given to the rhetorical flourishes of Bernard or the personal warmth of Aelred, Guerric was a master of the trivium and brought to his preaching both the calm rationality of the scholar and the monk's intense desire for transformation in Christ. His monastic formation is evident in his focus on Christology and community, and the distinctions he made in developing his ideas reveal his scholastic training. The 'three forms of Christ', which Guerric refers to as the *forma corporalis* (or *forma carni*), the *forma moralis*, and the *forma intellectualis* (corporal, moral and intellectual form), penetrate to the heart of Guerric's Christology, McGinn asserts, and is 'deeply Pauline and Augustinian in inspiration'.[26]

'OUR SUCCESSORS': CHANGING PERSPECTIVES[27]

Amadeus of Lausanne[28] (1110–1159) belongs chronologically among the 'first founders', yet his spirituality belongs to a slightly later, less austere age. As befitted a young man of his noble rank, he received a good education at the abbeys of Bonnevaux and Cluny and at the court of his kinsman, the future Holy Roman Emperor Conrad III Hohenstaufen. After twenty years as a monk of Clairvaux, in 1145 he became bishop of Lausanne – not an easy diocese to govern. His vestments, he wrote, once ran red with the blood of a murdered man whom he had struggled to protect. Amid political skullduggery and pastoral and administrative duties, Amadeus managed to write – perhaps to preach – eight homilies in praise of the Virgin Mary, almost his only surviving work. His Marian devotion, less Christocentric than Bernard's, reflects the popular, some-times sentimental, piety sweeping Western Europe in the mid twelfth century.

Isaac of Stella[29] (c. 1100–c. 1169) left his native England at the end of the first quarter of the twelfth century, drawn to the flourishing schools of France. That and his subsequent career mirror the intellec-tual ferment and political debates of the time. He studied at Abelard's Paraclete and at Chartres and taught at Poitiers and Chartres before entering Cîteaux in about 1142. Only five years later he was elected abbot of Stella. After some twenty years, Isaac left and, to the best of anyone's knowledge, spent the rest of his days at the monastery of Our Lady of Châteliers on Ré, a 'remote island closed round by the sea'[30] off the coast of La Rochelle. He had a knack for being on the wrong side of controversy. Two of his masters, Peter Abelard and Gilbert of Poitiers, were accused of heresy by his abbot, Bernard of Clairvaux, and he saw the Cistercian General Chapter yield to the implacable Henry II of England and withdraw its protection from Archbishop Thomas Becket of Canterbury, whose cause Isaac championed.

Fifty-five sermons on the liturgical year and two treatises in letter form, one on the *Office of the Mass* (*Epistola Ad Joannem Episcopum Pictaviensem De Officio Missae*) and another *On the Soul* (*Epistola de anima*) survive. Commentaries on the Song of Songs and on the Book of Ruth as well as a series of *Glossae morales* have been attributed to him, but without demonstrable foundation. His work reveals his mastery of the technical vocabulary and the systematic organisation of information being developed in the cathedral schools of his day, his 'lively interest in dialectics and metaphysics'[31] and his commitment to the ongoing conversion demanded by the monastic vocation. Of him, Bernard McGinn has written that cloister and classroom were 'complementary, not antagonistic. It is hard not to think that his theological studies had … led him to Citeaux.'[32] The influence of Pseudo-Dionysius is discernible in his images of divine darkness, 'dissimilar similitude' and the intensifying 'super' in speaking 'about the Ineffable, about whom nothing can properly be said'.[33]

Gilbert of Hoyland[34] (d. 1172), another Englishman, is best known as the abbot who took up the commentary on the Song of Songs left unfinished at chapter three, verse one, when Bernard of Clairvaux died. In forty-eight sermons Gilbert extended the commentary to chapter five, verse ten before he, too, died. From his exegesis the practical dimension of living virtuously is never absent. In addition, he wrote seven treatises and four extant letters, and possibly sermon commentaries on the Gospel of Matthew.

Nothing is known of his origins, his education or his entry into monastic life. His monastery, Swineshead in the fenlands of eastern England known as Hollandia, was a foundation of the Savigniac abbey of Furness in Cumbria. Aelred, newly elected abbot of Rievaulx, is known to have sent a group of monks to Swineshead to help the monks make the transition to Cistercian customs after the Orders merged in 1147. If Gilbert was one of those sent, he had been formed as a Cistercian.[35] His friendship with Aelred, between 1143 and 1147 abbot of Revesby, which lay only 15 miles north of Swineshead, has led to the hypothesis that Gilbert may have been one of the Clairvaux monks who founded Rievaulx. It is entirely possible, on the other hand, that he began his monastic life as a Savigniac either in Normandy or in England. Some of his sermons were preached, or written, for nuns,[36] and care for nuns was characteristic of Savigniac, not of Cistercian, houses. Seven fairly short treatises deal more with practical issues of monastic living than with theological speculation, as do four extant letters.[37] That he entered monastic life somewhere in France is suggested by his retirement to L'Arrivour, near Troyes, around 1167.

Geoffrey of Auxerre[38] (c. 1120–post 1188) is known more for his career than for his literary output, much of which remains unpublished. A student of Peter Abelard at Paris when Bernard preached his sermon *De conversione ad clericos*, he was one of a group who followed the abbot back to Clairvaux.[39] There, in 1145, he became Bernard's secretary, collected his letters and, as the abbot's health deteriorated, kept notes on his activities and miracles which he turned over to William of Saint Thierry to aid him in writing of the *Life* designed to secure Bernard's canonisation by Rome once he died. After William predeceased Bernard, Geoffrey himself composed Books Three through Five.

As the abbot's secretary, he learned ecclesiastical politics and collected hagiographical material by observing his abbot as he preached against Albigensians in Toulouse, rallied troops for the Second Crusade in the Rhineland and attempted to secure the condemnation of Gilbert of Poitiers at the 1148 Synod of Reims.[40] In 1159 Geoffrey became abbot of Igny, only to be recalled to Clairvaux three years later as its fourth abbot. The match was evidently not a happy one, for when he visited Rome in 1165, Pope Alexander III requested his resignation. Subsequently he replaced two of his successors at Clairvaux, serving as abbot of Fossanova and Hautecombe in Savoy before, apparently, retiring to Cîteaux. Geoffrey composed a commentary on the Song of Songs (*Expositio in Cantica canticorum*), and another on the Apocalypse (*Super Apocalypsin*), as well as two letters, one on the hotly debated question of how the body of Christ is present in the eucharistic elements (*De conversione aquae cum vino in sanguinem Domini*), and another on the Lord's Prayer (*Epistola ad Josbertum continens notulas in Orationem dominicam*).

Baldwin of Forde[41] (d. 1190) was typical of his age in building an ecclesiastical career on the foundation of the study of law. After serving some ten years as archdeacon of Totnes in the English diocese of Exeter, he interrupted the pattern by entering Forde Abbey (then Devon, now Dorset). Elected abbot in 1175, he resumed his ecclesiastical career, and was promoted seven years later to the see of Worcester. In 1184 he was consecrated as archbishop of Canterbury. Gervase of Canterbury considered him learned in both sacred and secular studies, but viewed his archiepiscopate with misgivings, perhaps an indication of tension between the Benedictines of Canterbury and their new Cistercian archbishop.[42] Gerald of Wales, who accompanied Baldwin through Wales as he preached the Second Crusade, claimed that 'by the purity of his personal life he was an inspiration to his people',[43] but also alleged that at each stage of his career, he moved further beyond his competence.[44] Baldwin's modern editor, David N. Bell, assesses him as 'deeply learned, unquestionably ascetic, godly and gullible ... too lax, too lenient, and too easily led',[45] heavy-handed and frequently at odds with the Benedictines of Canterbury.[46] His literary works, produced almost

entirely at Forde, include sermons reworked at Canterbury into tractates, a *Commendation of Faith* (*Sermones De Commendatione fidei*)
and a treatise on the Eucharist (*De sacramento altaris*). After crowning
Richard the Lionhearted at Canterbury in 1189, Baldwin followed him
to the Holy Land, where he died a year later during the siege of Acre.

'BURGEONING WITH NEW BRANCHES': THE THIRTEENTH CENTURY[47]

Idung of Prüfening, sometime between 1153 and 1174, authored
two works: a debate in dialogue form on the respective virtues of the
Cistercian and Cluniac observances (*Dialogus duorum monachorum*),
and an argument on four questions of practical interest to monks of
his day (*Argumentum super quatuor quaestionibus*). From these texts,
R.B.C. Huygens has sketched a biography of this 'shadowy monk'.[48] His
orthography and references to the Benedictine abbot of Admont, the
Benedictine abbess of Niedermünster and a canon of Reichersberg place
him in the Holy Roman Empire. The criticisms exchanged between
Black Monk and White indicate that before becoming a Cistercian, he
had been a Benedictine *conversus* (adult vocation). Both works reveal
a solid classical and patristic education, and his four questions suggest
training in canon law and involvement in some of the burning issues
of the day: whether a monk can also be a cleric; whether a monk may
preach in a parish church; whether nuns should observe the same, or
stricter, cloister as monks; and whether intention alone makes the
monk.

John of Forde[49] (c. 1145–1214), in 120 sermons surviving in only one
manuscript, completed the commentary on the Song of Songs begun by
Bernard of Clairvaux and continued by Gilbert of Hoyland. While serving
under Baldwin as prior, he wrote a *Life of Blessed Wulfric of Haselbury*
(*Vita beati Wulfrici anachoretae Haselburgiae*), a hermit living not far
from Forde. In 1191, some five years after becoming the founding abbot
of Bindon, Forde's daughter house in Dorset, he returned to Forde as
abbot. Forde apparently thrived under his leadership, for it founded a
second daughter house at Dunkeswell in 1201. Over the ensuing years,
perhaps because he had been trained in law, he became something of
an insular trouble-shooter for the General Chapter. Named confessor
to King John in 1204, he resigned in frustration after three years.[50] The
final years of his abbacy were clouded by the interdict laid on England in
1208 by Innocent III, by the king's crippling taxation to sustain his Irish
campaign and by a punitive royal fine levied on the Cistercians. The

effects, spiritual and temporal, John recorded in *A Lamentation on the General Interdict*[51] and a melancholy account *Of the Persecution of the Cistercians in England* in which he tells of the sale of 'oxen ... calves and heifers, sheep and any other animals we had, estates and rents, even the very clothes the community had to wear, not to mention our food itself, our books, and our sacred vessels'.[52] He died before having the satisfaction of seeing the barons' revolt against John's prodigal and rapacious policies.

Adam of Perseigne[53] (d. 1221) entered the Cistercian Order, probably at Pontigny, after being, perhaps, both a canon regular and a Benedictine. Once he became abbot of Perseigne in Normandy – probably in 1188 – the events of his life become considerably clearer. His reputation as what is today called a spiritual director and his role in distilling and passing to future generations the Cistercian literature of the 'golden age' is attested by his broad correspondence. His numerous public roles, both royal and monastic, led to the thankless tasks of advising Richard the Lionhearted, attempting to broker peace between Philip Augustus of France and John of England and being dispatched to Italy to look into the ecclesiastically destabilising writings of the one-time Cistercian Joachim of Fiore, and perhaps to the Holy Land.[54] Critical editions of Adam's reflective works – a *Mariale*, Soliloquy and *Book of Mutual Love* – have still to be made.

Hélinand of Froidmont[55] (c. 1160–1237) abandoned the French royal court to enter monastic life, much as his father and uncle had fled their native Flanders for France in the wake of the assassination of Charles the Good. Except for a journey to Toulouse, he seems to have remained in the area of Beauvais. After completing his studies at the cathedral – under a student of Peter Abelard – he indulged his talents for poetry and music as a minstrel, or *trouvère*. His best-known work, the Old French *Les Vers de la mort* (*Verses on Death*), hints at his reasons for leaving a scintillating courtly life for the austere Cistercian noviciate at Cold-Mountain, Froidmont, a daughter house of Clairvaux. After his change of heart, he wrote, 'I've left all play and badinage.'[56] General Chapter looked askance at monks writing verse,[57] but the far from frivolous verses – 'one of the great works of the twelfth century'[58] and much recited in the early thirteenth century[59] – reminded listeners of the inevitability of death and judgement and may have inspired the grim late medieval *danses macabres*. In addition to vernacular verses, Hélinand composed Latin sermons, a chronicle of events between 634 and 1180, in fact 1204 (*Chronicon*), three treatises, *De cognitione sui* (*On Self-Knowledge*), *De bono regimine principis* (*On Good Princely*

Rule) and *De reparatione lapsi* (*On Reconciling a Lapsed Brother*), and an account of the martyrdom of four monks of the Thebaid.

Stephen of Lexington, or Lexinton[60] (*c.* 1193–1260), the youngest of four sons of Richard of Lexinton, now Laxton, Nottinghamshire, studied the liberal arts at Paris and theology at Oxford. While attending a lecture by the saintly Edmund Rich (later, as archbishop of Canterbury, exiled at the Cistercian abbey of Pontigny, where he died and is buried), he and six companions were moved by the appearance of the Cistercian abbot of Quarr to enter monastic life. In 1223 he was made abbot of Quarr's daughter house at Stanley in Wiltshire. A Savigniac foundation, Quarr had come into the filiation of Clairvaux in 1147, giving the abbot of Clairvaux far too many daughter houses to be able to visit as was required by the Charter of Charity. At the General Chapter of 1227 and again in 1128, Stephen was deputised as visitor to the Irish houses founded by the conquering Normans in the untamed marches. Dismayed at the rowdy and irregular observances he observed, he expressed Anglo-Norman disapproval of native Irish customs by laying down the law in a series of letters. 'He did not approach the Irish situation as a problem of souls, but as a problem of regulations, of standards and role, of rules to be applied and observed.'[61] Plans for further Irish reform were laid aside in 1229, at his election to the abbacy of Savigny. In that capacity he became responsible for visiting some thirty daughter houses as well as, at papal behest, the Benedictines of Redom and houses of the Grandmontines. He narrowly escaped capture en route home from a 1241 council called by Pope Gregory IX against the Holy Roman Emperor Frederick II. The less fortunate abbot of Clairvaux died in captivity. In 1243, as monastic debate over the value of sending young monks out for higher studies heated up, Stephen was elected abbot of Clairvaux. Vexed at seeing the mendicant Orders siphon off the brightest and the best vocations, Stephen founded the Collegium Sancti Bernardi on a piece of Claravallian property in Paris. Conflict led to his deposition from office in 1256, his reinstatement, redeposition and retirement to Ourscamp, where he died.

Stephen of Sawley, or Salley (d. 1252) served successively as abbot of Sawley (Yorkshire), Newminster (Northumbria) and Fountains (York). He died while on visitation at a daughter house of Fountains in Lincolnshire, Vaudy, where he was buried. His surviving works – *Meditationes de gaudiis beatae Mariae Virginis* (*Meditations on the Joys of Blessed Mary*), *Triplex exercitium* (*Threefold Exercise*), *Speculum Novitii* (*Mirror for Novices*) and *De informatione mentis circa psalmarum diei et noctis* (*Preparing the Mind for the Divine Office*) – were all written with the practical aim of inculcating attentiveness and devotion in monks, whether during their years of formation or during their hours at liturgical worship. Unknown or misattributed, these works were discovered, edited and translated by Léopold Delisle. While his name appears occasionally in charters and General Chapter documents, little is known of his life beyond the offices he held. His works display a polished style, a classical education, intimate knowledge of Scripture and the Church Fathers and a familiarity with several twelfth-century Cistercian writers.

Women Cistercian writers appear last, not because they have been segregated from their brothers as is still too often done in monastic histories and scholarly conferences, but because the women's literature flowered in the thirteenth and fourteenth centuries. By then the giants among male Cistercian writers had been replaced by monks and lay brothers who sometimes manifest a lesser talent and different piety – monks and lay brothers who, like Goswin of Villers, composed hagio-biographies of holy Cistercian nuns and lay brothers[62] and, just perhaps, by monks whose work has yet to be discovered by moderns.

Beatrice of Nazareth[63] (1200–1268) was born in Tienen/Tirlemont, in the diocese of Liège, to a 'modest' merchant family. Her parents, Gertrud and Bartholomew, were known for their piety and good works and for encouraging all their children to enter religious life. Despite the modesty of their means, her father is credited with 'founding' three abbeys[64] and moving four of his five children successively into them. Bartholomew, apparently the manager of the abbey estates, entered Bloemendaal as a lay brother along with his remaining two daughters and one son – the other being already a Premonstratensian canon. After being there six years he 'constructed' another Cistercian house of nuns, Maagdendaal, and 'transferred to it himself with all his progeny';[65] fourteen years later, in 1236, he 'founded' yet another Cistercian abbey, Nazareth, and '[t]ogether with his aforementioned progeny the veteran knight went there henceforth to serve the Lord, his Creator'.[66] Most likely, Bartholomew raised money and/or helped with the construction of these successive houses. This peripatetic upbringing, coupled with her youthfulness, delicate physique and intense piety, may explain a certain instability in the adolescent Beatrice which she later outgrew. Sent to be schooled by the Beguines of Léau (Lewis, Zoutleeuw) at seven, when her mother died, Beatrice went from there to the Benedictine, soon to be Cistercian, nuns of Bloemendaal (Florival). Despite being underage, she insisted on being admitted to the noviciate. Professed in 1216, she was sent to the abbey of Rameya (La Ramée) to study manuscript writing with Ida of Nivelles, under whose direction Beatrice had the first of several mystical experiences.

Later serving as novice mistress and prioress, Beatrice kept a diary which became the basis of a Latin *Vita Beatricis* written not long after her death in 1268. The anonymous writer calls himself the nuns' brother and fellow servant. Probably their chaplain, he asserts that he wrote at the nuns' request, likely because the community hoped to avoid the attention of the inquisition by turning their prioress's Flemish diary into a polished Latin *Vita*. It includes a Latin version of the *Van seven manieren van heileger Minne* (*De caritate Dei et vii eius gradibus*) in which Beatrice describes the seven stages of the loving experience of God.

Gertrud the Great (1256–1302?) was placed in the monastery of Helfta, near the city of Magdeburg, at the tender age of four or five and remained there for the rest of her outwardly uneventful life. That she became a choir nun hints that she came from a 'good', possibly noble, family. That she was allowed to enter at so young age suggests that the Helfta nuns were not recognised as Cistercians by the General Chapter, but had chosen independently to follow the customs of the White Monks, except on the point of child oblature. Gertrud's *Revelations*, *Herald of God's Loving-Kindness* (*Legatus Memorialis Abundantiae Divinae Pietatis*) and *Spiritual Exercises* (*Exercitia spiritualia*),[67] all written after a series of visions she experienced early in 1281, reveal the breadth of her reading, her familiarity with Scripture and the quality of her Latin – a testament to the excellence of Helfta's liturgy, library and school. They also disclose the illnesses she suffered and established her reputation as a mystic. Central to them is liturgy and a loving response to *pietas*, the loving, dutiful generosity of God. Only Book Two of *The Herald* came from her hand; Book One is an account of her life, Books Three through Five were assembled from her notes by nuns of her community.

'BY WHAT STAGES THEIR MONASTERY AND
THEIR LIFESTYLE TOOK ITS BEGINNING': THE
GUARDIANS OF TRADITION[68]

Cistercian literature after the 'golden age' ranges from allegorical poetry, for example the edifying 'romances' of Guillaume de Digulleville (c. 1295–c. 1258), a monk of Chaalis, to scholastic textual criticism.[69] Three very similar genres especially stand out and provide insight into the daily lives, spiritualities and expectations of Cistercians.

Historiae. These retrovisionary and frequently idealised accounts of the Order's history allow scholars to glimpse the developing Cistercian myth through the eyes of monks of the thirteenth and later centuries. The best known and most complete is the *Exordium Magnum* of Conrad of Eberbach (d. 1221), which is part history and part a series of *exempla*.[70]

Exempla. Edifying 'examples' of monastic lives well lived, these resemble histories but contain a higher incidence of visions and miraculous interventions. Those most often read are the *Dialogus miraculorum* (*Dialogue of Miracles*) collected by Caesarius of Heisterbach (*c*.1180–*c*.1240) and the *Liber de miraculis* (*Book of Miracles*) by Herbert of Clairvaux – also called Herbert of Torres, or Mores – compiled around 1178 and heavily pilfered by Conrad of Eberbach.[71] Until recently overlooked by historians, *exempla* collections are now being studied for the information they provide on the details of daily routines never systematically committed to parchment.

Vitae. Hagiographic biographies hold up as models individual monks and nuns who led ordinary monastic lives of prayer and work, solitude and community but were remembered for their extraordinary holiness. The piety and literary quality of these *Lives* vary enormously, yet they provide a privileged view into the aspirations and daily lives of the monk and nun in the choir stall and attest to the fervour of their monastic conversion and the remarkable geographical expansion of the Order during the twelfth and thirteenth centuries.[72]

* * *

Between the thirteenth and the twenty-first centuries, a great number of Cistercians continued writing. One thinks immediately of Thomas Merton (1914–1968), the monk of Gethsemani Abbey whose books explored the Cistercian past, plumbed the modern psyche and protested against political hypocrisy. The thirteenth century, however, provides a convenient cut-off date for this brief overview. Those interested in exploring further are referred to the *Dictionnaire des auteurs cisterciens*, cited in note 1, below.

Notes

1   É. Brouette, A. Dimier and E. Manning (eds.), *Dictionnaire des auteurs cisterciens*, La documentation cistercienne 16 (Rochefort, 1975–9).

2   'primi huius ecclesie fundatores', *Exordium Parvum*, prologue; ed. Waddell, *Narrative*, pp. 232–59 (p. 233).

3   C. Stercal, *Stephen Harding: A Biographical Sketch and Texts* (Kalamazoo, MI, 2008; pub. in Italian 2001).

4   Waddell, *Narrative*, pp. 261–73. Waddell reviews the authorship of and scholarship on the several versions of this distinctive document.

5   William of Malmesbury, *Gesta Regum anglorum* 4.20; ed. and trans. R.A.B. Mynors *et al.*, *Gesta Regum Anglorum: The History of the English Kings*, 2 vols. (Oxford, 2007), vol. 1, pp. 576–84. See H.E.J. Cowdrey, 'Quidam frater Stephanus nomine, anglicus natione': The English Background of Stephen Harding', *Revue bénédictine*, 101 (1991), 322–40, repr. in *The New Monastery: Texts and Studies on the Earliest Cistercians*, ed. E.R. Elder, CF 60 (Kalamazoo, MI, 1998), pp. 57–77. On Stephen's companion and their travels, see Cowdrey, 'Peter, Monk of Molesme and Prior of Jully', in *Cross Cultural Convergences in the Crusader Period*, ed. M. Goodich, S. Menache and S. Schein (New York, 1995), pp. 59–73. See also Wim Verbaal's chapter in this volume.

6   *Exordium Cistercii* 2.9; Waddell, *Narrative*, p. 402; *VP* 4.19; *PL* 185:237.

7   For editions and translations of the works mentioned, see the primary sources listed at the end of this volume.

8   D.N. Bell, *The Image and Likeness: The Augustinian Spirituality of William of Saint Thierry*, CS 78 (Kalamazoo, MI, 1984); B. McGinn, 'William of St. Thierry', in *Growth*, pp. 225–74; and P. Verdeyen, *La théologie mystique de Guillaume de Saint-Thierry* (Paris, 1990).

9   A. Wilmart, 'La série et la date des ouvrages de Guilluame de Saint-Thierry', *Revue Mabillon*, 14 (1924), 157–67.

10 Now thought to have been the *Theologia 'scholarium'* and student notes. See C.J. Mews, 'Peter Abelard's "Theologia" Re-Examined', *RTAM*, 52 (1985), 109–58 and 'Bernard of Clairvaux and Peter Abelard', in B. P. McGuire (ed.), *A Companion to Bernard of Clairvaux* (Leiden, 2011), pp. 133–68 (p. 158).

11 *Epistola Guillelmi abbatis* (*Letter of Abbot William*), *Ep* 326 inter Bernardi; *PL* 182:531–3; ed. P. Verdeyen, CCCM 89A (Turnhout, 2007), pp. 3–15.

12 A. Squire, *Aelred of Rievaulx: A Study* (London, 1969; repr. Kalamazoo, MI, 1981); M.L. Dutton's introductions to Cistercian Publications' translations of Aelred's works; A. Hallier, *The Monastic Theology of Aelred of Rievaulx* (Spencer, MA and Shannon, 1969; first pub. in French 1959); J.R. Sommerfeldt, *Aelred of Rievaulx: Pursuing Perfect Happiness* (New York, 2005). For a complete, if outdated, listing, see A. Hoste, *Bibliotheca Aelrediana: A Survey of the Manuscripts, Old Catalogues, Editions and Studies Concerning St. Aelred of Rievaulx* (Steenbrugge, 1962) and P.-A. Burton, *Bibliotheca Aelrediana secunda: une bibliographie cumulative (1962–1996)* (Louvain-la-Neuve, 1997).

13 M.L. Dutton, 'Introduction', in *Walter Daniel: The Life of Aelred of Rievaulx and The Letter to Maurice*, trans. F.M. Powicke and J.P. Freeland, CF 57 (Kalamazoo, MI, 1994) pp. 7–88.

14 C. Brooke, 'Gregorian Reform in Action: Clerical Marriage in England, 1050–1200', *Cambridge Historical Journal*, 12 (1956), 1–21; A.L. Barstow, *Married Priests and the Reforming Papacy: The Eleventh-Century Debates* (New York, 1982).

15 The Peterborough Chronicle (*Chronicon Angliae Petriburgense*, ed. J.A. Giles [1845], p. 99), cited Dutton, 'Introduction', p. 40.

16 *Vita Aelredi* 30; ed. and trans. F.M. Powicke (London, 1950); rev. and repr. in *Walter Daniel: The Life of Aelred of Rievaulx*, p. 119.

17 *Vita Aelredi* 20.

18 *De spirituali amicitia*, e.g. Liber 1 (*PL* 195:661: 'et in Christo inchoetur, et secundum Christum servetur, et ad Christum finis ejus et utilitas referatur ...'); 2 (672: 'a Christo inchoantur, per Christum promoventur, in Christo perficiuntur').

19 B. McGinn, 'The Other Voices of Cîteaux', in *Growth*, pp. 309–23 (p. 311).

20 Studies are fewer than Guerric deserves. See McGinn, *Growth*, pp. 276–84; and J. Morson, *Christ the Way: The Christology of Guerric of Igny*, CS 25 (Kalamazoo, MI, 1976).

21 'Introduction', in *Guerric of Igny: Liturgical Sermons*, trans. monks of Mount Saint Bernard, 2 vols., CF 8 and CF 32 (Spencer, MA, 1971), vol. 1, cites in evidence the contemporary life of Hugh of Marchiennes; *Vita Hugonis, Abbatis Marchianensis*, ed. E. Martène and U. Durand, *Thesaurus Novus Anecdotorum*, 3 (Paris, 1717), cols. 1708–36 (cols. 1722–4).

22 See Conrad of Eberbach's late twelfth-century *Exordium Magnum*, dist. 3, chapters 8–9; ed. B. Griesser (Rome, 1961), pp. 163–6.

23 See *Ep* 89 and 90 of Bernard of Clairvaux; Letters 92 and 93 in B. Scott James (trans.), *The Letters of St Bernard of Clairvaux*, intro. B.M. Kienzle (Stroud and Kalamazoo, MI, 1998; first pub. 1953).

24 *Vita Hugonis* 16; 3, col. 1723.

25 Igny was the fourth daughter house of Clairvaux and the mother house of Signy, William of Saint Thierry's Cistercian home. See Bernard's *Ep* 141, an attempt to convince the first abbot, Humbert, to remain in office (*PL* 182:296; SBOp 7, pp. 338–9), and Bernard, *Humb*; *PL* 183:513–18; SBOp 5, pp. 440–7.

26 McGinn, *Growth*, p. 280. See his discussion of Guerric in 'Other Voices from Cîteaux', pp. 276–84.

27 'successoribus notris', *Exordium Parvum*, prologue; Waddell, *Narrative*, p. 233.

28 T. Merton, 'Father and Son Cistercians of the Twelfth Century: Blessed Amadeus of Hauterive, "the Elder", and Saint Amadeus, Bishop of Lausanne', *CSQ*, 43 (2008), 379–90; R. Clair, 'Saint Pierre II de Tarentaise et Saint Amédée de Lausanne', *Cîteaux*, 25 (1974), 287–98; and C. Waddell's introduction to *Magnificat: Homilies in Praise of the Blessed Virgin Mary*, trans. M.-B. Saïd *et al.*, CF 18A (Kalamazoo, MI, 1978).

29 B. McGinn, *The Golden Chain: A Study in the Theological Anthropology of Isaac of Stella*, CS 15 (Spencer, MA and Washington, DC, 1972), bibliography, pp. 246–53. See also McGinn's introduction to *Isaac of Stella: Sermons on the Christian Year 1*, trans. H. McCaffery, CF 11 (Kalamazoo, MI, 1979); McGinn, 'Isaac of Stella on the Divine Nature', *Analecta Cisterciensia*, 29 (1973), 1–53; and McGinn, *Growth*, pp. 284–96.

30   Isaac, S 18.1; PL 194:1750: 'in hanc semotam, et inclusam Oceano insulam nudi ac naufragi, nudam nudi Christi crucem amplexi'.

31   É. Gilson, *The Mystical Theology of Saint Bernard*, CS 120 (London 1940; repr. Kalamazoo, MI, 1990; first pub. in French 1934), p. 6.

32   McGinn, 'Introduction', *Isaac of Stella: Sermons 1*, p. xiv.

33   S 22.10; PL 194:1762: 'de ineffabili fari volumus, de quo nihil proprie dici potest', *Isaac of Stella: Sermons 1*, p. 180.

34   E. Mikkers, 'De vita et operibus Gilberti de Hoylandis', *Cîteaux*, 14 (1963), 33–43, 265–79; J. Leclercq, 'La première rédaction des sermons in Cantica Canticorum de Gilbert de Hoyland', *Revue bénédictine*, 62 (1952), 289–91; and McGinn, *Growth*, pp. 298–303.

35   Mikkers, 'De vita et operibus', pp. 36–7.

36   S 16–18, according to A. Dimier (*Dictionnaire des auteurs cisterciens*, pp. 291–2); S 15–22, according to L.C. Braceland, 'Introduction', in *Gilbert of Hoyland: Sermons on the Song of Songs 1*, CF 14 (Kalamazoo, MI, 1978), p. 11: 'a recognizable series which comments on Canticle 3:3–11'.

37   *Tractatus Ascetici*; PL 194:251–89; *Epistolae* 289–98; trans. L.C. Braceland, *Gilbert of Hoyland IV: Treatises, Epistles, and Sermons*, CF 38 (Kalamazoo, MI, 1981). Two sermons on the Gospel of Matthew, with a prologue, contained in MS Bodley 87, the Bodleian Library, Oxford, identified as being by 'Master Gilbert, abbot' were also edited by Braceland in this volume. The attribution to Gilbert of Hoyland, suggested by Leclercq and Lubac in 1953 and 1959, was strengthened in Braceland's opinion by the 'light and friendly style reminiscent of Gilbert of Hoyland'.

38   F. Gastaldelli, *Ricerche su Goffredo d'Auxerre: Il compendio anonimo del 'Super Apocalypsim'* (Rome, 1970); J. Leclercq, 'Les écrits de Geoffroy d'Auxerre', *Revue bénédictine*, 62 (1952), 277–88; and H. Lange, *Traités du XIIe siècle sur la symbolique des nombres: Geoffroy d'Auxerre et Thibault de Langres* (Copenhagen, 1978).

39   *VP* 4.2.10; *PL* 185:327.

40   Geoffrey's own two works against Gilbert of Poitiers appear in *PL* 185:587–96 and 595–617; U.-R. Blumenthal, 'Cardinal Albinus of Albano and the Digesta pauperis scolaris Albini. MS. Ottob.lat.3057', *Archivum Historiae Pontificiae*, 20 (1982), 7–49; Blumenthal, *Papal Reform and Canon Law in the 11th and 12th Centuries* (Aldershot, 1998), pp. 64–6 includes an appendix on them; N.M. Häring, 'The Writings against Gilbert of Poitiers by Geoffrey of Auxerre', *Analecta Cisterciensia*, 22 (1966), 3–83.

41   D.N. Bell, 'The Ascetic Spirituality of Baldwin of Ford', *Cîteaux*, 31 (1980), 227–50.

42   W. Stubbs (ed.), *Gervase of Canterbury: Historical Works*, 2 vols. (London, 1879–80), vol. II, p. 400.

43   J. Dimock (ed.), *Itinerarium Kambriae* (London, 1868), p. 147; trans. L. Thorpe, *The Journey through Wales* (Harmonsworth, 1978), pp. 205–6.

44   *Itinerarium Kambriae* 2.14, p. 149; Thorpe, *The Journey through Wales*, p. 206.

45 Bell, 'Introduction', in *Baldwin of Forde: Spiritual Tractates*, 2 vols., CF 38 and 41 (Kalamazoo, MI, 1986), vol. I, p. 9.

46 *Ibid.*, p. 12.

47 'cum novos in ramos novella coepisset pullulare plantatio', *Exordium Cistercii* 12; Waddell, *Narrative*, p. 402.

48 J.F. O'Sullivan, 'Introduction', in *Cistercians and Cluniacs: The Case for Cîteaux*, CF 33 (Kalamazoo, MI, 1977), p. 146.

49 H. Costello, 'The Idea of the Church in the Sermons of John of Ford', *Cîteaux*, 21 (1970), 236–64; Costello, 'John of Ford and the Quest for Wisdom', *Cîteaux*, 23 (1972), 141–59; C.J. Holdsworth, 'John of Ford and the Interdict', *English Historical Review*, 78 (1963), 705–14; Holdsworth, 'John of Ford and English Cistercian Writings 1167–1214', *Transactions of the Royal Historical Society*, fifth series, 11 (1961), 117–36; and H. Costello and C.J. Holdsworth (eds.), *A Gathering of Friends: The Learning and Spirituality of John of Forde*, CS 161 (Kalamazoo, MI, 1996).

50 *S* 76.8–9.

51 *S* 41.

52 *S* 76.2.

53 T. Merton, *The Feast of Freedom: Monastic Formation according to Adam of Perseigne* (Gethsemani Abbey, KY, [n.d.]), repr. as introduction to *The Letters of Adam of Perseigne 1*, trans. G. Perigo, CF 21 (Kalamazoo, MI, 1976); K. Romanuik, 'Mary, Mediatrix of All Graces, in the Work of Adam of Perseigne', *CSQ*, 33 (1998), 185–90.

54 A.J. Andrea, 'Adam of Perseigne and the Fourth Crusade', *Cîteaux*, 36 (1985), 21–37.

55 R. Pernoud, *Poètes et romanciers du moyen-âge* (Paris, 1958), pp. 847–61; J. du Halgouët, 'Poètes oubliés, Hélinand le Trouvère', *COCR*, 20 (1958), 31–135; E.R. Smits, 'Editing the *Chronicon* of Helinand of Froidmont: The Marginal Notes', *Sacris Erudiri*, 32 (1991), 269–89; B.M. Kienzle, 'Deed and Word: Helinand's Toulouse Sermons', in *Erudition at God's Service*, ed. J.R. Sommerfeldt, CF 98 (Kalamazoo, MI, 1987), pp. 267–76 and 277–90; Kienzle, 'Cistercian Views of the City in the Sermons of Helinand of Froidmont', in *Medieval Sermons and Society: Cloister, City, University*, ed. J. Hamesse *et al.* (Louvain-la-Neuve, 1998), pp. 165–82; Kienzle, 'Hélinand de Froidmont et la prédication cistercienne dans le Midi (1145–1229)', in *La prédication en Pays d'oc (XIIe–début XVe siècle)*, ed. J.-L. Biget *et al.* (Toulouse, 1997), pp. 37–67; and Kienzle, 'Mary Speaks against Heresy: An Unedited Sermon of Hélinand for the Purification, Paris, B.N. ms. lat. 14591', *Sacris Erudiri*, 32 (1991), 291–308.

56 'Por ce ai changié mon corage / Et ai laissié et gieu et rage', *Verses on Death* 1; ed. and trans. J.L. Porter, *Helinand of Froidmont: Verses on Death*, CF 61 (Kalamazoo, MI and Spencer, MA, 1999), pp. 50–1.

57 W.D. Paden, '*De Monachis rithmos facientibus*: Hélinand de Froidmont, Bertran de Born, and the Cistercian General Chapter of 1199', *Speculum*, 55 (1980), 669–85 (esp. pp. 674–7). Paden suggests (p. 680) that 'such diffusion through the vernacular of his vision of a corrupt and parasitic

church may well have increased the uneasiness of spirit felt by those entrusted with the maintenance of religious order. Perhaps a sign of the disturbing effects of his poem may be read in the anonymity with which it was transmitted by the scribes of all twenty-four known manuscripts, save one ... It seems likely that the Vers helped provoke the condemnation of *rythmi* by the [Cistercian] General Chapter of 1199.'

58 B. Duculot, 'Le bienheureux Hélinand de Froidmont poète du XIIe siècle à la télévision et au theatre du XXe siècle', *Cîteaux*, 16 (1975), 109–11 (p. 110).

59 According to Vincent of Beauvais: *Speculum historiale* 29.108, *ad annum* 1208; *PL* 212:478.

60 C.H. Lawrence, 'Stephen of Lexington and Cistercian University Studies', *Journal of Ecclesiastical History*, 2 (1960), 164–78; B.W. O'Dwyer, 'The Impact of the Native Irish on the Cistercians in the Thirteenth Century', *Journal of Religious History*, 3 (1967), 287–301; O'Dwyer, 'The Crisis in the Cistercian Monasteries in Ireland in the Early Thirteenth Century', *Analecta Cisterciensia*, 31 (1975), 267–304; 32 (1975), 3–112; E. Kwanten, 'Le collège Saint-Bernard à Paris, sa fondation et ses débuts', *Revue d'histoire ecclésiastique*, 43 (1948), 443–72; P. Dautrey, 'Croissance et adaptation chez les Cisterciens au treizième siècle: les débuts du collège des Bernardins de Paris', *Analecta Cisterciensia*, 32 (1977 for 1976), 122–215; and C. Obert-Piketty, 'La promotion des études chez les cisterciens à travers le recrutement des étudiants du collège Saint-Bernard de Paris au moyen âge', *Cîteaux*, 39 (1988), 65–78.

61 B.W. O'Dwyer, 'Introduction', *Stephen of Lexington: Letters from Ireland, 1228–1229*, CF 28 (Kalamazoo, MI, 1982), p. 5.

62 M. Cawley, *Send Me God: The Lives of Ida the Compassionate of Nivelles, Nun of la Ramée, Arnulf, Lay Brother of Villers, and Abundus, Monk of Villers, by Goswin of Bossut* (Turnhout, 2003 and University Park, PA, 2005).

63 R. De Ganck, *Beatrice of Nazareth in Her Context*, CS 121 (Kalamazoo, MI, 1991); De Ganck, *Towards Unification with God*, CS 122 (Kalamazoo, MI, 1991); vol. II contains an exhaustive bibliography on Beatrice and the *mulieres religiosae* of her generation; M.A. Sulivan, 'An Introduction to Beatrice of Nazareth', in *Hidden Springs: Cistercian Monastic Women*, ed. J.A. Nichols and L.T. Shank, CS 113 (Kalamazoo, MI, 1995), pp. 345–60; R. Bradley, 'Love and Knowledge in *Seven Manners of Loving*', in *Hidden Springs*, ed. Nichols and Shank, pp. 361–76; A. Hollywood, 'Inside Out: Beatrice of Nazareth and Her Hagiographer', in *Gendered Voices: Medieval Saints and Their Interpreters*, ed. C.M. Mooney (Philadelphia, PA, 1999), pp. 78–98; E.M. Wiberg Pedersen, 'The Incarnation of Beatrice of Nazareth's Theology', in *New Trends in Feminine Spirituality: The Holy Women of Liège and Their Impact*, ed. J. Dor *et al.* (Turnhout, 1999), pp. 61–79; Pedersen, 'Image of God – Image of Mary – Image of Woman: On the Theology and Spirituality of Beatrice of Nazareth', *CSQ*, 29 (1994), 209–20; M. Casey, 'Beatrice of Nazareth (1200–68): Cistercian Mystic' and 'Beatrice of Nazareth:

The Seven Modes of Love (a Translation)', *Tjurunga: Australasian Benedictine Review*, 50 (1996), 44–70 and 71–82; and J.H. Winkelman, 'Over Beatrijs visioen en de imperfectie van het menselijke interpretatievermogen', *Amsterdamer Beiträge zur älteren Germanistik*, 36 (1992), 181–96. See also Elizabeth Freeman's chapter in this volume.

64 On Beatrice's father's activities, see R. De Ganck, 'The Three Foundations of Bartholomew of Tienen', *Cîteaux*, 37 (1986), 49–75.

65 *Life* of Beatrice 1.10.

66 *Ibid.*

67 Her *Insinuationes divinae pietatis* was first edited in 1536 at Cologne and again at Poitiers in 1877.

68 'quibusque temporius, cenobium et tenor uite illorum exordium sumpserit', *Exordium Parvum*, prologue; Waddell, *Narrative*, p. 233.

69 For example, Nicolas Maniacoria, a twelfth-century monk of Tre Fontane, near Rome, *Libellus de corruptione et de correptione psalmorum et aliarum quarundam scripturarum*, see A. Wilmart, 'Nicolas Manjacoria: Cistercien à Trois Fontaines', *Revue bénédictine*, 63 (1953), 3–17.

70 Conrad of Eberbach, *Exordium Magnum Cisterciense*; trans. B. Ward and P. Savage, *The Great Beginning of Cîteaux*, ed. E. R. Elder, CS 72 (Collegeville, MN, 2012). On the need for a new edition and on the manuscript tradition – including the supposed loss of the original Eberbach codex and its recovery – see F. Gastaldelli, 'A Critical Note on the Edition of the Exordium Magnum Cisterciense', *CSQ*, 39 (2004), 311–19 (also published in Italian, German and French; p. 311).

71 See P. Savage, 'Introduction', *The Great Beginning of Cîteaux*, pp. 17–24: 'Conrad's Sources'; M. Casey, 'Herbert of Clairvaux's *Book of Wonderful Happenings*', *CSQ*, 25 (1990), 37–64.

72 'Biographies spirituelles', in *Dictionnaire de spiritualité ascétique et mystique: doctrine et histoire*, ed. M. Viller et al., 17 vols. (Paris, 1932–95), vol. 1, cols. 1658–9.

15 The spiritual teaching of the early Cistercians

BERNARD MCGINN

In his *Sermo de diversis* 121 Bernard of Clairvaux told his monks: 'We are in the school of Christ (*In schola Christi sumus*), and there we learn two teachings: the one that the one true Master teaches us himself, that is, love; and the other through his ministers, that is, fear.'[1] The appeal to being in the 'school of Christ' was a mark of the self-identity of the Cistercian Order.[2] Manifested in the abbot of Clairvaux,[3] and also illustrated by three other major early Cistercian theologians influenced by him (William of Saint Thierry, Aelred of Rievaulx and Isaac of Stella),[4] the 'great miracle', as Bernard put it,[5] of the success of the Cistercians made a lasting impact on the medieval world. The institutional, political and cultural roles of the Cistercians are presented in other essays in this volume; here I will concentrate on their spiritual theology during the fifty years between c. 1120 and 1170.[6] However much scholars continue to study the Cistercian Order, if the early Cistercians still reach a wide audience, it is fair to say it is largely because of their spiritual teaching, what they learned 'in the school of Christ'.

The goal of learning in Christ's school was not restricted to monastics. Bernard and his confreres believed that all the baptised are called to deeper knowledge and more intimate contact with God, even to the embrace of the Divine Word. In *SC* 83.1 Bernard says that all Christians are called to marriage with the Word, though monastics have a privileged highway to the goal. Although the White Monks were the virtuosi of the religious life, they felt an obligation to speak, both to other monks and (as history has shown) to non-monastics.

When we speak of learning in the school of Christ as a mark of the Cistercians this does not mean that we need to think of the twelfth-century Cistercian writers as constituting a 'school' in the intellectual or doctrinal sense. The major Cistercian authors of the twelfth century were distinctive, although they shared institutional, personal, intellectual and spiritual bonds centred on the figure of Bernard of Clairvaux. William of Saint Thierry was one of Bernard's closest friends;

Aelred of Rievaulx had contact with Bernard, who persuaded him to write his major work, the *Speculum caritatis*. Isaac of Stella was somewhat younger, but had met Bernard and was deeply inspired by him (see *S* 52.15). What tied these Cistercian mystics together was not just their links to Bernard, but also the fact that they shared a commitment to the same form of monastic life and its imperative of realising the goal of human living – the restoration of the *imago Dei* given to Adam in the beginning, severely deformed in the Fall, but once again made accessible to humans through the saving work of Christ. Their teaching (*doctrina*) about this saving truth includes correct knowledge (*scientia*) about faith, but aims at the higher gift of wisdom (*sapientia*), the 'savoury knowing' that reforms, transforms and unites a person to God.[7] The four Cistercians treated here were intent on exploring the dynamics of this process of restoration, though they did so in their own ways. Early Cistercian spiritual theology consists of a series of variations on a few central themes.

These Cistercian were theologians, though not scholastic theologians. As Jean Leclercq showed more than a half-century ago, monastic theology had its own teaching context, characteristics, genera and objectives.[8] Monastic theology was the product of an environment in which the abbot and novice master were responsible for helping their monks find God, especially through spiritual guidance, liturgical prayer and the study of the Bible. Its literary forms were closely tied to Scripture, finding expression especially in biblical commentaries and sermons for the major feasts, though treatises and letters were also employed. The Cistercians were masters of the spiritual, or mystical, interpretation of the Bible, penetrating beneath the surface, or literal, meaning of the text to the depths of its doctrinal and spiritual teaching.[9] Building on the writings of the Fathers and influenced by the classical literary heritage, the theology of the monks was not opposed to the Augustinian notion of believing in order to understand (*credo ut intelligam*), but insisted that the ultimate goal of belief was to attain deeper experience of God (*credo ut experiar*). Monastic theology was rhetorical, synthetic, symbolical; it was rarely analytical or dialectical in the manner of the schools. This did not mean that monks like Bernard and his followers were not precise and often original dogmatic theologians. Bernard's ability as a dogmatic theologian is evident in his letter-treatise against Abelard (*Ep* 190). Although filled with the rhetorical attacks typical of Bernard's polemics, the abbot's rebuttals of Abelard's trinitarian and Christological teachings are insightful and carefully argued. With William and Isaac we also find elements of a more speculative theology, but a speculation in the service of lived experience. The Cistercian emphasis on experience is summarised by Bernard, who told the monks in the third of his *Sermones super Cantica canticorum*: 'Today we are reading in the book of experience' (*Hodie legimus in libro experientiae*).[10] It is important to remember, however, that Bernard and the other Cistercians insisted that individual experience was not the norm, but was to be normed by faith (*SC* 28.8–9 and especially Quad 5.5). William once said in regret, 'When I reckon up the [spiritual] wealth of others I blush for myself and sigh because what I contemplate in another I would prefer to experience in myself' (*Ep frat* 194). The emphasis on personal appropriation of the divine mystery is central to the spiritual theology of the White Monks.

Our Cistercian authors were focused on how humans attain deeper consciousness of God here below as preparation for the full union-vision of the coming life. Theological anthropology and mystical teaching about the path to God form the core of their teaching. This does not mean, however, that they were indifferent to the basis of anthropology and mystical teaching in the fundamentals of Christian faith regarding God, Christ and Church. The Cistercians showed less interest in two other theological areas popular with many monastic theologians: the doctrine of creation and the theology of history. The theology of history was a prominent concern for traditional Benedictines, such as Rupert of Deutz and Hildegard of Bingen, as well as among the reformed canons of the twelfth century (e.g., Anselm of Havelberg, Hugh of Saint Victor, Gerhoh of Reichersberg). Bernard shows some interest in the history of salvation (e.g., *SC* 33; *QH* 6), as does Isaac (e.g., *S* 26, *S* 37, and *S* 53), but this is not a central theme. The synthetic nature of Cistercian theology makes it difficult, even artificial, to excerpt particular doctrines from the seamless web of their writings, but it is important to see how their theology (i.e., in the proper sense of the doctrine of God), Christology and ecclesiology demonstrate that the early Cistercians anchored their spiritual teaching in the central teachings of medieval Christianity.

The Cistercians did not engage much in thinking about *theologia* as a discipline, with the exception of Isaac and his concern for a Dionysian model of three forms of *theologia* (as in *S* 22.9 and *S* 23.9). But they were concerned with the relation of faith and reason, especially in light of contemporary Early scholasticism with its new 'scientific' mode of relating the deposit of faith to academic investigation. Cistercian reservations about the new theology, though sometimes sharp, as with Bernard's and William's attacks on Abelard, were not directed at school theology *as such*, but rather against a theology that was seen as perverting the proper relation between faith and reason. Bernard had good relations with more moderate schoolmen, like Hugh of Saint Victor and Peter Lombard. What Bernard and the other Cistercians insisted upon was that in fallen humans the *scientia* pursued by reason could often go astray and therefore always needed to be guided by humility and the truth given in revelation. Isaac, trained in the northern French schools in the 1120s and 1130s, shows the most confidence in the potential of speculative reason, but even he was compelled to retreat, as can be seen in his noted S 46, also known as the *Apologia*.

William spelled out an original position on the relation of faith and reason in the two trinitarian treatises he wrote against Peter Abelard, the *Aenigma fidei* and the *Speculum fidei*. In the former work (*Aenig* 40–1) William distinguishes three modes of faith which *mutatis mutandis* can be said to characterise the Cistercian approach. The three theological virtues of faith, hope and charity that re-energise the trinitarian image of the soul are rooted in faith and 'three degrees of understanding in the progress of faith'. The first is diligent investigation of what is to be believed; the second is 'how to think and talk correctly about what is rightly believed', while the third is 'the experience of the realities in perceiving God'. The second level, that of 'faith seeking understanding', is where the *ratio fidei* is at work, not a work of human reasoning from below, but a grace from above that guides and corrects the human mind so that it can truly 'understand' (*intelligere* from *intus legere*), that is, '"read within" in the affection of his heart what he believes'. William and Bernard felt (rightly or wrongly) that Abelard's dependence on human reason negated the necessity of the *ratio fidei* in spiritually effective penetration of belief.

Rooted in the New Testament doctrine that God is love (e.g., 1 John 4.16), the Cistercian teaching about God as one and three centres around the transcendent divine charity/love that is the source and the goal of all created being. Each of our four early Cistercians has a developed doctrine of God as love.[11] Especially noteworthy is Aelred's *Speculum caritatis*, which studies charity both as the reality of God and the power that draws us back to Him. In Book 1.19 he says of God:

> Charity alone is his unchangeable and eternal rest, his eternal and unchangeable tranquillity, his eternal and unchangeable Sabbath. It was the sole cause why he created what was to be created, why he rules what is to be ruled ... advances what is to be advanced and perfects what is to be perfected ... His charity is his very will and also his very goodness; all this is nothing but his very being.

The White Monks were not as concerned as the schoolmen with spelling out a detailed doctrine of the divine nature and attributes, although there are important passages in their writings that explore the proper ways to speak of God (e.g., Bernard, *Csi* 5.6–8). Perhaps the most penetrating investigation of the divine nature in the early Cistercians is a series of sermons for Sexagesima Sunday by Isaac (*S* 18–23), a metaphysical and deeply negative (apophatic) account of God as the 'One, Simple, Immobile' *supersubstantia*, who nonetheless unfolds as the three persons of the Trinity.[12] The abbot of Stella recognises how the *ratio fidei* is what allows us to break our silence and say something, however halting, about God: 'When we wish to speak about the Ineffable, about whom nothing can be properly said, it is necessary to be silent, or to use altered terms' (*S* 22.10). The mystery of the Trinity is often treated by our four thinkers. Although Bernard does not give the Trinity a central role, there is still a considerable trinitarian theology scattered over his writings;[13] but it is fair to say that William provides the most powerful trinitarian theology. As Odo Brooke put it, 'the great contribution of William of Saint Thierry is to have evolved a theology of the Trinity which is essentially mystical, and a mystical theology which is essentially trinitarian'.[14]

Developed out of Augustine's *De trinitate*, William's Spirit-centred mysticism is one of the high points of Cistercian, indeed, of all medieval theology. In his two treatises on the Trinity (*Aenig* and *Spec*), as well as in numerous passages on how the soul becomes one with the Father and the Son in the loving bond of their own union, that is, the Holy Spirit (e.g., *Contemp* 11; *Ep frat* 235–7, 274–5, 262–3; *Cant* 109), William stresses the communitarian aspect of the three persons, a transcendent sharing communicated to humanity through the Son's taking on flesh and the Spirit's being poured out in our hearts (Rom. 5.5). William's insistence on the importance of the three persons as subsistent relations and his emphasis on the Father as the source and origin of the whole divinity underline the constitutive role of each of the three persons in our growing likeness (*similitudo*) to God. His mystical theology is Spirit-centred, both in an innertrinitarian sense, because the Spirit is the one who makes the three persons one, and in an extratrinitarian way, since the Spirit is sent to bring us to where we were always destined to be. Our union with God is not a mere sharing in God's union; it *is* God's own union, though received in our limited being. As the kiss, embrace, love and oneness of the mutually constituted Father and Son, the Holy Spirit: 'becomes for a human person in relation to God, in an appropriate manner, what by consubstantial unity he is for the Son in relation to the Father and for the Father in relation to the Son' (*Ep frat* 263). Our oneness of spirit with God is intersubjective and circumincessive, or interpenetrating, precisely because it is realised within 'the place' of God's own oneness. The Father is 'where' the Son is and the Son is 'where' the Father is (see Matt. 11.27, a favourite text of William and the other Cistercians), precisely because that 'where' is the Holy Spirit. It is also 'where' we are called to be.

The Christology of the early Cistercians is more concerned with Christ's saving work than it is with ontological questions of the union of the divine and human natures in the Godman.[15] The redemption theology of the Cistercians, along with the slightly earlier contribution of Anselm, can be said to be decisive for later Western views of Christ's saving action. Once again, the core of Cistercian Christology is traditional in adhering to the patristic formula that God became man so that man might become God (e.g., Bernard, *V Nat* 1.2), but the way in which the White Monks understood the economy of salvation had new elements that were to be decisive, not only in the later Middle Ages, but for centuries beyond. In this dimension of theology, Bernard was once again the central figure. First of all, the abbot of Clairvaux created his own, more concrete, answer to the Anselmian question *Cur deus homo?* (Why the Godman?) by showing how through the Fall humans were entrapped in a carnal world that allowed them no access to God and the world of the spirit *unless* God condescended to take on flesh and attract carnal humans to begin the ascent to the spiritual realm (*SC* 1–8, especially 4–6). A presentation of Bernard's understanding of Christ's saving work is found in his attack on Abelard's redemption theology in *Ep* 190.11–26. 'Carnal love of Christ' (*amor carnalis Christi*; see, e.g., *SC* 20.4) is the necessary starting point for the restoration of the *imago Dei*. The other early Cistercians agreed with Bernard (and broke with many patristic and earlier medieval authors) in emphasising that human love of the exemplary human, Jesus Christ, not an eschewing of our carnal nature, was the starting point for beginning the path to loving God in a spiritual way.[16] Cistercian emphasis on devotion to the events of the human life of Jesus was part of a broader spiritual groundswell in the twelfth century and on, but no religious Order contributed more to this new theology and piety than the White Monks. The Cistercians, however, were also Benedictines whose lives were formed by liturgical celebration, so it is no surprise that Bernard, and after him Aelred and Isaac (we do not have William's sermons), emphasised the need to appropriate the meaning of the mysteries of Christ's life as relived in the cycle of feasts of the liturgical year. Christ was not a figure of the

historic past; he was at work in each believer through effective participation in the annual re-presentations of the mysteries of salvation from
Advent through the feast of All Saints. As Isaac puts it: 'This Nativity of
Christ, and also the life, death, Resurrection and Ascension are indeed
begun, but are not yet completed' (*S* 42.20).[17] For Bernard the Word's
taking flesh for our salvation and the need for ascending from carnal
to spiritual love of Christ implied an emphasis on the Nativity and the
Ascension in his preaching. The abbot of Clairvaux preached on all the
mysteries of Christ's life, but it is interesting to see a breakdown of his
Sermones per annum (other sermons in the *De diversis* would expand
the list): seven sermons on Advent; six on the eve of the Nativity; five
on the Nativity itself, and ten on the feasts after Christmas. Bernard
preached no less than seventeen sermons on the Lenten Psalm 90 'Qui
habitat', but only five sermons on Holy Week. He has five sermons on
Easter week and six on the Ascension. Also popular with the abbot was
the feast of All Saints (five sermons) and the Dedication of a Church
(six sermons). William shared Bernard's view of the need for starting
with a 'carnal love' of the events of Christ's life, but was more prophetic
of late medieval piety in the intensity of his devotion to Christ on the
cross (see *Med* 10). Unlike Bernard, William also taught what later
came to be called the 'absolute predestination of Christ', that is, that
the Word would have become incarnate even if Adam had not sinned
(e.g., *Med* 10.7–8).Emphasis on the human life of Jesus was doubtless a
factor in Cistercian theology and devotion to Mary, though this too was
part of a broad movement in twelfth-century piety. Bernard has come
down in history as an influential Mariologist on the basis of his Marian
homilies (e.g., *Ann; Asspt; Miss*). There is no reason to downplay this
aspect of his thought, though it is important to put it in a Christological
perspective.[18]

Early Cistercian theology was also concerned with ecclesiology
and the doctrine of the sacraments, though in its own way. Once again
Bernard of Clairvaux is representative. The abbot's view of the Church
was both spiritual and practical. The higher, spiritual aspect is seen in
his reflections on the Church as Christ's supernal bride, predestined
from eternity and composed of both angels and saved humans – the
mother of all believers (e.g., *SC* 9–10; *Ded* 5). Bernard's practical ecclesiology is set forth especially in the treatise of instruction he wrote for
his former pupil, Pope Eugenius III (*Csi*), in his letter-treatise on the
conduct and office of bishops (*Ep* 42) and in his work on the monastic
rule and its relation to other Church offices (*Pre*). In addition, Bernard's
letters have been seen as a *speculum ecclesiae*, a collection designed

to instruct the varied members of Christ's Body about their obligations and opportunities for spiritual advancement. The Cistercian sense of the communion of saints was richly developed by Isaac into a treatment of the Church as the mystical body of Christ that was among the most profound of the Middle Ages (see *S* 11, *S* 15, *S* 34, *S* 42 and *S* 55). The White Monks were not as much concerned with exploring the definition, constitution and numbering of the sacraments, a major concern for contemporary scholastics. They tended to emphasise the *magnum sacramentum/mysterium* of Christ's presence in the whole ritual life of the community. This is not to say that the Cistercians neglected the theology of the sacraments, especially the need to defend the proper understanding of individual sacraments, as we can see from Bernard's *Ep* 77 to Hugh of Saint Victor on baptism (actually another attack on Abelard), as well as William's treatise on the Eucharist, *De sacramento altaris*.

The dense web of themes of early Cistercian theology found in sermons, commentaries, treatises and letters treated God, Christology and ecclesiology, not as topics for abstract perusal, but as the foundation for a way of life based on the proper grasp of what it meant to be created in the image and likeness of God (Gen. 1.26), as well as an honest recognition of our present sinful misery and need for Christ's grace as the beginning of the road back to ultimate felicity. Cistercian theological anthropology was traditional in understanding man's nature as *imago et similitudo Dei* as an *imago trinitatis* in which the three higher powers of the soul (usually the Augustinian triad of memory, understanding and will) mirrored the three persons in God. Also traditional was the Christological dimension, which understood Genesis in the light of Paul's teaching on the Word as the true *imago patris* (Col. 1.15–16; 2 Cor. 4.4), so that humans are made after the image (*ad imaginem*) and their restoration is a process of Christoformity – *Transformamur cum conformamur* ('We are transformed as we are being conformed', *SC* 62.5).

True to the character of monastic theology, there is no single Cistercian theology of humans as *imago et similitudo*, but a series of variations among and within the authors. In his *De gratia et libero arbitrio* Bernard placed the image nature in human freedom, analysing three aspects of image as *liberum arbitrium* (free choice), 'a self-determining habit of soul' (*Gra* 1.2): the freedom from necessity bestowed by nature but imprisoned by sin; the freedom from sin restored by Christ; and the freedom from misery to be attained in heaven and at times briefly tasted in this life through mystical elevation to God (*Gra* 3.6–7). In *SC* 80–2, however, the abbot lays out a somewhat different account of image and likeness, an example of what he calls *diversa sed non adversa* ('different but not opposed'). William penned an important anthropological treatise, *De natura corporis et animae*, which contains a trinitarian account of the image and likeness. William distinguishes between *imago* as an originating participation in the Trinity and *similitudo* as a perfecting participation in the dynamic relation of the persons by which we can come to resemble God in how we love (see also *Aenig* 6). Isaac wrote the most systematic of the Cistercian treatments. His *Epistola de anima* contains a detailed account of the intellectual and appetitive powers of the soul, including the stages by which the powers ascend to God, an analysis of the union of soul and body and various trinitarian analogies. Aspects of Isaac's *Epistola de anima* had a major impact on later thinking since they were taken over in an eclectic, probably Cistercian, tract of the 1170s, the *De spiritu et anima*, which was widely read because it circulated under Augustine's name. Many of Isaac's sermons also contain theological anthropology.[19]

The Cistercian interest in anthropology, however, was always practical – one needs to know the truth about human nature in order to know how to relate to God. The starting place for this realised anthropology is expressed in the Delphic maxim: *Cognosce teipsum* ('Know yourself'), which for the Cistercians meant recognising the dignity of human creation and the present misery of sinful human existence (see, e.g., *SC* 34–8; Isaac, *S* 2.13). Hence, the need for humility, the foundational virtue for the return process, and also for conversion (*conversio*), which could be conceived both generally as turning away from sin, and more specifically as conversion to the monastic life.[20] The early Cistercians, like many later mystical teachers, were particularly concerned with analysing how the ascent to God (which is one and the same as the interior journey to meet God in the depths of the soul) is effected.

The journey utilises the two fundamental powers of the soul, *sensus*, that is, the capacity for knowing, from sense knowledge through to the knowing of God in *intelligentia/intellectus*, and *affectus*, all forms of attraction, willing and loving. The description of how these powers and their manifestations are brought into play is presented in a wide range of mystical itineraries. Sometimes these take on a cosmic dimension, as in Isaac's *Epistola de anima* 8:

> Just as in the visible world there are as it were mounting steps: earth, water, air, ether or the firmament, and the highest heaven ...

so too there are five stages to wisdom for the soul as it makes its pilgrimage in the world of its body: sense knowledge, imagination, reason, discernment and understanding. For rationality is led to wisdom by five steps, just as the power of desire is led to charity by four. Through these nine stages the soul which lives in the spirit journeys into itself by the powers of knowledge and desire as if on internal feet.

Most of the Cistercian itineraries, however, are simpler than Isaac's and generally based on three or four stages. Bernard, for example, famously spoke about the three kisses suggested in Song of Songs 1.1 – the kiss of the feet in penance, the kiss of the hands in virtuous action and the kiss of the mouth of mystical union (*SC* 3–4, 6–9). His *De diligendo deo* is based on the progress of four stages of love toward God, beginning with a person's love of self for the sake of self, moving on to love of self for the love of God, love of God for his own sake and culminating in love of self only for God's sake. Div 101 has a four-stage ascent of the transformation from carnal to spiritual love. Bernard also spoke of the progress of three forms of love (*amor carnalis, amor rationalis, amor spiritualis*: *SC* 20.9), a triple pattern that William richly developed in his *Epistola ad fratres de Monte Dei*, also known as the *Epistola aurea* (see especially 40–1, and 141; also *Cant* 21–3). In Book 3 of the *Speculum caritatis* Aelred distinguished three sabbaths: the sabbath of the love of self, that of love of neighbour and that of love of God leading to mystical rapture.

Although the cognitive dimensions of the mystical path were not neglected by the Cistercians, it is primarily love and desire that drive the process of reformation and ascent, as is especially evident in Bernard's masterwork, the *Sermones super Cantica*.[21] In *SC* 83.4 Bernard declares:

> It is love alone of all motions, perceptions, and affections of the soul by which the creature, though not in equal measure, can repay something to the Creator, weigh back from the same measure .... When God loves, he wants only to be loved; he loves for no other reason than to be loved, knowing that those who have loved him are made blessed in that love.

Bernard specifies ascending levels of love, beginning with that of mercenaries, moving through the love of children, but culminating in the marital love of man and woman, the best model here below of the purity, impetuosity, mutuality and satisfaction of the soul's 'conversion to the Word, its reformation through him, its conformation to him' (*SC* 83.2). The marital model for the highest form of love between God and the soul is most marked in Bernard, due to his use of the Song of Songs as the primary biblical reference for the mystical way.

Like Bernard, William saw the Song of Songs as the mystical guidebook par excellence; his unfinished commentary *Expositio super Cantica canticorum* is one of the jewels of medieval mystical exegesis. William's Spirit-centred view of the path to union does not neglect the role of the Word Incarnate, the Divine Lover made flesh, but it does find that the 'lying together' (*accubitus*) and 'embrace' (*amplexus*) of the soul and Christ on their mutual 'little flowery bed' (*lectulus floridus noster*: S. of S. 1.15) must be understood as a union in and through the Holy Spirit as noted above. Gregory the Great had been the first to use the phrase 'Love itself is a form of understanding.' The Cistercians, especially William, adopted this theme as a way of expressing the interpenetration of loving and knowing in mystical transformation. In *Spec* 101 William describes three stages in love's progress:

> This process takes place more powerfully and worthily when the Holy Spirit ... so draws the human will to himself that the soul loving God, and perceiving him in the act of loving, is transformed suddenly and totally, not indeed into the nature of divinity, but still into a certain form of beatitude above what is human.

This transition from the level of soul (*anima*), through that of intellectual soul (*animus*), to the status of spirit (*spiritus*) involves an experience of God in the act of love that is real and 'concrete', almost like sense knowing, and also a form of connatural knowing – both a *sensus amoris* and the kind of *intelligentia amoris* enshrined in the saying *amor ipse intelligentia est* ('Love itself is a form of understanding'). The phrase appears only four times in William, but the teaching, as reflected in the use of *sensus amoris* and *intelligentia amoris*, is central to his thought. In one place William describes it as follows: 'At times, when grace overflows to secure and manifest experience of something of God in a new way, a kind of sensible reality is suddenly present to the sensation of enlightened love, something that no corporeal sense could hope for, no reason conceive, no intellect be fit for save the intellect of enlightened love' (*Cant* 94). It is through this transformation and new way of knowing 'that a person is made one spirit with God [1 Cor. 6.17] to whom he is drawn' (*Spec* 99).

Isaac is less erotically charged than Bernard and William, though the transformation of love plays its part in his mystical thought (see his discussion of the forms of marriage in *S* 5 and *S* 9). Aelred provides a new option for the transformation of human love in the service of loving God – that of spiritual friendship (*spiritualis amicitia*). Aelred's *Speculum caritatis* provides a summary of the main lines of Cistercian thought about charity as the essence of God, the motive of creation and the power by which the soul can return to its source. Nevertheless, Aelred's most original work was the dialogue he devoted to spiritual friendship, a conversation in which the abbot and his dearest friends investigate how intimate human friendship (among male monks) is not only a model (as in Bernard's view of the marriage of man and woman), but also a real instrument for learning how to love God. Although Aelred depended on classical works on friendship (e.g., Cicero), as well as a long tradition of patristic and medieval literature, his treatise was innovative, profound and still attractive to readers. For Aelred the truest friendship can only be realised in Christ, an insight that leads him to the daring transposition of 1 John 4.16 that if God can be said to be the love we call *caritas*, can we really deny him the title of *amicitia*? The first book of *De spirituali amicitia* begins with the famous line: *Ecce ego et tu; et spero quod tertius inter nos Christus sit* ('Here we are, you and I, and I hope that Christ may be the third among us').

The transformation of love also means the 'ordering of charity' (*ordinatio caritatis*, based on S. of S. 2.4: *Ordinavit in me caritatem*). This ancient theme in Christian mysticism was richly developed in the twelfth century. Learning how to love God for himself alone allows us to love all other persons and things in relation to God, thus re-establishing the order destroyed by sin and the triumph of disordered selfish love (*cupiditas*). This ordering also involves the proper balance between love of God in contemplation and active love of neighbour. The ordering of charity is a frequent theme in Bernard, especially in *SC* 49–50, commenting on S. of S. 2.4 and discussing the relation of *caritas in affectu* (love of God in affection) and *caritas in actu* (love of neighbour in action).[22] For Bernard the delights of the love of God are always higher, but the obligation to help the neighbour often means that we must forego contemplation. William's treatment of S. of S. 2.4 in his *Cant* 120–30 has original aspects, but culminates in emphasising the same essential message that 'true love of self and neighbour is nothing else but love of God (*Cant* 121).[23]

The transformation of love that leads to union is inseparable from the prayer and contemplation that is the daily life of the monk, and at least the aspiration of all the faithful. The ascent of love and knowledge to union could involve the experience of ecstatic states beyond ordinary consciousness (*exstasis/raptus/excessus mentis/sacra ebrietas*). The early Cistercians recognised the reality of such transports, often referring to Paul's famous rapture to the third heaven in 2 Cor. 12.2–4.[24] Nevertheless, states of ecstasy, rapture, 'passing beyond' and spiritual drunkenness were special gifts of God; love of God and of neighbour were the core of the transformation process.

Reasons of space preclude a discussion of the Cistercian theology of prayer. It is worth noting that while our authors often discuss *contemplatio*, unlike the Victorines, the Cistercians did not construct accounts of the various stages of contemplation, but used the term generically as 'concentrated attention to God', in the manner of Gregory the Great. Contemplation, of course, immediately calls to mind the notion of 'seeing God' (*visio Dei*), as promised in the beatitude, 'Blessed are the pure of heart for they shall see God' (Matt. 5.8). The Cistercians were traditional in their teaching that full vision and union would come only in heaven, so that the most to be hoped for here below was a partial and brief experience, a seeing that is more an adhering in love. According to Bernard, 'Inhering in God is nothing else than that seeing of God which is given with special happiness only to the pure of heart ... "It is good for me to adhere to God" [Ps 72.28]. He adheres by seeing; he sees by adhering.'[25] William had a special predilection for the biblical theme of seeing God face-to-face (e.g., Gen. 32.30; 1 Cor. 13.12; 2 Cor. 3.18). In the third of his *Meditationes* he has an extended treatment of the soul's longing for face-to-face vision, even in this life. Later, in *Cant* 155, he addresses God:

> You see her first and make her [the soul] able to see you. Standing
> before her, you make her able to stand up to you until the mutual
> drawing together of you who have mercy and she who loves
> completely and destroys the barrier of sin, the wall dividing you,
> and there is mutual vision, mutual embrace, mutual joy and one
> spirit.

The theme of 'one spirit' (*unus spiritus*: 1 Cor. 6.17) may be described as a leitmotif of our Cistercian mystics. Eschewing any notion that the created spirit could ever become totally one with God, the White Monks held out the hope that even in this life the soul and God could at times achieve a total unity of willing, a oneness of knowing and loving. In his *De diligendo deo* Bernard spoke of this as a deification – *Sic affici deificari est* ('To be drawn in this way is to be deified', *Dil* 10.28).[26] After using three examples of seeming fusion, such as water mingling with wine, to indicate the reality of the union, the abbot nonetheless closes by reminding his reader, 'The substance [i.e., of the soul] will remain, but in another form, another glory, another power.' The same careful teaching about the nature of mystical union is found in the other stars of the early Cistercian firmament. William's teaching on Spirit-centred union some-times uses formulae about being one with God that go beyond Bernard, but he too was careful to underline the distinction that remains between Creator and creature (e.g., *Cant* 20; *Ep frat* 263).[27] In their teaching about uniting with God the major Cistercian authors formed the basis for the main tradition on mystical union for centuries to come.

Notes

1 Bernard of Clairvaux, *Div* 121. I will refer to the works of Bernard and the other Cistercians using the standard abbreviations (see the List of abbreviations at the beginning of this volume).

2 É. Gilson, *The Mystical Theology of Saint Bernard*, CS 120 (London 1940; repr. Kalamazoo, MI, 1990; first pub. in French 1934), chapter 3.

3 The literature on Bernard is large. A good sense of the range of his the-ology can be found in: *Saint Bernard Théologien* (Rome, 1953); *La dot-trina della vita spirituale nelle opere di San Bernardo di Clairvaux* (Rome, 1991); and J.R. Sommerfeldt (ed.), *Bernardus Magister*, CS 135 (Spencer, MA, 1992).

4 For William, select studies include, O. Brooke, *Studies in Monastic Theology*, CS 37 (Kalamazoo, MI, 1980); D.N. Bell, *The Image and Likeness: The Augustinian Spirituality of William of Saint Thierry*, CS 78 (Kalamazoo, MI, 1984); R. Thomas, *Guillaume de Saint-Thierry: homme de doctrine, homme de prière* (Sainte-Foy, Quebec, 1989); and P. Verdeyen, *La théologie mystique de Guillaume de Saint-Thierry* (Paris, 1990). For Aelred, A. Hallier, *The Monastic Theology of Aelred of Rievaulx*, CS 2 (Spencer, MA, 1969; first pub. in French 1959); and A. Squire, *Aelred of Rievaulx* (London, 1969). On Isaac, B. McGinn, *The Golden Chain: The Theological Anthropology of Isaac of Stella*, CS 15 (Washington, DC, 1972); and D. Deme (ed.), *The Selected Works of Isaac of Stella* (Aldershot, 2007). See also E. Rozanne Elder's and Wim Verbaal's chapters in this volume.

5 Bernard, *Ded* 1.2.

6 The treatment of these four Cistercians depends in part on McGinn, *Growth*, chapters 5–7. Reasons of space make it impossible to consider other twelfth-century Cistercians, notably Guerric of Igny (c. 1085–1157) and Gilbert of Hoyland (d. 1172), but see Elder's chapter in this volume. Among general accounts of the early Cistercians, see L. Bouyer, *The Cistercian Heritage* (London, 1958; first pub. in French 1955).

7 For the relation of reformation, transformation and union, see Bernard, *Gra* 14.49.

8 J. Leclercq, *The Love of Learning and the Desire for God* (New York, 1961; first pub. in French 1957).

9 On Bernard's view of exegesis, e.g., *SC* 23. Isaac of Stella has interesting reflections on exegesis in *S* 16.1–5.

10 *SC* 3.1. Bernard's appeals to experience are frequent; e.g., *SC* 4.1, 9.3, 21.4–5, 22.2, 31.4, 50.6, 52.1–2, 69.6–7 and 84.6–7.

11 On God as *caritas*, see Bernard, *SC* 8, 83–5; *Dil* 1 and 35; William, *Nat am*; Isaac, *S* 34.26–31.

12 *S* 18–26 are translated in *Isaac of Stella: Sermons for the Christian Year 1*, CF 11 (Kalamazoo, MI, 1979), pp. 149–217. For an analysis, B. McGinn, 'Isaac of Stella on the Divine Nature', *Analecta Cisterciensia*, 29 (1973), 3–56.

13 See M. Stickelbroeck, *Mysterium Venerandum: Der trinitarische Gedanke im Werk des Bernhard von Clairvaux* (Münster, 1994).

14 Brooke, *Studies in Monastic Theology*, p. 8.

15 There are occasional references to issues of Christological ontology; see Isaac, *S* 40.14–18.

16 The *amor carnalis Christi* also appears, for example, in William (e.g., *Cant* 16), and especially in Aelred's *De Jesu puero duodenni*.

17 For more on Isaac's view of the process of redemption: *S* 5 and 28–9.

18 On Bernard's view of Mary, see M.B. Pranger, *Bernard of Clairvaux and the Shape of Monastic Thought: Broken Dreams* (Leiden, 1994), chapter 4.

19 Isaac's anthropological sermons include *S* 4, 16, 17, 32, 46 and 51. Aelred also wrote a treatise *De anima*, though it is not very original.

20 Bernard preached a sermon *De conversione* to the clerics of Paris.

21 For an analysis, see M. Casey, *Athirst for God: Spiritual Desire in Bernard of Clairvaux's Sermons on the Song of Songs*, CS 77 (Kalamazoo, MI, 1987).

22 Bernard treats the *ordinatio caritatis* in, e.g., *Dil* 14.38; *Div* 50; *Ep* 85.3.

23 For the *ordo caritatis* in Isaac, see *S* 4.16–19, 25.10 and 54.5; in Aelred, e.g., *Spec* 3.18.

24 For discussions, see Bernard, *SC* 7.3, 49.1–4, 85.13 and *Dil* 10.27; William, *Cant* 38, 46, 117, 132, 137 and 140; Isaac, *S* 4.9–10 and 5.20.

25 *SC* 7.7; for more on seeing God, consult *SC* 31–2, 41.3 and 82.2.

26 Deification language is also found in the other Cistercians; e.g., Isaac, *S* 2.13 and 32.10; William, *Cant* 97 and *Nat corp* 2.3.

27 For Isaac's teaching on union, see especially *S* 4.8–12, 5.17–24, 9.8–20 and 37.29–31; for Aelred, see *Spec* 3.6.

16 Cistercians in dialogue: bringing the world into the monastery

WIM VERBAAL

The long twelfth century was one of those periods when fundamental changes occurred at a high speed. Robert of Molesme and his followers' founding of the *Novum Monasterium* in 1098 is often considered the expression of a general tendency toward renewal. Spiritual asceticism is most commonly thought to be the driving force behind the foundation as this seems to have stimulated many initiatives that were taken around 1100.

There is little doubt that Robert's project must be positioned within the overall spiritual climate around 1100. But this does not explain the huge success of the new foundation some decades later. Nor does it offer any explanation for the crisis and the serious regression towards the end of the century, when Cîteaux handed over the torch to new currents of spiritual poverty such as those of the Franciscans and the Dominicans.

The early history of Cîteaux demands a more profound understanding of the backgrounds against which the Order developed. Its success during the greater part of the twelfth century can only be due to the fact that the Cistercians offered an answer to certain urgent demands in the surrounding world. Likewise, regression and failure at the end of the century seem to point toward a disruption of this dialogue. During the first century of its existence, important shifts took place within Cîteaux that had a lasting influence on its dialogue with the world. In order to shed light upon these inner changes, we will first have to identify the Order's interlocutors and the social developments which incited a demand for new solutions.

The foundation of Cîteaux by Robert at a time when he was abbot in Molesme has directed the scholarly attention to the monastic context specifically. Robert's entire pursuit is interpreted as a renewal of traditional monastic life. Unsurprisingly, the prevailing emphasis on the supposed conflicts between Cîteaux and Cluny has led to the dialogue with the great sister congregation being considered as a formative force for the new initiative.[1] However, scholars tend to focus their efforts on factual history and pay little attention to the solutions offered by Cîteaux to recent challenges and to the new demands in contemporary society, to which Cluny did not have an answer.

The monastic dialogue with Cluny may be of some importance for the origins of Cîteaux, but it does not offer an explanation for its growth later in the twelfth century. This success was due to the personality of Bernard of Clairvaux. Without his intervention Cistercian history would have taken another course and probably not have known the expansion it did. Reading Bernard's works, we find that the dialogue with Cluny is present, but for the abbot of Clairvaux this is clearly not a chief concern. Around 1130 the competition with Cluny had been decided largely in favour of Cîteaux. Bernard does not seem to consider Cluny a serious threat; at most it was a rival in ecclesiastical nominations. The true danger he saw elsewhere.

The expansion of Cîteaux coincides with the rise of the schools in France. From 1115 to 1150 the educational system undergoes a spectacular development: around 1100 Guibert of Nogent could still recall the want of competent teachers.[2] A few decades later an abominable competition is waged among the *magistri* to attain personal recognition, attract students and gain prospects of a lucrative position. Perhaps no one saw as clearly as Bernard the actual needs underlying this flourishing of the schools. Yet, simultaneously, he clearly saw their shortcomings. Thanks to his intervention Cîteaux was able to offer an alternative to the schools, and for most of the twelfth century Cîteaux could be considered a monastic counterpart to the emerging scholastics. The dialogue with the schools was the second formative force in early Cistercian history.

THE MONASTIC DIALOGUE

In order to understand Cîteaux's dialogue with Cluny, the major representative of the Benedictine tradition, we must consider the background of the Cluniac reform. The monastic renewal of Cluny results both from the Carolingian reform and from the social changes that took place under the Ottonians. A sounder, centralised organisation was its issue. With Cluny the monastic communities were submitted to a stronger central authority; this corresponded to the demand for an authoritative spirituality as it was pursued in the political structures of the Carolingian and Ottonian world.

Besides, monastic life fulfilled a clearly circumscribed role in the social order. According to the famous tripartition of feudal society expressed by Adalberon of Laon in his *Carmen ad Rodbertum regem* (*c.* 1027), monks had the task of praying for the entire society, just as nobility had the duty to defend it and farmers to feed it.[3] Monastic life had a social obligation, liturgy, to which individual life was subjected. Entering a monastery was not only an individual choice. Handing over one's child as an oblate to a monastic community meant a self-evident sacrifice of society in exchange for salvation.

This group and community thinking came under great pressure during the eleventh century. The authority of central government was questioned and the annihilation of individuals into the community became a less obvious choice. The foundation of Cîteaux may be interpreted as an expression of this renewed feudal society, in which central authority is no longer self-evident but rather based upon the principle of a *primus inter pares*. Its sound monastic organisation relied on the Christian virtue of *caritas* as a unifying force. Thus the founders of Cîteaux took a road similar to that of Anselm of Canterbury, who, in his monastic correspondence, elaborated on *amicitia* as a binding force for spiritual communities.

These shifts had an impact on the interpretation of monastic communal life. A life by which the individual was absorbed, and even somehow lost, was no longer acceptable in a world in which individuals came to claim rights of their own. In Cîteaux monastic life was considered a community of individuals who had chosen to submit to its customs. Therefore the stress was not on authority or respect for superiors, but on the obedience and responsibility of the individual monk. The shift is light but significant: instead of the authorities to which one submitted, it was now the person who submitted who took centre stage. Simultaneously, and parallel to this inner shift, the social role of monastic life changed. In fact, Cîteaux did not fit the social tripartition with its distribution of tasks and duties. Instead it focused on the individual salvation of its constituting members. Thus, liturgy somewhat lost its value as the sole, day-consuming monastic duty, while personal prayer, meditation and manual work gained importance. The role of manual labour highlights the difference from Cluniac tradition. At Cluny the principle of the three classes was recognised in so far as monks were dedicated to liturgy while labour was intended for the lay brothers. At Cîteaux manual work became part of monastic life: not completely eliminating the tripartition but at least blurring its boundaries.

The fact that the monastic community was interpreted in a different way and seen as the sum of constituent members, who had made a voluntary choice, can be related also to the changed condition of admission: the Cistercian Order never accepted oblates, for voluntariness could only be a result of maturity. Entry into monastic life was reserved for those of an adult age, that is, fifteen years at least. Though nothing changed in the basic principle of sacrificing one's individual life, it took on a more personal and intentional dimension. Emphasis was shifted from the act itself to the inner intention. Thus Cîteaux tapped into the same currents as the contemporary schools.

THE SCHOLASTIC DIALOGUE

The twelfth century witnessed a spectacular increase in the general impact of schools. An important shift had occurred in the course of the tenth and eleventh centuries. Monastic schools held a central position in education till far into the tenth century, but around 1000 they lost this primacy to schools that emerged in the shadow of the cathedrals. Once again political and social developments seem decisive. Ottonian politics rested heavily on episcopal authority and the importance of the bishoprics began to grow. A need for schooled clerics grew out of the emerging chancelleries and administrative centres. While monasteries began to confine their educational programmes to internal training, the episcopal sees developed into regular centres of schooling.

Whereas monastic schooling had always paid more attention to grammar and rhetoric, the cathedral schools focused on dialectics. Apart from this shift in focus, teaching methods differed too. In monastic education, schooling in Latin had been a central concern, and its models were the (mostly) pagan poets of Antiquity and the Church Fathers. The dialectic tendency of the cathedral schools, however, redirected attentions toward internal logic, based upon rationalistic arguments. Ultimately, this rational and logic approach brought about one of the most important intellectual revolutions in European history. While the older monastic education was founded on authoritative models, both classical and patristic, dialectic reasoning began to question the authorities. After Berengar of Tours (d. 1088) and the first eucharistic controversy, traditional authorities had to be supported by dialectics, were they to maintain their relevance. Slowly Western thinking emancipated itself from an obedient to a self-conscious acceptance of the articles of faith. The intellectual mind freed itself from the authorities of both classical Antiquity and the Church Fathers.

Simultaneously, the number of students at the cathedral schools grew considerably during the first decades of the twelfth century. An increasing part of the population, notably the younger, became schooled to some extent and could lay claim to the much coveted title of *magister*.

Mutual rivalry kept pace with this growing population of ambitious students. Their choices were pragmatic and orientated towards making a career. They did not feel any need to follow one particular master. The students developed into a mobile mass that escaped the traditional social and local boundaries, and study became a material means of promotion. Spiritual and even intellectual aspects came under threat, which caused deep indignation in highly placed intellectuals such as John of Salisbury.

In their turn the school masters strived for renown. They tried to attract students (and revenues) in order to gain popularity and qualify for a lucrative position in the ecclesiastical or secular hierarchy. As a consequence, violent arguments and academic envy as well as a vigorous search for originality and sophistication became inherent elements of intellectual life, posing serious dangers for orthodoxy.

Cîteaux was forcefully confronted with these developments. Since it accepted only adults, the necessity for a proper basic education disappeared. Novices at Cîteaux had supposedly received training at the schools. Each entry of a new member brought with it the entry of the schools, the new rationalistic approach, the dialectic attitude towards authorities, the experience of academic jealousy and competition as well as the personal ambitions for an ecclesiastical or secular career. Besides, these former students were young adults that had tasted liberty, travelled across the world and, undoubtedly, were not unacquainted with love.

This public created a different community from the more traditional one at Cluny. It also demanded another approach. Cîteaux did not need to bother with education in the same way as Cluny, but was obliged to actively take into account the higher training enjoyed by these new monks. The ingenuity of the Order demonstrated itself in the fact that it dared to enter into a dialogue with the schools. It offered a kind of parallel schooling, of higher spiritual training, which presented itself as a crowning of the secular schooling, leading to not a worldly, but a spiritual career.

A CHANGING DIALOGUE

These two major dialogues of Cîteaux with key social currents did not occur at the same moment, nor did they conform to the same scheme. Clearly, during its first century, different generations in the Order reacted differently to contemporary challenges, according to its leaders' priorities.

The first generation

Robert of Molesme (d. 1111) seems to have searched for a concrete way to realise his spiritual ambitions with a remarkable predilection for a hermit's life but within a community. Alberic (d. 1108) had to secure survival for the young community. It had to be confirmed in its ambition and stabilised as a group. He succeeded: within a few years, his successor contemplated the foundation of a first daughter house. Surely this was primarily due to Stephen's policy, but it was based on Alberic's achievements. Stephen Harding (d. 1134) saw the evolution of the small community into a true Order with different daughters who, in turn, founded new communities. His was the task to channel this growth and to draw up rules that prevented the loss of the original ideal. The young Order needed a proper identity, which was strong enough to hold up against other related initiatives.

The dialogue of this first generation was orientated towards the existing monastic tradition, notably Cluny. Dissatisfaction with the social role as it was manifested by Cluniac monastic life lies beneath its arguments. The idea that monks had the duty to pray for knights and farmers no longer satisfied. Robert's quest for a more rigid life shows him looking for a way towards personal salvation. His ambition for poverty was not primarily motivated by the search for a monastic ideal, but by a desire for personal purification. Therefore he pushed out his frontiers. Poverty became a means of personal penitence, not social compensation.

Personal salvation through poverty received its institutionalisation from Alberic. The emphasis on individual salvation within communal life is also clear in the rupture with the traditional tripartition of tasks. Manual and agricultural work became an integral part of monastic life, helping the individual monk to achieve his salvation, and was thus invested with a purifying influence. Manual *labor* was placed on a level closer to that of liturgy. Liturgy did not lose anything of its significance for the monks, but its importance for the daily rhythm decreased; it was no longer a means of salvation for the entire society but rather a spiritual reunion of the community members in Christ. Liturgical activities, praying and singing of psalms, were imbued in all aspects of monastic life. Each task had to be ventured upon as an opportunity for personal prayer and meditation.

Stephen faced the challenge of making the organisation of a young and growing congregation meet the demands that pertained to the individual salvation of its members. Significantly, he introduced *caritas* as a unifying force. His interpretation of love as capable of uniting individuals shows a new understanding of spirituality that comes very close to Anselm's use of *amicitia*. Stephen had experienced the force of *caritas* in his own spiritual friendship with Peter of Jully. During a common pilgrimage to Rome, they took up the daily habit of reciting the entire psalter, alternating each verse. Both entered Molesme and they decided to recite daily half of the psalter each. As Stephen became abbot of Cîteaux, Peter, who had returned with Robert to Molesme, took over his friend's part and again committed himself to a daily psalter recital.

Stephen wanted a similar love-unity within the young Order. He tried to achieve this by imposing his personal influence and authority as an abbot, believing he would be able to prescribe this bond of mutual love to his monks. It shows him belonging to an older generation, which could not fully imagine the new disregard for authority. Contemporary society took another turn and his assumption proved untenable.

The second generation

The following generation was less concerned with viability. Similar problems appeared at every foundation, but from now on there was a well-structured organisation within which to solve these problems. The second generation faced other challenges. Theirs was the task of guaranteeing the growth of the Order without losing its original ideas. Two tendencies may be distinguished: firstly a lively attention to the Order's expansion and its impact on the social order; secondly a continued concern for internal structure: the coherence of the Order and each individual community.

The second generation is dominated by the personality of Bernard of Clairvaux (d. 1153). He took initiatives that gave a fundamentally new incentive to the development of the Order and gave birth to its particular spirituality. Bernard was the first true author of the Order. His gifts as a writer created a proper Cistercian literary voice and helped him to achieve results that Stephen could never achieve by his sole authority. Bernard's texts were read throughout the Order. His voice reached every individual. Meditative and ruminative reading made his words penetrate into every individual mind. Thus Bernard nourished the inner motives of the monks, arriving at an inner depth that Stephen prescribed but never attained.

Furthermore, for conversion Bernard addressed notably the young, the students at the schools. His first 'catch' was the entire student population of the cathedral school of Châlons-sur-Marne, probably patronised by its bishop, William of Champeaux. Undoubtedly, the famous conflict with Peter Abelard can be traced back to a pedagogic rivalry for impact on the young: the years of success of Abelard's Paraclete, 1124–7, coincide with a serious decline of new entries to Clairvaux, while after Abelard's departure for the monastery of St Gildas in 1127 Clairvaux retains its fabulous increase, immediately resulting in new foundations. Again, in the winter of 1140–1, a failed preaching to the students in Paris definitively determined Bernard's further involvement in the charge of heterodoxy against Abelard.

Bernard's focus on the students obliged monastic communities to develop into centres of a new intelligentsia. This demanded a proper spiritual approach and guidance, conveyed in Bernard's writings, which clearly anticipate an intellectual public. The abbot's *preaching* activities outside the monastery constitute another new element. The Order's first generation did not venture out into the world to preach. But Bernard was an active preacher even in his early career. He wanted to make an impact on society. This desire for influence may be explained by his wish to find a response among the young, aware of their personal ambitions. However, it also contributed to construe a society in which Cîteaux played a structural part through the formation of ecclesiastical dignitaries.

In spite of Bernard's monumental presence (or perhaps thanks to it), the second generation counts some of the most important Cistercian writers. Guerric of Igny (d. 1157) and Aelred of Rievaulx (d. 1166) were Bernard's immediate disciples. Isaac of Stella (d. 1168) was more of an indirect follower. Their focus was on the internal coherence of the communities that had been entrusted to their guidance. Besides, Aelred must have had a considerable social influence, although this cannot be properly assessed, owing to the loss of his correspondence.[4]

Otto of Freising (d. 1158) is a typical second-generation Cistercian. After studies at the schools of Paris and Chartres, he entered the monastery of Morimond. He became its third abbot but was soon nominated bishop of Freising. As such, he remained a supporter of the new spiritual currents that he had come to know in the canons of Saint Victor, the Premonstratensians and the Cistercians. Both his career and his historical writings express the new spiritual intellectuality that Cîteaux founded during its second generation.

In Bernard's footsteps the second generation took up a dialogue with the intellectual evolutions at the schools. Of primary concern were the dangers for spiritual growth inherent in the dialectical approach to religious matters. This could lead to serious tensions within the individual, as illustrated by Bernard's friend William of Saint Thierry (d. 1148). William's was a more theoretical mind than Bernard's and his works reveal the problems he experienced in balancing his intellectual and his ascetic dispositions. Apparently he had difficulties bringing his inner voices into harmony. He seemed to compensate for this tension in individual mystic ecstasy. Bernard is more balanced than William in his confrontation with intellectual challenges. He strives after a deepening of rationality by appealing to human experience. He constantly refers to individual experiences and to the world familiar to his public. He wanted them to continuously put rational truth to the test as a lived reality in order to avoid being captured by pure theory. However, he never denied the importance of rationality for spiritual growth.

Guerric, Isaac and Otto introduced the voice of the schools into the monastery. Guerric and perhaps Isaac had been masters. In them, the tension between the intellectual voice of the school and the spiritual one of Cîteaux seems absent. Their works attest to a sound basic balance. Aelred was less acquainted with recent developments at the schools. Nonetheless, for him, rationality did not lose any of its importance. He gives it an even more affective interpretation than Bernard did.

Otto of Freising's career shows how Cîteaux could satisfy the ambitions of young students. The election of Eugenius III constituted the climax, but the number of Cistercian bishops and cardinals increased throughout the twelfth century. This ecclesiastical policy and its success, however, was not the primary motif for Cîteaux's answer to the intellectual challenges of its day. Bernard wanted to be a master in the intellectual and affective life of his monks. In his last book, *De consideratione*, dedicated to Eugenius III, he considered responsibility within the Church hierarchy against the background of a celestial hierarchy, based upon the works of Pseudo-Dionysius the Areopagite. Ecclesiastical ambition must be seen in the light of spiritual truth. If one wants to understand this spiritual truth, Bernard's writings still offer a considerable intellectual challenge to their readers. Of his disciples, Isaac of Stella seems to come closest to such intellectual claims.

Besides his answer to the ambitions of the young, Bernard had a strong focus on the affective education of his readers and monks. For this purpose he develops the notion of *abyssum caritatis*, the fathomless abyss of divine love, in which human love finds an unfulfilled fulfilment in divine love by endlessly longing for more. A movement of love is created, resulting in an affectivity that never halts. Bernard consciously made use of the Song of Songs, with its language of love and marriage, anticipating the affectivity of his young monks.

The dialogue of the Order thus shows a remarkable shift within its self-evaluation as regards the aims and nature of communal life. For the founders the community had to guarantee the salvation of its members. For the second generation the monastery developed into a community of education. Its members were formed in order to take up responsibility in a world and in a society that were notably interpreted in a spiritual way.

The third generation

The overwhelming success Cîteaux knew halfway into the twelfth century had far-reaching consequences for the next generation. Its increasing wealth and its influence within the Church and the world threatened to alienate the Order from its principles. Cîteaux guaranteed a successful ecclesiastical career; the poverty and the difficulties of the initial years began to assume a mythical air.

The new generation was aware of these dangers. The call for a more potent brand of asceticism grew stronger, as did the urge to reflect upon the Order's character. This led to a growth in moral didactic works, in which the novice was educated in what was considered to be the specific Cistercian spirituality of asceticism. This culminated in the *Monks' Mirror (Speculum monachorum)* by Arnulf of Bohéries (d. *c.* 1200), which taught the novice to live continuously with the image of concrete death in mind.

The new writers recurrently appealed to their own tradition and to Bernard's authority. He is not referred to, however, as the rational and spiritual master of his treatises and sermons, but as an example of mystical and visionary exaltation. After 1170 Bernard appears in Cistercian literature as a mythological personality, the central figure in all kinds of mystical anecdotes. The exemplary and anecdotic elements of the different versions of his Life begin to outbalance the intellectual intention of his writings. The miracle books by Conrad of Eberbach (d. 1221) and Caesarius of Heisterbach (d. *c.* 1240) are the most famous examples.

This shift in attention parallels a general decrease of intellectual level. It may even be its cause. We know of several reactions to this decrease by schooled monks; Cîteaux had become a favoured retreat for retired school masters. Alan of Lille (d. 1203), Peter the Chanter (d. 1197) and Everard of Ypres (d. *c.* 1200) are known to have retreated from the schools at a later age to enter Cistercian monasteries – an indication of the wealth the Order had come to enjoy. These masters often denounce the low level of intellectual life within their community.[5]

During the second half of the twelfth century the dialogue with the schools was entirely lost. This must be due, in part, to the violent and often very technical disputations of the scholarly world. At the same time, the growing importance of towns in the social structure might explain the loss of importance of an Order that focused primarily on agriculture. Yet it cannot be denied that the Cistercians turned toward themselves more than before. The Order felt the need to reflect upon its own identity and credibility, causing the focus to shift towards a rigid form of asceticism previously unknown. Thus, the Order lost contact with the evolutions that took place in the outside world. It was no longer able to answer new challenges.

Stephen of Lexington (d. 1260) tried to turn the tide. In 1244 he founded the *Collegium Sancti Bernardi* in Paris. Cistercian monks could be sent to the centre of scholastic science and participate in contemporary intellectual movements. Stephen hoped to restore the lost dialogue between the Order and society and to regain influence on the preaching against heretical currents. His action came too late. The initiative had been taken over by the mendicants. Cîteaux's twelfth-century growth and flourishing had become fatal.

The first three Cistercian generations show the tragedy of a spiritual movement that was one of the determining factors of the twelfth century. The first generation laid the foundations for an Order, which, by its innovative interpretation of the Rule of Benedict, answered new challenges to monastic tradition. The second generation enlarged the field of influence by opening up towards demands in contemporary society. Its members became the great pedagogues of the Order, who did not focus exclusively on monastic education but remained sensitive to the intellectual developments in the schools. The impact of the second generation led to the overwhelming success of the Order in the third quarter of the century, but it brought about its failure too. The new generations lost contact with the contemporary world. The dialogue with the outside world disappeared and all attention was focused on the inner situation. An extreme asceticism was restored, or rather introduced. Yet even here, Cîteaux was surpassed as Franciscan poverty offered a more fitting answer to the demands of the rising towns, just as the Dominicans gave a more appropriate embodiment to the new intellectuality. The Cistercian Golden Age was over.

Notes

1   But see Martha G. Newman's chapter in this volume.
2   Guibert de Nogent, *Monodiae* 1.4; ed. E.-R. Labande, *Guibert de Nogent: Autobiographie* (Paris, 1981), pp. 26–7.
3   Adalberon of Laon, *Carmen ad Rotbertum regem*, verses 275–305, with the famous verse: 'Nunc orant, alli pugnant aliique laborant' (296); ed.

C. Carozzi, *Adalbéron de Laon: Poème au roi Robert* (Paris, 1979), pp. 20–3.

4   See E. Rozanne Elder's chapter in this volume.

5   Everard of Ypres, *Dialogus Ratii et Everardi;* ed. N. Häring, 'A Latin Dialogue on the Doctrine of Gilbert of Poitiers', *Mediaeval Studies*, 15 (1953), 243–89.

17 Preaching

BEVERLY MAYNE KIENZLE

Cistercian sermons enjoyed a golden age as the Order expanded and flourished in the twelfth century. The sermon was the preferred literary genre for influential Cistercian commentary on the Song of Songs as well as other works of exegesis. Extant sermons are found as complete and polished literary works, reports, parables and *sententiae* – short summaries or outlines containing the major points of the sermon. These texts provide a guide to monastic spirituality and theology. Preaching, whether formal sermons or informal chapter talks, was centred in the liturgy of the community as described in the Rule of Benedict. Everyday preaching offers a glimpse of life within the monastery. Rarely did the preacher direct comments to life in the outside world. However, Cistercian preachers occasionally addressed audiences beyond the monastery, and even preached on crusade missions. The numerous editions of Cistercian sermons give testimony to the richness of medieval Cistercian preaching. Unfortunately, little evidence remains to elucidate the preaching done by medieval abbesses, with the exception of Innocent III's letter concerning abbesses preaching in northern Spain in the late twelfth century.

CISTERCIAN PREACHING AND THE LITURGY

Preaching was central to the community liturgy, as Chrysogonus Waddell emphasises: the sermon preached in chapter 'was itself a liturgical act, with the preacher breaking the bread received from Christ, ever present and acting through his word'.[1] The Cistercian usages describe how the Rule of Benedict was to be read in chapter, which usually took place after Prime and was followed by a commentary by the abbot or another monk appointed by the abbot. A parallel chapter was held for the lay brothers each week; the abbot or a designated monk spoke there. Cistercians delivered formal sermons to the community on the major liturgical feasts of the First Sunday of Advent, Christmas, Epiphany,

Palm Sunday, Easter, Pentecost, John the Baptist, Peter and Paul and the Dedication as well as the Marian feasts of Purification, Annunciation, Nativity and Assumption. Most extant sermons by major Cistercian writers correspond to those feasts. On those occasions and others at the abbot's discretion, the lay brothers generally joined the monks.[2]

There is evidence that the preacher simplified his style and probably used the vernacular in order for the lay brothers to understand. Isaac of Stella in one sermon says, 'I say this briefly in the vernacular.' Elsewhere he speaks of the need for simple speech; and he asserts that he must speak slowly and repeat for the lay brothers.[3] It is generally assumed that a monastic sermon was delivered to a monastic audience in Latin, but that monks preaching to the lay brothers or outside the monastery employed the vernacular. Exceptions to this were certainly possible and are difficult to detect. Sermons were translated from Latin into the vernacular and vice versa.[4] Sermons of Bernard of Clairvaux appear with the notation: 'delivered completely in French', and one of Hélinand of Froidmont's sermons is rubricated: 'This entire sermon was delivered in French.'[5]

The sermon genre also served for texts that were read, whether for private meditation or for public reading in the refectory and in the cloister before Compline.[6] The readings for the nocturns of Matins included sermons, which were primarily patristic. Moreover the genre of the sermon was employed for correspondence. The sermon in epistolary form served as a sort of imagined conversation taking the place of an actual discourse;[7] at times a sermon recorded a conversation that had already taken place. These varying functions of the sermon can be seen in the manuscripts and collections where they are found.

THE TERMINOLOGY AND THE LITERARY FORM OF CISTERCIAN SERMONS

Cistercian writers generally used the word *sermo* for talks or sermons preached in chapter and for sermons intended to be read. Isaac of Stella even defines *sermo* as a type of reading and part of the necessary spiritual exercises: 'There are three: reading meditation and prayer. By reading or by a sermon, which is itself a certain type of reading, God speaks to you.'[8] The word *sermo* also denotes speech or discourse in a general sense and in addition can refer to the words one utters.[9] Nonetheless, among monastic authors who refer to their preaching, the word *sermo* predominates over others such as *tractatus* or *omilia* from the fourth century onwards.[10] A few of many possible examples will illustrate the tendency. Guerric of Igny's sermons are called *spiritales sermones*, and their collection is a *libellus sermonum*.[11] Aelred of Rievaulx describes a feast-day sermon he delivered in chapter as a *sermo*. Aelred's biographer, Walter Daniel, praises the *sermones* Aelred preached to various audiences.[12] John of Forde often uses the term *sermo* when making the transition from one sermon to the next.[13] Amadeus of Lausanne, whose 'homilies' on Mary are clearly compiled as a literary work, begins one homily by alluding to the preceding *sermo*.[14] Finally, Hélinand of Froidmont inserts a sermon into his *Chronicon*, saying: 'I remember that I composed a sermon for the community of brothers in this way.'[15]

While the word *sermo* was used widely, the term *sententia* is generally used to designate short outline-like compositions that were jotted down before or after sermons.[16] The *sententiae* frequently have a simple, numerical structure, and the shortest *sententiae* are often no more than the list of the sermon's main points. Numbering the main points aided the preacher and the listener.[17] Moreover, certain allegorical compositions with a moral aim are called *parabolae*. Bernard of Clairvaux's *Parabolae* teach about spiritual growth and employ personified virtues which enter the action in order to aid the sinful soul to conversion. They may represent the substance of chapter talks and were perhaps intended for an early level of instruction in spirituality and the monastic life.[18]

In addition to these forms of preaching, a sermon may be extant in one or more phases of its redaction. One of Bernard of Clairvaux's letters points to a sermon that began as a private conversation but was probably delivered later as a public talk during the intermediate phase of its redaction. Bernard and William of Saint Thierry at times met with William of Champeaux, bishop of Châlons, to discuss the Scriptures. A letter from Bernard to 'G', probably William of Saint Thierry or possibly William of Rievaulx, explains how a conversation on Christ's infancy, his circumcision and its interpretation came to be recorded afterwards, then revised and circulated. The verbs *conferre, scribere, recogitare/corrigere* and *legendum praebere* describe the conversation, writing, revising and circulation of the text. A report of the conversation exists, as do short sermons with applications to monastic life and a longer sermon where the style and form are perfected, but concrete references to monastic life have been eliminated for the most part. Some of Bernard's sermons exist in the form of reports taken down by his secretaries.[19]

Sermons were collected in various ways reflecting the function of the book in which they were included: exegetical sermon series; books for private reading or study; collections made for reading in the refectory; sermons with and within letters and other theological works; groups of sermons by the same author, such as the series grouped and revised by Bernard of Clairvaux[20] and the *libellus sermonum* gathered by Guerric of Igny; sermons by different authors, such as the sermon collection from Foigny, probably dating to the thirteenth century, which gathers thirty-nine sermons by twenty-one monks whose names are given with their respective works.[21] An abbot might request that one of his monks put together chapter talks. The monks too might ask the abbot to pursue in written form a topic discussed in chapter; such is the case for Aelred of Rievaulx's homilies on the burdens of Isaiah. Finally, sermons were also collected after the preacher's death; Odo of Morimond's disciples put together his sermons after he died.[22]

For sermons transmitted in complete form, scholars address the question of whether the text reflects its original oral state, if there was one at all. Bernard's sermons on the Song of Songs have provoked debate over whether they were ever preached. Jean Leclercq's contention that they were not delivered is challenged by Christopher Holdsworth, whose painstaking analysis leads him to conclude convincingly that 'the text we have grows out of what Bernard actually said'.[23] Another scholar has asserted that the sermons on the Song of Songs at times imitate the discourse situation, and possibly fictional literary elements have been pointed out in the sermons of other Cistercian authors as well. The question of oral and written form has been addressed at some length for Guerric of Igny, Aelred of Rievaulx and John of Forde.[24]

Leclercq's work provides guidelines for identifying indications of orality in a monastic sermon. A sermon close to its oral form would be written in a simple style and would present theological arguments that are not too complex to be understood when heard. It would contain direct allusions to monastic life, and it would be short enough to have been delivered during the Cistercian day. The community would be addressed in the second-person plural and significant first-person singular references would be made in the body of the sermon, not in the openings and closings, which were tightly governed by literary convention.[25] Still it is difficult if not impossible to use solely intratextual evidence in order to conclude that a given sermon was delivered or not.

The typical monastic sermon began with a biblical or liturgical lection, and then one or more key words were selected from the lection and used repeatedly to develop a motif or theme, such as the spiritual meaning of loaves of bread. Bernard of Clairvaux bases his Rogation sermon on Luke 11.5–6 and centres on the three loaves of bread and what they mean for the monastic life. Bernard's two sermons for the Sixth Sunday after Pentecost, drawn from Mark 8.1–9, interpret each of the seven loaves with which Jesus fed the crowd. Bernard delights in describing his words as mouthfuls and morsels (*frustra, fragmenta*) slipping through his fingers.[26] Guerric of Igny also draws most of his Rogation sermon from the three loaves, but he elaborates a more extensive concatenation of threes than does Bernard.[27]

Cistercian authors tended to prefer a thematic approach to their sermons rather than the sequential exegesis common in patristic authors such as Gregory the Great or Bede. By word association preachers, like their patristic predecessors, adduce additional texts and authorities from Scripture and Christian authors. Methods of developing the theme vary. The lection may be interpreted according to more than one sense of Scripture. *Exempla* from the Bible, from the lives of the saints and monastic stories appear.

With the growth of the schools the twelfth-century sermon moved towards the greater formalisation that would come with thirteenth-century university preaching. Furthermore, at the end of the twelfth century, Cistercians developed aids to study with alphabetical indexing and a reference system for specifying portions of the text. These study aids were clearly designed to facilitate the writing and preaching of sermons.[28] In turn, they influenced its form. In the sermons of authors who had contact with the schools, we find more complex theological arguments, more divisions of the biblical theme and more complicated questions and devices for explaining and developing the lection. Hélinand of Froidmont's sermons, for example, use divisions and *distinctiones*, alphabetical orderings of the allegorical meanings of scriptural words.

THE CONTENT AND THEMES OF CISTERCIAN SERMONS

The twelfth-century monastic sermon generally deals with themes relevant to monastic life and theology; hence it is primarily inward-looking and experiential, that is, directed to life within the monastery and to the monks' inner spiritual progress. As such, it provides a guide to the study of monastic spirituality. Ultimately the monastic sermon has an eschatological purpose: contemplation leads the monk to purify his heart and life and to merit his reward in heaven; meditation on the heavenly Jerusalem is his path to final ascent there. Neglect of the Rule jeopardises that journey. Sermons provide information on the liturgy – readings, hymns and ritual practices such as processions.

Hélinand of Froidmont's second Palm Sunday sermon gives a tour of the monastery buildings as the procession moved around the grounds.[29] Occasionally sermons offer practical advice and complaints are made about the observance of the Rule. The rigorous monastic routine left some nodding over the books they read in the cloister, snoring during the reading in the oratory and sleeping during the sermons given in chapter.[30]

Seldom in the surviving sermons does the monastic preacher direct his comments to life in the outside world. It seems that for Bernard of Clairvaux, the more revised the sermon, the less it dealt with daily life, even within the monastery. Leclercq's study of the Circumcision sermons shows a weeding out of references to community life as the sermon approached its final revision.[31] That process informs us on Bernard's notion of how the monastic sermon in its literary form differed from daily monastic preaching.

Nonetheless, biographical information can sometimes be gleaned from monastic sermons. Bernard of Clairvaux refers to his illness, explaining that 'speaking' to the monks is his labour because he cannot do manual work with them.[32] Isaac of Stella speaks of the famous teachers to whom he and others flocked. Isaac was sometimes called *Magister*, and it is likely that he left England to study in France, perhaps under Abelard and then at Chartres, where he himself later taught.[33] Hélinand of Froidmont recounts his conversion, and in another sermon he mentions being in Paris as a young man.[34]

When monastic preachers were involved in the events of their age, their biographical information also sheds light on those happenings. Isaac of Stella alludes to his forced exile on the island of Ré following Henry II's reprisals against Cistercians who supported Thomas Becket, archbishop of Canterbury.[35] One of his sermons can be given an approximate date because he refers to Bernard of Clairvaux as having died and been canonised.[36] Isaac of Stella criticises the new militia, possibly the Knights of Calatrava founded in 1157. This new militia, which he calls a *monstrum novum*, tries to make conversions by force and proclaims that Christians who die in the slaughter are martyrs. Isaac also preaches against monasteries fighting over land and those he calls destroyers of truth, presumably heretics who distort the Scriptures and writings of the Fathers.[37] John of Forde's Sermon 41 on the Song of Songs laments the Interdict imposed on 23 March 1208 and states that the people have been without the sacraments for almost two years.[38] John's Sermon 76 describes the deprivations undergone by his monastery when it was forced to sell everything of value in order to pay the fines imposed by King John later in 1208.[39]

Cistercians participated in preaching campaigns for the Third and Fourth Crusades and against heresy.[40] Bernard of Clairvaux had preached the Second Crusade at Vézelay in March 1146, yet the crusades are absent from his sermons. He established the theological foundations for crusading and the military Orders in *De laude novae militiae* in the late 1120s, and some of his letters evidence the content of the crusading message. One letter (246) reports the success of his preaching campaign.[41] Bernard refused to lead the Third Crusade, but Baldwin, archbishop of Canterbury, took the cross and died at Acre in 1190. Baldwin preached in England and Wales and often carried a cross on his tour (1188–90). An extant sermon on the cross reflects the general content of preaching the cross, but not the event of that preaching. The image of *lignum*, wood, unites the whole of salvation history in an exegetical tradition that tied the wood of the cross to the tree in paradise and interpreted other instances of wood and trees in the Hebrew bible as types for the cross of Christ.[42] Several Cistercians preached the Fourth Crusade and Abbot Guy of Vaux-de-Cernay and a few others accompanied the crusaders. Innocent III also called on the Cistercians to support missionary activity in Prussia, Scandinavia and the Baltics. Generally the sermons delivered as part of such preaching missions are not extant and one must rely on other texts such as chronicles and letters, where available, to surmise the content of the preaching missions.

Similarly, to reconstruct preaching against heresy by Bernard of Clairvaux and other Cistercians, one draws again on chronicles, letters and reports.[43] Hélinand of Froidmont delivered sermons at the University of Toulouse's opening ceremonies and at the 1229 synod following the conclusion of the Albigensian crusade.[44] Those sermons contribute to what is known about Cistercian involvement in the campaign against heresy and in the founding of the University. Perhaps Hélinand's sermons reflect in part the movement from the contemplative spirituality of the Cistercians to the active life of the friars. He and other Cistercians were deeply involved in southern France as preachers and legates, bishops and negotiators. Hélinand's sermons overall include frequent criticism not only of heretical beliefs but also of practices such as excessive taxation, pillaging, seizure of ecclesiastic property, superfluous monastic construction and wrong-minded study.

Notes

1   C. Waddell, 'The Liturgical Dimension of Twelfth-Century Cistercian Preaching', in *Medieval Monastic Preaching*, ed. C. Muessig (Leiden, 1998), pp. 335–49 (p. 337).

2   *Usus conversorum* 11.2.6. See Waddell, *Lay*, p. 69; Choisselet/Vernet, pp. 189–90.

3   *S* 37.17; ed. A. Hoste *et al.*, *Isaac de l'Étoile: Sermons 2*, SCh 207 (Paris, 1974), p. 294: 'vulgari sermone breviter narro'. See also the discussion by A. Hoste, 'Introduction', in *Isaac de l'Étoile: Sermons 1*, ed. A. Hoste and G. Salet, SCh 130 (Paris, 1967), pp. 33–4; *S* 45.8; ed. A. Hoste *et al.*, *Isaac de l'Étoile: Sermons 3*, SCh 339 (Paris, 1987), p. 102, and *S* 50.2; *Sermons 3*, p. 180.

4   A. Hoste, 'Introduction', *Isaac de l'Étoile: Sermons 1*, p. 34.

5   J. Leclercq, 'Recherches sur les Sermons sur les Cantiques de S. Bernard', *Revue bénédictine*, 65 (1955), 71–89 (p. 82): 'totus gallice pronunciatus'; *PL* 212:543: 'Hic sermo totus gallice pronuntiatus est.'

6   Waddell, 'Liturgical Dimension', p. 342. On the Morimondo lectionary, see L. Light, *The Bible in the Twelfth Century: An Exhibition of Manuscripts at the Houghton Library* (Cambridge, MA, 1988), pp. 32–4.

7   On the reading of the bishop of Lodève's letter by individuals in the community of Silvanès, see B.M. Kienzle and S. Shroff, 'Cistercians and Heresy: Doctrinal Consultation in Some Twelfth-Century Correspondence from Southern France', *Cîteaux*, 41 (1990), 159–66.

8   Isaac of Stella, *S* 14.7; *Sermons 1*, p. 274: 'Tria sunt, lectio, meditatio, et oratio. Lectione vel sermone, qui et ipse quaedam lectio est, loquitur tibi Deus.'

9   See Aelred of Rielvaux, *Sermones I–XLVI: Collectio Claraevallensis prima et secunda*, ed. G. Raciti, CCCM 2A (Turnhout, 1989), *S* 23.16 and 19, pp. 187, 188.

10 C. Mohrmann, *Praedicare-tractare-sermo: études sur le latin des chrétiens*, 2 vols. (Rome, 1961), vol. ii, pp. 63–72; J. Longère, 'Le vocabulaire de la prédication', in *La lexicographie du latin médiéval et ses rapports avec les recherches actuelles sur la civilisation du moyen âge* (Paris, 1981), pp. 303–20.

11 J. Morson and H. Costello, 'Introduction', in *Guerric d'Igny: Sermons 1*, ed. J. Morson and H. Costello, SCh 166 (Paris, 1970), p. 20.

12 A. Squire, 'The Literary Evidence for the Preaching of Aelred of Rievaulx, II: The Homilies on Isaias', *Cîteaux*, 11 (1960), 165–79, 245–51, p. 249: 'recordamini sermonis illius quem in Apparitionis ad fratres habui in capitulo'. *Vita Ailredi*, ed. F.M. Powicke (London, 1950), p. xxxii: 'Sermones disertissimos et omni laude dignos in capitulis nostris et in synodis et ad populos peroravit.'

13 John of Forde, *Super extremam partem Cantici canticorum sermones cxx*, ed. E. Mikkers and H. Costello, 2 vols., CCCM 17 and 18 (Turnhout, 1970), *S* 11.8, p. 108; *S* 102.11, p. 696; other examples are found in 6.1, p. 65; 89.12, p. 609; 90.10, p. 616; 106.1, p. 716; 112.1 and 12, pp. 756 and 761.

14 Amadeus of Lausanne, *PL* 188:1319; trans. A. Dumas, *Amédée de Lausanne: huit homélies mariales*, intro. G. Bavaud, ed. J. Deshusses, SCh 72 (Paris, 1960), p. 110.

15 Hélinand of Froidmont, *PL* 212:721: 'sermonem in conventu fratrum edidisse me memini in hunc modum'.

16 For Bernard of Clairvaux's works, his editors define *sententiae* in the following manner: 'quae sive compendia sunt sive schemata orationum quas ipse habuit que edidi', SBOp 6.2, 'Ad lectorem'.

17 On the *sententiae*, see J. Leclercq, *The Love of Learning and the Desire for God* (New York, 1982; first pub. in English 1961; first pub. in French 1957), pp. 169–70; and C. Holdsworth's suggestion that they are 'the unrevised notes taken by some of [Bernard's] listeners', C. Holdsworth, 'Were the Sermons of St Bernard on the Song of Songs ever Preached?', in *Medieval Monastic Preaching*, ed. Muessig, pp. 295–318 (p. 316). However, I think it just as likely that they represent the sort of outline Bernard might have used as an aide-mémoire, composed before preaching, which Holdsworth, p. 315, also allows in Bernard's preparation for preaching.

18 See M.B. Bruun, *Parables: Bernard of Clairvaux's Mapping of Spiritual Topography* (Leiden, 2007).

19 J. Leclercq, *Études sur Saint Bernard et le texte de ses écrits* (Rome, 1953), pp. 45–83.

20 J. Leclercq, 'Were the Sermons on the Song of Songs Delivered in Chapter?', in *On the Song of Songs 2*, intro. Leclercq, trans. K. Walsh, CF 7 (1983), p. xiii.

21 *Historia Fusniacensis coenobii* (Bonnefontaine, 1670), pp. 1–224.

22 B.M. Kienzle, 'The Medieval Monastic Sermon', in *The Sermon*, Typologie des sources du moyen âge occidental 81–3 (Turnhout, 2000), pp. 298–300.

23 Holdsworth, 'Were the Sermons of St Bernard'. Earlier Emero Stiegman emphasised the literary character of the sermons in 'The Literary Genre of Bernard of Clairvaux's *Sermones Super Cantica Canticorum*', in *Simplicity and Ordinariness*, ed. J.R. Sommerfeldt, CS 61 (Kalamazoo, MI, 1980). Wim Verbaal replies to Holdsworth in 'Réalités quotidiennes et fiction littéraire dans les *Sermons sur le Cantique* de Bernard de Clairvaux', *Cîteaux*, 51 (2000), 201–18.

24 Kienzle, 'The Medieval Monastic Sermon', pp. 291–5.

25 See Leclercq, 'Were the Sermons', pp. xv–xxiv.

26 SBOp 5, pp. 121–3, 206–13.

27 Guerric of Igny, *Sermons*, pp. 260–70.

28 R. Rouse, 'Cistercian Aids to Study in the Thirteenth Century', in *Studies in Medieval Cistercian History*, ed. J.R. Sommerfeldt, CS 24 (Kalamazoo, MI, 1976), vol. II, pp. 123–34; M. and R. Rouse, '*Statim invenire*: Schools, Preachers, and New Attitudes to the Page', in *Authentic Witnesses: Approaches to Medieval Texts and Manuscripts*, ed. M.A. Rouse and R.H. Rouse (Notre Dame, IN, 1991), pp. 191–220.

29 *PL* 212:559–60.

30 Isaac of Stella, *S* 14; *Sermons 1*, p. 274.

31 Leclercq, *Études sur Saint Bernard*, pp. 55–62.

32 'Verumtamen quod aliquoties vobis loquimur praeter consuetudinem Ordinis nostri, non nostra id agimus praesumptione, sed de voluntate venerabilium fratrum et coabbatum nostrorum ... nec enim modo loquerer vobis, si possem laborare vobiscum', SBOp 4, p. 447.

33 *S* 48; *Sermons 3*, p. 146. See also Hoste, 'Introduction', *Isaac de l'Étoile: Sermons 1*, pp. 10–13.

34 *PL* 212:592–4; A.T. Thayer, 'Judith and Mary: Hélinand's Sermon for the Assumption', in *Medieval Sermons and Society: Cloister, City, University*, ed. J. Hamesse *et al.* (Louvain-la-Neuve, 1998), pp. 63–76.

35 *Sermo peregrinationis; Sermons 3*, pp. 294–302 and *Notes complémentaires*, pp. 316–19.

36 See *S* 52; *Sermons 3*, p. 235 and *Notes complémentaires*, p. 313.

37 *S* 37; *Sermons 2*, p. 299; *S* 48; *Sermons 3, 5*, pp. 158–60; and *Notes complémentaires*, pp. 310–11.

38 Mikkers and Costello (eds.), *Sermones*, vol. I, pp. 298–304.

39 *Ibid.*, vol. II, pp. 526–34.

40 P.J. Cole, *The Preaching of the Crusades to the Holy Land 1096–1270* (Cambridge, MA, 1991), esp. pp. 40–59, 65–71, 71–8; B.M. Kienzle, *Cistercians, Heresy and Crusade, 1145–1229: Preaching in the Lord's Vineyard* (Woodbridge, 2001).

41 G. Constable, 'The Second Crusade as Seen by Contemporaries', *Traditio*, 9 (1953), 245–7.

42 Baldwin composed a sermon or treatise on the cross, probably at the request of the canons of Waltham, who received a miraculous crucifix in 1177. D.N. Bell and J.P. Freeland, 'The Sermons on Obedience and the Cross by Baldwin of Forde', *CSQ*, 29 (1994), 241–90.

43 See Cole, *The Preaching of the Crusades*, esp. pp. 42–61; and the works of B.M. Kienzle.

44 See B.M. Kienzle, 'Hélinand de Froidmont et la prédication cistercienne dans le Midi', in *La prédication en Pays d'oc (XIIe–début XVe siècle)*, ed. J.-L. Biget *et al* (Toulouse, 1997), pp. 37–67.

Primary sources

Studies and translations of one or a few Cistercian sermons abound; the vastness of the genre makes it the predominant source for analysis of spirituality, theology, pastoral care, exegesis, to name only a few areas of research. Hence the bibliography here must be limited to editions and book-length translations of the primary texts themselves. Other works that prove essential to the study of Cistercian preaching are cited in the notes but not included here.

Note that J.B. Schneyer's *Repertorium der lateinischen Sermones des Mittelalters für die Zeit von 1150–1350*, 11 vols. (Münster, 1969–90), lists more than 2,000 unidentified Cistercian sermons (vol. VI, pp. 355–500).

Adam of Perseigne (*c.* 1145–1221)
Mariale (twelve Marian sermons); *PL* 211:699–754; trans. (French) R. Thomas, *Mariale* (Chambarand, 1963)

Aelred of Rievaulx (1110–*c.* 1167)
Homeliae de oneribus propheticis Isaiae (*Homilies on the Burdens of Isaiah*); *PL* 184:817–28 and 195:363–500; ed. G. Raciti, A. Hoste and C.H. Talbot, CCCM 2D (Turnhout, 2005), pp. 21–288

Sermones I–XLVI: Collectio Claraevallensis prima et secunda; ed. G. Raciti, CCCM 2A (Turnhout, 1989)
Sermones XLVII–LXXXIV: Collectio Dunelmensis, sermo a Matthaeo Rievallensi servatus, Sermones Lincolnienses; ed. G. Raciti, CCCM 2B (Turnhout, 2001); trans. (partial) A. Sulavik, 'Aelred of Rievaulx: Sermons on the Feasts of Saint Mary', *CSQ*, 32 (1997), 37–125; trans. (partial) T. Berkeley and M.B. Pennington, *Aelred of Rievaulx: The Liturgical Sermons. The First Clairvaux Collections*, CF 58 (Kalamazoo, MI, 2001)

Amadeus of Lausanne (1110–1159)
Eight homilies in praise of the Virgin Mary; *PL* 188:1303–46; trans. A. Dumas, *Amédée de Lausanne: huit homélies mariales*, intro. G. Bavaud, ed. J. Deshusses, SCh 72 (Paris, 1960); trans. G. Perigo, *Magnificat: Homilies in Praise of the Blessed Virgin Mary*, intro. C. Waddell, CF 18A (Kalamazoo, MI, 1978), repr. *Amadeus of Lausanne: Eight Homilies on the Praises of Blessed Mary*, intro. C. Waddell, CF 18B (Kalamazoo, MI, 1979)

Baldwin of Forde (d. 1190)
Sermones: De commendatione fidei (Commendation of Faith); ed. D.N. Bell, CCCM 99 (Turnhout, 1991); trans. D.N. Bell and J.P. Freeland, 'The Sermons on Obedience and the Cross by Baldwin of Forde', *CSQ*, 29 (1994), 241–90; trans. D.N. Bell and J.P. Freeland, *Baldwin of Forde: The Commendation of Faith*, CF 59 (Kalamazoo, MI, 2000)

Bernard of Clairvaux (1090–1153)
Ad clericos de conversione (On Conversion); SBOp 4, pp. 69–116; trans. M.-B. Saïd, *Sermons on Conversion*, CF 25 (Kalamazoo, MI, 1981)
In laudibus virginis matris (In Praise of the Virgin Mother); SBOp 4, pp. 13–58
Parabolae (Parables); SBOp 6.2; trans. M. Casey, *Bernard of Clairvaux: The Parables and The Sentences*, ed. M. O'Brien, CF 55 (Kalamazoo, MI, 2000)
Sententiae (Sentences) in three series; SBOp 6.2; trans. F.R. Swietek, *Bernard of Clairvaux: The Parables and The Sentences*, intro. J.R. Sommerfeldt, CF 55 (Kalamazoo, MI, 2000)
Sermones de diversis (Sermons on Diverse Topics); SBOp 6.1
Sermones per annum (Sermons for the Liturgical Year); SBOp 4 and 5 include seventeen sermons on *Qui habitat*, SBOp 4, pp. 383–492; trans. (partial) M.-B. Saïd, *Sermons on Conversion*, CF 25 (Kalamazoo, MI, 1981); trans. (partial) I. Edmonds, W. Beckett and C. Greenia, *Sermons for Advent and the Christmas Season*, intro. W. Verbaal, ed. J. Leinenweber, CF 51 (Kalamazoo, MI, 2007); trans. (partial) B.M. Kienzle and J. Jarzembowski, *Sermons for the Summer Season: Liturgical Sermons from Rogationtide and Pentecost*, CF 53 (Kalamazoo, MI, 1990)
Sermones super Cantica canticorum (Sermons on the Song of Songs); SBOp 1 and 2; English translations are published in four volumes by Cistercian Publications, Kalamazoo: *On the Song of Songs*, vol. I, intro. M.C. Halflants, trans. K. Walsh, CF 4 (1981); vol. II, intro. J. Leclercq, trans. K. Walsh, CF 7 (1983); vol. III, intro. E. Stiegman, trans. K. Walsh and I.M. Edmonds, CF 31 (1979); vol. IV, intro. J. Leclercq, trans. I.M. Edmonds, CF 40 (1980)

Geoffrey of Auxerre (*c.* 1120–*post* 1188)

Gastaldelli, F., 'Quattro sermoni *"ad abbates"* di Goffredo di Auxerre', *Cîteaux*, 34 (1983), 161–200

'Tre sermoni di Goffredo di Auxerre su San Benedetto', in F. Gastaldelli, 'Regola, spiritualita e crisi dell'ordine cisterciense in tre sermoni di Goffredo di Auxerre su San Benedetto', *Cîteaux*, 31 (1980), 193–225

Sermo ad praelatos in concilio convocatos (*Sermon for the Prelates Summoned to Council*); PL 184:1095–102

Super Apocalypsim (*On the Apocalypse*); ed. F. Gastaldelli, *Ricerche su Goffredo d'Auxerre. Il compendio anonimo del 'Super Apocalypsim'* (Rome, 1970); trans. J. Gibbons, *Geoffrey of Auxerre: On the Apocalypse*, CF 42 (Kalamazoo, MI, 2000)

Gilbert of Hoyland (d. 1172)

Sermo: De semine verbi Dei (*Sermon on the Seed of God's Word*); PL 184:288–90; trans. L.C. Braceland, *Gilbert of Hoyland: Treatises, Epistles and Sermons*, CF 34 (Kalamazoo, MI, 1981)

Sermo de eodem martyre (*Sermon on the Same Martyr*); ed. and trans. Braceland, *Gilbert of Hoyland: Treatises, Epistles and Sermons*

Sermo super evangelium secundum Matthaeum (*Sermon on the Gospel according to Matthew*); ed. and trans. Braceland, *Gilbert of Hoyland: Treatises, Epistles and Sermons*

Sermones super Cantica canticorum (*Sermons on the Song of Songs*); forty-eight sermons, ed. PL 184:9–252; trans. L.C. Braceland, *Gilbert of Hoyland: Sermons on the Song of Songs*, 3 vols., CF 14, 20 and 26 (Kalamazoo, MI, 1978–9)

Guerric of Igny (d. 1157)

Guerrici Abbatis Igniacensis Discipuli S. Bernardi Sermones per Annum (*Sermons for the Liturgical Year*); PL 185:11–220; trans. P. Deseille, *Guerric d'Igny: Sermons*, ed. and intro. J. Morson and H. Costello, 2 vols., SCh 166 and 202 (Paris 1970 and 1973); fifty-four sermons, trans. by Monks of Mount Saint Bernard, *Guerric of Igny: Liturgical Sermons*, 2 vols., CF 8 and CF 32 (Shannon and Spencer, MA, 1971); trans. (partial) T. Merton, *The Christmas Sermons of Bl. Guerric of Igny* (Gethsemani Abbey, KY, 1959)

Hélinand of Froidmont (*c.* 1160–1237)

Twenty-eight sermons, PL 212:481–720; forty additional sermons, ed. J.B. Schneyer, *Repertorium der lateinischen Sermones des Mittelalters für die Zeit von 1150–1350*, 11 vols. (Münster, 1969–90), vol. II (1970), pp. 617–22 (Helinandus of Perseigne); ed. B.M. Kienzle, 'Cistercian Preaching against the Cathars: Hélinand's Unedited Sermon for Rogation, B.N. ms. lat. 14591', *Cîteaux*, 39 (1988), 297–314; ed. B.M. Kienzle, 'Mary Speaks against Heresy: Hélinand of Froidmont's Unedited Purification Sermon, Paris B. N. ms. lat. 14591', *Sacris Erudiri*, 32 (1991), 291–308

Henry of Hautcrêt (d. 1231/2)

Fifty-one sermons entitled *Pentacontamonadius*, Fribourg, Bib. cant. L 303, fols. 31–81v, and Archives of Aragon, Ripoll 205, fols. 80–138. Three have been published by M. Meyer, 'Henri, abbé de Hautcret et ses homélies', *Archives de la Société du canton de Fribourg*, 1 (1850), 237–50

Isaac of Stella (c. 1100–c. 1169)
Sermons; *PL* 194:1689–1876; ed. D. Pezzini, *Isacco della Stella: I sermoni* (Milan, 2006–7); ed. and trans. A. Hoste and G. Salet, *Isaac de l'Étoile: Sermons 1*, SCh 130 (Paris, 1967); ed. and trans. A. Hoste, G. Salet and G. Raciti, *Isaac de l'Étoile: Sermons 2–3*, SCh 207 and 339 (Paris, 1974 and 1987); trans. H. McCaffery, *Isaac of Stella: Sermons on the Christian Year*, intro. B. McGinn, CF 11 (Kalamazoo, MI, 1979), vol. II is in preparation; trans. D. Deme, *The Selected Works of Isaac of Stella: A Cistercian Voice from the Twelfth Century* (Aldershot, 2007)

John of Forde (d. c. 1214)
Sermo in dominica in ramis palmarum (*Sermon for Palm Sunday*); ed. C.H. Talbot, 'Un sermon inédit de Jean de Ford', *COCR*, 7 (1940), 36–45
Super extremam partem Cantici canticorum sermones cxx (*One Hundred and Twenty Sermons on the Last Part of the Song of Songs*); ed. E. Mikkers and H. Costello, CCCM 17 and 18 (Turnhout, 1970); trans. W.M. Beckett, *John of Ford: On the Song of Songs*, intro. H. Costello, 7 vols., CF 29, 39 and 43–7 (Kalamazoo, MI, 1977–84); trans. (selected passages) H. Costello, *Sky-Blue is the Sapphire Crimson the Rose: Stillpoint of Desire in John of Ford*, CF 69 (Kalamazoo, MI, 2006)

Odo of Cheriton (1180/90–1247)
One hundred and ninety-three sermons listed in *Repertorium der lateinischen Sermones des Mittelalters für die Zeit von 1150–1350*, 11 vols., ed. J.B. Schneyer (Münster, 1969–90), vol. IV, pp. 483–98

Odo of Morimond (d. 1161)
Five sermons; *PL* 188:1645–58; unedited sermons listed in Schneyer, ed., *Repertorium*, vol. IV. 4, pp. 499–508

Ogerius of Locedio (d. 1214)
Fifteen sermons on the Last Supper; *PL* 184:879–950

Serlo of Savigny (d. 1158) and **Serlo of Wilton** (d. 1181)
Sermons; ed. and trans. L.C. Braceland, *Serlo of Savigny and Serlo of Wilton: Seven Unpublished Works*, CF 48 (Kalamazoo, MI, 1986); see also L.C. Braceland, *Supplement to Serlo of Savigny and Serlo of Wilton: Eight Unpublished Works*, CF 48, supplement (Kalamazoo, MI, 1986)

Other primary sources

Choisselet, D. and P. Vernet (eds.), *Les 'Ecclesiastica Officia' cisterciens du XIIe siècle. Texte latin selon les manuscrits édités de Trente 1711, Ljubljana 31 et Dijon 114: version française, annexe liturgique, notes, index et tables*, La documentation cistercienne 22 (Reiningue, 1989)
Waddell, C., *Cistercian Lay Brothers: Twelfth-Century Usages with Related Texts*, Cîteaux: Studia et Documenta 10 (Brecht, 2000)

18 Liturgy

NICOLAS BELL

The liturgical principles of the Cistercians were grounded, as with all other aspects of the Order, in the strict observance of the Rule of St Benedict. The singing of the psalms was central to Benedictine monasticism, and Benedict devoted several chapters of his Rule to an explanation of how the complete Psalter could be recited each week by dividing its contents between the various services of the day and night office. By the eleventh century, several abbeys under the influence of Cluny had sufficient endowments to enable their monks to pray and chant all day, leading to a perpetual cycle of worship which paid less attention to the spiritual reading and manual labour with which Benedict had balanced the life of prayer. It was in liturgical matters that the early reformers could most easily perceive decadence in the Cluniac congregations: the chief intention of the founders of Cîteaux was not to establish a new religious Order so much as to strip out the many liturgical accretions which had filled the monastic day, and thereby to maintain a more even balance between *ora et labora*. Their adherence to Benedict's prescriptions was very literal, and understandably attracted derision from some quarters, notably in Abelard's letter to Bernard.

When Robert and his twenty-one companions left Molesme in 1098 to establish the New Monastery that would later be named as Cîteaux, we may assume that they took with them the various liturgical books, vestments and vessels that they would require for worship. When Robert was recalled to Molesme the following year, his companions were allowed to retain all of the equipment he had brought with him (his *capella*), with the exception of a breviary which they were instructed to return to Molesme after making a copy.[1] A psalter written in Arras which Robert had owned in Molesme was among the books kept at Cîteaux, but a note added to it later records that its calendar and litany were unusable for the rite of the New Monastery.[2] There is no way of knowing precisely how services were ordered in the very early years, but it was under Stephen Harding's abbacy (1108/9–33) that major revisions were made to bring the liturgy in use at Cîteaux under a more systematic and uniform structure, primarily to ensure that the newly established daughter houses followed the same practices as the mother house. The chief concern was unity across all the houses, and in the *Carta Caritatis prior* it is specified that the monks in all the daughter houses shall have the same usages, chants and books as the mother house, 'so that there shall be no discord in our conduct, but we may live by one love [*caritas*], one rule, and similar traditions'.[3]

Stephen Harding was a meticulous editor, and took an almost antiquarian interest in seeking out the best sources for editions. He prepared a new edition of the vulgate Bible, consulting Jewish scholars in an attempt to remove contradictory passages from the Old Testament.[4] On some occasions in the Rule, Benedict uses the word *ambrosianum* as a synonym for *hymnus*; Stephen took this to refer exclusively to hymns composed by St Ambrose, and sent to Milan for the most authoritative versions of the texts it was assumed he had written.[5] For the chants of the mass and office, Stephen knew as well as anyone that the foremost ecclesiastical authority was the church of Metz, where the melodies were believed to have been preserved exactly as they had been dictated to Gregory the Great by the Holy Spirit in the form of a dove. He sent a delegation of his monks to Metz to bring back the authentic chant, and adopted their findings despite the fact that they found several of the melodies to be alien to the Burgundian tradition in which most of the early monks had been brought up.

We can see some of these results in the earliest liturgical book still extant, a complete breviary datable to 1132 and written for the newly founded daughter house of La Bussière in the diocese of Autun.[6] Some of its texts seem to derive from the traditions of monasteries in the Metz diocese, others (such as the biblical readings assigned as *capitula* in the Hours) from conventions more local to the province of Lyons. In comparison with the books in use in other Benedictine monasteries, though, the chief difference is seen in the omission of the many additional pieces which had come to fill the monastic day far beyond the prescriptions of Benedict's Rule. In the larger Benedictine houses there were numerous extra offices – for the dead, for the Virgin Mary and for locally venerated saints – while the mass was expanded by long processions with litanies and by new liturgical poetry such as tropes, composed as interpolations to the plainchant, and the sequence or *prosa* sung before the Gospel reading. As well as the omission of all of these elaborations, there is an interesting aspect of the structure of this breviary which was to become a distinctive feature of the later books of the Order. It was customary to treat the feasts of Stephen, John the Evangelist and Holy Innocents on 26, 27 and 28 December as part of the Christmas season and group them together with the other principal feasts of the liturgical year in the Temporal section of the book, but here they are placed with other saints' feasts at the very start of the Sanctoral, which ends with Thomas the Apostle on 21 December instead of starting with Advent, as would normally have been expected.

Unlike the services of the office, the Rule of Benedict gave no detailed instructions for the celebration of the mass, and there was as much variety in the ritual among Benedictine houses as there was in secular dioceses. This gave the Cistercians an incentive to compare the different traditions and produce a ritual of suitable austerity. Two Cistercian sacramentaries survive from this early period, from which it is clear that the chief model was not the fusion of Gelasian and Gregorian sacramentary traditions which was found in Molesme and its environs, but rather a simpler and more ancient Gregorian tradition with various supplementary material, perhaps more closely associated with Metz.[7] This version, which is perpetuated in the later books, provides a useful tool for identifying books as being Cistercian, for example through certain phrases in the canon of the mass which differ from those found in books conventionally used outside the Order. Evidence for the early recension of the chant melodies is rather limited, since the few manuscripts to survive from the time of Stephen Harding's reforms have generally been corrected at a later date, but an antiphoner preserved at the abbey of Westmalle in Belgium allows one to see traces of the original texts and melodies underneath the later revisions.[8]

It was the unfamiliar chant taken from the Metz tradition that caused most problems for the monks coming to terms with the new liturgy of Cîteaux and her daughter houses, and it was not long before Stephen Harding's revision of the liturgy was supplanted by a second layer of reform. In the 1140s an editorial commission was convened under the leadership of Bernard of Clairvaux with the purpose of revising the text and music of the gradual and antiphoner, the books of chants for the mass and Office. In a prologue to the new edition of the antiphoner, copied into several of the surviving manuscripts, Bernard explained that both the text and the music of the Metz liturgy were found to be 'corrupt, highly inconsistent, and contemptible in almost every respect'.[9] It is certainly very likely that the Metz manuscripts did not transmit a pure and ancient chant tradition, but Bernard's scathing comments in fact tell us more about his own temperament and the change in philosophy of the Order since the founding years. Whereas Stephen Harding's main concern was that the liturgy should conform with Benedict's Rule and be consistently enacted across the Order, Bernard required that all aspects of the monastic life should be conducted *regulariter*, including every detail of the words and music used in worship.

One principle of the Bernardine reforms was an insistence that no liturgical text should diverge from a strict understanding of biblical narrative. In the Christmas responsory *Quem vidistis pastores* the text with which the revisers were presented had the shepherds proclaiming that they had seen the new-born child in a choir of angels praising God ('natum vidimus in choro angelorum'), when in fact Luke's Gospel tells us that the choir of angels had already left the shepherds before they saw the child. Other chant traditions including the modern Roman editions simply amended this to 'natum vidimus et choros angelorum', but the Cistercian reformers preferred to remove the text altogether and replace it with verses taken directly from the Bible. The Apocrypha had been the source of several of the most familiar chant texts in use across Europe, but these were likewise outlawed by the Cistercians. More recent doctrine was not prohibited, though, and a great many new Marian antiphons were added to the repertory, most famously *Salve Regina*. There were also many other changes to the texts, for the sake of variety or concision. Where a phrase was repeated, as happens in several offertory chants, the repetition was removed; and in cases where the same chant was repeated each day through a festal season, new texts were supplied. Other changes allowed the replacement of an unfamiliar text from the Metz tradition with a more familiar one found in other books closer to home: now that the Metz books were no longer seen as sacrosanct, the editorial team felt able to revert to the words with which they were more familiar.[10]

Following Stephen Harding's introduction of the Ambrosian hymnal, the absence of many favourite hymns was clearly felt. Abelard had made it a chief complaint in a letter he wrote to Bernard sometime in the early 1130s: traditional hymns had been replaced by unknown ones, and a single hymn, *Eterne rerum conditor*, was prescribed to be sung at Vigils the whole year through.[11] The Bernardine commission reconsidered this matter, and observed that in fact Benedict uses the term *ambrosianum* only when writing about the hymn at Vigils, Lauds and Vespers: elsewhere in the Rule, he uses the more common term *hymnus*. The revisers therefore felt confident to reintroduce more familiar hymns at Prime, Terce, Sext, None and Compline, and composed fine new melodies for the Ambrosian hymns that remained.

The plainchant melodies which Stephen Harding's reform had brought from Metz required more careful attention from Bernard and his collaborators. The main intention of the earlier reform had been unity across the Order, combined with a desire for a sense of authenticity. Bernard's motivation lay more in a sense of reason, which in Cistercian ethics was closely associated with moderation. When asked by the Benedictine abbey of Montiéramey to compose an office for St Victor of Arcis-sur-Aube, whose relics they held, Bernard replied that 'if there is to be singing, the melody should be grave and not flippant or uncouth ... and it should never obscure but enhance the sense of the words'.[12] This aesthetic standpoint manifested itself in a series of theoretical principles which were applied to the chant as a means of filtering out impurities.

The method of revision is explained in several texts, at most length in a spirited treatise attributed to an Abbot Guido, and in abbreviated form as prologues to the antiphoner and gradual.[13] It is based on a literal understanding of the modal system, a tradition of music theory which had been developed over the previous two centuries as a means of understanding and categorising a much older and more diverse chant practice. The system is applied as 'a rule determining the nature and form of regular chant'.[14] Sounds are to be grouped into one of four unvarying identities, each of which divides into two forms, authentic and plagal. The four consequences of this nature are that a melody need never extend beyond ten notes (the principle of the decachord); that authentic and plagal forms of a mode may not encroach upon one another; that if these forms may not encroach, then neither may modes; and that modes may not be confounded by modifying the value of sounds with the use of a B flat.[15] Adherence to these rules will produce modally pure and therefore 'regular' chant. In addition, musical repetitions were removed, just as textual repetitions had been.

In practice, large numbers of chant melodies survived this process of sanitisation without any changes, since they happened already to conform, but there are many other cases where modal equivocation is employed quite deliberately to enrich the sonority of the music. These were considered deficient and forced into a single modal identity, often by transposing the offending portion of the chant. The long, florid melismas which add great beauty to the alleluia, the offertory and other important moments in the liturgy were perceived to be decadent and shortened to what was considered necessary. Thus Bernard felt that he had succeeded in providing a chant that was 'sober and sensible'.[16] The effect of this application of modal purity is sometimes a shortening or simplification of the sung portions of the mass and Office, but in practice the differences from the Benedictine liturgy of the time would have been much more evident in the suppression of the tropes and sequences which provided such a contrast to the plainchant in their music and their words.

The editing of the antiphoner and gradual was the most time-consuming part of the editorial project that took place under Bernard's leadership, but is best seen as one component of a programme to bring all of the liturgical and other activities of the monastery under a single unified philosophy. In a series of *Capitula*, or decisions of the General Chapter, dating probably from the abbacy of Stephen Harding, there is a summary list 'of which books it is not permitted to have variant texts', consisting of eleven books which must everywhere be the same as one another: 'missale, textus [i.e. the book of Gospel readings], epistolare, collectaneum, gradale, antiphonarium, hymnarium, psalterium, lectionarium, regula [i.e. the Rule of Benedict], kalendarium'.[17] The culmination of this endeavour can be seen in MS 114 of the Bibliothèque municipale in Dijon, a large volume mainly compiled between 1173 and 1191 to function as the exemplar from which all the books required by a new daughter house could be copied. Its grand title-page lists fifteen volumes which were required throughout the Order: a *breviarium* in three parts (which is in effect a lectionary in modern terms) followed by epistolary, evangeliary, missal, collectar, calendar, rule, consuetudinary, psalter, canticles, hymnal, antiphonal and gradual.[18] The last five have unfortunately been missing from the manuscript since the fifteenth century, but the close fidelity of later manuscripts to this exemplar allows us to be confident of the nature of its contents.

Work on Bernard's antiphoner and gradual was completed by 1147, and multiple copies were quickly made as the Order expanded.[19] Older Benedictine foundations that came under Cistercian rule often observed the principles of austerity by not commissioning new books, preferring to adapt their existing books by erasing surplus notes and cutting out the pages with feasts that were no longer permitted. It was a requirement that the musical notation should be clearly and consistently written on a four-line stave, a practice that was already becoming standard in parts of France but remained unknown in parts of Germany. The rapid growth of the Order across Europe makes it not unreasonable to give the Cistercians credit for the four-line stave and pitch-specific notation becoming the common currency of Europe for the next four centuries. These principles of clarity, as well as the simplified chant, were also adopted by the Dominicans, who otherwise followed the Roman cursus instead of the monastic rite. Similarly, the clear and distinctively Cistercian system of punctuation which is found in books as early as

Stephen Harding's Bible came to be standard in lectionaries and other books used for public reading, and influenced its use by other Orders.[20]

The Cistercian calendar was centrally controlled by Cîteaux, with the intention that any additions made to it should always be celebrated in like manner throughout the order. In the breviary of Stephen Harding's time there are very few proper offices for saints, though several more were acknowledged in simple commemorations. The reforms of Bernard's time led to a slight increase and to a clearer differentiation in rank between different feasts. Changes to the calendar were promulgated by the General Chapter, and took place with increasing frequency. Bernard was accorded a feast on his canonisation in 1174, the other Cistercian saints Peter of Tarentaise and Malachy in 1191. In the thirteenth century almost fifty feasts were newly introduced or raised in rank.[21] In practice, the application of these changes to the calendar was far less systematic than the General Chapter intended: it depended on abbots being present at the meetings, and their diligence in passing the necessary emendations on for inclusion in the books. In the case of a new office, this could be a substantial undertaking requiring the disbinding of the book, and we see various methods of incorporation in surviving books. With time, local saints came to be commemorated in local books, despite the clear contravention of the principles of uniformity which this entailed.[22]

Apart from these adaptations to the calendar, the prescriptions found in the Dijon manuscript were maintained virtually unchanged into the seventeenth century. Cistercian liturgical manuscripts have a remarkable uniformity in their content and appearance when compared with other Benedictine books, a tradition which continued when they first came to be printed: the breviary in Basle in 1484, a psalter two years later and the missal in Strasburg in 1487. The last edition of the *Liber usuum* before the suppression of the old rite was published in 1643 and remains very close to its earlier form as the *consuetudines* in the Dijon manuscript almost five centuries earlier. As well as the addition of new feasts, a few other concessions were made to standard practices outside the Order: the elevation of the host was reintroduced in 1152 and of the chalice in 1444, with genuflection at the elevation in 1232; and communion in both kinds was prohibited to the community from 1261 and to the deacon and subdeacon from 1437. By the end of the fourteenth century abbots had come to assume pontifical status, despite Bernard's arguments against this practice. The austerity of the early ordinances, which proscribed the use of gold or silk, demanding woollen vestments, a chalice of silver, thurible of base metal and a plain wooden crucifix in the sanctuary, soon came to be relaxed. Processions, at first reduced to Candlemas and Palm Sunday, were allowed by 1441 for all feasts of Sermon rank.

Other practices were never officially permitted, but are known to have been widespread because of the prohibitions which were issued against them by General Chapter. In 1217 the abbots of Neath and Flaxley reported to the General Chapter that their neighbours in Dore and Tintern Abbeys were singing in three- and four-part polyphony, 'in the secular style'. This led to the first of many condemnations of poly-phonic music issued by statute, which provide back-handed evidence that the plainchant was often elaborated in this way. A few manuscripts of polyphonic music have survived from Cistercian foundations, as well as books of tropes and sequences which were likewise not officially tolerated.[23]

Unlike some of the newer Orders, the Cistercians were exempted in the Council of Trent from having to conform to the Roman rite. Nevertheless, by the beginning of the seventeenth century the reform movement had sanctioned the adoption of many aspects of the rite, and the Roman mass rite was adopted wholesale in the Common Observance at the General Chapter meeting of 1618. In 1656 the reforms of Claude Vaussin introduced many more Roman feasts which had hitherto been omitted from the Cistercian rite, and suppressed several of the distinctive feasts; newer Roman feasts were added in the revision of 1871.[24] In the twentieth century, Strict and Common Observances have both used the old Cistercian mass rite and the Roman rite at different times and places, though the preference in recent times has been to follow the Roman rite for the mass and the Cistercian liturgy for the Office. The Trappists of Westmalle have pub-lished liturgical books closely modelled on those of Bernard's reform, which remain in use.

Notes

1   *Exordium Parvum* 7; ed. J. de la C. Bouton and J.B. Van Damme, *Les plus anciens textes de Cîteaux*, Cîteaux: Studia et Documenta 2 (Achel, 1974), p. 65; ed. Waddell, *Narrative*, pp. 242, 425.

2   Dijon, Bibliothèque municipale MS 30. See J. Marilier, *Chartes et documents concernant l'Abbaye de Cîteaux, 1098–1182* (Rome, 1961), p. 40.

3   *Carta Caritatis prior* 3; ed. Bouton and Van Damme, *Les plus anciens textes*, p. 92; ed. Waddell, pp. 276, 444.

4   The bible is Dijon BM MSS 12–15; its explanatory foreword is edited in Marilier, *Chartes et documents*, p. 56.

5 Stephen Harding's letter on this subject is published in Marilier, *Chartes et documents*, p. 55. The hymnal is edited by C. Waddell, *The Twelfth-Century Cistercian Hymnal*, 2 vols., Cistercian Liturgy Series 1–2 (Gethsemani Abbey, KY, 1984).

6 Berlin, Staatsbibliothek, MS lat. oct. 402; ed. C. Waddell, *The Primitive Cistercian Breviary* (Fribourg, 2007), which includes a list of other liturgical books from which the primitive rite is recoverable (pp. 31–2).

7 See Waddell, *The Primitive Cistercian Breviary*, pp. 66–8.

8 MS 12A–B. For a facsimile and study see A. Scarcez, *L'antiphonaire 12A–B de Westmalle dans l'histoire du chant cistercien au XIIe siècle* (Turnhout, 2011); see also C. Waddell, 'The Origin and Early Evolution of the Cistercian Antiphonary: Reflections on Two Cistercian Chant Reforms', in *The Cistercian Spirit*, ed. M.B. Pennington, CS 3 (Shannon, 1970), pp. 190–223.

9 'Prologus in antiphonarium', SBOp 3, pp. 511–16.

10 This is demonstrated in responsory verses, for example, by A. Scarcez, 'Les sources du responsorial cistercien', *Études grégoriennes*, 38 (2011), 137–80.

11 Abelard, Letter 10; E.R. Smits, *Peter Abelard: Letters IX–XIV. An Edition with an Introduction* (Groningen, 1983), pp. 239–47.

12 Bernard, *Ep* 398 to Abbot Guy of Montiéramey, edited most recently by C. Maître, *Bernard de Clairvaux: Office de Saint Victor, Prologue à l'antiphonaire, Lettre 398*, SCh 527 (Paris, 2009); quoted from the translation by B. Scott James. It is noteworthy that despite Bernard's words, the music supplied for this office does not conform to the rules imposed in Bernard's reform.

13 The treatise is edited, with a discussion of its authorship, by C. Maître, *La réforme cistercienne du plain-chant: étude d'un traité théorique*, Cîteaux: Studia et Documenta 6 (Brecht, 1995). For an edition and translation of the prologue to the antiphoner, see F.J. Guentner, *Epistola S. Bernardi de revisione cantus cisterciensis et Tractatus*, Corpus Scriptorum de Musica 24 ([Rome], 1974).

14 'Quid est tonus? Regula naturam et formam cantuum regularium determinans': the opening words of the *Tonale sancti Bernardi*; ed. C. Meyer, 'Le tonaire cistercien et sa tradition', *Revue de musicologie*, 89 (2003), 57–92.

15 These four rules are expounded at length by S.R. Marosszéki, *Les origines du chant cistercien*, ASOC, 8 (Rome, 1952) and C. Veroli, 'La revisione musicale Bernardina e il Graduale Cisterciense', *Analecta Cisterciensia*, 47 (1991), 3–141; 48 (1992), 3–104; 49 (1993), 147–256.

16 'sobriam tamen atque pudentem', Prologue to the antiphoner; ed. Guentner, *Tractatus*, p. 24.

17 Waddell, *Narrative*, pp. 187, 409.

18 The consuetudinary, or *Liber usuum*, is edited from this manuscript in Choisselet/Vernet.

19 For a convenient facsimile of a representative post-Bernard antiphoner from the abbey of Morimondo, see *Paris, Bibliothèque nationale de*

France, nouvelles acquisitions latines 1411: un antiphonaire cistercien pour le temporal, XIIe siècle (Poitiers, 1998) and *Un antiphonaire cistercien pour le sanctoral, XIIe siècle: Paris, Bibliothèque nationale de France, nouvelles acquisitions latines 1412* (Paris, 1999), both with indexes by C. Maître. A facsimile of a Cistercian gradual remains a desideratum.

20 On Cistercian punctuation see N.F. Palmer, 'Simul *cantemus, simul pausemus:* zur mittelalterlichen Zisterzienserinterpunktion', in *Lesevorgänge: Prozesse des Erkennens in mittelalterlichen Texten, Bildern und Handschriften,* ed. E.C. Lutz *et al.* (Zurich, 2010), pp. 483–569.

21 B. Backaert, 'L'évolution du calendrier cistercien', *COCR,* 11 (1950), 81–94, 302–16; 12 (1951), 108–27, provides a comprehensive account of the development of the calendar as reflected both in the central ordinances and in local practices.

22 See D.F.L. Chadd, 'Liturgy and Liturgical Music: The Limits of Uniformity', in *Cistercian Art and Architecture in the British Isles,* ed. C. Norton and D. Park (Cambridge, 1986), pp. 299–314.

23 See S. Grassin, 'Sur la pratique polyphonique chez les cisterciens', *Études grégoriennes,* 29 (2001), 129–66.

24 The most accessible introduction to these revisions is found in A.A. King, *Liturgies of the Religious Orders* (London, 1955), pp. 78–93.

Primary sources

Choisselet, D. and P. Vernet (eds.), '*Les Ecclesiastica officia' Cisterciens du'XIIème siècle,* La documentation cistercienne 22 (Reiningue, 1989).

Maître, C. (ed.), *Bernard de Clairvaux: Office de Saint Victor, Prologue à L'antiphonaire,* Lettre 398, SCh 527 (Paris, 2009).

Waddell, C. (ed.), *Narrative and Legislative Texts from Early Cîteaux,* Cîteaux: Studia et Documenta 9 (Brecht, 1999).

The Primitive Cistercian Breviary, Spicilegium Friburgense 44 (Fribourg, 2007).

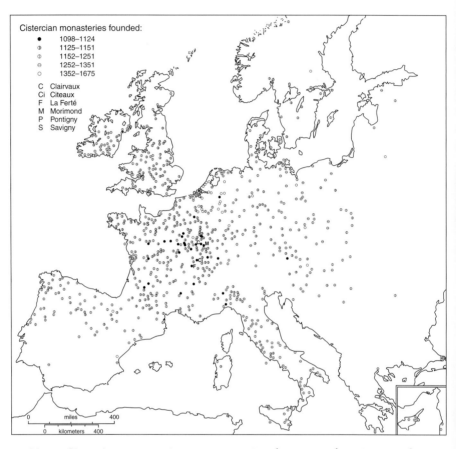

Map 1 Cistercian monasteries, 1098–1675. Based on a map from R.A. Donkin, *The Cistercians: Studies in the Geography of Medieval England and Wales* (Toronto, 1978).

Primary sources

Selected modern editions of Cistercian authors and translations of works mentioned

Adam of Perseigne (c. 1145–1221)

Book of Mutual Love; ed. G. Raciti, 'Un opuscule inédit d'Adam de Perseigne le "Livre de l'amour mutuel"', *Cîteaux*, 31 (1980), 297–341

Letters; ed. J. Bouvet, *Correspondance d'Adam, abbé de Perseigne (1188–1221)* (Le Mans, 1951; 1962), repr. *Adam de Perseigne: Lettres*, SCh 66 (Paris 1960); trans. (partial) G. Perigo, *The Letters of Adam of Perseigne 1*, intro. T. Merton, CF 21 (Kalamazoo, MI, 1976)

Mariale (twelve Marian sermons); *PL* 211:699–754; trans. (French) R. Thomas, *Mariale* (Chambarand, 1963)

Soliloquium (*Soliloquy*); ed. J. Bouvet, 'Le Soliloquium d'Adam de Perseigne', *Collectanea Cisterciensia*, 50 (1988), 113–71

Aelred of Rievaulx (1110–c. 1167)

De bello Standardii (account of the 1138 *Battle of the Standard* between English and Scottish troops); *PL* 195:701–12; trans. J.P. Freeland, *Aelred of Rievaulx: The Historical Works*, ed. M.L. Dutton, CF 56 (Kalamazoo, MI, 2005)

De Iesu puero duodenni (*On Jesus at the Age of Twelve*); *PL* 184:849–70; ed. C.H. Talbot and A. Hoste, CCCM 1 (Turnhout, 1971), pp. 249–78; trans. T. Berkeley, *Aelred of Rievaulx: Treatises*, intro. D. Knowles, CF 2 (Kalamazoo, MI, 1982; first pub. 1971)

De institutione inclusarum (*On the Institution of Recluses*); *PL* 32:1451–77 (*De vita eremitica ad sororem liber*); ed. C.H. Talbot and A. Hoste, CCCM 1 (Turnhout, 1971), pp. 637–82; trans. M.P. Macpherson, *Aelred of Rievaulx: Treatises*, CF 2 (Kalamazoo, MI, 1982; first pub. 1971)

De sanctimoniali de Wattun (tale of the *Nun of Watton*); *PL* 195:789–96; trans. J.P. Freeland, *Aelred of Rievaulx: Lives of the Northern Saints*, intro. M.L. Dutton, CF 71 (Kalamazoo, MI, 2006), pp. 109–122

De sanctis Hagulstaldensis ecclesiae (*On the Saintly Founders of the Church of Hexham*); ed. J. Raine, *The Priory of Hexham: Its Chronicles, Endowments and Annals*, Surtees Society 44 (Durham, 1863–4), pp. 173–203; trans. Freeland, *Lives of the Northern Saints*

De spirituali amicitia (*Spiritual Friendship*); *PL* 195:659–702; ed. A. Hoste and C.H. Talbot, CCCM 1 (Turnhout, 1971), pp. 287–350; trans. M.E. Laker, *Aelred of Rievaulx: Spiritual Friendship*, intro. C. Dumont, CF 1 (Spencer,

MA, 1974); trans. L.C. Braceland, *Aelred of Rievaulx: Spiritual Friendship*, ed. M.L. Dutton (Collegeville, MN, 2009)

Dialogus de anima (On the Soul); ed. C.H. Talbot, *Aelred of Rievaulx: De Anima*, Medieval and Renaissance Studies, Supplement 1 (London, 1952); ed. C.H. Talbot and A. Hoste, CCCM 1 (Turnhout, 1971), pp. 685–754; trans. C.H. Talbot, *Aelred of Rievaulx: Dialogue on the Soul*, CF 22 (Kalamazoo, MI, 1981)

Eulogium Davidis regis Scotorum (Eulogy of King David of Scotland); ed. W.M. Metcalfe, *Pinkerton's Lives of the Scottish Saints*, 2 vols. (Paisley, 1889), 2, pp. 269–85; trans. Freeland, *Aelred of Rievaulx: The Historical Works*

Genealogia regum Anglorum (The Genealogy of the Kings of England); PL 195:711–38; trans. Freeland, *Aelred of Rievaulx: The Historical Works*

Oratio pastoralis (Pastoral Prayer); ed. C.H. Talbot and A. Hoste, CCCM 1 (Turnhout, 1971), pp. 757–63; ed. and intro. M.L. Dutton, *CSQ*, 38 (2003), 297–308; trans. R.P. Lawson, *Aelred of Rievaulx: Treatises*; trans. M. DelCogliano, *CSQ*, 37 (2002), 453–66; trans. M. DelCogliano, *For Your Own People: Aelred of Rievaulx's Pastoral Prayer*, intro. M.L. Dutton, CF 73 (Kalamazoo, MI, 2008)

Speculum caritatis (The Mirror of Charity); PL 195:501–620; ed. A. Hoste and C.H. Talbot, CCCM 1 (Turnhout, 1971), pp. 3–161; trans. E. Connor, *Aelred of Rievaulx: The Mirror of Charity*, intro. C. Dumont, CF 17 (Kalamazoo, MI, 1990)

Vita Niniani Pictorum australium apostoli (Life of Ninian the 'Apostle of the North'); ed. A.P. Forbes, *Lives of S. Ninian and S. Kentigern*, The Historians of Scotland 5 (Edinburgh and Douglas, 1874), pp. 137–57; ed. W.M. Metcalfe, *Pinkerton's Lives of the Scottish Saints*, vol. 1, pp. 9–39; trans. Freeland, *Lives of the Northern Saints*

Vita sancti Edwardi regis et confessoris (Life of Saint Edward the Confessor); PL 195:737–90; trans. Freeland, *Aelred of Rievaulx: The Historical Works*

Sermons

Homeliae de oneribus propheticis Isaiae (Homilies on the Burdens of Isaiah); PL 184:817–28 and 195:363–500; ed. G. Raciti, A. Hoste and C.H. Talbot, CCCM 2D (Turnhout, 2005), pp. 21–288

Sermones I–XLVI: Collectio Claraevallensis prima et secunda; ed. G. Raciti, CCCM 2A (Turnhout, 1989)

Sermones XLVII–LXXXIV: Collectio Dunelmensis, sermo a Matthaeo Rievallensi servatus, Sermones Lincolnienses; ed. G. Raciti, CCCM 2B (Turnhout, 2001); trans. (partial) A. Sulavik, 'Aelred of Rievaulx: Sermons on the Feasts of Saint Mary', *CSQ*, 32 (1997), 37–125; trans. (partial) T. Berkeley and M.B. Pennington, *Aelred of Rievaulx: The Liturgical Sermons. The First Clairvaux Collections*, CF 58 (Kalamazoo, MI, 2001)

Amadeus of Lausanne (1110–1159)

Eight homilies in praise of the Virgin Mary; PL 188:1303–46; trans. A. Dumas, *Amédée de Lausanne: huit homélies mariales*, intro. G. Bavaud, ed. J. Deshusses, SCh 72 (Paris, 1960); trans. G. Perigo, *Magnificat: Homilies in*

Praise of the Blessed Virgin Mary, intro. C. Waddell, CF 18A (Kalamazoo, MI, 1978), repr. *Amadeus of Lausanne: Eight Homilies on the Praises of Blessed Mary*, intro. C. Waddell, CF 18B (Kalamazoo, MI, 1979)
Epistola ad filios suos ecclesiae lausannensis (Letter to His Sons in the Church of Lausanne); PL 188:1299–304

Arnulf of Bohéries (d. *post* 1200)
Speculum monachorum (Monks' Mirror); PL 184:1175–8

Baldwin of Forde (d. 1190)
Opera omnia; PL 204; ed. D.N. Bell, CCCM 99 (Turnhout, 1991); trans. D.N. Bell, *Baldwin of Forde: Spiritual Tractates*, 2 vols., CF 38 and 41 (Kalamazoo, MI, 1986)
De sacramento altaris (On the Sacrament of the Altar); trans. E. de Solms, *Baudouin de Ford: Le Sacrement de l'autel*, ed. J. Morson, intro. J. Leclercq, 2 vols., SCh 93 and 94 (Paris, 1963)
Sermones: De commendatione fidei (The Commendation of Faith); ed. D.N. Bell, CCCM 99 (Turnhout, 1991); trans. D.N. Bell and J.P. Freeland, 'The Sermons on Obedience and the Cross by Baldwin of Forde', *CSQ*, 29 (1994), 241–90; trans. D.N. Bell and J.P. Freeland, *Baldwin of Forde: The Commendation of Faith*, CF 59 (Kalamazoo, MI, 2000)

Beatrice of Nazareth (1200–1268)
De caritate Dei et vii eius gradibus (On the Love of God and its Seven Stages); ed. L. Reypens and J. Van Mierlo, *Beatrijs van Nazareth: Seven manieren van minne* (Leuven, 1926)
Vita Beatricis (based on Beatrice's diary); ed. L. Reypens, *Vita Beatricis: Autobiographie van de Z. Beatrijs van Tienen, O.Cist., 1200–1268* (Antwerp, 1964); Latin–English ed. R. De Ganck and J.B. Hasbrouck, *The Life of Beatrice of Nazareth, 1200–1268*, CF 50 (Kalamazoo, MI, 1991)

Bernard of Clairvaux (1090–1153)
Opera omnia; PL 180–5; ed. J. Leclercq, H.M. Rochais and C.H. Talbot, *Sancti Bernardi Opera* (SBOp), 8 vols. (Rome, 1957–77), vol. ix: *Index biblicus*, ed. G. Hendrix (Turnhout, 1998); rev. and repr. (with Italian trans.) F. Gastaldelli (ed.), *Opere di San Bernardo*, 6 vols. (Milan, 1984–87); rev. and repr. (with German trans.) G. Winkler (ed.), *Bernhard von Clairvaux: Sämtliche Werke* (Winkler), 10 vols. (Innsbruck, 1990–9)
Vita Sancti Malachiae; SBOp 3; Winkler i; ed. and trans. P.-Y. Émery, *Bernard de Clairvaux: Vie de Saint Malachie*, SCh 367 (Paris, 1990); trans. R.T. Meyer, *The Life and Death of Saint Malachy the Irishman*, CF 10 (Kalamazoo, MI, 1978)

Translations

Ad clericos de conversione; SBOp 4; Winkler iv; trans. M.-B. Saïd, *Sermons on Conversion*, CF 25 (Kalamazoo, MI, 1981)
Apologia ad Guillelmum abbatem; SBOp 3; Winkler ii; trans. M. Casey. *Cistercians and Cluniacs: St. Bernard's Apologia to Abbot William*, in *Bernard of Clairvaux: Treatises 1*, intro. J. Leclercq, CF 1A (Shannon,

1970); trans. C. Rudolph, *The 'Things of Greater Importance': Bernard of Clairvaux's 'Apologia' and the Medieval Attitude toward Art* (Philadelphia, PA, 1990).

De consideratione; SBOp 3; Winkler I; trans. J.D. Anderson and E.T. Kennan, *Five Books on Consideration: Advice to a Pope*, CF 37 (Kalamazoo, MI, 1986; first pub. 1976)

De diligendo Deo; SBOp 3; Winkler I; ed. and trans. P. Verdeyen and F. Callerot, *Bernard de Clairvaux: L'amour de Dieu. La grâce et le libre arbitre*, SCh 393 (Paris, 1993); trans. R. Walton, *On Loving God*, in *Bernard of Clairvaux: Treatises 2*, intro. E. Stiegman, CF 13 (Kalamazoo, MI, 1995; first pub. 1974)

De gradibus humilitatis et superbiae; SBOp 3; Winkler II; trans. M.A. Conway, *The Steps of Humility and Pride*, in *Bernard of Clairvaux: Treatises 2*, intro. M.B. Pennington, CF 13 (Kalamazoo, MI, 1995; first pub. 1974)

De gratia et libero arbitrio; SBOp 3; Winkler I; ed. and trans. P. Verdeyen and F. Callerot, *Bernard de Clairvaux: L'amour de Dieu. La grâce et le libre arbitre*, SCh 393 (Paris, 1993); trans. D. O'Donovan, *On Grace and Free Choice*, in *Bernard of Clairvaux: Treatises 3*, intro. B. McGinn, CF 19 (Kalamazoo, MI, 1995; first pub. 1974)

De laude novae militiae; SBOp 3; Winkler I; ed. and trans. P.-Y. Émery, *Bernard de Clairvaux: Éloge de la nouvelle chevalerie*, SCh 367 (Paris, 1990); trans. C. Greenia, *In Praise of the New Knighthood*, intro. M. Barber, CF 19 (Kalamazoo, MI, 2000; first pub. 1977)

De praecepto et dispensatione; SBOp 3; Winkler I; ed. and trans. F. Callerot et al., *Bernard de Clairvaux: Le précepte et la dispense*, SCh 457 (Paris, 2000); trans. C. Greenia, *On Precept and Dispensation*, intro. J. Leclercq, CF 1 (Shannon, 1970)

Epistula de baptismo (Ep 77); SBOp 7; Winkler II; trans. P. Matarasso, *On Baptism and the Office of Bishops: Two Letter-Treatises*, intro. M.G. Newman and E. Stiegman, CF 67 (Kalamazoo, MI, 2004)

Epistula de moribus et officio episcoporum; SBOp 7; Winkler II; trans. P. Matarasso, *On Baptism and the Office of Bishops: Two Letter-Treatises*, intro. M.G. Newman and E. Stiegman, CF 67 (Kalamazoo, MI, 2004)

Epistulae; SBOp 7 and 8; Winkler II and III; ed. and trans. H. Rochais, *Bernard de Clairvaux: Lettres (1–92)*, intro. M. Duchet-Suchaux, 2 vols., SCh 425 and 458 (Paris, 1997 and 2001); trans. B. Scott James, *The Letters of St Bernard of Clairvaux*, intro. B.M. Kienzle, CF 62 (Stroud and Kalamazoo, MI, 1998; first pub. 1953)

Homiliae super 'Missus est' (In laudibus Virginis Matris); SBOp 4; Winkler IV; ed. and trans. M.-I. Huille and J. Regnard, *Bernard de Clairvaux: À la louange de la Vièrge Mère*, SCh 390 (Paris, 1993); trans. M.-B. Saïd, *Magnificat: Homilies in Praise of the Blessed Virgin Mary*, intro. C. Waddell, CF 18A (Kalamazoo, MI, 1979)

Officium de Sancto Victore; SBOp 3; Winkler II; trans. E. Lenaerts-Lachapelle et al., *Bernard de Clairvaux: Office de Saint Victor, Prologue à l'antiphonaire, Lettre 398*, intro. C. Maître, SCh 527 (Paris, 2009)

Parabolae; SBOp 6.2; Winkler IV; trans. M. Casey, *Bernard of Clairvaux: The Parables and The Sentences*, ed. M. O'Brien, CF 55 (Kalamazoo, MI, 2000)

Prologus in Antiphonarium; SBOp 3; Winkler II; trans. E. Lenaerts-Lachapelle *et al.*, *Bernard de Clairvaux: Office de Saint Victor, Prologue à l'antiphonaire, Lettre 398*, intro. C. Maître, SCh 527 (Paris, 2009); trans. C. Waddell, *Prologue to the Cistercian Antiphonary*, in *Bernard of Clairvaux: Treatises 1*, intro. J. Leclercq, CF 1A (Shannon, 1970)

Sententiae; SBOp 6.2; Winkler IV; trans. F.R. Swietek, *Bernard of Clairvaux: The Parables and The Sentences*, intro. J.R. Sommerfeldt, CF 55 (Kalamazoo, MI, 2000)

Sermons

Sermones de diversis (Sermons on Diverse Topics); SBOp 6.1; Winkler IX; trans. P.-Y. Émery and F. Callerot, *Bernard de Clairvaux: Sermons divers*, 2 vols., SCh 496 and 518 (Paris, 2006 and 2007)

Sermones in psalmum 'Qui habitat'; SBOp 4; Winkler VII; trans. M.-B. Saïd, *Sermons on Conversion*, CF 25 (Kalamazoo, MI, 1981)

Sermones per annum; SBOp 4 and 5; Winkler VII and VIII; trans. M.-I. Huille, *Bernard de Clairvaux: Sermons pour l'année*, intro. M. Lamy, 2 vols., SCh 480 and 481 (Paris, 2004); trans. I. Edmonds, W. Beckett and C. Greenia, *Sermons for Advent and the Christmas Season*, intro. W. Verbaal, ed. J. Leinenweber, CF 51 (Kalamazoo, MI, 2007); trans. (partial) B.M. Kienzle and J. Jarzembowski, *Sermons for the Summer Season: Liturgical Sermons from Rogationtide and Pentecost*, CF 53 (Kalamazoo, MI, 1990)

Sermones super Cantica canticorum; SBOp 1 and 2; Winkler V and VI; ed. and trans. P. Verdeyen and R. Fasetta, *Bernard de Clairvaux: Sermons sur le Cantique*, 5 vols., SCh 414, 431, 452, 472 and 511 (Paris, 1996–2007); trans. pub. by Cistercian Publications, Kalamazoo, MI: *On the Song of Songs*, 1 (*S* 1–20), intro. M.C. Halflants, trans. K. Walsh, CF 4 (1981); 2 (*S* 21–46), intro. J. Leclercq, trans. K. Walsh, CF 7 (1983); 3 (*S* 47–66), intro. E. Stiegman, trans. K. Walsh and I.M. Edmonds, CF 31 (1979); 4 (*S* 67–86), intro. J. Leclercq, trans. I.M. Edmonds, CF 40 (1980)

Sermones varii; SBOp 6.1; Winkler IX; trans. P.-Y. Émery and F. Callerot, *Bernard de Clairvaux: Sermons variés*, SCh 526 (Paris, 2010)

Caesarius of Heisterbach (*c.* 1180–*c.* 1240)

Dialogus miraculorum (Dialogue on Miracles); ed. J. Strange, *Caesarii Heisterbacensis monachi Ordinis Cisterciensis Dialogus miraculorum*, 2 vols. (Cologne, 1851); ed. and trans. N. Nösges and H. Schneider, *Caesarius von Heisterbach: Dialogus Miraculorum – Dialog über die Wunder*, Fontes Christiani 86.1–5 (Turnhout, 2009); trans. H. von Essen Scott and C.C. Swinton Bland, *Dialogue on Miracles by Caesarius of Heisterbach* (London and New York, 1929)

Ernald (or Arnald) of Bonnevaux (d. *post* 1156)

Vita Prima, Book two; PL 185:267–302; ed. P. Verdeyen and C. Vande Veire, CCCM 89B (Turnhout, 2011); trans. (partial) G. Webb and A. Walker, *St Bernard of Clairvaux* (London, 1960)

Geoffrey of Auxerre (*c.* 1120–*post* 1188)
De conversione aquae cum vino in sanguinem Domini (letter to Henry of
Albano on the conversion of water and wine into the Lord's blood); ed.
C. Baronius, *Annales ecclesiastici ad annum 1188*, vol. XII (Antwerp,
1609), pp. 795–6
*Epistola ad Albinum cardinalem et episcopum Albanensem. De condemna-
tione errorum Gilberti Porretani* (letter on the condemnation of the errors
of Gilbert of Poitiers); *PL* 185:587–96
Epistola ad Josbertum continens notulas in Orationem dominicam (letter con-
taining notes on the Lord's Prayer); *PL* 185:617–20
Expositio in Cantica canticorum (*Exposition on the Song of Songs*); ed.
F. Gastaldelli, *Goffredo di Auxerre, Expositio in Cantica canticorum*, 2
vols. (Rome, 1974)
Fragmenta de vita et miraculis Sancti Bernardi (*Fragments on the Life and
Miracles of S. Bernard*); ed. R. Lechat, 'Fragmenta de vita et miraculis Sancti
Bernardi', *Analecta Bollandiana*, 20 (1932), 89–122; ed. and trans. R. Fassetta,
Notes sur la vie et les miracles de saint Bernard: fragmenta, SCh 548 (Paris,
2011)
Libellus contra capitula gilberti pictaviensis episcopi (against Gilbert of
Poitiers); *PL* 185:595–617
Super Apocalypsim (*On the Apocalypse*); ed. F. Gastaldelli, *Ricerche su Goffredo
d'Auxerre. Il compendio anonimo del 'Super Apocalypsim'* (Rome,
1970); trans. J. Gibbons, *Geoffrey of Auxerre: On the Apocalypse*, CF 42
(Kalamazoo, MI, 2000)
Vita Prima, Books Three to Five; *PL* 185:301–68; ed. P. Verdeyen and C. Vande
Veire, CCCM 89B (Turnhout, 2011); trans. (partial) G. Webb and A. Walker,
St Bernard of Clairvaux (London, 1960)

Sermons

Sermo ad praelatos in concilio convocatos (*Sermon for the Prelates Summoned to
Council*); *PL* 184:1095–102; ed. F. Gastaldelli, 'Quattro sermoni "*ad abbates*"
di Goffredo di Auxerre', *Cîteaux*, 34 (1983), 161–200; ed. F. Gastaldelli, 'Tre
sermoni di Goffredo di Auxerre su San Benedetto', in Gastaldelli, 'Regola,
spiritualita e crisi dell'ordine cisterciense in tre sermoni di Goffredo di
Auxerre su San Benedetto', *Cîteaux*, 31 (1980), 193–225

Gertrud of Helfta (the Great) (1256–1302?)
Exercitia spiritualia (*Spiritual Exercises*); ed. and trans. J. Hourlier *et al.*,
Gertrude la Grande: oeuvres spirituelles, 5 vols., SCh 127, 139, 143, 255
and 331 (Paris 1967–86), vol. I; trans. G.J. Lewis and J. Lewis, *Gertrud the
Great of Helfta: Spiritual Exercises*, CF 49 (Kalamazoo, MI, 1989)
Legatus memorialis abundantiae divinae pietatis (*Herald of God's
Loving-Kindness*); ed. and trans. J. Hourlier *et al.*, *Gertrude la Grande: oeu-
vres spirituelles*, 5 vols., SCh 127, 139, 143, 255 and 331 (Paris 1967–86),
vols. II–V; trans. A. Barratt, *The Herald of God's Loving-Kindness*, 2 vols.,
CF 35 (Books 1–2) and CF 63 (Book 3) (Kalamazoo, MI, 1991 and 1999),
Books 4 and 5 are projected

Gilbert of Hoyland (d. 1172)
Epistolae; PL 194:289–98; trans. L.C. Braceland, *Gilbert of Hoyland: Treatises, Epistles and Sermons*, CF 34 (Kalamazoo, MI, 1981)
Tractatus ascetici (*Ascetic treatises*); PL 184:251–90; trans. Braceland, *Gilbert of Hoyland: Treatises, Epistles and Sermons*
A critical edition of Gilbert's works (CCCM) is in preparation by M.L. Dutton.

Sermons

Sermo: De semine verbi Dei (*Sermon on the Seed of God's Word*); PL 184:288–90; trans. Braceland, *Gilbert of Hoyland: Treatises, Epistles and Sermons*
Sermo de eodem martyre (*Sermon on the Same Martyr*); trans. Braceland, *Gilbert of Hoyland: Treatises, Epistles and Sermons*
Sermo super evangelium secundum Matthaeum (*Sermon on the Gospel according to Matthew*); trans. Braceland, *Gilbert of Hoyland: Treatises, Epistles and Sermons*
Sermones super Cantica canticorum (*Sermons on the Song of Songs*); PL 184:9–252; trans. L.C. Braceland, *Gilbert of Hoyland: Sermons on the Song of Songs*, 3 vols., CF 14, 20 and 26 (Kalamazoo, MI, 1978–9)

Guerric of Igny (d. 1157)
Guerrici Abbatis Igniacensis Discipuli S. Bernardi Sermones per Annum (*Sermons for the Liturgical Year*); PL 185:11–220; trans. P. Deseille, *Guerric d'Igny: Sermons*, ed. and intro. J. Morson and H. Costello, 2 vols., SCh 166 and 202 (Paris 1970 and 1973); trans. by Monks of Mount Saint Bernard, *Guerric of Igny: Liturgical Sermons*, 2 vols., CF 8 and CF 32 (Shannon and Spencer, MA, 1971); trans. (partial) T. Merton, *The Christmas Sermons of Bl. Guerric of Igny* (Gethsemani Abbey, KY, 1959)

Guillaume de Digulleville/Deguileville (c. 1295–c. 1358)
Pèlerinage de Jésus Christ (a verse transposition of the Gospel); ed. J.J. Stürzinger, *Le pèlerinage Jhesucrist de Guillamme de Deguileville* (London, 1897); ed. P. Amblard, *La vie de Jésus selon Guillaume de Digulleville* (Paris, 1999)
Pèlerinage de l'âme (*The Pilgrimage of the Soul*); ed. J.J. Stürzinger, *Le pèlerinage de l'âme de Guillaume de Deguileville* (London, 1895); Middle English version; ed. R.P. McGerr (London and New York, 1989)
Pèlerinage de la vie humaine (*The Pilgrimage of Human Life*); ed. J.J. Stürzinger, *Le pèlerinage de vie humaine de Guillaume de Deguileville* (London, 1893); a Middle English translation by John Lydgate circulated widely in France and England; ed. A. Henry, *The Pilgrimage of the Lyfe of the Manhode*, 2 vols. (London and New York 1985 and 1988); ed. E. Clasby, *The Pilgrimage of Human Life* (New York, 1992)
Roman de la Fleur de Lys; ed. A. Piaget, *Romania*, 62 (1936), 317–58

Hélinand of Froidmont (c. 1160–1237)
Chronicon (*Chronicle*); PL 212:771–1082
De bono regimine principis (*On Good Princely Rule*); PL 212:735–42
De cognitione sui (*On Self-Knowledge*); PL 212:721–36
De reparatione lapsi (*On Reconciling a Lapsed Brother*); PL 212:745–60

Sanctorum Gereonis, Victoris, Cassii et Florentii Thebaeorum martyrum passio (account of the martyrdom of four monks of the Thebaid); ed. BHL 3446: *Sanctorum Gereonis, Victoris, Cassii et Florentii Thebaeorum martyrum passio ab Helinando scripta*; ed. AASS Octobris 5:36–40

Les Vers de la mort (*Verses on death*); ed. F. Wulff and E. Walbert, *Les vers de la mort, par Hélinand de Froidmont* (Paris, 1905); trans. J. Coppin, *Les vers de la mort d'Hélinand de Froidmont* (Paris, 1930); ed. and trans. J.L. Porter, *Helinand of Froidmont: Verses on Death*, CF 61 (Kalamazoo, MI and Spencer, MA, 1999)

Sermons

Twenty-eight sermons, *PL* 212:481–720; forty additional sermons, ed. J.B. Schneyer, *Repertorium der lateinischen Sermones des Mittelalters für die Zeit von 1150–1350*, 11 vols. (Münster, 1969–90), vol. II (1970), p. 617–22 (Helinandus of Perseigne); ed. B.M. Kienzle, 'Cistercian Preaching against the Cathars: Hélinand's Unedited Sermon for Rogation, B.N. ms. lat. 14591', *Cîteaux*, 39 (1988), 297–314; ed. B.M. Kienzle, 'Mary Speaks against Heresy: Hélinand of Froidmont's Unedited Purification Sermon, Paris B. N. ms. lat 14591', *Sacris Erudiri*, 32 (1991), 291–308

Henry of Hautcrêt (d. 1231/2)
Three sermons ed. M. Meyer, 'Henri, abbé de Hautcret et ses homélies', *Archives de la Société du canton de Fribourg*, 1 (1850), 237–50

Herbert of Clairvaux/Herbert of Torres, or Mores (d. c. 1180)
Liber de miraculis (*Book of Miracles*); *PL* 185:1273–384; a critical edition is in preparation by S. Mula *et al.*

Idung of Prüfening (wrote between 1153 and 1174)
Argumentum super quatuor quaestionibus (*Discussion of Four Questions*); ed. B. Pez, *Thesaurus anecdotorum novissimus*, 6 vols. (Augsburg, 1721–9), vol. II, pp. 507–42; ed. R.B.C. Huygens, 'Le moine Idung et ses deux ouvrages', *Studi Medievali*, third series, 13 (1972), 291–470; trans. J.F. O'Sullivan *et al.*, *Cistercians and Cluniacs: The Case for Cîteaux*, CF 33 (Kalamazoo, MI, 1977)

Dialogus duorum monachorum (*Dialogue between Two Monks*); ed. Martène and Durand, *Thesaurus novus anecdotorum*, 5 vols. (Paris, 1717), vol. V, pp. 1571–654; ed. R.B.C. Huygens, 'Le moine Idung et ses deux ouvrages'; trans. O'Sullivan *et al.*, *Cistercians and Cluniacs*

Isaac of Stella (c. 1100–c. 1169)
Epistola ad Joannem Episcopum Pictaviensem De Officio Missae (letter treatise on the Office of the Mass); *PL* 194:1889–96; trans. C. Waddell, 'On the Canon of the Mass', *Liturgy*, 11 (1977), 63–76; trans. D. Deme, *The Selected Works of Isaac of Stella: A Cistercian Voice from the Twelfth Century* (Aldershot, 2007)

Epistola de anima (letter treatise on the soul); *PL* 194:1875–90; trans. B. McGinn, *Three Treatises on Man: A Cistercian Anthropology*, CF 24 (Kalamazoo, MI, 1977), pp. 153–77; trans. Deme, *The Selected Works of Isaac of Stella*

Sermons on the liturgical year; *PL* 194:1689–876; ed. D. Pezzini, *Isacco della Stella: I sermoni* (Milan, 2006–7); ed. and trans. A. Hoste *et al.*, *Isaac de l'Étoile: Sermons*, 3 vols., SCh 130, 207 and 339 (Paris, 1967, 1974 and 1987); trans. H. McCaffery, *Isaac of Stella: Sermons on the Christian Year*, intro. B. McGinn, CF 11 (Kalamazoo, MI, 1979), vol. ii is in preparation; trans. Deme, *The Selected Works of Isaac of Stella*

John of Forde (*c.* 1145–1214)

Vita beati Wulfrici anachoretae Haselburgiae (*Life of Blessed Wulfric of Haselbury*); ed. M. Bell, *Wulfric of Haselbury* (London, 1933); trans. P. Matarasso, *John of Forde: The Life of Wulfric of Haselbury*, CF 79 (Collegeville, MN, 2011)

Sermons

Sermo in dominica in ramis palmarum (*Sermon for Palm Sunday*); ed. C.H. Talbot, 'Un sermon inédit de Jean de Ford', *COCR*, 7 (1940), 36–45

Super extremam partem Cantici canticorum sermones cxx (*One Hundred and Twenty Sermons on the Last Part of the Song of Songs*); ed. E. Mikkers and H. Costello, CCCM 17 and 18 (Turnhout, 1970); trans. W.M. Beckett, *John of Ford: On the Song of Songs*, intro. H. Costello, 7 vols., CF 29, 39 and 43–7 (Kalamazoo, MI, 1977–84); trans. (selected passages) H. Costello, *Sky-Blue is the Sapphire Crimson the Rose: Stillpoint of Desire in John of Ford*, CF 69 (Kalamazoo, MI, 2006)

Odo of Cheriton (1180/90–1247)

One hundred and ninety-three sermons listed in *Repertorium der lateinischen Sermones des Mittelalters für die Zeit von 1150–1350*, 11 vols., ed. J.B. Schneyer (Münster, 1969–90), vol. iv.4, pp. 483–98

Odo of Morimond (d. 1161)

Five sermons in *PL* 188:1645–58; unedited sermons listed in Schneyer, ed., *Repertorium*, vol. iv.4, pp. 499–508

Ogerius of Locedio (d. 1214)

Fifteen sermons on the Last Supper; *PL* 184:879–950

Otto of Freising (d. 1158)

Gesta Friderici Imperatoris (*The Deeds of Frederick Barbarossa*, written with Rahewin); ed. G. Waitz, B. von Simon and F.J. Schmale, *Ottonis Episcopi Frisingensis et Rahewini Gesta Frederici* (Berlin, 1965); trans. C.C. Mierow and R. Emery, *The Deeds of Frederick Barbarossa* (Toronto, 1994; first pub. New York, 1953)

Historia de duabus civitatibus (*History of the Two Cities*); ed. A. Hofmeister and W. Lammers, *Chronica, sive Historia de duabus civitatibus* (Darmstadt, 1961); trans. C.C. Mierow, *The Two Cities*, ed. and intro. A.P. Evans and C. Knapp (New York, 1966; first pub. 1928)

Rancé, Armand-Jean Bouthillier de (1626–1700)

Letters; ed. A.J. Krailsheimer, *Correspondance*, 4 vols. (Paris and Cîteaux, 1993); trans. (partial) A.J. Krailsheimer, *The Letters of Armand-Jean de Rancé, Abbot and Reformer of La Trappe*, 2 vols., CS 80 and 81 (Kalamazoo, MI, 1984)

Serlo of Savigny (d. 1158)

Sermons; ed. B. Tissier, *Bibliotheca Patrum Cisterciensium*, 8 vols. (Paris, 1660–69), vol. vi, pp. 107–30; ed. and trans. L.C. Braceland, *Serlo of Savigny and Serlo of Wilton: Seven Unpublished Works*, CF 48 (Kalamazoo, MI, 1986); see also L.C. Braceland (ed.), *Supplement to Serlo of Savigny and Serlo of Wilton: Eight Unpublished Works*, CF 48, supplement (Kalamazoo, MI, 1986)

Serlo of Wilton (d. 1181)

Poems; ed. J. Öberg, *Serlon de Wilton: Poèmes latins* (Stockholm, 1965); ed. (selection) P. Dronke, *Medieval Latin and the Rise of the European Love Lyric*, 2 vols. (Oxford, 1968; first pub. 1965), vol. ii, pp. 493–512

Sermons; ed. and trans. Braceland, *Serlo of Savigny and Serlo of Wilton: Seven Unpublished Works*; see also Braceland (ed.), *Supplement to Serlo of Savigny and Serlo of Wilton*

Stephen Harding (abbot of Cîteaux 1108/9–33, d. 1134)

Homily; ed. J. Marilier, *Chartes et documents concernant l'Abbaye de Cîteaux, 1098–1182* (Rome, 1961), item 23, pp. 54–5; trans. E.R. Elder, *The New Monastery: Texts and Studies on the Earliest Cistercians*, CF 60 (Kalamazoo, MI, 1998), pp. 45–6

Letter to the monks of Sherborne; see C. Waddell, 'An Exegesis of the Letter of Saint Stephen Harding', in E.R. Elder (ed.), *Noble Piety and Reformed Monasticism* (Kalamazoo, MI, 1981), pp. 10–39; repr. in *The New Monastery*, pp. 90–123

Monitum (preface to the reformed Cistercian hymnal); ed. C. Waddell, *The Twelfth-Century Cistercian Hymnal*, 2 vols. (Gethsemani Abbey, KY, 1984), ii, pp. 11–12; trans. C. Waddell, in E.R. Elder, *The New Monastery*, pp. 78–86

Stephen of Lexington (*c.* 1193–1260)

Letters; ed. B. Griesser, 'Registrum epistolarum Stephani de Lexington abbatis de Stanlegia et de Savigniaco', *ASOC*, 2 (1946), 1–118; 8 (1952), 182–378; trans. (partial) B.W. O'Dwyer, *Stephen of Lexington: Letters from Ireland, 1228–1229*, CF 28 (Kalamazoo, MI, 1982)

Stephen of Sawley (d. 1252)

De informatione mentis circa psalmarum diei et noctis (on the preparation of the mind for the Divine Office); ed. E. Mikkers, '*De informatione mentis circa psalmarum diei et noctis*', *Cîteaux*, 23 (1972), 245–88; trans. J.F. O'Sullivan, *Stephen of Sawley: Treatises*, intro. B.K. Lackner, CF 36 (Kalamazoo, MI, 1984)

Meditationes de gaudiis beatae Mariae Virginis (*Meditations on the Joys of Blessed Virgin Mary*); ed. A. Wilmart, '*Meditationes de gaudiis beatae Mariae Virginis*', *Revue d'ascétique et de mystique*, 10 (1929), 368–415; trans. O'Sullivan, *Stephen of Sawley: Treatises*

Speculum Novitii (*Mirror for Novices*); ed. E. Mikkers, 'Un *Speculum Novitii* inédit d'Etienne de Sallay', *ASOC*, 8 (1946), 17–68

Triplex exercitium (*Threefold Exercise*); ed. A. Wilmart, 'Le triple exercise d'Etienne de Sallai', *Revue d'ascétique et de mystique*, 11 (1930), 355–74

William of Saint Thierry (1080?–1148)

Aenigma fidei (*The Enigma of Faith*); PL 180:397–440; ed. P. Verdeyen, CCCM 89A (Turnhout, 2007), pp. 129–91; trans. M.-M. Davy, *Deux traités sur la foi* (Paris, 1959)

Brevis commentatio in Cantici canticorum priora duo capita (*Brief Commentary on the Song of Songs*); *PL* 184:407–36; ed. S. Ceglar and P. Verdeyen, CCCM 87 (Turnhout, 1997), pp. 155–96; trans. (excerpt) D. Turner, *Eros and Allegory: Medieval Exegesis of the Song of Songs*, CS 156 (Kalamazoo, MI, 1995), pp. 275–90

Commentarius in Cantica canticorum e scriptis Sancti Ambrosii (*Commentary on the Song of Songs from the Writings of Saint Ambrose*); *PL* 15:1947–2060; ed. A. van Burink, CCCM 87 (Turnhout, 1997), pp. 207–384

De contemplando deo (*On Contemplating God*); *PL* 184:367–80; ed. P. Verdeyen, CCCM 88 (Turnhout, 2003), pp. 153–73; ed. and trans. J. Hourlier, *Guillaume de Saint-Thierry: La contemplation de Dieu*, SCh 61 (Paris, 1999; first pub. 1959); ed. and trans. M.-M. Davy, *Deux traités de l'amour de Dieu* (Paris, 1953); trans. P. Lawson, *William of Saint Thierry: On Contemplating God, Prayer, and Meditations*, intro. J. Hourlier and J.M. Déchanet, CF 3 (Spencer, MA, 1971)

De natura corporis et animae libri duo (*On the Nature of the Body and the Soul*); *PL* 180:695–726; ed. P. Verdeyen, CCCM 88 (Turnhout, 2003), pp. 103–46; trans. B. Clark *et al.*, *Three Treatises on the Soul: A Cistercian Anthropology*, intro. B. McGinn, CF 24 (Kalamazoo, MI, 1977)

De natura et dignitate amoris (*On the Nature and Dignity of Love*); *PL* 184:379–408; ed. P. Verdeyen, CCCM 88 (Turnhout, 2003), pp. 177–212; ed. M.-M. Davy, *Deux traités de l'amour de Dieu* (Paris, 1953); trans. T.X. Davis, *William of Saint Thierry: On the Nature and Dignity of Love*, intro. D.N. Bell, CF 30 (Kalamazoo, MI, 1998)

De sacramento altaris (*On the Sacrament of the Altar*), with *Epistola ad Rupertum*; *PL* 180:341–66; ed. P. Verdeyen, CCCM 88 (Turnhout, 2003), pp. 47–91

Disputatio adversus Petrum Abaelardum (*Disputation against Peter Abelard*); *PL* 180:249–82; ed. P. Verdeyen, CCCM 89A (Turnhout, 2007), pp. 17–59

Epistola ad Fratres de Monte Dei/Epistola aurea (*Letter to the Brothers of Mont-Dieu/The Golden Epistle*); *PL* 184:307–54; ed. P. Verdeyen, CCCM 88 (Turnhout, 2003), pp. 225–89; ed. and trans. J. Déchanet, *Guillaume de Saint-Thierry: Lettre aux Frères du Mont-Dieu*, SCh 223 (Paris, 2004; first pub. 1976); trans. M.-M. Davy, *Un traité de la vie solitaire* (Paris, 1940); trans. T. Berkeley, *William of Saint Thierry: The Golden Epistle*, CF 12 (Spencer, MA, 1971)

Epistola Guillelmi abbatis (*Letter of Abbot William*), Ep 326 inter Bernardi; *PL* 182:531–3; ed. P. Verdeyen, CCCM 89A (Turnhout, 2007), pp. 3–15

Excerpta ex libris Sancti Gregorii Papae super Cantica canticorum (*Excerpts from the Books of St Gregory the Great on the Song of Songs*); *PL* 180:441–74; ed. P. Verdeyen, CCCM 87 (Turnhout, 1997), pp. 395–444

Expositio in epistolam ad Romanos (*Exposition on the Letter to the Romans*); *PL* 180:547–694; ed. P. Verdeyen, CCCM 88 (Turnhout, 2003); trans. Y.-A. Baudelet, *Guillaume de Saint-Thierry: Exposé sur l'Épître aux Romains'* 1, ed. P. Verdeyen, SCh 544 (Paris, 2011); trans. J.B. Hasbrouck, *William of Saint Thierry: Exposition on the Epistle to the Romans*, ed. J.D. Anderson, CF 27 (Kalamazoo, MI, 1980)

Expositio super Cantica canticorum (*Exposition on the Song of Songs*); *PL* 180:473–546; ed. P. Verdeyen, CCCM 87 (Turnhout, 1997), pp. 19–133; ed.

and trans. J.-M. Déchanet and M. Dumontier, *Guillaume de Saint-Thierry: Exposé sur le 'Cantique des Cantiques'*, SCh 82 (Paris, 2007; first pub. 1962); trans. C. Hart, *William of Saint Thierry: Exposition on the Song of Songs*, CF 6 (Spencer, MA, 1968)

Meditativae orationes (*Meditations*); *PL* 180:205–48; ed. P. Verdeyen, CCCM 89 (Turnhout, 2005), pp. 3–80; ed. and trans. J. Hourlier, *Guillaume de Saint-Thierry: Oraisons méditatives*, SCh 324 (Paris, 1985); ed. and trans. M.-M. Davy, *Meditativae orationes: texte et traduction* (Paris, 1934); trans. P. Lawson, *William of Saint Thierry: On Contemplating God, Prayer, and Meditations*, intro. J. Hourlier and J.M. Déchanet, CF 3 (Spencer, MA, 1971)

Speculum fidei (*The Mirror of Faith*); *PL* 180:365–98A; ed. P. Verdeyen, CCCM 89A (Turnhout, 2007), pp. 81–127; ed. and trans. J. Déchanet, *Guillaume de Saint-Thierry: Le miroir de la foi*, SCh 301 (Paris, 1982); trans. M.-M. Davy, *Deux traités sur la foi* (Paris, 1959); trans. J.-M. Déchanet, *Guillaume de Saint-Thierry: Le miroir de la foi* (Bruges, 1946); trans. T.X. Davis, *William of Saint Thierry: The Mirror of Faith*, intro. E.R. Elder, CF 15 (Kalamazoo, MI, 1979)

Vita Prima, Book One; *PL* 185:225–66; ed. P. Verdeyen and C. Vande Veire, CCCM 89B (Turnhout, 2011); trans. M. Cawley, *Bernard of Clairvaux: Early Biographies*, vol. 1, *William of Saint Thierry* (Lafayette, OR, 2000); trans. (partial) G. Webb and A. Walker, *St Bernard of Clairvaux* (London, 1960); trans. (excerpts) P. Matarasso, *The Cistercian World: Monastic Writings of the Twelfth Century* (London, 1993), pp. 15–41

Other Cistercian primary sources

For comments see Peter King's and Michael Casey's chapters in this volume.

Berman, C.H. (trans.), *Women and Monasticism in Medieval Europe: Sisters and Patrons of the Cistercian Reform* (Kalamazoo, MI, 2002)

Bouton, J. de la Croix and J.B. Van Damme (eds.), *Les plus anciens textes de Cîteaux*, Cîteaux: Studia et Documenta 2 (Achel, 1974)

Bronseval, Claude de, *Frère Claude de Bronseval: Peregrinatio Hispanica 1531–1533*, ed. M. Cocheril, 2 vols. (Paris, 1970)

Broun, D. and J. Harrison (eds.), *Chronicle of Melrose Abbey: A Stratigraphic Edition*, 2 vols. (Woodbridge, 2007–)

Canivez, J.-M. (ed.), *Statuta Capitulorum Generalium Ordinis Cisterciensis ab anno 1116 ad annum 1786*, 8 vols. (Louvain, 1933–41)

Choisselet, D. and P. Vernet (eds.), *Les 'Ecclesiastica Officia' cisterciens du XIIème siècle. Texte latin selon les manuscrits édités de Trente 1711, Ljubljana 31 et Dijon 114: version française, annexe liturgique, notes, index et tables*, La documentation cistercienne 22 (Reiningue, 1989)

Conrad of Eberbach, *Exordium Magnum Cisterciense*, ed. B. Griesser (Rome, 1961; repr. Turnhout, 1994); trans. J. Berlioz, *Conrad d'Eberbach: Le grand Exorde de Cîteaux ou Récit des débuts de l'Ordre cistercien* (Turnhout, 1998); trans. B. Ward and P. Savage, *The Great Beginning of Cîteaux*, ed. E.R. Elder, CS 72 (Collegeville, MN, 2012)

Cotheret, N., *Annales de Cîteaux*, ed. L. J. Lekai , 'Les *Annales de Cîteaux* de Nicholas Cotheret (1680–1753)', *Analecta Cisterciensia*, 40 (1984), 150–303; 41 (1985), 42–315; 42 (1986), 265–332; a reader-friendly version has been produced by L. J. Lekai, *Nicolas Cotheret's Annals of Cîteaux*, CS 57 (Kalamazoo, MI, 1982)

Georges, D., 'Proces Verbal de l'ètat spirituel & temporel de l'Abbaïe de la Trappe', in Pierre Maupeou, *La vie du très-reverend père dom Armand Jean Le Bouthillier de Rancé* (Paris, 1709), Book 4, pp. 251–71

Górecki, P. (ed.), *A Local Society in Transition: the Henryków Book and Related Documents* (Toronto, 2007)

Griesser, B. 'Die *Ecclesiastica Officia Cisterciensis Ordinis* des Cod. 1711 von Trient', *ASOC*, 12 (1956), 153–288

Griesser, B. (ed.), 'Consuetudines Domus Cisterciensis', *ASOC*, 3 (1947), 138–46

Guignard, P. (ed.), '*Les monuments primitifs de la règle cistercienne, publiés d'après les manuscrits de l'abbaye de Cîteaux* (Dijon, 1878)

Hermans, V. (ed.), *Actes des Chapitres Généraux des Congrégations Trappistes au XIXe siècle: 1835–1891* (Rome, 1975)

Johnson, A.O. and P. King (eds.), *The Tax Book of the Cistercian Order* (Oslo, 1979)

Konrad, N., *Die Enstehung der Österreichisch-Ungarischen Zisterzienser-kongregation (1849–1869)* (Rome, 1967)

Legendre O. (ed.), *Collectaneum exemplorum et visionum Clarevallense* (Turnhout, 2005)

Leloczky, J.D. (ed.), *Constitutiones et Acta Capitulorum Strictioris Observantiae Ordinis Cisterciensis (1624–1687)* (Rome, 1967)

Lucet, B. *Les codifications cisterciennes de 1237 et de 1257* (Paris, 1977)

Lucet, B. (ed.), *La codification cistercienne de 1202 et son évolution ultérieure* (Rome, 1964)

Manrique, A. (ed.), *Annales Cistercienses, Lyons 1642–59*, 4 vols. (Westmead, 1970)

Marilier, J.-M. (ed.), *Chartes et documents concernant l'Abbaye de Cîteaux: 1098–1182* (Rome, 1961)

Matarasso, P. (ed.), *The Cistercian World: Monastic Writings of the Twelfth Century* (Harmondsworth, 1998)

Séjalon, H. (ed.), *Nomasticon Cisterciense* (Solesmes, 1892)

Talbot, C.H. (ed.), *Letters from the English Abbots to the Chapter at Cîteaux 1442–1521* (London, 1967)

Tuyén, T. Nguyên-Dính-, 'Histoire des controverses à Rome entre la Commune et l'Étroite Observance de 1662 à 1666', *Analecta Cisterciensia*, 26 (1970), 3–247

Waddell, C. *Narrative and Legislative Texts from Early Cîteaux*, Cîteaux: Studia et Documenta 9 (Brecht, 1999)

The Primitive Cistercian Breviary (Fribourg, 2007)

The Twelfth-Century Cistercian Hymnal, 2 vols., Cistercian Liturgy Series 1–2 (Gethsemani Abbey, KY, 1984)

Twelfth-Century Statutes from the Cistercian General Chapter, Cîteaux: Studia et Documenta 12 (Brecht, 2002)

Waddell, C. (ed.), *Cistercian Lay Brothers: Twelfth-Century Usages with Related Texts*, Cîteaux: Studia et Documenta 10 (Brecht, 2000)

Zakar, P., *Histoire de la Stricte Observance de l'Ordre Cistercien depuis ses débuts jusqu'au Généralat du Cardinal Richelieu (1606–1635)* (Rome, 1966)

Other primary sources

Constable, G. (ed.), *The Letters of Peter the Venerable*, 2 vols. (Cambridge, MA, 1967)

Félibien des Avaux, A., 'Description de l'abbaye de la Trappe a Madame la Duchesse de Liancour', in *Reglemens de l'Abbaye de Nôtre-Dame de la Trappe* (Paris, 1718)

Jacques de Vitry, *Historia Occidentalis*, ed. J.F. Hinnebusch, *The Historia Occidentalis of Jacques de Vitry* (Fribourg, 1972)

Luscombe, D. (ed.), *Peter Abelard's 'Ethics'* (Oxford, 1971)

William of Malmesbury, *Gesta Regum Anglorum*; ed. R.A.B. Mynors, R.M. Thomson and M. Winterbottom, *Gesta Regum Anglorum: The History of the English Kings*, 2 vols. (Oxford, 2007)

Further reading

Introduction: withdrawal and engagement

Auberger, J.-B., *L'unanimité cistercienne primitive: mythe ou réalité?*, Cîteaux: Studia et Documenta 3 (Achel, 1986)

Bell, D.N., *Understanding Rancé: The Spirituality of the Abbot of La Trappe in Context*, CS 205 (Kalamazoo, MI, 2005)

Bouchard, C., *Holy Entrepreneurs: Cistercians, Knights, and Economic Exchange in Twelfth-Century Burgundy* (London and Ithaca, NY, 1991)

Bruun, M.B., *'Je ne comprends point cette sorte de mortification: Seventeenth-Century Fascination with the Trappists'*, *Transfiguration* 2010/11 (2012), 125–60

'The Wilderness as *lieu de mémoire*: Literary Deserts of Cîteaux and La Trappe', in *Negotiating Heritage: Memories of the Middle Ages*, ed. M. B. Bruun and S. Glaser (Turnhout, 2008), pp. 21–42

Burton, J. and J. Kerr, *The Cistercians in the Middle Ages* (Woodbridge and Rochester, NY, 2011)

Elm, K., P. Joerissen and H.J. Roth (eds.), *Die Zisterzienser: Ordensleben zwischen Ideal und Wirklichkeit* (Cologne, 1981)

Felten, F.J. and W. Rösener (eds.), *Norm und Realität: Kontinuität und Wandel der Zisterzienser im Mittelalter* (Berlin, 2009)

Freeman, E., *Narratives of a New Order: Cistercian Historical Writing in England, 1150–1220* (Turnhout, 2002)

Hall, J., 'The Legislative Background to the Burial of Laity and Other Patrons in Cistercian Abbeys', *Cîteaux*, 56 (2005), 363–71

Hall, J., S. Sneddon and N. Sohr, 'Table of Legislation Concerning the Burial of Laity and other Patrons in Cistercian Abbeys', *Cîteaux*, 56 (2005), 373–418

Harper-Bill, C., 'Cistercian Visitation in the Late Middle Ages: The Case of Hailes Abbey', *Historical Research*, 53 (1980), 103–14

Jamroziak, E., *The Cistercian Order in Medieval Europe: 1090–1500* (Harlow, in press)

'Making and Breaking the Bonds: Yorkshire Cistercians and Their Neighbours', in *Perspectives for an Architecture of Solitude: Essays on Cistercians, Art and Architecture in Honour of Peter Fergusson*, ed. T.N. Kinder (Turnhout, 2004), pp. 198–206

Survival and Success on Medieval Borders: Cistercian Houses in Medieval Scotland and Pomerania from the Twelfth to the Late Fourteenth Century (Turnhout, 2011)

Jamroziak, E. and J. Burton (eds.), *Religious and Laity in Western Europe 1000–1400: Interaction, Negotiation, and Power* (Turnhout, 2006)

Kasper, C. and K. Schreiner (eds.), *Zisterziensische Spiritualität: Theologische Grundlagen, funktionale Voraussetzungen und bildhafte Ausprägungen im Mittelalter* (St. Ottilien, 1994)

Krailsheimer, A.J., *Armand-Jean de Rancé, Abbot of La Trappe: His Influence in the Cloister and the World* (Oxford, 1974)

Lackner, B. K., 'The Liturgy of Early Cîteaux', in *Studies in Medieval Cistercian History presented to Jeremiah F. O'Sullivan*, ed. M.B. Pennington, CS 13 (Shannon, 1971), 1–34

Lekai, L.J., *The Cistercians: Ideals and Reality* (Kent, OH, 1977)
  'Ideals and Reality in Early Cistercian Life and Legislation', in *Cistercian Ideals and Reality*, ed. J.R. Sommerfeldt, CS 60 (Kalamazoo, MI, 1978), pp. 4–29

Müller, A. and K. Stöber (eds.), *Self-Representation of Medieval Religious Communities* (Berlin, 2009)

Newman, M.G., *The Boundaries of Charity: Cistercian Culture and Ecclesiastical Reform 1098–1180* (Stanford, CA, 1996)

Rudolph, C., 'The Principal Founders and the Early Artistic Legislation of Cîteaux', in *Studies in Cistercian Art and Architecture*, 3, ed. M.P. Lillich (Kalamazoo, MI, 1982), pp. 1–45

Schneider, A., A. Wienand, W. Bickel and E. Coester (eds.), *Die Cistercienser: Geschichte, Geist, Kunst* (Cologne, 1974)

Sonntag, J., *Klosterleben im Spiegel des Zeichenhaften: Symbolisches Denken und Handeln hochmittelalterlicher Mönche zwischen Dauer und Wandel, Regel und Gewohnheit* (Münster, 2008)

Untermann, M., *Forma Ordinis: Die mittelalterliche Baukunst der Zisterzienser* (Munich and Berlin, 2001)

Waddell, C., 'The Cistercian Dimension of the Reform of La Trappe', in *Cistercians in the Late Middle Ages*, ed. E.R. Elder, CS 64 (Kalamazoo, MI, 1981), pp. 102–61

Ward, B., 'The Desert Myth', in *One Yet Two: Monastic Tradition East and West*, ed. B.M. Pennington, CS 29 (Kalamazoo, MI, 1976), pp. 183–99

Wardrop, J., *Fountains Abbey and Its Benefactors*, CS 91 (Kalamazoo, MI, 1987)

1 Foundation and twelfth century

Auberger, J.-B., *L'unanimité cistercienne primitive: mythe ou réalité*, Cîteaux: Studia et Documenta 3 (Achel, 1986)

Berman, C.H., *The Cistercian Evolution: The Invention of a Religious Order in Twelfth-Century Europe* (Philadelphia, PA, 1999)

Bouchard, C., *Holy Entrepreneurs: Cistercians, Knights, and Economic Exchange in Twelfth-Century Burgundy* (London and Ithaca, NY, 1991)

Bredero, A.H., *Bernard of Clairvaux: Between Cult and History* (Grand Rapids, MI, 1996)

Burton, J. and J. Kerr, *The Cistercians in the Middle Ages* (Woodbridge and Rochester, NY, 2011)

Constable, G., *The Reformation of the Twelfth Century* (Cambridge, 1998)

Elder, E.R. (ed.), *The New Monastery: Texts and Studies on the Earliest Cistercians*, CF 60 (Kalamazoo, MI, 1998)

France, J., *Separate but Equal: Cistercian Lay Brothers 1120–1350*, (Collegeville, MN and Kalamazoo, MI, 2012)

Kienzle, B.M., *Cistercians, Heresy, and Crusade in Occitania, 1145–1229: Preaching the Lord's Vineyard* (Rochester, NY, 2001)

Lackner, B.K., *The Eleventh-Century Background of Cîteaux* (Washington, DC, 1972)

Letèvre, J.A., 'Que savons-nous du Cîteaux primitif?', *Revue d'histoire ecclésiastique*, 51 (1956), 4–51

Lekai, L.J., *The Cistercians: Ideals and Reality* (Kent, OH, 1977)

Lester, A., *Making Cistercian Nuns: Gender, Society and Religious Reform in Medieval Champagne* (Ithaca, NY, 2011)

McGuire, B.P., *The Difficult Saint: Bernard of Clairvaux and His Tradition*, CS 126 (Kalamazoo, MI, 1991)

Mahn, J.-B., *L'ordre cistercien et son gouvernement, des origines au milieu du XIIIe siècle (1098–1265)* (Paris, 1951)

Newman, M.G., *The Boundaries of Charity: Cistercian Culture and Ecclesiastical Reform 1098–1180* (Stanford, CA, 1996)

   'Text and Authority in the Formation of the Cistercian Order: The Early Cistercians Read Gregory the Great', in *Reforming the Church before Modernity: Patterns, Problems and Approaches*, ed. L. Hamilton and C. Belitto (Farnham, 2005), pp. 173–98

Pranger, M.B., *Bernard of Clairvaux and the Shape of Monastic Thought: Broken Dreams* (Leiden, 1994)

Rudoph, C., *The 'Things of Greater Importance': Bernard of Clairvaux's 'Apologia' and the Medieval Attitude toward Art* (Philadelphia, PA, 1990)

Van Engen, J., 'The "Crisis of Cenobitism" Reconsidered: Benedictine Monasticism in the Years 1050–1150', *Speculum*, 61 (1986), 269–304

2 The Cistercian Order 1200–1600

Elder, E.R. (ed.), *Cistercians in the Late Middle Ages*, CS 64 (Kalamazoo, MI, 1981)

Freeman, E., '"Houses of a Peculiar Order": Cistercian Nunneries in Medieval England, with Special Attention to the Fifteenth and Sixteenth Centuries', *Cîteaux*, 55 (2004), 245–86

Grundmann, H., *Religious Movements in the Middle Ages* (Notre-Dame and London, 1995; first pub. in German 1935)

King, A.A., *Cîteaux and Her Elder Daughters* (London, 1954)

King, P., *The Finances of the Cistercian Order in the Fourteenth Century*, CS 85 (Kalamazoo, MI, 1985)

   Western Monasticism, CS 185 (Kalamazoo, MI, 1999)

Lekai, L.J., *The Cistercians: Ideals and Reality* (Kent, OH, 1977)

Nichols, J.A. and L.T. Shank (eds.), *Hidden Springs: Cistercian Monastic Women*, 2 vols. CS113 (Kalamazoo, MI, 1995)

Norton, C. and D. Park (eds.), *Cistercian Art and Architecture in the British Isles* (Cambridge, 1986)

Oram, R. (ed.), *Life on the Edge: The Cistercian Abbey of Balmerino (Scotland)*, thematic issue of *Cîteaux*, 59 (2008)

3 The Cistercian Order since 1600

Bell, D.N., *Understanding Rancé: The Spirituality of the Abbot of La Trappe in Context*, CS 205 (Kalamazoo, MI, 2005)

Bouton, J. de la Croix, *Les moniales cisterciennes: Livre premier: Histoire externe: Deuxième partie: du XVIe siècle à nos jours* (Grignan, 1987)

Friedlander, C., *Décentralisation et identité cistercienne 1946–1985. Quelle autonomie pour les communautés?* (Paris, 1988)

Guerout, G., 'La communauté de La Trappe face à la Révolution, 13 février 1790–3 juin 1792', *Cîteaux*, 40 (1989), 376–477

Kervingant, M. de la Trinité, *A Monastic Odyssey*, CS 171 (Kalamazoo, MI, 1999)

Kinder, T.N. (ed.), *Réformes et continuité dans l'Ordre de Cîteaux: de l'Étroite Observance à la Stricte Observance* (Brecht and Cîteaux, 1995)

Konrad, N., *Die Enstehung der Österreichisch-Ungarischen Zisterzienserkongregation (1849–1869)* (Rome, 1967)

Krailsheimer, A.J., *Armand-Jean de Rancé, Abbot of La Trappe: His Influence in the Cloister and the World* (Oxford, 1974)

Lehner, U.L., *Enlightened Monks: The German Benedictines 1740–1803* (Oxford, 2011)

Lekai, L.J., *The Cistercians: Ideals and Reality* (Kent OH, 1977), pp. 91–204
  Nicholas Cotheret's 'Annals of Cîteaux': Outlined from the French Original (Kalamazoo, MI, 1982)

Pacaut, M., *Les moines blancs: histoire de l'ordre de Cîteaux* (Paris, 1993), pp. 309–63

Tescari, A. (ed.), *The Cistercian Order of the Strict Observance in the Twentieth Century, vol. I, From 1892 to the Close of the Second Vatican Council; vol. II, From the Second Vatican Council to the End of the Century* (Rome, 2008)

Tuyén, T. Nguyên-Dính-, 'Histoire des controverses à Rome entre la Commune et l'Étroite Observance de 1662 à 1666', *Analecta Cisterciensia*, 26 (1970), 3–247

Un homme et son temps: l'Abbé de Rancé. Actes du colloque de La Trappe 23–29 octobre 2000, pour le troisième centenaire de la mort de Rancé (Bégrolle-en-Mauges, 2004)

Waddell, C., 'The Cistercian Dimension of the Reform of La Trappe', in *Cistercians in the Late Middle Ages*, ed. E.R. Elder, CS 64 (Kalamazoo, MI, 1981), pp. 102–61

Zakar, P., *Histoire de la Stricte Observance de l'Ordre Cistercien depuis ses débuts jusqu'au Généralat du Cardinal Richelieu (1606–1635)* (Rome, 1966)

Useful information can be found on the official websites of both Orders: www.ocist.org and www.ocso.org. From the latter can be downloaded the document *Observantiae: Continuity and Reforms in the Cistercian Family*, which deals with the period discussed in this chapter.

4 Centres and peripheries

Flanagan, M.T., 'Irish Royal Charters and the Cistercian Order', in *Charters and Charter Scholarship in Britain and Ireland*, ed. M.T. Flanagan and J.A. Green (Basingstoke, 2005)

France, J., *The Cistercians in Scandinavia*, CS 131 (Kalamazoo, MI, 1992)

Goez, E., *Pragmatische Schriftlichkeit und Archivpflege der Zisterzienser: Ordenszentralismus und regionale Vielfalt, namentlich in Franken und Altbayern (1098–1525)* (Münster, 2003)

Jamroziak, E., *The Cistercian Order in Medieval Europe: 1090–1500* (Harlow, in press)

'Making and Breaking the Bonds: Yorkshire Cistercians and Their Neighbours', in *Perspectives for an Architecture of Solitude: Essays on Cistercians, Art and Architecture in Honour of Peter Fergusson*, ed. T.N. Kinder (Turnhout, 2004), pp. 198–206

Survival and Success on Medieval Borders: Cistercian Houses in Medieval Scotland and Pomerania from the Twelfth to the Late Fourteenth Century (Turnhout, 2011)

Jamroziak, E. and J. Burton (eds.), *Religious and Laity in Western Europe 1000–1400: Interaction, Negotiation, and Power* (Turnhout, 2006)

McGuire, B.P., *The Cistercians in Denmark, Their Attitudes, Roles, and Functions in Medieval Society*, CS 35 (Kalamazoo, MI, 1982)

'Norm and Practice in Early Cistercian Life', in *Norm und Praxis in Alltag des Mittelalters und der frühen Neuzeit*, ed. G. Jaritz (Vienna, 1997), pp. 107–24

Oberste, J., *Visitation und Ordensorganisation: Formen sozialer Normierung, Kontrolle und Kommunikation bei Cisterziensern, Prämonstratensern und Cluniazensern (12.–frühes 14. Jahrhundert)* (Münster, 1995)

Pressouyre, L. (ed.), *L'espace cistercien* (Paris, 1994)

Tsougarakis, N.I., *The Latin Religious Orders in Medieval Greece, 1204–1500* (Turnhout, 2012)

5 The Cistercian community

Cassidy-Welch, M., *Monastic Spaces and Their Meanings: Thirteenth-Century English Cistercian Monasteries* (Turnhout, 2001)

Constable, G., 'Famuli and Conversi at Cluny', *Revue bénédictine*, 83 (1973), 326–50

Donnelly, J.S., *The Decline of the Medieval Cistercian Laybrotherhood* (New York, 1949)

France, J., *Separate but Equal: Cistercian Lay Brothers 1120–1350* (Collegeville, MN and Kalamazoo, MI, 2012)

Newman, M.G., 'Crucified by the Virtues: Monks, Lay Brothers, and Women in Thirteenth-Century Cistercian Saints' Lives', in *Gender and Difference in the Middle Ages*, ed. S. Farmer and C.B. Pasternak (Minneapolis, MN, 2003), pp. 182–208

Williams, D.H., *The Cistercians in the Early Middle Ages* (Leominster, 1998)

6 Constitutions and the General Chapter

Berman, C.H., *The Cistercian Evolution: The Invention of a Religious Order in Twelfth-Century Europe* (Philadelphia, PA, 1999)

Cocheril, M., *Dictionnaire des monastères cisterciens*, La documentation cistercienne 18 (Rochefort, 1976)

McGuire, B.P., 'Bernard's Concept of a Cistercian Order: Vocabulary and Context', *Cîteaux*, 54 (2003), 225–49

'Charity and Unanimity: The Invention of the Cistercian Order. A Review Article', *Cîteaux*, 51 (2000), 285–97

The Difficult Saint: Bernard of Clairvaux and His Tradition, CS 126 (Kalamazoo, MI, 1991)

Friendship and Community: The Monastic Experience 350–1250, CS 95 (Kalamazoo, MI, 1988)

Waddell, C., 'The Myth of Cistercian Origins: C.H. Berman and the Manuscript Sources', *Cîteaux*, 51 (1999), 299–360

7 Nuns

Berman, C.H., 'Cistercian Nuns and the Development of the Order: The Abbey of Saint-Antoine-des-Champs outside Paris', in *The Joy of Learning and the Love of God*, ed. E.R. Elder, CS 160 (Kalamazoo, MI, 1995), pp. 121–56

'Cistercian Women and Tithes', *Cîteaux*, 49 (1998), 95–128

'The Economic Practices of Cistercian Women's Communities: A Preliminary Look', in *Studiosorum Speculum: Studies in Honor of Louis J. Lekai, O.Cist*, ed. F.R. Swietek and J.R. Sommerfeldt, CS 141 (Kalamazoo, MI, 1993), pp. 15–32

'The Labors of Hercules, the Cartulary, Church and Abbey for Nuns of La Cour-Notre-Dame-de-Michery', *Journal of Medieval History*, 26 (2000), 33–70

'Were There Twelfth-Century Cistercian Nuns?', *Church History*, 68 (1999), 824–64

Berman, C.H. (trans.), *Women and Monasticism in Medieval Europe: Sisters and Patrons of the Cistercian Reform* (Kalamazoo, MI, 2002)

Bonis, A., S. Dechavanne and M. Wabont (eds.), *Cîteaux et les femmes* (Paris, 2001)

Bouton, J. de la Croix, *Les moniales cisterciennes*, 4 vols. (Grignan, 1987)

Boyd, C.E., *A Cistercian Nunnery in Medieval Italy: The Story of Rifreddo in Saluzzo, 1220–1300* (Cambridge, MA, 1943)

Degler-Spengler, B., 'The Incorporation of Cistercian Nuns into the Order in the Twelfth and Thirteenth Century', in *Hidden Springs: Cistercian Monastic Women*, ed. J.A. Nichols and L.T. Shank, 2 vols., CS 113 (Kalamazoo, MI, 1995), vol. I, pp. 85–134

France, J., *The Cistercians in Medieval Art* (Stroud, 1998), chapter 9, 'The Nuns'

The Cistercians in Scandinavia, CS 131 (Kalamazoo, MI, 1992), pp. 159–84 on nuns

Freeman, E, 'A Cistercian Monk Writes to a Cistercian Nun: John Godard's Treatise for the Abbess of Tarrant, England, c. 1250', *CSQ*, 45 (2010), 331–51

'"Houses of a Peculiar Order": Cistercian Nunneries in Medieval England, with Special Attention to the Fifteenth and Sixteenth Centuries', *Cîteaux*, 55 (2004), 245–87

Kulke, W.-H., *Zisterzienserinnenarchitektur des 13. Jahrhunderts in Südfrankreich* (Munich and Berlin, 2006)

Lekai, L.J., *The Cistercians: Ideals and Reality* (Kent, OH, 1977), chapter 22, 'Cistercian Nuns'

Lester, A.E., 'Cares beyond the Walls: Cistercian Nuns and the Care of Lepers in Twelfth- and Thirteenth-Century Northern France', in *Religious and Laity in Western Europe 1000–1400: Interaction, Negotiation, and Power*, ed. E. Jamroziak and J. Burton (Turnhout, 2006), pp. 197–224

'Cleaning House in 1399. Disobedience and the Demise of Cistercian Convents in Northern France at the End of the Middle Ages', in *Oboedientia: Zu Formen und Grenzen von Macht und Unterordnung im mittelalterlichen Religiosentum*, ed. S. Barret and G. Melville (Münster, 2005), pp. 423–43

Nichols, J.A. and L.T. Shank (eds.), *Hidden Springs: Cistercian Monastic Women*, 2 vols., CS 113 (Kalamazoo, MI, 1995)

Thompson, S., 'The Problem of the Cistercian Nuns in the Twelfth and Early Thirteenth Centuries', in *Medieval Women*, ed. D. Baker (Oxford, 1978), pp. 227–52

Waddell, C., 'One Day in the Life of the Savigniac Nun: Jehanne de Deniscourt', *CSQ*, 26 (1991), 134–51, reconstruction of a day in the life of a Cistercian nun, based on Stephen of Lexington's visitation register

Williams, D.H., *The Cistercians in the Early Middle Ages* (Trowbridge, 1998), chapter 20, 'The Nunneries'

8 Agriculture and economies

Berman, C.H., *The Cistercian Evolution: The Invention of a Religious Order in Twelfth-Century Europe* (Philadelphia, PA, 1999)

'Cistercian Women and Tithes', *Cîteaux*, 49 (1998), 95–128

Medieval Agriculture, the Southern-French Countryside, and the Early Cistercians: A Study of Forty-Three Monasteries (Philadelphia, PA, 1986)

'Two Medieval Women's Control of Property and Religious Benefactions in France: Eleanor of Vermandois and Blanche of Castile', *Viator*, 41 (2010), 151–82

Boyd, C.E., *A Cistercian Nunnery in Medieval Italy: The Story of Rifreddo in Saluzzo, 1220–1300* (Cambridge, MA, 1943)

Constable, G., *Monastic Tithes from Their Origins to the Twelfth Century* (Cambridge, 1964)

Donkin, R.A., *The Cistercians: Studies in the Geography of Medieval England and Wales* (Toronto, 1978)

Donnelly, J.S., *The Decline of the Medieval Cistercian Laybrotherhood* (New York, 1949)

Pressouyre, L. and P. Benoit (eds.), *L'hydraulique monastique: milieux, réseaux, usages* (Grâne, 1996)

9 Art

Bony, P., 'An Introduction to the Study of Cistercian Seals: The Virgin as Mediatrix, then Protectrix on the Seals of Cistercian Abbeys', *Studies in Cistercian Art and Architecture*, 3, ed. M.P. Lillich, CS 89 (Kalamazoo, MI, 1987), pp. 201–40

Cahn, W., 'The Rule and the Book: Cistercian Book Illumination in Burgundy and Champagne', in *Monasticism and the Arts*, ed. T. Vernon (Syracuse, NY, 1984), pp. 139–72

Frings, J. and J. Gerchow, *Krone und Schleier: Kunst aus mittelalterlichen Frauenklöstern* (Munich, 2005)

Heslop, T.A., 'Cistercian Seals in England and Wales', in *Cistercian Art and Architecture in the British Isles*, ed. C. Norton and D. Park (Cambridge, 1986), pp. 266–83

Hörsch, M., 'Tendenzen der Zisterzienser-Literatur der letzten zehn Jahre unter besonderer Berücksichtigung kunsthistorischer Studien zu den Ordensklöstern in Mitteleuropa', *Cîteaux*, 58 (2007), 131–70

Kratzke, C., *Das Zisterzienserkloster Dargun in Mecklenburg-Vorpommern: Studien zur Bau- und Kunstgeschichte* (Petersberg, 2004)

Laabs, A., *Malerei und Plastik im Zisterzienserorden: Zum Bildgebrauch zwischen sakralen Zeremoniell und Stiftermemoria 1250–1430* (Petersberg, 2000)

Lillich, M.P. (ed.), *Studies in Cistercian Art and Architecture*, 6 vols., CS 66, CS 69, CS 89, CS 134, CS 167, CS 194 (Kalamazoo, MI, 1982–2005)

Norton, C., 'Early Cistercian Tile Pavements', in *Cistercian Art and Architecture in the British Isles*, ed. C. Norton and D. Park (Cambridge, 1986), pp. 228–55

'Table of Cistercian Legislation on Art and Architecture', in *Cistercian Art and Architecture in the British Isles*, ed. C. Norton and D. Park (Cambridge, 1986), pp. 317–93

'*Varietates Pavimentorum*: contribution à l'étude de l'art cistercien in France', *Cahiers archéologiques*, 31 (1983), 68–113

Reilly, D., 'Bernard of Clairvaux and Christian Art', in *A Companion to Bernard of Clairvaux*, ed. B.P. McGuire (Leiden, 2011), pp. 279–304

Rudolph, C., *The 'Things of Greater Importance': Bernard of Clairvaux's 'Apologia' and the Medieval Attitude toward Art* (Philadelphia, PA, 1990)

Violence and Daily Life: Reading, Art and Polemics in the Cîteaux 'Moralia in Job' (Princeton, NJ, 1997)

Schumann, D. (ed.), *Sachkultur und religiöse Praxis* (Berlin, 2007)

Talbot, C.H., 'The Cistercian Attitude towards Art: The Literary Evidence', in *Cistercian Art and Architecture in the British Isles*, ed. C. Norton and D. Park (Cambridge, 1986), pp. 56–64

Zakin, H.J., 'French Cistercian Grisaille Glass', *Gesta*, 2 (1974), 17–28

Załuska, Y., *L'enluminure et le scriptorium de Cîteaux au XIIe siècle* (Nuits-Saint-Georges, 1989)

10 Libraries and scriptoria

Bell, D.N., 'Cistercian Scriptoria in England: What They Were and Where They Were', *Cîteaux*, 57 (2006), 45–68

An Index of Authors and Works in Cistercian Libraries in Great Britain, CS 130 (Kalamazoo, MI, 1992)

'The Libraries of Religious Houses in the Late Middle Ages', in *The Cambridge History of Libraries in Britain and Ireland: I*, ed. T. Webber and E. Leedham-Green (Cambridge, 2004), pp. 126–51

'The Library of Cîteaux in the Fifteenth Century: *Primus inter pares* or *Unus inter multos?*', *Cîteaux*, 50 (1999), 103–34

'Monastic Libraries: 1400–1557', in *The Cambridge History of the Book in Britain: III*, ed. L. Hellinga and J.B. Trapp (Cambridge, 1999), pp. 229–54

'Printed Books in English Cistercian Monasteries', *Cîteaux*, 53 (2002), 127–62

'A Treasure-House for Monks: The Cistercian General Chapter and the Power of the Book from the Twelfth Century to 1787', *Cîteaux*, 58 (2007), 95–122

What Nuns Read: Books and Libraries in Medieval English Nunneries, CS 158 (Kalamazoo, MI, 1995)

'What Nuns Read: The State of the Question', in *The Culture of Medieval English Monasticism*, ed. J.G. Clark (Woodbridge, 2007), pp. 113–33

Bondéelle-Souchier, A., *Bibliothèques cisterciennes dans la France médiévale: répertoire des abbayes d'hommes* (Paris, 1991)

'Les moniales cisterciennes et leurs livres manuscrits dans la France d'ancien régime', *Cîteaux*, 45 (1994), 193–337

Dimier, A., 'Les premiers cisterciens étaient-ils ennemis des études?', *Studia Monastica*, 4 (1962), 69–91

Doyle, A.I., 'Production by the Monastic Orders in England (c. 1375–1530): Assessing the Evidence', in *Medieval Book Production: Assessing the Evidence*, ed. L.L. Brownrigg (Los Altos Hills, CA, 1990), pp. 1–19

'Publication by Members of the Religious Orders', in *Book Production and Publishing in Britain 1375–1475*, ed. J. Griffiths and D. Pearsall (Cambridge, 1989), pp. 109–23

Schneider, A., 'Skriptorien und Bibliotheken der Cistercienser', in *Die Cistercienser: Geschichte, Geist, Kunst*, ed. A. Schneider, A. Wienand, W. Bickel and E. Cöster (Cologne, 1974), pp. 399–433

Sharpe, R., 'Library Catalogues and Indexes', in *The Cambridge History of the Book in Britain: II*, ed. N. Morgan and R.M. Thomson (Cambridge, 2008), pp. 197–218

'The Medieval Librarian', in *The Cambridge History of Libraries in Britain and Ireland: I*, ed. T. Webber and E. Leedham-Green (Cambridge, 2004), pp. 218–41

Talbot, C.H., 'The English Cistercians and the Universities', *Studia Monastica*, 4 (1962), 197–220

11 Cistercian architecture or architecture of the Cistercians?

Aubert, M. and A. de Maillé, *L'architecture cistercienne en France*, 2 vols. (Paris, 1948)

Cassidy-Welch, M., *Monastic Spaces and Their Meanings: Thirteenth-Century English Cistercian Monasteries* (Turnhout, 2001)

Coomans, T., *L'abbaye de Villers-en-Brabant: construction, configuration et signification d'une abbaye cistercienne gothique* (Brussels, 2000)

'Cistercian Nuns and Princely Memorials: Dynastic Burial Churches in the Cistercian Abbeys of the Medieval Low Countries', in *Sépulture, mort et représentation du pouvoir au moyen âge/Tod, Grabmal und Herrschaftsräpresentation im Mittelalter*, ed. M. Margue (Luxembourg, 2006), pp. 683–734, 775–98

Coppack, G., *The White Monks: The Cistercians in Britain 1128–1540* (Stroud, 1998)

Elm, K., P. Joerissen and H.J. Roth (eds.), *Die Zisterzienser: Ordensleben zwischen Ideal und Wirklichkeit*, 2 vols. (Cologne, 1980–2)

Fergusson, P., *Architecture of Solitude: Cistercian Abbeys in Twelfth-Century England* (Princeton, NJ, 1984)

Fergusson, P. and S. Harrison, *Rievaulx Abbey: Community, Architecture, Memory* (New Haven, CT and London, 1999)

Hall, J. and C. Kratzke (eds.), *Sepulturae cistercienses: Burial, Memorial and Patronage in Medieval Cistercian Monasteries*, thematic issue of *Cîteaux*, 56 (2005)

Kinder, T.N., *Cistercian Europe: Architecture of Contemplation* (Grand Rapids, MI, 2002)

Kinder, T.N. (ed.), *Perspectives for an Architecture of Solitude: Essays on Cistercians, Art and Architecture in Honour of Peter Fergusson* (Turnhout, 2004)

Kratzke, C., *Das Zisterzienserkloster Dargun in Mecklenburg-Vorpommern: Studien zur Bau- und Kunstgeschichte* (Petersberg, 2004)

Kulke, W.-H., *Zisterzienserinnenarchitektur des 13. Jahrhunderts in Südfrankreich* (Munich and Berlin, 2006)

Lillich, M.P. (ed.), *Studies in Cistercian Art and Architecture*, 6 vols., CS 66, CS 69, CS 89, CS 134, CS 167, CS 194 (Kalamazoo, MI, 1982–2005)

Lindemann-Merz, G., *Infirmarien – Kranken- und Sterbehäuser der Mönche: Eine architekturhistorische Betrachtung der Infirmariekomplexe nordenglischer Zisterzienserklöster* (Munich, 2009)

Norton, C. and D. Park (eds.), *Cistercian Art and Architecture in the British Isles* (Cambridge, 1986)

Plouvier, M. and A. Saint-Denis (eds.), *Pour une histoire monumentale de l'abbaye de Cîteaux 1098–1998*, Cîteaux: Studia et Documenta 8 (Vitreux, 1998)

Pressouyre, L. (ed.), *L'espace cistercien* (Paris, 1994)

Pressouyre, L. and P. Benoit (eds.), *L'hydraulique monastique: milieux, réseaux, usages* (Grâne, 1996)

Pressouyre, L. and T.N. Kinder (eds.), *Saint Bernard et le monde cistercien* (Paris, 1990)

Robinson, D., *The Cistercians in Wales: Architecture and Archaeology, 1130–1540* (London, 2005)

Rüffer, J., *Orbis Cisterciensis: Zur Geschichte der monastischen ästhetischen Kultur im Mittelalter* (Berlin, 1999)

Stalley, R., *Cistercian Monasteries of Ireland* (New Haven, CT and London, 1987)

Untermann, M., *Forma Ordinis: Die mittelalterliche Baukunst der Zisterzienser* (Munich and Berlin, 2001)

van der Meer, F., *Atlas de l'ordre cistercien* (Paris and Brussels, 1965)

12 Bernard of Clairvaux: his first and greatest miracle was himself

Arabeyre, P., J. Berlioz and P. Poirrier (eds.), *Vies et légendes de saint Bernard de Clairvaux: création, diffusion, réception (XIIe–XXe siècles)* (Brecht and Cîteaux, 1993)

Aubé, P., *Saint Bernard de Clairvaux* (Paris, 2003)

Bertrand, D. and G. Lobrichon (eds.), *Bernard de Clairvaux: histoire, mentalités, spiritualité*, SCh 380 (Paris, 1992)

Bredero, A.H., *Bernard of Clairvaux: Between Cult and History* (Grand Rapids, MI, 1996)

Casey, M., 'Reading Saint Bernard: The Man, the Medium, the Message', in *A Companion to Bernard of Clairvaux*, ed. B.P. McGuire (Leiden, 2011), pp. 62–107

Commission d'histoire de l'ordre de Cîteaux (ed.), *Bernard de Clairvaux* (Paris, 1953), esp. chronological tables, pp. 567–619

Dinzelbacher, P., *Bernhard von Clairvaux: Leben und Werk des berühmten Zisterziensers* (Darmstadt, 1998)

Holdsworth, C., 'Bernard as Father Abbot', in *A Companion to Bernard of Clairvaux*, ed. B.P. McGuire (Leiden, 2011), pp. 169–219

McGuire, B.P., 'Bernard's Life and Works: A Review', in *A Companion to Bernard of Clairvaux*, ed. B.P. McGuire (Leiden, 2011), pp. 18–61

  The Difficult Saint: Bernard of Clairvaux and His Tradition, CS 126 (Kalamazoo, MI, 1991)

McGuire, B.P., (ed.), *A Companion to Bernard of Clairvaux* (Leiden, 2011)

Picard, A. and P. Boglioni, 'Miracle et thaumaturgie dans la vie de saint Bernard', in *Vies et légendes de saint Bernard de Clairvaux: création, diffusion, réception (XIIe–XXe siècles)*, ed. P. Arabeyre, J. Berlioz and P. Poirrier (Brecht and Cîteaux, 1993), pp. 36–59

Vacandard, E., *Vie de Saint Bernard*, 2 vols. (Paris 1920; first pub. 1895)

Williams, W., *Saint Bernard of Clairvaux* (Westminster 1952; first pub. 1935)

13 Bernard of Clairvaux: work and self

Bruun, M.B., *Parables: Bernard of Clairvaux's Mapping of Spiritual Topography* (Leiden, 2007)

Evans, G.R., *The Mind of St Bernard of Clairvaux* (Oxford, 1993)

Gilson, É., *The Mystical Theology of Bernard of Clairvaux*, CS 120 (Kalamazoo, MI, 1990; first pub. in French 1934; first pub. in English 1940)

Holdsworth, C., 'Bernard as Father Abbot', in *A Companion to Bernard of Clairvaux*, ed. B.P. McGuire (Leiden, 2011), pp. 169–219

Leclercq, J., *The Love of Learning and the Desire for God* (New York, 1961 and later; first pub. in French 1957)

  Monks and Love in Twelfth-Century France (Oxford, 1979)

Lubac, H. de, *Medieval Exegesis: The Four Senses of Scripture*, 3 vols. (Grand Rapids, MI and Edinburgh, 1998–2009; first pub. in French 1959–63)

McGinn, B., 'Bernard of Clairvaux: "That Contemplative"', in *The Presence of God*, vol. II, *The Growth of Mysticism: Gregory the Great through the Twelfth Century* (New York, 1995), pp. 158–224

Morris, C., *The Discovery of the Individual, 1050–1200* (New York, 1972)

Pranger, M.B., *Bernard of Clairvaux and the Shape of Monastic Thought: Broken Dreams* (Leiden, 1994)

'The Concept of Death in Bernard's Sermons on the Song of Songs', *Cîteaux*, 42 (1991), 85–93

'Killing Time: An Essay on the Monastic Notion of Speed', in *Medieval Monastic Preaching*, ed. C. Muessig (Leiden, 1998), pp. 319–33

'Mystical Tropology in Bernard of Clairvaux', *Bijdragen: tijdschrift voor filosofie en theologie*, 52 (1991), 428–35

'The Virgin Mary and the Complexities of Love-Language in the Works of Bernard of Clairvaux', *Cîteaux*, 40 (1989), 112–38

Rudolph, C., *The 'Things of Greater Importance': Bernard of Clairvaux's 'Apologia' and the Medieval Attitude toward Art* (Philadelphia, PA, 1990)

Vacandard, E., *Vie de Saint Bernard, abbé de Clairvaux*, 2 vols. (Paris, 1920; first pub. 1895)

14 Early Cistercian writers

The introductions to the translations in the Cistercian Fathers Series, Cistercian Publications, Kalamazoo, MI (see 'Cistercian Primary Sources')

Bell, D.N., 'The Ascetic Spirituality of Baldwin of Ford', *Cîteaux*, 31 (1980), 227–50

The Image and Likeness: The Augustinian Spirituality of William of Saint Thierry, CS 78 (Kalamazoo, MI, 1984)

Boquet, D., *L'ordre de l'affect au moyen âge: autour de l'anthropologie affective d'Aelred de Rievaulx* (Caen, 2005)

Brouette, É., A. Dimier and E., Manning (eds.), *Dictionnaire des auteurs cisterciens*, La documentation cistercienne 16 (Rochefort, 1975–9)

Burton, P.-A., *Aelred de Rievaulx (1110–1167): essai de biographie existentielle et spirituelle* (Paris, 2010)

Bibliotheca Aelrediana secunda: une bibliographie cumulative (1962–1996) (Louvain-la-Neuve, 1997)

Casey, M., 'Beatrice of Nazareth (1200–68): Cistercian Mystic' and 'Beatrice of Nazareth: The Seven Modes of Love (a Translation)', *Tjurunga: Australasian Benedictine Review*, 50 (1996), 44–70 and 71–82

'Herbert of Clairvaux's *Book of Wonderful Happenings*', *CSQ*, 25 (1990), 37–64

Costello, H., 'The Idea of the Church in the Sermons of John of Ford', *Cîteaux*, 21 (1970), 236–64

Costello, H. and C.J. Holdsworth (eds.), *A Gathering of Friends: The Learning and Spirituality of John of Forde*, CS 161 (Kalamazoo, MI, 1996)

Cowdrey, H.E.J., '*Quidam frater Stephanus nomine, anglicus natione*: The English Background of Stephen Harding', *Revue bénédictine*, 101 (1991), 322–40; repr. in E.R. Elder (ed.), *The New Monastery: Texts and Studies on the Earliest Cistercians*, CF 60 (Kalamazoo, MI, 1998), pp. 57–77

'Stephen Harding and Cistercian Monasticism', *Cîteaux*, 49 (1998), 209–19

De Ganck, R., *Beatrice of Nazareth in Her Context*, CS 121 (Kalamazoo, MI, 1991)

'The Three Foundations of Bartholomew of Tienen', *Cîteaux*, 37 (1986), 49–75

Towards Unification with God, CS 122 (Kalamazoo, MI, 1991)

Elder, E.R., 'Bernard of Clairvaux and William of Saint Thierry', in *A Companion to Bernard of Clairvaux*, ed. B.P. McGuire (Leiden, 2011), pp. 108–32

Elder, E.R. *Noble Piety and Reformed Monasticism*, CS 65 (Kalamazoo, MI, 1981)

Elder, E.R. (ed.), *Goad and Nail*, CS 84 (Kalamazoo, MI, 1985)

Hallier, A., *The Monastic Theology of Aelred of Rievaulx* (Spencer, MA, 1969; first pub. in French 1959)

Häring, N.M., 'The Writings against Gilbert of Poitiers by Geoffrey of Auxerre', *Analecta Cisterciensia*, 22 (1966), 3–83

Holdsworth, C.J., 'John of Ford and English Cistercian Writings 1167–1214', *Transactions of the Royal Historical Society*, fifth series, 11 (1961), 117–36

Hollywood, A., 'Inside Out: Beatrice of Nazareth and Her Hagiographer', in *Gendered Voices: Medieval Saints and Their Interpreters*, ed. C.M. Mooney (Philadelphia, PA, 1999), pp. 78–98

Hoste, A., *Bibliotheca Aelrediana: A Survey of the Manuscripts, Old Catalogues, Editions and Studies Concerning St. Aelred of Rievaulx* (Steenbrugge, 1962)

Kienzle, B.M., 'Cistercian Views of the City in the Sermons of Helinand of Froidmont', in *Medieval Sermons and Society: Cloister, City, University*, ed. J. Hamesse, B.M. Kienzle, A. Thayer and D.L. Stoudt (Louvain-le-Neuve, 1998), pp. 165–82

'Deed and Word: Helinand's Toulouse Sermons', in *Erudition at God's Service*, ed. J.R. Sommerfeldt, CF 98 (Kalamazoo, MI, 1987), pp. 267–76 and 277–90

Leclercq, J., *The Love of Learning and the Desire for God* (New York, 1961 and later; first pub. in French 1957)

McGinn, B., *The Golden Chain: a study in the Theological Anthropology of Isaac of Stella*, CS 15 (Spencer, MA, 1972)

The Presence of God, vol. II, *The Growth of Mysticism: Gregory the Great through the Twelfth Century* (New York, 1994)

McGuire, B.P., *Brother and Lover: Aelred of Rievaulx* (New York, 1994)

Merton, T., 'Father and Son Cistercians of the Twelfth Century: Blessed Amadeus of Hauterive, "the Elder", and Saint Amadeus, Bishop of Lausanne', *CSQ*, 43 (2008), 379–90

The Feast of Freedom: Monastic Formation according to Adam of Perseigne (Gethsemani Abbey, KY, [n.d.]), repr. as introduction to *The Letters of Adam of Perseigne 1*, trans. G. Perigo, CF 21 (Kalamazoo, MI, 1976)

Morson, J., *Christ the Way: The Christology of Guerric of Igny*, CS 25 (Kalamazoo, MI, 1976)

Nemes, B.J., 'Gertrude of Helfta's "Legatus divinae pietatis": Text Production and Authorship in the Revelatory Literature of Helfta', in *Companion to Medieval Northern German Mysticism*, ed. E.A. Andersen and H. Lähnemann (Leiden, in press)

Nichols, J.A. and L.T. Shank (eds.), *Hidden Springs: Cistercian Monastic Women*, CS 113 (Kalamazoo, MI, 1995)

Paden, W.D., '*De Monachis rithmos facientibus*: Hélinand de Froidmont, Bertran de Born, and the Cistercian General Chapter of 1199', *Speculum*, 55 (1980), 669–85

Pedersen, E.M. Wiberg, 'Image of God – Image of Mary – Image of Woman: On the Theology and Spirituality of Beatrice of Nazareth', *CSQ*, 29 (1994), 209–20

   'The Incarnation of Beatrice of Nazareth's Theology', in *New Trends in Feminine Spirituality: The Holy Women of Liège and Their Impact*, ed. J. Dor, L. Johnson and J. Wogan-Browne (Turnhout, 1999), pp. 61–79

Sommerfeldt, J.R., *Aelred of Rievaulx: Pursuing Perfect Happiness* (New York, 2005)

Squire, A., *Aelred of Rievaulx: A Study*, CS 50 (Kalamazoo, MI, 1981; first pub. 1969)

Stercal, C., *Stephen Harding: A Biographical Sketch and Texts* (Kalamazoo, MI, 2008; pub. in Italian 2001)

15 The spiritual teaching of the early Cistercians

Bell, D.N., *The Image and Likeness: The Augustinian Spirituality of William of Saint Thierry*, CS 78 (Kalamazoo, MI, 1984)

Bouyer, L., *The Cistercian Heritage* (London, 1958; first pub. in French 1955)

Brooke, O., *Studies in Monastic Theology*, CS 37 (Kalamazoo, MI, 1980)

Casey, M., *Athirst for God: Spiritual Desire in Bernard of Clairvaux's Sermons on the Song of Songs*, CS 77 (Kalamazoo, MI, 1987)

Gilson, É., *The Mystical Theology of Saint Bernard* (London 1940; repr. Kalamazoo, MI, 1990; first pub. in French 1934)

Hallier, A., *The Monastic Theology of Aelred of Rievaulx* CS2 (Spencer, MA, 1969; first pub. in French 1959)

Hiss, W., *Die Anthropologie Bernhards von Clairvaux* (Berlin, 1964)

Köpf, U., *Religiöse Erfahrung in der Theologie Bernhards von Clairvaux* (Tübingen, 1980)

Leclercq, J., *The Love of Learning and the Desire for God* (New York, 1961 and later; first pub. in French 1957)

McGinn, B., *The Golden Chain: The Theological Anthropology of Isaac of Stella*, CS 15 (Spencer, MA, 1972)

   'Isaac of Stella on the Divine Nature', *Analecta Cisterciensia*, 29 (1973), 1–53

   The Presence of God, vol. II, *The Growth of Mysticism: Gregory the Great through the Twelfth Century* (New York, 1994)

Pranger, M.B., *Bernard of Clairvaux and the Shape of Monastic Thought: Broken Dreams* (Leiden, 1994)

Sommerfeldt, J.R. (ed.), *Bernardus Magister*, CS 135 (Spencer, MA, 1992)

Spiritualité cistercienne: histoire et doctrine (Paris, 1998)

Squire, A., *Aelred of Rievaulx: A Study*, CS 50 (Kalamazoo, MI, 1981; first pub. 1969)

Stickelbroeck, M., *Mysterium Venerandum: Der trinitarische Gedanke im Werk des Bernhard von Clairvaux* (Münster, 1994)

Verdeyen, P., *Guillaume de Saint-Thierry: premier auteur mystique des Pays-Bas* (Turnhout, 2003)

La théologie mystique de Guillaume de Saint-Thierry (Paris, 1990)

16 Cistercians in dialogue: bringing the world into the monastery

Bautier, R.-H., 'Paris au temps d'Abélard', in *Abélard en son temps*, ed. J. Jolivet (Paris, 1981), pp. 21–77

Boquet, D., *L'ordre de l'affect au moyen âge: autour de l'anthropologie affective d'Aelred de Rievaulx* (Caen, 2005)

Bredero, A.H., 'Cluny et Cîteaux: les origines de la controverse', in *Cluny et Cîteaux au douzième siècle: l'histoire d'une controverse monastique*, ed. A.H. Bredero (Amsterdam, 1985)

Brouette, É., A. Dimier and E. Manning (eds.), *Dictionnaire des auteurs cisterciens*, La documentation cistercienne 16 (Rochefort, 1975–9)

Canivez, J.-M., 'Albéric ou Aubry', in *Spiritualité cistercienne: histoire et doctrine* (Paris, 1998), pp. 221–4

Constable, G., 'Renewal and Reform in Religious Life: Concepts and Realities', in *Renaissance and Renewal in the Twelfth Century*, ed. R. Benson and G. Constable (Cambridge, 1982), pp. 37–67

Cowdrey, H.E.J., '*Quidam frater Stephanus nomine, Anglicus natione*: The English Background of Stephen Harding', *Revue bénédictine*, 101 (1991), 322–40

'Stephen Harding and Cistercian Monasticism', *Cîteaux*, 49 (1998), 209–19

Debuisson, M., 'La provenance des premiers cisterciens d'après les lettres et les *vitae* de Bernard de Clairvaux', *Cîteaux*, 43 (1994), 5–118

Foreville, R. (ed.), *Les mutations socio-culturelles au tournant des XIe–XIIe siècles* (Paris, 1984)

Fossier, R., 'L'essor économique de Clairvaux', in *Bernard de Clairvaux*, ed. Commission d'histoire de l'ordre de Cîteaux (Paris, 1953), pp. 77–93

'L'installation et les premières années de Clairvaux', in *Bernard de Clairvaux*, ed. Commission d'histoire de l'ordre de Cîteaux (Paris, 1953), pp. 95–114

'Le modèle cistercien', in *Saint Bernard et le monde cistercien*, ed. L. Pressouyre and T.N. Kinder (Paris, 1992), pp. 65–6

Jolivet, J., *Arts du langage et théologie chez Abélard* (Paris, 1969)

Leclercq, J., *The Love of Learning and the Desire for God* (New York, 1961 and later; first pub. in French 1957)

McGuire, B.P., 'The First Cistercian Renewal and a Changing Image of Saint Bernard', in McGuire, *The Difficult Saint: Bernard of Clairvaux and His Tradition*, CS 126 (Kalamazoo, MI, 1991), pp. 153–87

'A Lost Clairvaux Exemplum Collection Found: The Liber Visionum et Miraculorum Compiled under Prior John of Clairvaux (1171–1179)', *Analecta Cisterciensia*, 39 (1983), 26–62

Mikkers, E., 'Robert de Molesme', in *Spiritualité cistercienne: histoire et doctrine* (Paris, 1998), pp. 430–32

Morson, J., 'Arnulphe (Arnoul) de Boheries', in *Dictionnaire des auteurs cisterciens*, ed. É. Brouette, A. Dimier and E. Manning, La documentation cistercienne 16 (Rochefort, 1975–9)

Reilly, D., 'Education, Liturgy and Practice in Early Cîteaux', in *Understanding Monastic Practices of Oral Communication*, ed. S. Vanderputten (Turnhout, 2011), pp. 79–108

Riché, P., *Écoles et enseignement dans l'Occident chrétien de la fin du Ve siècle au milieu du XIe siècle* (Paris, 1979)

   'La vie scolaire et la pédagogie au Bec au temps de Lanfranc et de saint Anselme', in *Les mutations socio-culturelles au tournant des XIe–XIIe siècles*, ed. R. Foreville (Paris, 1984), pp. 213–27

Rijk, L. de, 'Peter Abälard: Meister und Opfer des Scharfsinns', in *Petrus Abaelardus (1079–1142): Person, Werk und Wirkung*, ed. R. Thomas (Trier, 1980), pp. 125–38

Southern, R.W., *St. Anselm: A Portrait in a Landscape* (Cambridge, 1990)

Stercal, C., *Stephen Harding: A Biographical Sketch and Texts*, CS 226 (Kalamazoo, MI, 2008; first pub. in Italian 2001)

Verbaal, W., 'The Council of Sens Reconsidered: Masters, Monks or Judges?', *Church History*, 74 (2005), 460–93

   Een middeleeuws drama (Kapellen-Kampen, 2004)

   'The Preaching of Community: Bernard of Clairvaux's Sermons and the School of Experience', *Medieval Sermon Studies*, 48 (2004), 75–90

   '*Teste Quintiliano*: Jean de Salisbury et Quintilien: un exemple de la crise des autorités au XIIe siècle', in *Quintilien ancien et moderne*, ed. P. Galand (Turnhout, 2010), pp. 155–70

   'Tussen het klooster en de school', in *De Duinenabdij van Koksijde: Cisterciënzers in de Lage Landen*, ed. D. Vanclooster (Tielt, 2005), pp. 25–45

Verdeyen, P., *Guillaume de Saint-Thierry: premier auteur mystique des Pays-Bas* (Turnhout, 2003)

17 Preaching

Casey, M., 'An Introduction to Aelred's Chapter Discourses', *CSQ*, 45 (2010), 279–314

Holdsworth, C., 'Were the Sermons of St. Bernard on the Song of Songs Ever Preached?', in *Medieval Monastic Preaching*, ed. C. Muessig (Leiden, 1998), pp. 295–318

Kienzle, B.M., 'Mary Speaks against Heresy: An Unedited Sermon of Hélinand for the Purification, Paris, B.N. ms. lat. 14591', *Sacris Erudiri*, 32 (1991), 291–308

Kienzle, B.M. (ed.), *The Sermon*, Typologie des sources du moyen âge occidental 81–3 (Turnhout, 2000)

Mohrmann, C., *Praedicare-tractare-sermo: études sur le latin des chrétiens*, 2 vols. (Rome, 1961)

Muessig, C. (ed.), *Medieval Monastic Preaching* (Leiden, 1998)
Stiegman, E., 'The Literary Genre of Bernard of Clairvaux's *Sermones Super Cantica Canticorum*', in *Simplicity and Ordinariness*, ed. J.R. Sommerfeldt, CS 61 (Kalamazoo, MI, 1980), pp. 68–93
Verbaal, W., 'Réalités quotidiennes et fiction littéraire dans les *Sermons sur le Cantique* de Bernard de Clairvaux', *Cîteaux*, 51 (2000), 201–18
Waddell, C., 'The Liturgical Dimension of Twelfth-Century Cistercian Preaching', in *Medieval Monastic Preaching*, ed. C. Muessig (Leiden, 1998), pp. 335–49

18 Liturgy

Backaert, B., 'L'évolution du calendrier cistercien', *COCR*, 11 (1950), 81–94, 302–16; 12 (1951), 108–27
King, A.A., *Liturgies of the Religious Orders* (London, 1955)
Maître, C., (ed.), *Bernard de Clairvaux: Office de Saint Victor, Prologue à l'antiphonaire, Lettre 398*, SCh 527 6 (Paris ,2009)
Marosszéki, S.R., *Les origines du chant cistercien*, *ASOC*, 8 (Rome, 1952)
Scarcez, A., *L'antiphonaire 12A–B de Westmalle dans l'histoire du chant cistercien au XIIe siècle* (Turnhout, 2011)

Index

abbess
  and lay brothers, 107
  as organiser, 114, 119
  authority, 106
  General Chapter, 32, 42, 60, 102, 106
  preaching, 245
  seal, 136
  spiritual advice for, 106
  visitation, 105–6
abbot, 29, 72, 81–2, 176, 219, 245–6, 248
  and donors, 11, 15
  and foundations, 93
  and nuns, 32–3, 105–8
  as *vicarius Christi*, 81, 191–2, 195
  authority, 15, 29, 54, 57, 75, 81, 91, 159–60, 176, 195, 239
  burial, 159
  commendatory, 41, 43–4, 51, 55, 76, 165
  conspiracies against, 71
  deposition, 34, 39, 70–1, 82, 96, 136
  election, 54, 70, 83, 96
  General Chapter, 15, 27, 35, 40–1, 52, 69–70, 81, 88–90, 94–6, 146, 264
  hospitality, 16–17
  insignia, 82
  lists, 26
  residence, 16–17, 29, 41, 163
  resignation, 72–3, 81–2, 205
  seal, 136–7
  tension with lay brothers, 34–5
  tension with other abbots, 40, 53
  visitation, 29, 31, 70–1, 74, 90, 93–4, 107–8, *see also* visitation
abstinence from meat, 51, 53–5
Acre, 206, 251
Adalberon of Laon, 235

Adam of Perseigne, 207
Adam of Smailholm, 73
Admont, 206
Advent, 224, 245, 260
Aelred of Rievaulx, 3, 32, 83, 201–2, 240–1, 248
  De spirituali amicitia, 202, 229
  Homeliae de oneribus propheticis Isaiae, 202, 248
  on friendship, 201–2, 229, 239
  on love, 202, 227, 229
  preaching, 201–2, 247
  sermons, 201–2, 247–8
  Speculum caritatis, 202, 219, 221–2, 227, 229
Africa, 58–60
agriculture, 29, 66, 112–21, 238, 243
  crops, 66, 115, 117
  documents, 113
  forestry, 117, 121, 164
  granges, 2, 35, 82, 84–5, 91, 112–20, 151–2, 163–4
  lay brothers, 116, 119–20
  lay sisters, 116, 119–20
  mills, 2, 112, 114, 117–19, 163–4
  nuns, 107–8, 114–15, 118–21
  pastoralism, 11, 107–8, 112, 114–19
  viticulture, 114, 116–17, 119
Alan of Lille, 242
Alberic of Cîteaux, 26–7, 29, 36, 87–8, 92, 199, 238
Albert of Buxhövden, 68
Alcobaça, 158, 167n. 1
Alexander III, 33–4, 173–4, 178, 205
Alexander VII, 54
Alfonso VIII, 42, 116
Alfonso X, 13
Algeria, 58
Alice of Parc-aux-Dames, 106
allegory, 195, 210, 247, 249

All Saints, Feast of, 224
altar, 12, 83–4, 129, 135, 158–9
Altenberg, 73–4, 147, 158
Altzella, 147
Amadeus of Lausanne, 203, 247
  homilies in praise of Virgin Mary,
  203, 247
Ambrose of Milan, 126, 200, 259
Amelungsborn, 67
Amiens, Treaty of, 58
Anacletus II, 33–4, 176–7, 179
Anders Sunesen, 95
Annunciation, 194–6, 246
Anselm of Canterbury, 180, 223, 235,
  239
  Cur deus homo, 223
Anselm of Havelberg, 220
Anthony, 5
Anthropology (academic discipline),
  3, 226–30
Anthropology (theological), 226–30
Antioch, 66
Antiquity, 4, 145, 149, 206, 209, 219,
  229, 236
Apocrypha, 261
apostolic life, 26, 36, 108
Aragon, 70
archaeology, 2–4, 130, 133, 152–3,
  163–5
  nuns, 165–6
architecture, 151–66, 187
  abbatial residence, 16–17, 163
  ambulatory, 39, 156–9
  and liturgy, 132, 154, 158, 160–1
  apse, 39, 155–6
  armarium, 141, 143, 161
  Baroque style, 56, 165
  benefactors, 158–60
  the 'Bernardine' plan, 152, 156–7,
  160
  brick, 39, 153–4
  burials, 14–16, 158–9
  chancel, 39
  chapel, 15–17, 39, 121, 135,
  156–9
  chapter house, iv, 15–16, 41, 71,
  83, 159, 161–2, 142–3
  choir, 85, 104, 133, 154–5, 158–9
  church, iv, 12, 14–16, 39, 56, 76,
  96, 104, 125, 128–30, 132–3, 141,
  143, 151–64, 201
  'Cistercian model plan', the, 161–4
  Classic style, 165

cloister, 7, 41, 84–5, 142, 161–3,
  166, 246, 250
craftsmen, 160
crypt, 156
dormitory, 7, 29, 53, 82, 143, 161,
  164
Ecclesiastica Officia, 161
first generations, 31, 156–7
forma Ordinis, 153–7, 159–60,
  166–7
gate house, 83, 161, 163
Gothic revival, 165
Gothic style, 39, 97, 137, 151–2,
  154, 158–60
guest house, 16–17, 83, 161, 163
infirmary, 151, 161, 163–4
kitchen, 16, 142, 161, 163
latrine block, 161
lay brothers, 16, 85, 157, 160–1, 164
lay people, 161
legislation, 96, 153, 160
nave, 15, 39, 85, 133, 156, 159
novices, 41, 83, 161
nuns, 121, 124n. 51, 135, 152, 159,
  165–6
private chambers, 147–8, 164
refectory, 7, 9, 53, 133, 161, 163,
  206
Renaissance style, 165
Rococo style, 165
Romanesque style, 151, 154
sacristy, 9, 143, 146, 161
scholarship on, 2, 151–3, 161–7
scriptorium, 135, 142, 161
storeroom, 161
tower, 153, 156, 159
transept, iv, 39, 133, 156, 158–9,
  162
transformations, 158–60
unity and diversity, 125–6, 153–5,
  160
warming room, 142, 161
westwork, 159
Arcis-sur-Aube, 262
armarium, 141, 143, 161
Arnolfini, Octave, 53
Arnulf of Bohéries, *Speculum
  monachorum*, 242
Arras, 258
art, 125–37, 153
  Bernard of Clairvaux on, 31,
  127–30, 136, 186–7
  crucifixes, 129, 265

devotional images, 125–8, 153
illuminations, 30–1, 105, 125–7,
   129–30, 135, 154
legislation, 91–2, 96, 125, 129, 133,
   153
manuscripts, 126–7, 129–30, 133–5,
   142–3
murals, 104, 153
nuns, 104, 125, 136
Pontigny, 133–5
Romanesque style, 31
sculptures, 125, 128–9, 135–6, 153
seals, 125, 136–7
Stephen Harding, 30–1, 126–8
Wienhausen, 135–6
windows, 12, 125, 129, 132–5, 153,
   155, 159
Ascension, 187, 224
asceticism, 5–6, 9–10, 26, 88, 91, 116,
   125, 205, 233, 241–3
Asia, 59–60
Assumption, 246
Aubert, Marcel, 152
Augustine of Hippo, 3, 126, 134, 140,
   198, 202–3, 219, 222, 225–6
   De trinitate, 222
Augustinian Canons, 13, 179
Austria, 56, 106, 144
Austro-Hungarian Congregation, 57
Austro-Hungarian Empire, 58
Avignon, 73, *see also* papacy, the

Baldwin of Forde, 205–6
   De sacramento altaris, 206
   Sermones de commendatione fidei,
   206
Baldwin, Archbishop of Canterbury,
   251
Balmerino, 43
Baltic region, 67–8, 251
Bartholomew of Tienen, 42, 209
Basle, Council of, 146
Bavaria, 75
Beatrice of Nazareth, 42, 44–5, 104,
   209–10
Beaubec, 130
Beaulieu (Cyprus), 67
Beaulieu (England), 158
Beauvais, 207
Bebenhausen, 16, 159
Bede, 126, 146, 249
Beguines, 107, 209
Belgium, 58, 103, 106, 144, 165

Bell, David N., 126, 205
Belleéglise, 114
Belmont, 66
Benedict XII, 41, 45, 52, 97, 136,
   see also Jacques Fournier
Benedict, Rule of, 7, 12, 16, 26, 29,
   31–2, 34, 36, 45, 54, 56, 58, 69,
   74, 80–6, 87–93, 95, 112, 126,
   140, 148, 153, 174, 176, 186, 191,
   199, 243, 245, 249–50, 258–61,
   263
   departure from, 84–6, 91
   labor manuum, 81, 84, 112,
   258, *see also* manual labour
   lectio divina, 81, 85, 126,
   see also lectio divina
   opus Dei, 80, 85, 112, 258–61,
   see also liturgy
Benedictines, 3, 39, 45, 65, 67, 80–2,
   84, 95, 113, 136–7, 153–4, 159,
   179, 191, 199–200, 205–9, 220,
   223, 259–60
benefactors, 10–17, 31–2, 38,
   65, 76, 113, 121, 158–60,
   see also donations
Berengar of Tours, 236
Berman, Constance H., 28, 31, 88–9
Bernard of Clairvaux, 2, 27, 43, 56,
   75, 80, 88–90, 141, 144, 186–98,
   199–200, 202, 205, 218–31, 234,
   261
   and Peter Abelard, 176, 186–8, 201,
   203, 219–21, 223, 225, 239–40,
   258
   and Stephen Harding, 30–2, 95,
   260–1
   and the Church. 31, 33, 128,
   174, 176–8, 181, 262–4,
   see also Bernard of Clairvaux
   ecclesiology *De consideratione*, 178
   Apologia, 127–30, 176, 221
   appearance, 173
   as a chimaera, 176, 190–1
   as abbot, 175–6, 180–1, 186–7,
   189–95
   as brother, 82–3, 181, 191–3
   as peacemaker, 178
   canonisation, 33, 173, 201, 205,
   250, 264
   Christology, 188, 196–8, 223–4
   commemoration of, 43, 152, 264
   De consideratione, 187, 222, 224,
   241

Bernard of Clairvaux (*cont.*)
  De conversione ad clericos, 204
  De diligendo deo, 187, 227, 230
  De gradibus humilitatis et superbiae, 187
  De gratia et libero arbitrio, 225
  De laude novae militiae, 251
  De praecepto et dispensatione, 224
  ecclesiology, 224–5, *see also De consideratione*
  exegesis, 195, 197, 248–9
  Holy Week, 224
  Homilia super 'Missus est', 194–5, 224
  letters, 176, 187, 190, 200, 205, 223–5, 247
  life, 174–83
  liturgical reform, 260–5
  miracles, 178–82, 205
  Nativity, 224
  on Advent, 224
  on Annunciation, 194–6
  on art, 127–9, 186–7
  on Ascension, 187, 224
  on Circumcision, 250
  on contemplation, 31, 187, 192, 230–1
  on Easter, 224
  on Feast of All Saints, 224
  on friendship, 31
  on humility, 31, 187
  on love, 3, 31, 187, 227–30
  on Nativity, 187, 196–8
  on Pentecost, 249
  on repentance, 31
  on Rogation, 248
  on the degrees of love, 227
  on the kiss, 195, 227
  on the wilderness, 6–7, 10
  on Virgin Mary, 188, 194–6, 203, 224
  Parabolae, 187, 245, 247
  preaching, 31, 173, 177, 180–1, 186, 204–5, 224, 239–40, 246
  representation, 33, 43, 103, 136, 173, 178–81, 183, 190–3, 242, *see also Vita Prima*
  scholarship on, 136–7, 179–80, 187–9, 192, 248, 250
  seal, 136
  Sermo de diversis, 218, 224
  Sermo in annuntiatione domini, 224
  Sermo in assumptione B. Mariae Virginis, 224
  Sermo in dedicatione ecclesiae, 224
  Sermo in nativitate domini, 198
  Sermo in vigilia nativitatis domini, 223
  Sermo super psalmum 'Qui habitat', 220, 224
  Sermones super Cantica canticorum, 82–3, 187, 190–6, 204, 206, 218, 220, 223–30, 241, 248
  sermons, 187, 223, 246–51
  significance, 30–2, 151, 174–5, 188–9, 234, 239–42
Berthold, bishop of Livonia, 68
Bible, the, *see also* exegesis edition
  exposition, 2, 5, 31, 181, 188, 193–8, 219, 227–8, 230, 245, 248–9, 251, 261
  manuscripts, 126, 130–1, 134–5, 140, 144
  reading, 81
  references to, 3, 5, 35, 182, 191, 209–10, 219, 227–8, 230, 261
  translations, 44
Bindon, 206
Black Death, 40, 50, *see also* plague
Blanche of Castile, 114, 119, 121
Blencot, 145
Bloemendaal, 42, 209
Boglioni, Pierre, 179–80
Bohemia, 44, 65
Bologna, 39
Bonparte, Napoleon, 57–8
Bonaventure, 145
Boniface IX, 73
Bonnevaux, 116, 203
book production, 104, 142–3, 147–8, *see also* printing
book collections, 145–6
books, 12, 26, 57, 104, 140–9, 207, 250, 258
  collections, 140–2, 144–6, 148–9
  donations, 12, 141–3
  storage, 143, 146–7, 149
Bordesley, 141, 153
Borwin, 38
Bouchard, Constance, 12, 30
Braceland, Lawrence C., 214n. 37
Brandenburg, 38
Bredero, Adriaan, 179–80
Bronnbach, 147

Brooke, Odo, 222
Buckfast, 145–6
Burgundy, 13, 16, 26, 30, 71, 73, 118,
    126, 151, 259
burials, 17, 38
    architecture, 14–16, 158–9
    of lay people, 15–16, 38, 158–9
    of monks 159
Byland, 132

Caduin, 166
Caesarius of Heisterbach, 33, 83, 85,
    90, 242
    Dialogus miraculorum, 83, 211
Calixtus II, 27–8, 88
Cambron, 106
Canada, 59
Candlemas, 265
Canivez, J.-M., 100
Canvern, 116
Carta Caritatis, 27–9, 31–2, 52,
    69–70, 81–2, 87–90, 92–3, 105,
    157, 199–200, 208, 259
    scholarship on, 27–8, 92
Carthusians, 13, 44, 57, 146
Casamari, 39, 58
Castile, 42, 70, 102
Catalonia, 70
Cathars, 34, 205
Causse de Larzac, 116
cemeteries, 14, 16, 159, *see also* burial
Chaalis, 43, 45, 117, 210
Châlons-sur-Marne, 178, 239
Champagne, 30, 135
Champagnes, 108
chapel, 15, 39, 121, 156, 159
chapter, 96, 245–8, 250
chapter house, 15, 41, 71, 83, 142–3,
    159, 161–2
charisma, 9, 26, 30, 35–6, 52
charity, 13, 43–5, 89–90, 93, 105, 108,
    121, 201
    nuns, 44, 108, 121
Charles I of Sicily, 13
Charles the Good, 207
Chartres, 203, 240, 250
Châteliers, Our Lady of, 203
Châtillon-Sur-Seine, 174
Chełmno, 104
Cheney, Christopher, 146
Chorin//Mariensee, 38–9, 159
Christ, 5, 34, 81, 83, 104, 135, 137,
    153, 178, 187, 191, 196–8,

201–5, 225, 229, 238, 245,
    see also imitation of Christ
    adoration of, 104, 188
    and friendship, 201
    as spouse, 44, 218, 224, 227–8,
        see also Song of Songs
    human life of, 202, 223–4
    passion of, 104, 135, 192, 194–7,
        224, 251
    school of, 218–19
    typology, 193
chronicles, 16, 29, 71, 73, 80, 145,
    157, 207, 251
Church, the, 33–4, 65, 67, 76, 87, 115,
    173–4, 177–8, 181, 183, 186, 189,
    198, 241–2, *see also* ecclesiology
    as mystical body of Christ, 225
churches, 81, 112–13, 202, 206,
    see also architecture, church
Cicero, 145, 229
Circumcision, 250
Cîteaux, 234, 281
    900th anniversary, 153
    after the dissolution, 57
    and Clairvaux, 30–2, 40, 43
    and *Exordium Parvum*, 28
    and the General Chapter, 40, 69, 73,
        88, 90, 94
    books, 146
    as centre of the Order, 40, 44, 52,
        54, 57–8, 69–70, 72–3, 91, 102,
        240, 264, *see also* Cîteaux and
        the General Chapter
    church, 153–4, 157
    crisis, 41, 54, 233, 243
    eighteenth century, 58
    expansion, 233–4, 242
    female filiation, 32, 42, 105
    fifteenth century, 43, 146–7
    filiation, 29–30, 69, 88, 91, 94, 113,
        133, 175
    foundation, 5–6, 8, 25–9, 31, 35–6,
        80, 87, 89–90, 125–6, 140, 174,
        233, 235–7, 258
    fourteenth century, 41
    land, 51, 119
    library, 147
    manuscripts, 30–1, 125–7
    nineteenth century, 58–9
    plan, 151
    recruitment, 30, 113, 174–5, 204,
        233–4, 237, 240–2
    seventeenth century, 51, 53–4

Cîteaux (*cont.*)
  sixteenth century, 44, 52
  twentieth century, 59
  under Alberic of Cîteaux, 92, 199
  under Armand Jean du Plessis de
    Richelieu, 54
  under Claude Vaussin, 54
  under Edmond de la Croix, 53
  under Jean de Cirey, 43
  under Raynard de Bar, 89
  under Stephen Harding, 16, 30–1,
    199, 235–6, 239, 259–60
  viticulture, 119
cities, Cistercians in, 39, 41, 96–7,
    107–8, 120, 143, 208, 243
Clairvaux, 113, 118, 175, 179
  after the dissolution, 57
  and Cîteaux, 30–2, 40, 43
  and *Exordium Cistercii*, 28
  as Jerusalem, 175
  as proto-abbey, 69, 88, 91
  church, 154, 157
  crisis, 54
  female filiation, 105, 108
  fifteenth century, 43, 147
  filiation, 30–1, 39, 53, 65, 69, 90,
    113, 156–7, 175, 207–8
  foundation, 30–1, 174–5, 186
  land, 118
  library, 147
  manuscripts, 116, 130
  plan, 151
  recruitment, 30, 113, 130, 175,
    239–40
  seventeenth century, 54
  sixteenth century, 41, 108
  thirteenth century, 39
  under Bernard of Clairvaux, 30–1,
    129, 156–7, 173, 186, 202–5,
    239–40
  under Denis Largentier, 53
  under Geoffrey of Auxerre, 34, 205
  under Pierre de Virey, 43
  under Stephen of Lexington, 38–9,
    208
Clanchy, Michael, 176
Clement IV, 40, 52
cloister, 7, 41, 44, 84–5, 135, 142,
    161–3, 246, 250
clothing, 51, 83, 91, 93, 116, 127, 207
Cluny, 12–14, 67, 87, 153, 203, 206, 237
  architecture, 156–7
  criticism of, 127–8, 156, 186–7, 258

organisation, 69, 177, 234–5
response to, 89–90, 233–6, 238,
    see also Idung of Prüfening,
    Dialogus duorum monachorum
Cognosce teipsum ('Know yourself'),
    226
College of St Bernard, 39, 41, 54,
    96–7, 143, 208, 243
Collège Saint Bernard, see College of
    St Bernard
Collegium Sancti Bernardi,
    see College of St Bernard
Colligatio Galilaeensis, 42
Cologne, 38, 44
commendatory abbot, 41, 43–4, 51,
    53, 55, 76, 165
Common Observance, 53–5, 58–60,
    62, 265
confession, 105, 180, 194
congregations, 42–5, 52–3, 57–60, 87,
    159
  General Chapter on, 44, 204
  novices, 44
Congregation of Saint Bernard of
    Alcobaça, 57
Conrad III, 203
Conrad of Eberbach, 38, 193, 211, 242
  Exordium Magnum Cisterciense,
    38, 89, 102, 193, 211
Conrad of Mazovia, 68
Constance, Council of, 146
Constantinople, 38, 106
contemplation, 6, 31, 36, 154, 187,
    192, 229–31, 249
Coppack, Glyn, 163
Counter-Reformation, 109, 166
craftsmen, 160
Croix, Edmond de la, 53
crucifixes, 129, 265
crusader states, the, 65
crusades, 31, 34, 36, 39–40, 113, 205,
    245
  Albigensian, 34, 251
  Baltic, 67–8
  Second, 176–7, 182, 186, 205
  Third, 248–9
  Fourth, 251
Curtius, E.R., 4
Cyprus, 67, 70

Dante, *Paradiso*, 43
d'Aungerville,Richard, 144
David, 193

David I, 201
decline, 41, 44, 50–2, 56–7, 60, 75, 85,
  96–7, 121, 144, 146, 240, 243
  scholarship on, 25–6, 75, 97
Dedication, 96, 224, 246
Deer, 73
definitors, 40, 54
Delisle, Léopold, 209
Denmark, 65
Depaquy, Jean, 149
De regularibus et monialibus, 52
Desert Fathers, 5–6, 56
Deuteronomy, 5, 89
Devotio Moderna, 42, 108
dialectics, 204, 219, 236–7, 240
diffinitorium, 40
Dijon, 95, 174, 263–4
Dimier, Anselme, 152
dissolution, 56–7, 109
distinctiones, 40, 144
diversity, 2–16, 32–3, 35, 52, 59, 126,
  153–5, 160, 167
Doberan, 15, 38–9, 67, 147, 158
Dominicans, 41, 94, 96, 143, 233, 243,
  263, *see also* mendicants
donations, 10–17, 30–1, 34, 38, 40,
  75–6, 113, 115–16, 119, 121,
  141–3, 158–9
  ceremony, 11–12
Dore, 43, 265
dormitory, 7, 29, 53, 82, 143, 161, 164
Drinkwater, Geneva, 144
Duby, Georges, 118, 152
Duissern, 38
Dundrennan, 68, 72
Dünamünde, 68

Easter, 13, 105, 224, 246
Eberbach, 147, 154
Ebrach, 32
Ecclesiastica Officia, 16, 83, 103, 161
ecclesiology, 3, 220, 224–5
Edme de Saulieu, 41
Edmund Rich, 208
education, 38–9, 41, 56–7, 74, 96–7,
  145–6, 203–4, 206, 208–9, 234,
  236–7, 240–2
  distrust of learning, 85, 144, 208
  nuns, 42, 104–5, 209–10
  school of Christ, 218–19
Edward I, 13
Edward III, 43
Egeln, 109

Eleanor of Castile, 116
Elne, 120
Engelhard of Langheim, 33, 106
England, 58–9, 74, 102–3, 105, 107–9,
  126, 143–6, 165, 201–4, 206–7
Enlart, Camille, 151
Epiphany, 245
Ernald of Bonneval, 179
Ernald, abbot of Melrose, 72
Esrum, 14
Esser, Karl-Heinz, 152
Estonia, 67
Eugenius III, 28, 187, 224, 241
Everard of Ypres, 242
exegesis, 31, 193, 196–8, 204, 228,
  245, 247–9
exempla, 33, 85, 106, 191, 211, 249
Exodus, 6
Exordium Cistercii, 5–6, 26–8, 89, 92
  scholarship on, 27–8
Exordium Parvum, 6, 16, 27–9, 92
  scholarship on, 27–8
experience, 31, 36, 188, 192, 200, 210,
  219–21, 228–30

familiares, 13–14
fast, 16, *see also* abstinence from meat
Félibien des Avaux, André, 8–10
Fergus, lord of Galloway, 66, 68
Feuillants, 44–5
filiation, 29–30, 32–3, 39, 50, 69–73,
  75, 89–91, 94, 102, 113, 125
Flanders, 42, 107, 207
Flaxley, 140, 144, 265
Flines, 159
Florence, 43
Foigny, 248
Fontenay, 118, 147, 151, 154–5, 157,
  167n. 1
Fontfroide, 151
food, 16–17, 45, 51, 55, 91, 112, 127,
  207
Forde, 205–6
forestry, 117, 121, 164
forma Ordinis, 153–7, 159–60, 166–7
Fossanova, 39, 205
foundation documents, 1–6, 88–91,
  129
  scholarship on, 1–5, 25–8, 66, 90
foundation, 1–6, 14–16, 25–36, 38,
  42–3, 45, 58, 60, 65–8, 70–4, 80–1,
  87–8, 126, 157, 165, 175, 182,
  204, 206, 208–9

foundation (*cont.*)
  Baltic region, 67–8
  British Isles, the, 65
  Central-Eastern Europe, 65
  Greece, 66–7
  Middle East, 66–7
  nuns, 38, 41–2, 100–5, 114–17, 119,
    121, 135, 209
  Scandinavia, 65
  scholarship on, 1–5, 26–8, 31,
    88–90, 112, 233–4
Fountains, iv, 16, 74, 147, 153–4,
    157–9, 162–3, 167n. 1, 208
France, 15, 34, 40, 42–3, 50–1, 54,
    57–8, 65, 105, 107–8, 116, 138n.
    15, 144, 147, 152, 165, 176–7,
    207, 234, 250–1, 263
Franciscans, 94, 96, 143, 145, 188,
    233, 243, *see also* mendicants
Franquevaux, 41
Frederick Barbarossa, 34
Frederick II, 208
French Revolution, the, 53, 55, 57, 97,
    122n. 7, 125, 133, 148, 165
Fribourg, 57
friendship, 31, 95, 177, 201–2, 229,
    235, 239
Frisia, 70
Froidmont, 207
Fulgens sicut stella, 41, 52, 97, 108
Furness, 160, 204

Galicia, 70
gate house, 83, 161, 163
Gaudry, Bernard of Clairvaux's uncle,
    181
gender studies, 165, 251
General Chapter, 7–8, 33, 45, 50–3,
    61, 65, 73, 75–6, 87–98, 113, 203,
    206
  attendance, 40–1, 52, 69–70, 90–1,
    94
  early General Chapters, 27, 31, 33,
    69, 88–9
  eighteenth century, 53–5
  for nuns, 32, 42, 60, 102
  format, 40, 69–70, 72, 90, 94–5
  fourteenth century, 40–1, 52, 73–4,
    76
  nineteenth century, 58
  on art, 91–2, 96, 125, 129–30, 133
  on architecture, 153
  on books, 126, 140, 146–8, 263

  on clothing, 91
  on congregations, 43, 52–3
  on education, 39, 143–4, 146
  on filiation, 90, 93–4
  on food, 91
  on foundation of monasteries, 93
  on hospitality, 16
  on intercession, 13
  on lapses, 50–3, 85, 96, 148
  on lay brothers, 35, 85, 91, 96, 107
  on lay burials, 14–15, 158–9
  on libraries, 146–7
  on liturgy, 126, 263–5
  on manual labour, 91
  on novices, 84
  on nuns, 41–2, 100–3, 105–8, 210
  on polyphony, 265
  on private chambers, 147–8
  on the Strict and the Common
    Observance, 53–5, 58–9
  on uniformity, 33, 35, 52–3, 59–60,
    93–4, 125, 151, 160, 263–5
  on verse, 207
  on visitation, 71, 74, 90, 93–4, 106,
    108, 208
  on withdrawal, 3, 91
  on women, 91, *see also* General
    Chapter, on nuns
  purpose, 90
  scholarship on, 35, 69, 90, 92, 96,
    100
  seventeenth century, 50, 52–4, 265
  statutes, 1–2, 27–8, 35, 40, 69–71,
    87, 90, 92, 94, 96
Genoa, 178
Geoffrey of Auxerre, 34, 173, 178–9,
    182–3, 204–5, *see also* Clairvaux,
    under Geoffrey of Auxerre
  Vita Prima, 179
Geoffrey, bishop of Chartres, 179,
    181
Georges, Dominique, 7–10
Gerald of Wales, 34
Gerard, Bernard of Clairvaux's
    brother, 82–3, 180–1, 192–3, 195
Gerhoh of Reichersberg, 179, 220
Germany, 15, 65, 68, 75, 107, 109,
    135, 144, 147, 165, 177, 263
Gertrud of Hackeborn, 42
Gertrud of Helfta, 44–5, 104, 210
  Exercitia spiritualia, 44, 210
  Herald of God's Loving-Kindness,
    104, 210

Gertrud the Great, *see* Gertrud of
    Helfta
Gervase of Canterbury, 205
Gethsemani, 59, 211
Gilbert Foliot, 173, 183
Gilbert of Hoyland, 204, 206
    *Sermones super Cantica
    canticorum*, 204, 206
    sermons for nuns, 204
Gilbert of Poitiers, 203, 205
Gilbert Scagrave, 146
Gilbert, abbot of Glenluce, 72
Gilchrist, Roberta, 165
Gilson, Étienne, 3
glass, *see* windows
Godric, Saint, 140
Good Friday, 13
Goswin of Villers, 209
grammar, 145, 236
Grandselve, 120
granges, 2, 35, 82, 84–5, 112–15,
    117–20, 151–2, 163–4
    and lay brothers, 84–5, 91, 119
Greece, 66–7, 70
Gregory IX, 208
Gregory the Great, 126–7, 140–27n. 1,
    200, 228, 230, 249, 259
    Moralia in Job, 126–7
Gregory XVI, 59
grisaille, see windows
Guerric of Igny, 32, 202–3, 240–1,
    247–9
    Christology, 202–3
    libellus sermonum, 248
    sermons, 202, 248–9
guest house, 16–17, 83, 161, 163
Gui, Bernard of Clairvaux's brother,
    181
Guibert of Nogent, 234
Guillaume de Digulleville, 43, 210
    Pélerinage de la vie humaine, 43
Guise, Isabelle d'Orléans, Mme de, 9
Guy de Beauchamp, 141
Guy of Vaux-de-Cernay, 251

Hadersleben, 42
Hailes, 17, 159
Hainaut, 107
Hamburger, Jeffrey, 165
Haskin, Charles Homer, 188
Hautecombe, 205
Heiligengrabe, 147
Heiligenkreuz, 57, 135, 158–9

Heilig-Kreuz, 105
Heilsbronn, 74
Heisterbach, 155
Helfta, 42, 104, 210
Hélinand of Froidmont, 207–8,
    246–7
    sermons, 246–7, 249–51
Henry II, 34, 203, 250
Henry of Ghent, 145
Henry the Bearded, 15
Henry the Lion, 67
Herbert of Clairvaux, 211
heretics, 31, 36, 181, 188, 243, 251
Herkenrode, 166
Herman of Stratford, 17
Herman of Tournai, 101–2, 107
hermits, 5–6, 43, 175, 199, 206, 238
hierarchy
    between abbeys, 71–2, 94, 241
Hildegard of Bingen, 220
Hill, Bennett D., 2
Himmerod, 146
Hohenstaufen, the, 40
Holdsworth, Christopher, 36n. 1,
    179–80, 248, 253n. 17
Hollandia, 204
Holme Cultram, 72, 147
Holy Innocents, feast of, 260
Holy Land, the, 66, 106, 206–7
Holy Saturday, 13
Holy Spirit, the, 222–3, 228, 259
Holy Week, 224
Honorius II, 176
Hope, William St John, 152, 164
hospitality, 9, 14, 35, 82–3, 94
    accomodation, 9, 16–17, 161
    food, 16–17
    guest master, 83
    ritual, 16
Huerta, 155
Hugh of Die, 27
Hugh of Melrose, 73
Hugh of Saint Victor, 220–1, 225
humility, 16, 31, 42, 56, 84, 187, 191,
    221, 226
Hungary, 56–7, 65, 70
Huygens, R.B.C., 206
Hvide family, 15, 65
hydraulic systems, 118–19, 152, 163

Iberia, 57, 65, 106
Ida of Gorseleeuw, 44, 104
Ida of Nivelles, 106, 210

ideals, 1, 3, 11, 25–6, 32–6, 52, 81, 96, 118, 136, 238
ideals and reality, 1, 3, 26
Idung of Prüfening, 101, 206
  Dialogus duorum monachorum, 206
Igny, 202, 205, 213n. 25
illumination, 30–1, 126–7, 129–30
image of God, 2, 219, 225–6
imitation of Christ, 26, 31, 191, 202
In suprema, 54–5
incarnation, 31, 195, 228
infirmary, 151, 161, 163–4
Innocent II, 33–4, 115, 176–8, 186
Innocent III, 39, 67–8, 206, 245, 251
Instituta Generalis Capituli, 71, 92–3, 106, 140, *see also* General Chapter, statutes
intercession, 13–14, 17, 68, 106, 121, 141, 143, 158–9, 235
Ireland, 58–9, 65, 69–70, 74, 106, 208
Islamic culture 133
Isaac of Stella, 32, 203–4, 218–29, 240–1, 246, 250
  Epistola de anima, 203, 226
  sermons, 203, 221–2, 224–6, 229, 246, 250
Italy, 39, 44, 51, 74, 76, 106, 108, 147, 151, 165, 177

Jacques de Pontaillier, 147
Jacques de Thérines, 45
Jacques de Vitry, 38, 102, 106
Jacques Fournier, 97, *see also* Benedict XII
James I, 43
James I of Aragon, 13
Janauschek, Leopold, 100
Jansenism, 54
Japan, 60
Jean de Cirey, 43, 45
Jean de la Barrière, 44–5
Jerome, 126
Jerusalem, 44, 66, 175, 249
Joachim of Fiore, 207
John Cassian, 56, 126
John Climacus, 56
John, King, 206–7, 250
John of Forde, 146, 206–7, 247–8, 250
  sermons, 248, 250
  Super ... cantici canticorum sermones cxx, 206
John of Hallis, 43

John of Salisbury, 179, 237
John the Baptist, Feast of, 246
John the Evangelist, feast of, 260
Josbert de la Ferté, 181
Joseph II, 56
Jubin, 67
Jully, 32

Kaisheim, 147
Kalamazoo, International Congress on Medieval Studies, 152
Kamp, 147
Kienzle, Beverly M., 248
Kinder, Terryl N., 153
King John, 206–7, 250
Kirchheim, 75
kitchen, 16, 142, 161, 163
Knights of Calatrava, the, 250
knowledge of God, 227–30
Knowles, David, 2, 142
Kołbacz, 68, 73, 155
Korea, 60

L'Arrivour, 204
La Bussière, 104, 259
La Celle, 67
La Charmoye, 53
La Ferté, 27, 66, 69, 88, 91, 126, 154, 199
  church, 154
La Ramée, 42, 104, 106, 209
La Rochefoucauld, François, Cardinal de, 53–4
La Trappe, 7–10, 55–9
landscape history, 163
Langres, 178
language, 73–5
  English, 140
  Flemish, 210
  French, 44, 74, 106, 140–1, 207, 246
  German, 44, 75, 104
  Italian, 44
  Latin, 56, 74–5, 85, 104, 140, 210, 236, 246
  preaching, 246
  Spanish, 44
  vernacular, 44, 73–5, 207, 215n. 57, 246
Largentier, Denis, 53
Las Huelgas, 42, 102, 109, 116, 159
Lateran Council, Fourth, 95
Latvia, 67
Lausanne, 203

lay brothers, 9, 34–5, 55, 84–6, 91–2, 94, 107, 112–13, 116, 175, 201, 209, 235, 245–6
  agriculture, 91, 113, 116, 119–20
  architecture, 157, 160–1, 163–4
  at nunneries, 107, 119–20
  chapter, 245–6
  liturgy, 112, 120, 245–6
  recruitment, 84, 91, 116, 119–20, 175, 201, 209
  tensions, 34–5, 85, 120
lay people, 10–17, 32, 41, 44, 51, 65–6, 68, 75, 107, 135, 158–9, *see also* burials, commendatory abbot, hospitality
lay sisters, 107, 112, 116, 119–20
  tensions, 120
Le Clos Vougeot, 119
Le Lys, 117, 119, 121
Leclercq, Jean, 3, 35, 96, 179–80, 219, 248, 250
lectio continua, 126
lectio divina, 56, 81, 85, 126, 141, 149
Leeds, International Medieval Congress, 152
Lefèvre, Jean, 27
legislation. , *see* General Chapter
Lehnin, 146
Lekai, Louis J., 1
Łekno, 68, 74
Leland John, 145
Lent, 140
Leo XIII, 59
Leon, 42, 70
Leonius, abbot of Dundrennan and Rievaulx, 72
lepers, 108
Les Écharlis, 148–9
Lestrange, Augustin de, 57–9
letters, 3, 9, 28, 31, 33, 89, 106, 136, 176, 187, 223–5, 235, 246–8, 251, 261
Liancourt, Jeanne de Schomberg, Duchesse de, 9
Libelli diffinitionum, 70
Libellus antiquarum definitionum, 70
Libellus novellarum definitionum, 70
Liber usuum, 140, 264
liberal arts, 208
libraries, 57, 75–6, 106, 140–9, 250–1
  armarium, 141
  book collections, 140–2, 144–6, 148–9

buildings, 146–7, 149
donations, 141–2
nuns, 106
Lincoln, 175
Lithuania, 57
liturgy, 3, 14, 80, 101, 113, 155, 209, 219, 223, 235, 238, 249, 258–65
  Abbot Guido, 262
  Ambrosian hymnal, 259, 261
  and architecture, 126, 154, 158, 160–1, 165
  Benedictines, 223, 262–3
  books, 12, 26, 75, 104, 109, 126, 140–1, 148, 161, 258, 263–5, *see also Ecclesiastica Officia*
  breviary, 259
  calendar, 264
  chant, 260, 263
  Cîteaux, 259–61
  commemoration, 12–15, 33, 68, 264
  Common Obrservance, 265
  Compline, 80, 246, 261
  Eterne rerum conditor, 261
  feasts, 13, 245–6, 265, *see also individual feasts*
  Gelasian sacramentary, 260
  Gregorian sacramentary, 260
  Lauds, 80, 261
  lay brothers, 120, 245–6
  legislation, 52, 126, 263–5
  liturgical year, 13, 187, 197, 202–3, 223, 245–6, 248–9, 260, 265, *see also individual feasts*
  litanies, 259
  manuscripts, 103–4, 125–6, 260, 263–4
  mass, 13–14, 69, 103, 105, 107, 120–1, 259–60, 262, 265
  mass for the dead, 16, 108, 253n. 17
  Matins, 246
  Metz, 259–61
  modal system, 263
  Night Office, 80
  None, 80, 261
  notation, 263
  Novum Psalterium B. Virginis Mariae, 148
  nuns, 103–4, 107, 121, 210
  Office, the, 45, 80, 84–5, 96, 189, 245–6
  opus Dei, 80, 85, 140
  Peter Abelard, 258
  polyphony, 265

liturgy (*cont.*)
  Prime, 80, 245, 261
  processions, 245, 265
  punctuation, 263
  Quem vidistis pastores, 261
  reform under Bernard of Clairvaux,
    28, 104, 260–5
  reform under Claude Vaussin, 265
  reform under Stephen Harding, 200,
    258–64
  Roman rite, 265
  Rule of Benedict, 80, 258–61, 263
  saints' feasts, 259, 264
  Salve Regina, 261
  Sanctoral, 260
  scholarship on, 152, 165, 209, 265
  seventeenth century, 56, 265
  Sext, 80, 261
  Strict Observance, 265
  Temporal, 260
  Terce, 80, 261
  transformations, 264–5
  tropes, 259
  Vespers, 80, 261
  vessels, 12, 91, 129, 207, 258, 264–5
  vestments, 12, 125, 129, 203, 258,
    264
  Vigils, 261
Livonia, 67–8, 70
Loccum, 68, 147
Lombardy, 57
London, 74, 280
Longpont, 158
Louis IX, 38, 114, 117, 121
Louis the Pious, 87
Louis VI, 130, 177
Louis VIII, 13
Louis XIV, 8–9
Love
  extra-mural, 227, 237
  of God, 3, 187, 194–5, 197, 202,
    218, 221–4, 226–31
  within the Order, 31, 59, 76, 81,
    89–90, 93, 95, 235, 238–9, 241,
    259, *see also Carta Caritatis*
Low Countries, the, 103, 107
Lubac, Henri de, 188–9, 197–8
Lucan, 145
Lund, 95
Lunéville, Treaty of, 58
Lyons, 259
Lysa, 74
Løgum, 154

Maagdendaal, 42, 209
Madrid, 44
Magerau, 157, 166
Maillé, Aliette Marquise de, 152
Malachy of Armagh, 179, 183, 264
Malogranatum, 44
Manasses II of Orléans, 115
Manerbio, 118
manual labour, 31, 34–5, 45, 53, 55,
  81, 84, 91, 96, 102, 107–8, 112,
  115, 117, 119, 235, 238, 250, 258,
  see also agriculture
manuscripts, 3, 30–1, 57, 75, 103–7,
  125–7, 129–30, 133, 135, 137,
  142–3, 149, 209, 260
  nuns, 107
Marienfeld, 147
Mariensee/Chorin, 38–9, 159
Martha and Mary, 192
Marti, Suzan, 165
Martial, 145
Martin V, 43
Martin Vargas, 42–3
martyr, 69, 135, 208, 250
mass, 13–14, 69, 103, 105, 107, 119–
  21, 158, 203, 259–60, 262, 265
mass for the dead, 2–16, 121
Matthew, abbot of Melrose, 71
Matthew, chancellor of the king of
  Sicily, 13
Maubuisson, 114, 119, 159
Maulbronn, 160, 167n. 1
Mazan, 116
McCrank, Lawrence, 147
McGinn, Bernard, 202–4
Meaux, 132, 144–5
Mechtild of Hackeborn, 104
  Book of Special Grace, 104
Mecklenburg, 15, 67
Medingen, 105
Mellifont, 65
Melrose, 15–16, 70–3, 160
mendicants, 38, 159, 208, 243
Merton, Thomas, 60, 211
metaphysics, 204
Metz, 39, 178, 259–61
  liturgy, 259–61
Michael, Saint, 135
Middle East, 66–7
Milan, 177–8, 259
militia Christi, 5–6, 92
mills, 2, 112, 114, 116–19, 163–4
mission, 66–8, 74, 251

Mistassini, 59
mixt, 94
Mogiła, 74
Mohrmann, Christine, 3
Molesme, 25–9, 32, 80, 87, 92–3, 233,
    239, 258, 260
monastic offices
    abbess, 106–7, *see also* abbess
    abbot, 29, 72, 81–2, 107, 176, 191–2,
        195, 219, *see also* abbot
    cantor, 71–2, 104
    career, 72–3, 82, 203, 205, 240
    cellarer, 82–3
    deacon, 264
    chaplain, 107, 210
    gate keeper, 83
    guest master, 83
    novice master/mistress, 57, 72,
        83–4, 201, 210
    precentor/precentrix, 143
    prior/prioress, 26, 28, 42, 72, 82, 87,
        107, 114–15
    sacristan, 72–3
    secretary, 26, 179, 205, 247
    subdeacon, 264
monastic sites, 3–5, 30–1, 91, 112–13,
    163
Monte Cassino, 13
Montiéramey, 262
Montpellier, 39
Montreuil, 102, 107
Morimond, 66, 69, 91, 154, 175, 240
    church, 154
    filiation, 66
Morin, 113
Moses, 5
Mount Melleray, 59
Mount Saint Bernard, 59
music, *see* liturgy
Muslims, 36
mysticism, 36, 42, 44, 187, 210, 220,
    222, 225–31, 241–2

Naples, 57
Nativity, 196–8, 224, 245–6
Navarre, 70
Nazareth, 42, 209
Neath, 265
necrologies, 12–13
necropolis, 15, 38, 68, 159
New Melleray, 59
Newenham, 106
Newman, Martha G., 5

Newminster, 208
Niedermünster, 206
Nonenque, 116
Norbert of Magdeburg, 180
Norbert of Xanten, 177
Normandy, 130, 204
North America, 149, *see also* United
    States, the
Norway, 65, 70
novices, 53–4, 83–4, 161, 175, 208,
    237, 242
cella novitiorum, 83
nunneries, 15, 25, 27, 30, 32–4, 38,
    41–2, 75, 91, 114–21, 135–6, 152,
    159, 165–6, 209
nuns, vii–1, 32–3, 41, 44–5, 54, 58, 60,
    93, 96, 100–9, 114–21, 125, 135,
    159, 206, 209, 211
    agriculture, 107–8, 115
    and monks, 104, 106
    architecture, 124n. 51, 135, 152,
        159, 165–6
    art, 104–5, 125, 135–6
    charity, 44, 108, 121
    dissolution, 109
    education, 42, 104–5, 209–10
    fifteenth century, 108, 135–6
    filiation, 27, 32–3, 38, 102
    foundations, 38, 41–2, 100–5,
        114–17, 119, 121, 135, 209
    fourteenth century, 108, 135–6
    general chapters, 32, 42, 54, 102
    in cities, 102, 108, 120
    intercession, 15, 120, 141, 143, 159
    lay brothers and lay sisters, 107,
        120
    legislation, 41–2, 54, 100, 105–6,
        108, 135–6, 210
    libraries, 106, 109
    liturgy, 103–4, 210
    manual labour, 34, 107–8, 115–17
    manuscripts, 107
    nineteenth century, 58–9
    printed works, 44
    recruitment, 32, 54, 119–20, 209–10
    scholarship on, 30, 100–1, 152,
        165–6
    sermons for, 204
    seventeenth century, 54
    sixteenth century, 108–9, 135–6
    sources, 103, 107, 211
    spirituality, 44, 104–5, 135, 209–10
    supervision of, 6, 33, 100, 105–6, 204

nuns (*cont.*)
  thirteenth century, 38, 42, 100, 114,
    135–6
  twelfth century, 32–3, 101, 118, 120
  twentieth century, 60
  visitation, 33, 41, 100, 105–6, 108
  wealth, 15, 34, 75, 105, 107–8,
    114–15, 119–21, 135–6
  writers, 209–10
Nuremberg, 74

Obazine, 113, 133–4
obedience, 29, 56, 81, 83–4, 93, 105,
  176, 235–6
oblate, 84, 199, 210, 235
Obodrites, 67
Odo of Morimond, 248
Oka, 59
Office, the, 45, 84–5, 189, 245–6,
  258–61
Orderic Vitalis, 29, 80
organisation, 25, 29, 31–2, 69–72, 75,
  88–9
Origen, 198
Osek, 68
Othe, 117
Otto of Freising, 240–1
Ourscamp, 39, 151, 154, 157, 208
Ovid, 145
Oxford, 39, 143, 208

Paden, William D., 215n. 57
Palazzo Vecchio, 43
Palm Sunday, 246, 250, 265
papacy, the 28, 32, 39–41, 43, 45,
  53–4, 58, 67, 73, 76, 87–8, 102–3,
  108, 115, 159, 187, 201, 208
  the schism, 33–4, 73, 176–7, 179, 186
Papal States, 57–8
Paraclete, the, 203, 240
paradise, 7, 10, 141, 251
Paris, 8, 39, 41, 44, 96–7, 119–20, 143,
  176, 179, 204, 208, 212n. 8, 240,
  250, 252n. 10, 278
Parma, 57
Parvus fons, 40–1, 52
pastoralism, 107–8, 114, 116–19, 164
patristic fathers, 206, 223
  as authority, 5, 188, 198, 219, 236,
    249–50
  lectio divina, 81, 246
  manuscripts, 126–7, 144
  references, 2–3, 5, 209, 229

patrons, *see* benefactors
Paul I, Tsar, 58
Peder of Roskilde, 15
Pelplin, 13
penitence, 9–10, 180, 238
Pentecost, 13, 246, 249
perambulation, 11
Perseigne, 55, 207, 295
Peter Abelard, 204, 207, 250
  and Bernard of Clairvaux, 176,
    186–8, 201, 203, 220–1, 223, 225,
    239–40, 258, 261
  and William of Saint Thierry,
    200–1, 220–1
  liturgy, 258, 261
Peter and Paul, Feast of, 246
Peter de Bruys, 181
Peter Lombard, 141, 221
  Sentences, 145
Peter of Ivrea, 66
Peter of Jully, 32, 239
Peter of Tarentaise, 264
Peter the Chanter, 242
Peter the Venerable, 177
Petit, Jean, 55
Philip Augustus, 207
Philip III, 13
Philip of Harvengt, 80
Philippines, the, 60
Picard, André, 179–80
Piedmont, 57
Pierre de Virey, 43
Pietism, 189
Pius IX, 59
Pius VII, 58
plague, 41, 108, 146
Poblet, 159, 167n. 1
Poitiers, 203
Poitou, 130
Poland, 56–7, 65, 74–5, 104, 152
Pomerania, 73
ponds, 119, 163
Pont-aux-Dames, 118
  Pontigny, 34, 69, 88, 91, 117, 133–5,
    149, 151, 154, 157, 167n. 1, 199,
    207–8
  church, 133
poor, the, 8, 13, 43–4, 84
Port-Royal, 9, 54, 115, 119
Portugal, 44, 57, 70, 165
poverty, 26, 31, 34, 42, 56, 85, 108, 153,
  174, 186, 196, 233, 238, 242–3
Prairies, 59

prayer, 29, 45, 69, 173, 180, 219,
229–30, 238, 246
and the Office, 103
books, 104–5
intercessory, 11–14, 17, 30, 106,
121, 141, 143, 155–9, 235
ora et labora, 80, 84, 258
preaching, 31, 177, 186, 224, 240, 243,
251
Aelred of Rievaulx, 201, 247
against Cathars, 34, 205
against heretics, 31, 243, 250–1
Bernard of Clairvaux, 31, 173,
175–7, 180–1, 186, 204–5, 239–40,
246–7, 251
crusades, 31, 176–7, 186, 205, 245,
251
language, 246
lay brothers, 245–6
liturgy, 245–6, 249–50, 265,
see also individual feasts
mission, 251
oral vs. written form, 248, 250
scholarship on, 248, 250
terminology, 246–7
universities, 249
Premonstratensians, 13, 121, 240
Pribislav, 38, 67
printing, 44, 56, 147–8, 264
processions, 103, 105, 249–50, 259,
265
proto-abbeys, *see also* Clairvaux, La
Ferté, Morimond and Pontigny,
57, 69–71, 73, 75, 91
proto-abbots, 40, 52, 54, 69, 91
Provence, 67
Prussia, 67–8, 251
Psalter, the, 140–1, 148, 239, 258,
261–4, *see also* liturgy, books
manuscripts, 126
Pseudo-Dionysios, 204, 220, 241
punishment, 15, 29
Purification, 246

Quarr, 208

Rancé, Armand-Jean de, 7–10, 55–6,
58–9
Raynard de Bar, 28, 89
recruitment
of lay brothers and lay sisters,
84, 91, 116, 119–20, 175, 201,
209

of monks, 27, 30, 32, 38–242
of nuns, 32, 54, 119, 209–10
refectory, 7, 9, 53, 133, 161, 163, 246,
248
reform, *see also* liturgy, reform
and foundation, 26, 28, 36, 80–1,
89, 112–13, 115–16, 153
architecture, 159–60
Council of Trent, 52–3
Cluny, 69
eleventh century, 25, 85, 115
fifteenth century, 52, 108, 146, 165
fourteenth century, 41–2, 108
Fourth Lateran Council, 95
in nunneries, 41
scholarship on, 25–6, 75
seventeenth century, 52–6, 165,
265, *see also* La Trappe
twelfth century, 31–2, 36, 65, 69,
113, 201
under Armand-Jean de Rancé, 7–10,
56
under Benedict XII, 41, 45, 97, 108
under Clement IV, 52
under Denis Largentier, 53
under Edmond de la Croix, 53
under Jean de Cirey, 43
under Jean de la Barrière, 44
under Martin Vargas, 42–3
under Stephen of Lexington, 74, 208
Reformation, 15, 44, 51, 108–9, 165
Reformed Congregation of Saint
Bernard, 53
Reichersberg, 206
Reigny, 11
Reims, 178
Synod of, 205
relics, 14, 159, 262
Resurrection, 224
Revesby, 201, 204
Rewley, 143
rhetoric, 3–4, 6, 10, 173, 177, 189,
191, 196, 202, 209, 219, 236
Rhineland, 73–4, 105, 200, 205
Richard I, the Lionhearted, 13, 40,
206–7
Richard of Middleton, 145
Richard of Saint Victor 130
Richelieu, Armand Jean du Plessis de,
54–5
Riddagshausen, 147
Rievaulx, 39, 68, 70–2, 142, 155,
157–8, 163, 201, 204

Rifreddo, 108, 114, 117
ritual, 11–12, 161, 190, 193–4, 225,
    249, 260
Robert Grosseteste, 146
Robert Kilwardby 145
Robert of Molesme, 5–6, 26–7, 29,
    36, 80, 87–8, 140, 186, 199, 233,
    238–9, 258
Roermond, 159
Rogation, 248
romances, 141
rosary devotion, 104
Roscrea, 59
Royaumont, 38, 114, 118, 158–9
Ruffin, Jacques-Christophe, 149
ruminatio, 81, 239
Rupert of Deutz, 220
    De divinis officiis, 200
Russia, 58

saints, 14, 35, 259–60, 264
Salamanca, 39, 44
Salem, 57, 147
Sallust, 145
Salvatio, 66
San Bernardo alla Terme, 58
San Galgano, 39
Santa Croce in Gerusalemme, 58
Santa Maria in Trastevere, 176
Sant, Angelo, 176
Savigny, 38, 105, 113, 204, 208
Scandinavia, 65, 103, 106, 109, 143,
    146, 152, 165, 251
Scarborough, 40
Schimmelpenninck, Mary, 8
scholasticism, 145, 202, 210,
    220, 225, 234, 236–7, 243,
    see also schools, universities
Schöntal, 147
schools, 176, 203–4, 221, 234, 236–7,
    239–43, 249, *see also* universities
Scotland, 43, 65, 69–71, 73, 91, 132,
    201–2
scriptorium, 135, 142, 161
sculptures, 125, 128–9, 135
seal, 12, 43, 125, 136–7
Sedlec, 158–9
Segeberg, 68
Sénanque, 154
Seneca, 145
Sens, Council of, 186
Sept-Fons, 59
sermons, *see also individual authors*

biblical exposition, 245, 247–9
content, 249–51
for nuns, 204
for the liturgical year, 187, 197,
    202–3, 245–6
genres, 199–200, 246–8
structure, 249–50
terminology, 246–7
transmission, 245–8
servants, 14, 161
Settimo, 43
sewers, 163
Sharpe, Edmund, 151
Sharpe, John, 146
Sherborne, 199
Sicily, 70, 177
sign language, 143
Signy, 147, 200
silence, 9, 55, 102, 181, 222
Silvanès, 115
Silvanus, abbot of Dundrennan and
    Rievaulx, 72
Simon of Waverley, 106
Sixtus IV, 51
Slade, William, 145
solitude, *see wilderness*
Song of Songs, 44, 204, 203–6, 241,
    245, 250, *see also works by
    individual authors*
Sorø, 15, 65
South America, 60, 149
Spain, 44, 57–8, 108–9, 165, 245
Speculum Virginum, 130
Spencer, 59
spirituality, 3, 31, 33, 56, 145, 148,
    186, 203, 218–31, 234, 239, 242,
    245, 247, 249, 251
St Antoine, 114
St Antoine des Champs, 120
St Bénigne, 113
St Gertrude, 42
St Gildas, 240
St Just, 103–4
St Mary Graces, 74
St Sixte, 59
Saint Thierry, 200
St Thomas an der Kyll, 104
St Victor, 240
stabilitas loci, 186
Stanley, 38, 208
statutes, 87–98, *see also* General
    Chapter
Statutes on Unity and Pluralism, 60

Stella, 203
Stephen Harding, 16, 26–32, 36, 42,
    87–9, 92–3, 95, 126, 128, 174,
    199–200, 238–9, 259, 261, 264
  and art, 126–8
  and Bernard of Clairvaux, 30–2, 95,
    199–200, 260–1
  and *Carta Caritatis*, 29, 31, 87, 89,
    93
  and *Exordium Parvum*, 89
  liturgical reform, 200, 258–60
  works, 200
Stephen Langton, 146
Stephen of Lexington, 38–9, 45, 74,
    105, 208, 243
  visitation report , 105
Stephen of Sawley, 208–9
Stephen, Feast of, 260
Stradell, Richard, 43
Strasburg, 264
Stratford Langthorne, 118
Strict Observance, 53–60, 62, 165, 265
*Studies in Cistercian Art and
    Architecture*, 152
Styria, 70
Suger of St Denis, 187
Summa Cartae Caritatis, 28, 89–91
Sutton, John, 146
Sweden, 65, 91
Swineshead, 204
Swiss-German Congregation, the, 58
Switzerland, 57–8, 103, 106, 165

Tarrant, 106
Tart, 32, 42, 102
taxation, 40, 73, 76, 206, 251
Teutonic Knights, 68
Thame, 118
  exposition, Victorines, 141, 230,
    see also St Victor, Hugh of Saint
    Victor, Richard of Saint Victor
Theobald, count of Blois, 179
Thibaut of Beaumont, 114, 118
Thomas à Kempis
  Imitatio Christi, 191
Thomas Aquinas, 145
Thomas Becket, 34, 141, 203, 250
Thomas de Burton, 144
Thomas of Villers, 106
Thomas the Apostle, feast of, 260
Thoronet, 151, 163f
Tienen, 42, 209
tiles, 129–33

Tintern, 157–8, 265
tithes, 1, 32, 34, 81, 112, 117
  exemption from, 32, 34, 114–15
Totnes, 205
Toulouse, 39, 45, 205, 207
  University of, 251
tourism, 151
Tournai, 202
Trappists, 55, 57–61, 88, 165, 179,
    265, *see also* La Trappe, Strict
    Observance
Trent, Council of, 44, 52, 265
Trinity, the, 219, 221–3, 225
Tripoli, 66
Trzebnica, 15
Turner, Victor, 26
Tuscany, 57
typology, 5, 193

UNESCO World Heritage list, 151,
    167n. 1
union with God, 44, 222, 230–1
United States, 58–60, 149
unity, 1–2, 6, 10, 12, 25–9, 33–5, 53–5,
    70, 76, 81, 93–4, 126, 130, 136,
    159, 230, 239, 259, 262, 264,
    see also General Chapter, on
    uniformity
unity and diversity, 2, 34–5, 50,
    59–60, 68, 75, 125–6, 153–5,
    160
universities, 38, 45, 144–6, 249, 251,
    see also schools
Untermann, Matthias, 153
Upper German Congregation, 57
urban cellars, 164
Urban VI, 73

Vacandard, Elphège, 188–9, 192
Valdemar IV Atterdag, 14
Valdemar the Great, 67
Vallombrosa, 26
Valmagne, 116
Val-Richer, 7
Valsainte, 57–9
Vatican Council, Second, 59
Vaucelles, 149, 157
Vaudy, 208
Vauluissant, 117
Vaussin, Claude, 54, 265
Vaux-de-Cernay, 54
Venice, 44, 67
Verbaal, Wim, 253n. 23

Vézelay, 251
Victor of Arcis-sur-Aube, Saint, 262
Victorines, 141, 230, *see also* St
    Victor, Hugh of Saint Victor,
    Richard of Saint Victor
Vienna, 74
Vietnam, 60
Villard de Honnecourt, 156
Villers, 106, 155–7
Viollet-le-Duc, Eugène 151
Virgin Mary, 13, 135–7, 148, 188,
    194–6, 203, 208, 224, 259
  dedication to, 93
  liturgy, 13, 259
  representation, 135–6
Visigothic culture, 133
visitation, 7–9, 17, 27, 29, 31, 33, 41,
    44–5, 49, 50, 52, 54–5, 59, 69–71,
    74, 81, 88, 90–1, 93–4, 96, 105,
    108, 208
  legislation, 33, 41, 71, 100
  provincial, 74
  nuns, 33, 41, 100, 105–6, 108
  reports, 7–8, 55, 71, 105
  transfer of information via, 71, 73
Vita Prima, 33, 88, 174–83, 205,
    see also Ernald of Bonneval,
    Geoffrey of Auxerre, William of
    Saint Thierry
vitae, 106, 211
viticulture, 114, 116–17, 119
Voisins, 115
Vulgata, 259

Waddell, Chrysogonus, 4, 28, 92, 245
Wągrowiec, 74–5
Waldsassen, 147
Wales, 205, 251
Walter Daniel, 83, 201, 247
  Life of Aelred, 201
Walter Espec, 68, 72, 201
Walter Map, 4, 34
Warcisław Świętobrzyc, 66
Weber, Max, 26
Wechterswinkel, 32, 106
Wenceslas II, 38
Westmalle, 59, 260, 265
Westphalia, Peace of, 56
Wienhausen, 105, 107, 135–6, 166
wilderness, 3–10, 17, 28, 89, 211
William de Courcy, 72
William de Hinet, 173

William Gainsborough 145
William of Champeaux, 88, 173, 239,
    247
William of Conches, 201
William of Malmesbury, 29, 80, 199
William of Rievaulx, 247
William of Saint Thierry, 3, 32,
    88, 127, 178, 180, 200–1, 205,
    218–31, 240–1, 247
  Aenigma fidei, 201, 221–3, 226
  and Peter Abelard, 200–1, 220–1
  Christology, 223–4
  De contemplando deo, 200, 222
  De natura corporis et animae, 201,
    226
  De natura et dignitate amoris, 200
  De sacramento altaris, 200, 225
  Epistola ad fratres de Monte Dei,
    201, 220, 222–3, 227, 231
  *Expositio super Cantica
    canticorum*, 201, 222–3, 228–31
  Meditativae orationes, 200, 224,
    230
  on contemplation, 230–1
  on love, 179, 224, 227–30
  on the Trinity, 221–3, 226
  Speculum fidei, 201, 221–3, 228
  Vita Prima, 88, 178–81, 201, 205
wills, 3
Wilmart, André, 200
windows, 12, 125, 129, 132–5, 153,
    159
wine, *see* viticulture
Wintney, 106–7
withdrawal, 4–10, 186,
    see also wilderness
women Cistercian writers, 44, 104–5,
    209–10, *see also* Beatrice of
    Nazareth, Gertrud of Helfta
Worcester, 205
World War, First, 59, 151–2
World War, Second, 59–60, 152
Worms, 74
Würzburg, 32
Wydenbosch, Nicolas, 148

Yorkshire, 11, 16, 39, 201

Zbraslav, 38, 44
Zinna, 148
Zirc, 57
Zwettl, 146

CAMBRIDGE COMPANIONS TO RELIGION

Other titles in the series

THE CAMBRIDGE COMPANION TO AMERICAN JUDAISM
edited by Dana Evan Kaplan (2005)
9780521822046 hardback   9780521529518 paperback

THE CAMBRIDGE COMPANION TO KARL RAHNER
edited by Declan Marmion and Mary E. Hines (2005)
9780521832885 hardback   9780521540452 paperback

THE CAMBRIDGE COMPANION TO FRIEDRICH SCHLEIERMACHER
edited by Jacqueline Mariña (2005)
9780521814485 hardback   9780521891370 paperback

THE CAMBRIDGE COMPANION TO THE GOSPELS
edited by Stephen C. Barton (2006)
9780521807661 hardback   9780521002615 paperback

THE CAMBRIDGE COMPANION TO THE QUR'AN
edited by Jane Dammen McAuliffe (2006)
9780521831604 hardback   9780521539340 paperback

THE CAMBRIDGE COMPANION TO JONATHAN EDWARDS
edited by Stephen J. Stein (2007)
9780521852906 hardback   9780521618052 paperback

THE CAMBRIDGE COMPANION TO EVANGELICAL THEOLOGY
edited by Timothy Larsen and Daniel J. Trier (2007)
9780521846981 hardback   9780521609746 paperback

THE CAMBRIDGE COMPANION TO MODERN JEWISH PHILOSOPHY
edited by Michael L. Morgan and Peter Eli Gordon (2007)
9780521813129 hardback   9780521012553 paperback

THE CAMBRIDGE COMPANION TO THE TALMUD AND RABBINIC
LITERATURE
edited by Charlotte E. Fonrobert and Martin S. Jaffee (2007)
9780521843904 hardback   9780521605083 paperback

THE CAMBRIDGE COMPANION TO LIBERATION THEOLOGY, SECOND
EDITION
edited by Christopher Rowland (2007)
9780521868839 hardback   9780521688932 paperback

THE CAMBRIDGE COMPANION TO THE JESUITS
edited by Thomas Worcester (2008)
9780521857314 hardback   9780521673969 paperback

THE CAMBRIDGE COMPANION TO CLASSICAL ISLAMIC THEOLOGY
edited by Tim Winter (2008)
9780521780582 hardback   9780521785495 paperback

THE CAMBRIDGE COMPANION TO PURITANISM
edited by John Coffey and Paul Lim (2008)
9780521860888 hardback   9780521678001 paperback